FORTUNE'S MERRY WHEEL
The Lottery in America

FORTUNE'S
MERRY WHEEL
The Lottery in America

AAAAAAAAAAAAAAAAAAAAAAAAAAAAAAAAAAAAAAA

John Samuel Ezell

HARVARD UNIVERSITY PRESS
Cambridge, Massachusetts   1960

Publication of this book has been aided by a grant from the Ford Foundation

Library of Congress Catalog Card Number: 60–8448

Printed in the United States of America

For

Jean

John and Margaret

Preface

Mankind has always been fascinated by the hope of discovering a way to eliminate the need to work for a living. Of the hundreds of products of man's fertile imagination in this regard, none has had a longer or more interesting career than the lottery. To most Americans, however, the lottery is associated with the less sophisticated countries of the world. They little know that it once played a mighty role in the fortunes and dreams of literally hundreds of thousands of their forebears. Not only their kinsmen but also their governments, large and small, viewed the device as an easy road to financial salvation. In the pages that follow I have endeavored to show the forces that produced the lottery, why it came to America, its impact upon American life, why it declined, and what its future may be.

Curiously, scholars and textbooks have ignored this phenomenon, a vital influence for three centuries. Thus, tracing the history of the lottery in the United States has been unusually difficult because of the absence of preliminary spadework by other writers. The story has had to be pieced together from hundreds of diverse sources. Since from a very early date lotteries could not be held without specific legislative approval, the session laws of the individual colonies and states were the obvious starting point — but a tedious one in the absence of any comprehensive collection of such statutes. Facts garnered from contemporary newspapers, magazines, diaries, and correspondence; histories of states, local communities, churches, educational systems and institutions; minutes of churches and other organizations; and antiquarian writings of myriad varieties helped fill in the detail. I have tried to keep documentation to a minimum in the pages that follow and have used reference notes mainly to indicate those sources of a more unorthodox nature. The bibliographical essay at the end of the book will furnish the key to the numerous types of governmental publications and similar primary works used in the preparation of this study.

I am profoundly grateful to Professor Arthur M. Schlesinger, Sr., of Harvard University for first calling the role of the lottery in American history to my attention. Among the friends and colleagues who have given their encouragement and assistance in preparing this work, he deserves the greatest share of my appreciation. I would also like to thank specifically Ted R. Worley of the Arkansas Historical Commission; John H. Caldwell of the Arkansas Supreme Court Library; Dorothy Salmon of the Kentucky State Law Library; Elizabeth L. Mallalieu of the State Library of Nebraska; Raymond M. Jones of the Ohio Supreme Court Library; Walter B. Posey and Margaret Des Champs of Emory University; Henrietta M. Larson of the Harvard Graduate School of Business Administration; Grace M. Sherwood, Rhode Island State Record Commissioner; Julia Baylis Starnes of the Mississippi State Library; Josephine Soukup of Norman, Oklahoma; and Arthur A. Weeks of Birmingham, Alabama.

The materials necessary for this work were gathered in a large number of libraries. Although all were uniformly helpful, I owe special debts of gratitude to the staffs of the Harvard University libraries, especially the Law Library; the Boston and New York Public libraries; the Carnegie Library of Pittsburgh; and the Library of Congress. Appreciation is also due the *William and Mary Quarterly*, the *New England Quarterly*, and the *Maryland Historical Magazine* for allowing reproduction of material that first appeared under my name in their pages. The University of Oklahoma Faculty Research Fund generously financed much of the cost of preparing this manuscript. To the many others who have not been named but who gave aid and encouragement, I express my indebtedness.

Norman, Oklahoma   J. S. E.
November 1959

Contents

Tables

Illustrations

following page 80

All from the Bella C. Landauer Collection in The New-York Histori-cal Society, by courtesy of The New-York Historical Society, New York City.

FORTUNE'S MERRY WHEEL
The Lottery in America

Chapter I

The Background of the Lottery

According to the lot shall the possession thereof be divided between the many and few.[1]

In November 1955, Congressman Paul A. Fino, Republican Representative from New York, wrote in *Coronet:* "A simple, painless and honorable way for the U.S. Government to earn at least $10,000,000,-000 a year lies within the reach of Congress." He continued, "Congress can create a national lottery, and states could legalize off-track betting and bingo . . . [which] carefully supervised and controlled, would provide a harmless release for man's gambling instinct and collect desperately needed funds for useful public welfare activities." He realized "that these words may shock a good many conscientious and sincere Americans, because they have developed an automatic reaction against gambling," but concluded that in "our modern life with security built in, opportunities for daring are limited. Routine characterizes most of our lives. Buying a lottery or parimutuel ticket, or playing bingo is an avenue of escape from routine and boredom."[2]

Representative Fino was sincere in his proposal and bolstered it with many favorable and mitigating facts. What he may or may not have known, however, was that outside of his time and place in history he said nothing which had not been said many times before and in many other centuries. Such propositions have always met varying degrees of opposition, needless to say. In the seventeenth century, for example, Sir William Petty wrote, "A lottery is properly a tax upon unfortunate self-conceited fools. The world abounds in such fools; it is not fit that every man that will may cheat every man that would be cheated. Rather it is ordained that the Sovereign should have guard of these fools, even as in the case of lunatics and idiots."[3]

His words and Representative Fino's are but reflections of two sides of a controversy as old as time and probably as enduring. Underlying the long history of the lottery are disagreements on two fundamental premises — is gambling a basic, or natural, "instinct"? If so, to what degree does a state have the right and responsibility to regulate and control such a drive? As in the case of many social problems, abuses connected with the lottery cloud the issue even more. The right of a government to guard its citizens' welfare has never been argued. But what should be the law has been, and to no small degree. In the United States these questions have been further complicated by arguments over classifying the lottery — that is, gambling *per se* — as good or bad.

Perhaps no system has taken such advantage of this perennial dilemma of man as has the lottery. A chance to get rich quickly is irresistible, especially if the opportunity involves only a small amount of money and effort. Games of chance go back as far as written records. The word "lot," originating from the Teutonic root "hleut," was used to designate the object, such as a disk, pebble, or bean, which was drawn or cast to decide, under divine guidance, disputes, division of property, and the like. The Romance languages produced the Italian "lotteria" and the French "loterie," both meaning a game of chance. It is seen in old English as "hlot," in Dutch as "lot," in German as "loos," and in Danish as "lod." However, the twentieth century accepts the term "lottery" as generally meaning a scheme for distributing prizes by lots, especially one in which the lots or chances are sold.[4]

Lotteries prevailed in Roman times on a lavish scale. At Saturnalias and banquets, guests received varied gifts decided by lots. As his "apophoreta" Nero chose a house or a slave, while Heliogabalus increased the suspense and element of chance in his drawings by offering an equal opportunity for a gold vase or for six flies. The descendants of the Romans, however, extended the function of lotteries beyond mere entertainment. Festivals carried the custom down to the time of the feudal princes and merchants of Europe, who adopted it, especially in Italy, as a source of profit as well as pleasure. It was used primarily to encourage the sale of merchandise, and the "lotto" of Florence and the "seminario" of Genoa were well known in their day. Venice went even further and created a government monopoly in lotteries which yielded considerable revenue.

Francis I of France saw no reason why this wealth should find its way exclusively into the pockets of private promoters and issued the first letters patent for a "loterie" in 1539. During the same century funds were raised in this manner to erect a bridge between the Louvre and the Faubourg St. Germain.[5] So pronounced was popular response that what had been tried primarily as a last resort came to be viewed as an easy way to raise money for public improvements, and the raffle assumed an important place in the French government's fiscal structure. This was especially true after the citizenry, disgusted by the wild and uncurbed spending of their monarchs and weary of enormous taxes, refused to pay the increasing levies. But the public's natural cupidity was too strong to resist the lotteries. Some groups protested, but, supported by Jules Cardinal Mazarin as well as by public desire, the schemes continued. Le Comte de Pontchartrain raised the expenses of the War of the Spanish Succession by this means, and Jacques Necker, in his *Administration des finances*, estimated that the public lotteries cost the people 4,000,000 *livres* per year.[6]

In 1776 the "Great Loterie Decrees" suppressed ventures established by private individuals and combined various charitable, religious, and military projects into the *Loterie royale*. This scheme usually reserved five twenty-fourths of the money taken in for profit and expenses and gave the remaining nineteen twenty-fourths back in prizes, a much greater percentage than in Vienna, Frankfort, and other leading cities. Although the *Loterie royale* was ultimately abolished in 1836, the plan was used on many occasions for raising funds for charity and the fine arts. In some novel instances it was made a means of determining the amount and times for repayment of government loans.

The English Channel proved no barrier to the charms of this device. In England, as elsewhere in Europe, the practice followed a definite pattern. At first the people engaged in raffles similar to those used today by some charitable and church organizations. Next, enterprising individuals, noting the readiness with which the public parted with its money, saw an opportunity to make a large profit by so disposing of their merchandise. The government, in order to curb the subsequent abuses and to share in the easy money, assumed control of the lotteries by requiring all of them to have royal sanction.

British authorities, probably dazzled by the rich profits being reaped by the French, used the technique first to raise funds for the repair of several harbors. A lottery chartered by Queen Elizabeth in 1566 and drawn in 1569 provided for 40,000 tickets selling at ten shillings each and offering "plate and certaine sorts of merchaundizes" as prizes.[7]

With what was probably the third such public license, the lottery may be said to have entered American history.[8] Late in the winter of 1611 the Virginia Company of London was experiencing considerable difficulty in supporting its settlement at Jamestown. Upon petitioning the king for relief, it was granted a new charter on March 12, 1612. Articles XVI-XIX authorized the treasurer of this merchant group to conduct "one or more lottery or lotteries, to have continuance, and to endure and be held for the space of one whole year, next after the opening of the same, — to continue and be further kept during our will and pleasure only."[9] To supervise the undertaking the company was to choose the necessary commissioners, who should swear, "That none of our loving subjects, putting in their names, or otherwise adventuring in the said general lottery or lotteries may be, in anywise, defrauded or deceived of their said monies, or evil or indirectly dealt withal in their said adventures."[10] The drawings were to be held in London or elsewhere within the realm of England and the prizes were to be whatever the company "in their discretion shall see convenient."

So eager was the group to exercise the right that almost immediately Sir Thomas Smith, treasurer of the company, sent its publisher, William Welby, to Stationers' Hall to register a broadside calling public attention to the lottery. On April 8, 1612, Sir Edwin Sandys, an influential Puritan and member of the company, wrote the Mayor of Sandwich urging him to further "an enterprise tending so greatly to the enlargement of the Christian truth, the honor of our nation, and the benefit of the English people."[11] A tract, entered on May 1, proclaimed "the former successe and present estate of Virginia's Plantation"[12] and announced that lots would be drawn in London, with tickets sold in the other large cities.

To stir up popular enthusiasm the predecessor of the singing commercial was used, and the ballad, "London's Lotterie," to the tune of "Lusty Gallant," proclaimed the need of colonizing and civilizing the immense wilderness, later to be the United States of America. The first three stanzas show what is noticeable throughout the entire twenty-one, that the prizes are given a secondary stress, with the chief appeal to patriotism and religion.[13]

> London, live thou famous long,
>   thou bearst a gallant minde:
> Plenty, peace, and pleasures store
>   in thee we dayle find.
> The Merchants of *Virginia* now,
>   hath nobly tooke in hand,
> The bravest golden Lottery,
>   that ere was in this Land.
>
> A gallant House well furnisht foorth
>   with Gold and Silver Plate,
> There standes prepard with Prizes now,
>   set foorth in greatest state.
> To *London,* worthy Gentlemen,
>   goe venture there your chaunce:
> Good lucke standes now in readinesse,
>   your fortunes to advance.
>
> It is to plant a Kingdome sure,
>   where savadge people dwell;
> God will favour Christians still,
>   and like the purpose well.
> Take courage then with willingnesse,
>   let hands and hearts agree:
> A braver enterprize then this,
>   I thinke can never bee.

After six weeks delay, the "five thousand pounds in prizes certayne, besides rewards of causaltie, began to be drawn, in a new built house at West end of Paul's the 29. of June 1612; But of which Lottery for want of filling uppe the number of Lots, there were then taken out and throwne away three score thousande blanckes, without abating of any one prize; and by the twenteth of July, all was drawne and finished." [14] A contemporary account, in the 1631 edition of Stow's *Chronicle,* reported: "This lottery was so plainly carried and honestly performed that it gave full satisfaction to all persons." The first prize of four thousand crowns, "in fayre plate, which was sent to his house in a very stately manner," fell to Thomas Sharplisse, a tailor of London. Two others went to the Church of St. Mary Colechurch, London, which drew "twoe spones price twentye shillinge" for an investment of six pounds, and St. Mary's Woolchurch, Hawe, which won ten shillings with fifty twelve-pence lots.[15] Such participation expressed the tacit approval, at least, of the Anglican Church and helps explain the later toleration of American churches.

Still starved for funds, the Virginia Company announced July 17 the second "little standing lottery" at twelve pence a ticket, the drawings to take place next Candlemas. Public interest lagged, however, and in the spring of 1613 the sponsors issued a broadside address:

> Whereas sundrie the aduenturers to Virginia in their zeale to that memorable work, the plantation of that country with an English Colonie, for the establishing of the Gospell there, and the honour of our Kind and country, haue published a little standing Lotterie . . . and therein haue proportioned to the aduenturers more than the one halfe to be repaid in money or faire prizes without abatement, besides sundry other Welcomes and Rewards. . . . Which we did purpose to draw out in Candlemas Tearme last: yet now seeing that the slow bringing in of their money hath crossed our intents, either because there was no certaine day nominated for the drawing thereof, or for some lewd aspersions that no good successe was likely to ensue to this action.
> In consideration whereof, we do certifie all men, that we do purpose (God Willing) to begin the drawing . . . the 10. day of May next . . .[16]

By using their influence, the promoters obtained from the Privy Council a letter to the various city companies urging them or their individual members to risk "such reasonable sumes of money as each of them may conveniently and can willingly spare." With this letter went forms for registering the names of the persons and the amount ventured. This appeal bore fruit in at least two instances. At a meeting on April 15, 1614, a Mr. Warden Dale, with forceful reasoning concerning the advancement of Christianity and the good of the Commonwealth, persuaded the assembled members of the Court of Assistants of the Grocers' Company each to signify in writing how much he would personally risk. The Merchant Taylors' Company voted at its meeting on May 6, 1614, to invest £50.[17]

During the winter of 1614–15 the Virginia Company tried to increase the returns by a concentrated program of publicity in the towns outside London. As a further spur it issued a lottery puff that resembles those of later years. In addition to pictures of the items to be gained, down the center of the page "Welcomes," "Prizes," "Rewards," and "Addition of new Rewards" were listed. Under "Welcomes" were such enticements as one hundred crowns for the first-drawn blank. The person buying the greatest number of tickets would get four hundred crowns; the next, three hundred; down to the fourth greatest, one hundred. As a final encouragement everyone bringing in three pounds of ready money would receive a silver spoon worth six shillings, eight pence, or that sum in cash. Anyone who invested twelve pounds, ten shillings, and left the prizes would become a stockholder in the company.[18] The company's roster showed that some took advantage of this latter opportunity. The lottery, finally drawn on November 17, 1615, was the last of such magnitude to be conducted in London. Henceforth the Virginia Company concentrated on holding smaller ones in various cities.

In a letter of December 19, 1616, to the Mayor of Salisbury, the company outlined its method of operation. It stated that, although its agents took an oath to deal honorably, the Mayor's presence to supervise the drawings and thus remove any doubt of their honesty was desired. He was to have the key to the awards and personally to mix them with the blanks. In addition he was to appoint "men of care" to supervise the daily drawings, and a child of the Mayor's own choosing would perform the actual selection of numbers.[19]

In May 1619 management of the enterprise was placed in the hands of an agent, Gabriel Barbour. He proved very adept, as seen in his report from Exeter in October 1619, promising to pay £2,500 by the following February and £1,000 more, if necessary, in March. He noted his business was prospering "exceedingly in these western parts, where (I think) twill hold till Christide; I perceive small Towns and great markets doth exceed the best Cities . . ."[20]

In a short time, however, the cities and towns began to complain vigorously that the excitement of the lottery had demoralized business and industry. This led the company to consider other methods of support at the meeting held December 1, 1619, whereupon, "findinge no other means as yett to accrew vnto the Company," it was ordered that the lotteries should continue until midsummer of 1620. On July 7, 1620, the treasurer reported "ffower wayes ther are of gettinge in monneys, the first & most certaine is by the Lotteries wch must be continued till the end of this yeare . . ."[21] The criticisms had become so bitter that on November 4, 1620, Sir Edwin Sandys suggested that the company issue a printed defense of the undertakings, "now of late very much disgraced that itt may be deliuered of many fowle aspersions vniustly cast uppon itt by malignant tounges: notwithstandinge itt is evident that the money thereof arisinge hath sent allredie to Virginia 800 Personns to the great advancement of that Plantation." [22]

Such explanations proved unavailing, and the Privy Council, at the request of the House of Commons, ordered on March 21, 1620/21, that a proclamation be sent throughout the kingdom announcing the halting of the lotteries:

Now forasmuch as we are given to understand, that although wee in granting the sayd License, had our eye fixed upon a religious and Princely end and designe, yet the sayd Lotteries, hauing now for a long time been put in vse, doe dayly decline to more and more inconuenience, to the hinderance of multitudes of Our Subjects,

Wee whose care continually waiteth upon the generall welfare of our people, haue thought it expedient, for the generall good of Our Subjects, to suspend the further execution of the saide Lotteries, vntill upon further deliberation and aduisement, we shall be more fully informed of the inconueniences and evils thereby arising, and may ordaine due remedy for the same . . .[23]

In view of later accusations against lotteries, and as the proclamation was not specific, the reason for the revocation of the grant is important. Modern investigation has proved that the decision was probably made on grounds other than the morality of the device. Personality conflicts existed within the company, and Sandys's efforts to wring the utmost in returns from the lotteries gave his enemies an opportunity to attack his administration of them. General Manager Barbour was particularly criticized for his allegedly high-handed manner of appointing aides and his failure to place them under oath. Barbour was also accused of misappropriating from seven to eight thousand pounds and bribing the auditor to conceal his theft. The conclusions generally reached are that intervention resulted basically from the bitter squabbling that finally culminated in the death of the company or from a protest by the House of Commons that the lotteries were illegal because of a lack of parliamentary sanction.[24]

Regardless of the cause, the loss of the lottery franchise was a telling blow for the Virginia Company. As one member said, the schemes had been the "reall and substantiall food, by which Virginia hath been nourished." It had, indeed, been the one dependable fount of revenue. In his estimate of the expenses for the fiscal year, 1620–21, Sandys counted upon this source for £8,000 out of a total budget of £17,800. That this was not an unusual proportion is seen from a statement in 1621 that the colony "hath in these latter years been chiefly Supported by his Ma^ts [Majesty's] most gracious graunt of the vse of the Lotteries." [25] A public report on all the proceeds and expenditures from the lottery funds presented in November 1621 computed the sun collected at about £29,000, "though it was by diuers reported to haue bin a farr greater Somme." This amount, obtained from the "Runninge Lotteries," did not include the large ones held in London, whose proceeds cannot be estimated accurately. About these the Marquess of Flores stated in a letter to the King of Spain, dated London, August 16, 1612: "I reported to Y. M. that they have obtained from a lottery sixty thousand ducats for Virginia; now permission has been granted for another lottery worth 120.000 ducats, and they will make great haste to finish it and will send more than two thousand men to that country . . ." [26] In November 1613 Sir John Sammes mentioned the "greate sommes of money amounting to £8,000 or thereaboute wch have bene gotten by the lottorie." [27]

The revocation of this license did not mean that England was through with lotteries; on the contrary, they were destined to enjoy a long and vigorous life. Beginning in 1627, a series was authorized to raise funds for building an aqueduct to serve London. Likewise, monopoly privileges were issued to court favorites and other special groups; in 1664, for example, the king ordered that "no lotteries are to be allowed except as appointed by Sir Anthony Des Marces, to whom the management of the same is granted for the benefit of the Royal Fishing Company."

The exclusive feature did not prevent the growth of abuses, however, and all such undertakings were suppressed after December 29, 1699. The reason, as stated in the act's preamble, was later to become familar to Americans.

. . . several evil-disposed persons, for divers years past, have set up many mischievous and unlawful games, called *lotteries,* not only in the Cities of *London* and *Westminster* . . . but in most of the eminent towns and places in *England,* and in the Dominion of *Wales,* and have thereby most unjustly and fraudulently got to themselves great sums of money from the children and servants of several gentlemen, traders and merchants, and from other unwary persons, to the utter ruin and impoverishment of many families, and to the reproach of the *English* laws and government, by cover of several patents or grants under the great seal of *England* for the said lotteries, or some of them . . .[28]

The ban lasted only ten years, however. From 1709 to 1826 the British government authorized annual lotteries. These yielded a yearly profit of £346,765 from 1793 to 1824.

As before, the old abuses grew in their wake. Contractors, often purchasing tickets at a premium of 40 per cent, resold them, sometimes in fractions of parts, through "Morocco men," so-called because of their red leather books, who traveled throughout the country. Another practice was to insure, for a small sum, the fate of the tickets. This amounted to a bet that a certain number would or would not be drawn on a certain day, or would or would not win a prize. The drawings usually lasted thirty days, so ample opportunity was afforded for speculation of this sort.

The government took notice of these deviations by various legislative controls. In 1721 unlicensed ventures were prohibited with a fine of £500 and a year in jail, and in 1782 a system of certificating lottery-office keepers sought to strengthen the official monopoly. In 1802 the "Little Go Act" was aimed primarily at itinerant lottery wheels that flourished in the intervals between state drawings. To cripple the "insurance" racket, "Perceval's Act" of 1806 limited the drawings to one day. Evidence indicates, however, that the acts never succeeded in completely stamping out either "insurance" or private undertakings until all lotteries were abolished.[29]

The legal lotteries were used not only for general revenue, but also occasionally for specific projects, such as purchasing a picture gallery, improving London, or for the benefit of private individuals.[30] But year after year the introduction of the annual lottery act had led to parliamentary debate aimed at persuading the Chancellor of the Exchequer to discontinue this means of finance. He invariably replied that it was impossible to renounce a sum which must be supplied by some other tax, which in all probability would operate more oppressively on the people and would certainly not be as cheerfully paid. By 1826, however, the growing opposition led by Lord Lyttleton succeeded in having all such schemes prohibited. Energetic efforts were made to revive them, and in 1831, by a blunder, a law permitting drawings to be held for the improvement of Glasgow was enacted, but this was corrected by a special act three years later. Another exception was the Arts Union Lottery, legalized in 1846.[31]

Thus, the lottery had a long, if not honorable, career prior to and during the period of English colonization. More important, it played a key role in the social and economic history of England. Strong opposition did not appear there until well after the American colonies had achieved independence. Thus it is not surprising that colonists faced with similar economic problems proposed similar solutions and that this was a practice the emigrants saw fit to transport to the new world. The American lottery was obviously the offspring of the English parent, and soon proved that in its case heredity was accentuated by environment.

Chapter II

The Lottery Crosses to America

> Now a Lot is a serious thing not to be trifled with; the Scripture saith not only (as some would have it) of *Extraordinary Lots,* but of a Lot in general, that *the whole disposing* (or Judgement) *thereof is of the Lord,* Prov. 16.33.[1]

The American lottery, though a European import, soon rooted itself in the everyday life of the colonies. Many reasons account for the ease of this transplantation: the prevalence of lotteries in the old countries, the pressure of economic necessity co-existent with establishing new homes and governments, the general lack of moral opposition to the system — all stimulated the commonly accepted gambling instinct.

Like most imported customs, the American lottery basically followed the same pattern as the European. Some variations, however, resulted from frontier conditions, the unique needs of the people, and the shifting attitudes of the British and colonial governments. A well-established system in the old world, the lottery in its sophisticated form was not adaptable to a frontier society. But it could nonetheless fill a definite need in America, and so it reverted to a simpler form. Fundamentally, though, lotteries in America, as in England, fell into two categories: drawings by individuals for personal profit and those legally sanctioned for public benefit. Likewise, the official attitude toward them was characterized by four stages: (1) laissez faire; (2) legal sanction for some drawings with no restriction on others; (3) outlawing of unauthorized lotteries; (4) and complete prohibition. Though all colonies did not necessarily progress in this order or experience every stage, the trend was evident.

The lottery itself underwent a gradual transition. Nourished by diverse factors, it changed from the singular effort of an individual to the involved manipulations of many — growing from simple undertakings to a large complex business. The same conditions that had motivated the early raffles fed the growing system until it evolved into one gigantic enterprise — the Louisiana Lottery. This colossus embraced many businesses, controlled legal agencies, spent millions annually, and finally was destroyed only by the power of the United States government.

The lottery in the United States must be traced in sociological order rather than chronological — a common necessity when dealing with institutional development in a new country. The story of the United States is a history of many frontiers constantly shifting and in various stages of physical and cultural development. But as in other lands private lotteries, originated strictly by individual initiative, appeared first. In their European homes the colonists had become accustomed to selling their goods by this method for handsome profits and in turn to investing small sums in the schemes of their friends or governments. What could be more natural when one arrived at a new home with goods or land but little money than to dispose of one's property by the means most likely to produce the greatest return? Land and buildings, in particular, presented a problem if the owner wanted to obtain a reasonable price. The perennial currency shortage made it difficult for even the moderately wealthy to accumulate much of a cash reserve.

Thomas Jefferson, writing of lotteries of this sort, said:

An article of property, insusceptible of division at all, or not without great diminution of its worth, is sometimes of so large a value as that no purchaser can be found while the owner owes debts, has no other means of payment, and his creditors no other chance of obtaining it but by its sale at a full and fair price. The lottery is here a salutory instrument for disposing of it, where men run small risks for the chance of obtaining a high prize.[2]

As the settlements became better established, the procedures grew more sophisticated, but the idea was the same. A few examples from broadsides and newspaper advertisements sufficiently show this. In 1719 Joseph Marion sold by lottery two brick houses situated on large lots in the North End of Boston. For one he issued 100 tickets at five pounds each. The Philadelphia *American Weekly Mercury* for February 23, 1720, carried a notice of a raffle with 350 tickets at twenty shillings each, with a "new brick house, corner of Third and Arch streets" as a prize. John Blood offered through the New York *Post-Boy*, February 10, 1746, 2,000 chances at thirty shillings each to dispose of a brick house, an annuity of five pounds, numerous lots in New Jersey, and some cash awards. The *Pennsylvania Journal*, June 11, 1761, rather elaborately announced:

> The method of disposing of landed Estates by way of lottery, having been in practice in most Countries time out of mind, and as no Lotteries have been more common in *America*, in particular, it is presumed the following Scheme for disposing of 46 Acres . . . on the South West End of *Pettys'* Island . . . will be equally acceptable to the Publick with any Lottery yet set on foot on the continent . . .[3]

The most common type of private scheme, however, was the merchandising raffle. In 1727, for example, the *American Weekly Mercury* announced a drawing in the home of John Stevins of Perth Amboy, New Jersey. There were 278 prizes in all and only five blanks to each winning number. The awards consisted of "501£ of Silver and Gold work, wrought by *Simeon Soumain of New York*," with the highest being an "Eight Square Tea-Pot, six Tea-Spoons, Skimmer and Tongues valued at 18£. 3s. 6d." The chances sold at six shillings "York" money, or seven shillings "Jersey" money, and could be purchased in New York, New Jersey, and Pennsylvania.[4]

The *Virginia Gazette*'s columns also carried numerous and interesting accounts of this nature. In 1737 Alexander Kerr advertised a raffle of diamonds in his Williamsburg jewelry store, and in April of the same year, Mrs. Mary Stagg announced a ball with the added note, "There will be several valuable Things set up to be raffled for." How well this attraction worked is seen by her announcing the following March a "public Assembly" with the prizes including a young Negro. Mrs. Stagg's rival for public favor, Mrs. Barbara de Gaffenreidt, proclaimed a ball and assembly for the same period with a contest for a *"likely young* Virginia *Negro Woman, fit for House business and her Child."* [5]

William Dunlap, relative of Benjamin Franklin by marriage, raffled off a large number of books, "several Sets of the genteelest Pictures now in Taste in *England*," numerous pieces of silverware, rings, china, "a curious large *Orrery* with its Apparatus, the most complete Machine of its kind ever seen in America," a reflecting telescope, and a parcel of land.[6] This collection was surpassed in oddity and variety by the prizes featured in another drawing designed to sell "new and curious Goods, viz. a most elegant collection of Pictures, in green and gold Frames, ditto black and gold Frames, and a new and large collection of fancy Pieces, done by the greatest masters in the world . . . Drawing Books . . . ; with a large collection of the newest maps . . . in the very finest colours; [and] a large variety of copper Plate writings, by the ablest Penmen in England." In addition to these treasures there were many "curiosities lately imported from London and elsewhere," guns and pistols, and a fine assortment of jewelry, including diamonds and garnets. "Adventurers in this lottery may depend that every Article will be rated at the lowest Prices the Proprietor sells them out of his shop." [7]

Despite an abundance of the local variety, the buying of English lottery tickets continued in America until the Revolution. A letter to Jared Ingersoll of New Haven, dated London, November 20, 1761, informed him: "This day No. 53,697 in the Present State Lottery Register'd at this office in your name was Drawn a Blank." In a postscript the agent expressed willingness to buy more chances for him.[8] William Strahan, a London printer, did more than supply foreign news to David Hall, a newspaper partner of Benjamin Franklin, for he wrote on February 13, 1768: "Dear Davie, The Lottery is now finished; and I am very sorry to tell you that five of them came up Blanks . . . The other (No. 38,998) was drawn a Prize of £20 . . . for which I have given you Credit. Shall I purchase more Ticketts for you in the ensuing Lottery notwithstanding former Success?" [9]

In a letter from London, May 20, 1775, former Governor Horatio Sharpe of Maryland told John Ridout, who had served as his secretary, "My compliments to Dr. Scott and let him know that he will soon be in Fortune's cup. I will send the numbers of the tickets by the first opportunity after my purchase." Later he wrote, "The Act for a lottery is passed and you may dream of thousands till it is ended, for I shall make a gambling purchase for you, Dr. Scott and myself." [10]

This traffic, however, was not restricted to one direction, but in some instances at least, it seems the American product was less acceptable. William Byrd III of Virginia, falling into financial difficulties, offered to dispose of his vast property holdings by means of a lottery. The scheme involved 839 parcels of land near the present city of Richmond, including several forges, mill sites, fisheries, ferries, and so forth, to a value of £56,796. His plan was to sell 10,000 chances at home and abroad for £5 each, of which 839 would bring prizes and the rest would be blanks. In April 1768 Thomas Adams wrote Colonel Byrd from London:

Inclosed you have a Note of the Lottery Tickets sold. I still hope to dispose of the Whole before the Time of drawing. I little expected to have met with any opposition in a thing of this sort here, but I have been informed by some Tradesmen of Note who had promised to take a good many of me, that they had been spoken to & Caution'd by some Merch'ts in ye trade, but would not say who they were, not to be concern'd and excused themselves by saying they should be glad to do it if they could without giving offence to those Gentlemen — a narrowness of Soul that does not exist in any other Mortal but a Virginia Tobacco Merch't.[11]

Another instance was that of James Manning, head of the school which later became Brown University, who wrote an English friend in May 1772, "Wd: a well concerted scheme of a Lottery to raise 1,000 or 2[000] £ ster: meet wt: Encouragmt: by ye Sale of Tickets in England?" His correspondent replied discouragingly, "We have our fill of these cursed gambling Lotteries in London every year; they are big with ten thousand Evils. Let the Devils Children have them all to themselves: Let us not touch or taste." [12] However, the Reverend Manning, a Baptist, did not see fit to take this advice.

In fact, his attitude was typical of religious groups other than the Quakers. Extensive use of lotteries to raise money was made by churches. Proponents had little difficulty in finding religious authorities, including the Bible, to quote in their behalf. In a textbook used at Harvard and Yale in the seventeenth and eighteenth centuries, William Ames, "The Reverend and Faithful Minister of Christ," attempted to answer the question: "What is to bee thought of publicke Lotteries, wherein many Prizes, or rewards, are proposed to bee gotten by Lott?" His reply was sufficiently general to allow wide interpretation: "They might haply bee so ordered, that they might be lawful. Namely if there were any need of a contribution to some pious use." Since a word of warning seemed necessary, however, he added, "those also which cast the Lots should . . . come to the Lottery, not out of an hope of gayning, but out of an intention of bestowing something." [13] Promoters found little difficulty in swaddling their productions in the mantle of public-spiritedness, and it remained only for the purchaser to clear his motives with his conscience. Parenthetically, many more participants ended by "bestowing" rather than "gayning."

The term "lottery" itself had no bad connotations, seen in the fact that, beginning in 1744, the German-American printer, Christopher Sower of Germantown, Pennsylvania, issued a "Lottery of the Pious, or the Spiritual Treasure Casket," which eliminated the "hope of gayning" except in a religious sense. It consisted of a deck of 381 cards, with Scriptural and poetical verses on them, numbered like lottery tickets. People would use them on Sunday afternoons, drawing cards from this little treasury of good and beautiful thoughts and contemplating their meanings. If during the week one felt gloomy, he turned to the game, assured of a promise of consolation. A secular vendor would have probably headlined this as "Every number a Winner!" It is interesting to note that Charles Wesley at a later date used much the same idea in his Scriptural cards,[14] and that twentieth-century gift catalogues list similar items.

All was not sweetness and light, however. The Quakers and a few individuals had consistently opposed the lottery's use on moral grounds. Prominent in the latter group were the Mathers of Massachusetts. Increase Mather, statesman and theologian, in his *Testimony against Several Prophane and Superstitious Customs* (1687) had criticized the device mainly on the score of impiety. "He that makes use of a Lot," he said, "wholly commits his affair to a superior Cause than either nature or art, therefore unto God. But this ought not to be done in a Sportful Lusory way."[15] His son, Cotton, wrote in his diary on July 30, 1690: "Understanding that many, especially of our young People gave themselves a *Liberty,* to do Things not of *good Report,* especially, in using the scandalous Games of *Lottery* I sett myself, in the Lecture, to bear my Testimony against their Miscarriages, with a Sermon, on Act 16.2. *One well-reported of.*"[16]

It is not clear whether Cotton Mather's message inspired his colleagues among the Congregational ministry, or whether increasing evils of the lotteries themselves attracted clerical attention, but, under the title "Judgement of the Ministers, Met at Boston, May 1699," the practice was again denounced. The ministers' reasoning was packed with good "Yankee common sense":

Not only the undertakers of a lottery, have a certain gain unto themselves, but so likewise have they, who in the lottery draw tickets of benefit; and every one who ventures, does it with a desire to fall upon those tickets in drawing. It is very certain, that for this benefit, none of these can pretend that they do any one thing beneficial to human society. They only hire the undertakers to transfer the estates of others unto themselves, without any service done by them to the interest of any under heaven.

In a lottery so contrived, that when all the prizes are drawn, they do not make up, and fetch out, near the whole sum that was deposited by the adventurers, there is a plain cheat upon the people. The undertakers in such a lottery only resolve to pillage the people of such a considerable sum, and invite a number to assist them in their actions, in hopes of going shares with them in the advantage; and such is the corruption of mankind, that the mere hope of getting the riches of other men without doing the service of any thing for it, will engage men to run the hazard of being losers.[17]

Public opinion remained indifferent, and Cotton Mather returned to the battle in 1713. In *A Flying Roll, Brought Forth, to Enter into the House and Hand of the Thief,* he assailed the lottery in almost identical terms with those used by the ministers in 1699, probably indicating his help in drawing up that document. Once more he stressed the fact that nothing useful accrued to the community and added, "This is not an equal Thing, for Estates to be transferr'd at this rate, and no Service to *Humane Society* done for it." Since such schemes did not return as much as they brought in they were cheats, and he listed them among methods of theft.[18]

The only group consistently to oppose lotteries was the Society of Friends. Here, too, disapproval of the practice was part of the Quakers' hatred for all forms of gambling and most types of amusement.[19] Because of the generally low regard in which the Society of Friends was held in the early settlements, however, its opinion was largely ignored. An exception was Pennsylvania where a constant struggle between the Quakers and the rest of the population was carried on for over half a century. The Quaker-dominated first General Assembly of Pennsylvania (1682) passed the code known as the "Great Law," a section of which struck at such drawings. It declared: "That if any person be Convicted of playing at Cards, Dice, Lotteries, or such like enticing, vain, and evil Sports and Games, such persons shall, for every such offence, pay five shillings, or Suffer five Days Imprisonment (at hard labour) in the house of Correction." [20]

But the English sovereigns, William and Mary, took an unexpected stand and nullified this act in 1693. The Friends, not to be outdone, passed new antilottery legislation in 1693, 1700, and 1705, only to have each act meet a similar fate. Probably these were disallowed not only because raffles were banned, but also because such bills were usually coupled with attacks on other activities considered harmless by the British government. If these official checks had a depressing effect upon the Quakers, it did not change their minds. At the yearly meeting in Philadelphia in 1716 a resolution provided "that care be taken to prevent Friends' children and all professing Truth, from going to or being any way concerned in plays, games, lotteries, music and dancing." [21]

Gradually, another kind of opposition had been developing in the colonies. With the extravagant use of the lottery by any and all who desired to instigate one, dishonesty and corruption became prevalent. The only regulation on private lotteries was the degree of cupidity or gullibility of the patrons. Ticket purchasers had no security other than the instigators' good faith, sufficient so long as the communities were small enough for them to know the sponsors personally. But when the towns grew larger and more and more people floated lotteries, the opportunity for fraud multiplied. Unscrupulous individuals either gave inferior goods as prizes or manipulated the drawings so that all the worthwhile items remained undrawn. On increasingly frequent occasions the promoter, after collecting from the adventurers, fled from the colony without holding the contest. In one case in Connecticut the winners found that the four farms dangled as prizes had been secretly sold in advance.

Another source of discontent, undoubtedly, was the merchants. Their protests that such unorthodox methods of business diverted large sums from regular commercial channels, making competition difficult, were potent factors in the various assemblies' decisions to regulate lotteries. This feeling and the shifting in official opinion were reported by Samuel Sewall, a Salem merchant, in a letter to William Dummer, August 12, 1719: "I dined with the Court [the Massachusetts legislature] last Friday, where many express'd their dislike of the lotteries practiced of late, as differing little from Gaming for Money; and as being really pernicious to Trade. Taking notice of no less than four Lotteries in the inclosed News-Letter, I would propound it to consideration, whether it will not be expedient to put some stop to the progress of it?" [22]

The ostensible reason most governments cited for banning unlicensed lotteries was the harmful effect upon the lower classes.
These games appealed particularly to the poor. Flushed with great
expectations, they neglected their less exciting pursuits to loiter
around the taverns where the raffles commonly were held.[23] In 1719
the Massachusetts General Court denounced the lotteries as tempting "the Children and Servants of several Gentlemen, Merchants and
Traders, and other unwary People . . . into a vain and foolish Expence of money" and forbade any person "publicly or privately" to
"exercise, keep open, show or expose to be play'd at, drawn at, or
thrown at," or to "draw, play or throw at, any such Lottery, or any
other Lottery, either by Dice, Lotts, Cards, Balls, or any other
Numbers or Figures, or any other Way whatsoever." The pains taken
to include all such schemes indicate the many varieties being employed. All were branded "common and publick nuisances," and
any promoter would be fined £200, half to go to the government
and half to the informer. Henceforth, lotteries to be legal in Massachusetts had to have legislative authorization.[24]

The royal province of New York followed suit in 1721, when the
wave of merchandising schemes was checked by imposing on privately initiated raffles a penalty of double the amount to be raised.[25]
In Connecticut, too, the abuses lotteries engendered caused the government to take remedial steps. On January 22, 1727, Governor
Joseph Talcott issued a proclamation stating:

> Forasmuch as sundry persons in the counties of Fairfax and New Haven
> have of late presumed, without any lawful lycence, to set up lotteries, and
> to vend off their goods by lottery, to the very great abuse of many of his
> Majesty's subjects, who have inadvertently been drawn in to venture and
> loose their moneys . . . and to the occasioning of very great disorders,
> tumults, and mispence of precious time, I therefore . . . prohibit and
> strictly forbid all persons . . . to set up any lottery . . .

But the proclamation failed because it did not fix definite penalties.
A short time later the deputy governor reported that the sale of
goods by lottery was "growing to a prodigious rate." [26] As a result,
the Connecticut legislature in May 1728 decreed forfeiture of a sum
equal to the value of the property to be sold, which drastically curtailed such activity in that colony for the next nineteen years.

The Quaker legislature of Pennsylvania, still smarting from previous rebuffs, won the next round by an act of February 1729, pro-

hibiting *all* lottery drawings on a penalty of £100, half the fine going to the governor and half to the informer. This became law through the crown's failure to review it within the prescribed period. But the Friends soon found that although they had their law, they could not make it work. The Proprietor, despite the statute, attempted to dispose of one hundred thousand acres of Pennsylvania land by means of a raffle in 1735. Because of public indifference, undoubtedly spurred by Quaker opposition, the scheme was not drawn, but purchased tickets were recognized as titles to land. The minutes of the Friends' meeting that year stated, "In answer to that part of the report from Chester Quarterly Meeting relating to lotteries, this meeting is of opinion that Friends should be careful not to engage in anything of that kind." [27]

Instead of ending lotteries, the Pennsylvania law was soon made to serve as a sort of license, for the governor would agree to remit his half of the fine for cases he considered worthy. On such occasions, a friend of the sponsor would act as informer, return his half, and thus void the whole penalty. As shall be seen, the governor was quite liberal in this respect.[28]

The citizens of Rhode Island, however, were under no such religious or secular injunction. Individuals could freely initiate their own raffles until 1732, when the legislature restrained them on the grounds that they led many "unwary" persons "into a foolish expense of money, which may tend to the great hurt of this government, if not timely prevented." All lotteries had to cease by April 30, 1733, under penalty of £500.

It was probably this delay that caused passage of a Massachusetts law the same year against raffles "projected and tickets disposed of within this province, reserving the drawing of the lots in some of the neighboring colonies or provinces." Thus, the statute complained, the "good and wholesome design and true intent and meaning" of the legislative act of 1719 was "very much eluded and evaded." The penalty for holding illegal lotteries was raised to £500, a penalty of £100 was set for publishing information about them, and one of £200 for selling tickets. Any undertaking "allowed by act of Parliament or . . . of this province" was specifically excluded.[29]

New Jersey was going through much the same cycle. It, too, was the scene of numerous private lotteries, their notices appearing in the newspapers as early as 1727.[30] By 1748 the province was swamped with these ventures. Advertisements showed the number and variety of purposes served by the lotteries: a Presbyterian meetinghouse and parsonage at "Amwell"; an effort in New Brunswick to pay the debts of the imprisoned Peter Cochran; a brick steeple and bells for St. Mary's at Burlington; a parsonage at "Elizabeth-Town"; a parsonage and land at Hanover; a landing at Raritan; and a church and parsonage at Newark.

Faced by such conditions, the Assembly acted for "the more effectual preventing of Lotteries, playing of cards and Dice, and other Gaming for lucre of Gain . . . ," stating the familiar charges that such schemes were causing many persons "as well as Children and Servants" to lose large sums. Promoters henceforth forfeited £500, and anyone buying or selling tickets was fined £100. There is considerable evidence to indicate that Quaker opposition had a hand in this law.

Most New Jersey instigators, however, now began to operate from the no man's land of Biles, Petty, and Fish islands in the Delaware River. An announcement by William Dunlap, printer, offered to provide free boats to Petty Island for anyone wishing to watch his drawing. An apology by the managers of a church venture indicated the difficulties of this outlaw business: the project had been postponed because of the "fluctuating condition the ice was in, it was impracticable . . . to pass the river Delaware to the place appointed for drawing the Trenton Lottery on the Pennsylvania side." [31]

This case also illustrates why the Quakers had much with which to be unhappy in Pennsylvania. Here the public's hunger for the lottery was not satisfied by authorized drawings as in other colonies. Instead, all were forbidden. But the citizens were not to be denied, and before the legislature succeeded in taking control from the governor at least fifty-two quasi-legal lotteries were held with his connivance. Besides appeasing the people's desire for excitement, they served the same general purposes as did those in other colonies — raising funds for schools, bridges, roads, churches, and so on. Some even benefited institutions outside the province, such as the lotteries held in 1749, 1750, and 1761 for the College of New Jersey. An idea of the general acceptability can be gathered by the number of churches using this method of evasion. Before 1763 the total religious projects were: Presbyterian, nine; Episcopal, five; Lutheran, three;

High Dutch Reformed, one; and at least one for an unidentified denomination.

The most famous of these early drawings were for the "College, Academy and Charitable School of Philadelphia," later the University of Pennsylvania, the first nonsectarian college in America. Beginning in 1755 it was the recipient of funds from nine different raffles. Other schools benefiting from lotteries were the Lutheran Free School at Reading in 1757, the German Union School in Philadelphia, and the Germantown Public School in 1761.

This open flaunting of the law and mounting predilection for easy money did not go unchallenged. In the fall of 1758 a writer, signing himself "Pennsylvanicus," began a series in the *Pennsylvania Journal* attacking lotteries as irreligious and ruinous to society. After two articles — on November 30, 1758, and January 25, 1759 — he was answered by another writer, who cited the authorized schemes for the College of New Jersey and of the governments of New York and Connecticut as proof that such undertakings were not the "enemys of *Religion* and of the *Poor*, the abettors and patrons of the most contagious and dangerous vice." The rebuttal continued, "Is the use of Lots forbidden by God in scripture? By no means; he ordered his chosen tribes to use them in the division of their inheritance. Are they contrary to the Christian revelation? So far from it, that we know they were used by the apostles themselves . . ."

"Pennsylvanicus" replied on February 8 that he had been moved by a disinterested regard for the welfare and good of his country to write his former pieces "without the least intention of raising the *Passion* of any person." In this he had been disappointed. As for his "angry opponent, who seems *touched to the Quick*," the examples drawn were "no proof that *Lotteries are Justifiable*." New Jersey had declared them ruinous and placed heavy penalties upon buyers and sellers, yet "to elude this salutary law it is well known, the managers of several lotteries have drawn them out of the province on *Biles-Island*. But this is another instance of our authors knowledge of logic. Will *examples alone,* and especially examples against law, prove the virtue, legality or morality of any act. If so, theft, adultery and even murder itself may be justified . . ."[32]

He admitted his opponent's accusation of an ulterior motive to destroy Pennsylvania's lottery-supported college and defended this by saying that the school was an enemy of the people and would continue to aid the Proprietors in their tyrannical acts. If it were impoverished by the loss of this revenue, another institution, based upon local interests, loyal to the people's cause, and publicly supported might be established. On the last day of 1758 David James Dove, a former English professor of the academy, issued a pamphlet, *The Lottery: A Dialogue between Mr. Thomas Trueman and Mr. Humphry Dupe,* attacking the schemes for the academy and other institutions as "manifestly no better than public frauds." These charges were called to the attention of the trustees by the faculty, but it was refused permission to answer them on the grounds that the persons behind the attacks were "low creatures, who wrote from Passion and Resentment," and unworthy of attention.

In denouncing "An Act for More Effectual Suppressing of Lotteries and Plays," passed by the Pennsylvania lower house on June 2, 1759, the Provincial Council reported to the governor their conviction that the measure was "principally intended" to destroy the College, Academy, and Charity School of Philadelphia. Since enemies had tried before and failed, they reminded him that no lotteries had been carried on except for the "most necessary and charitable purposes," such as fortification of the city, defense of the province in time of war, and to finish the Episcopal church. Of the law of 1730, they added:

That this had the Effect intended by deterring Persons from erecting Lotteries for private and bad purposes, and no lottery has been drawn since but for a Publick use, of which the present and preceding Governors have been so far convinced that they have both Licensed and encouraged them by Remitting their part of the Fine. This act is therefore unnecessary, and should it take Place no Lotteries can be erected tho' for the most useful and Laudable Purposes.

As a final slap at the lower house, the Council concluded that "the Enacting, adjudging, and declaring all Lotteries in General, whether publick or private, to be Common and Publick Nuisances, was a high reflection on the Wisdom of the King, Lords and Commons, who frequently Erected them by Act of Parliament for public Utility." [33]

Despite these objections, the Assembly determinedly placed penalties on such ventures. Once more, however, the law was abrogated by the king, primarily because it also suppressed stage plays. The Privy Council for Plantation Affairs informed the legislature that the act would have been allowed if it had confined itself to lotteries, even though the penalties were drastic and the statute seemed aimed at destroying the proprietor-sponsored school.

Following this veto Pennsylvania was once more flooded with illegal lotteries. In 1761 alone there were twenty-seven, an all-time high, benefiting such purposes as improvements in Philadelphia, bridges over the Conestoga and Octorara creeks, payment to the Tulephauken Rangers for their services, and numerous schools and churches. A drawing to erect public baths and pleasure grounds in Philadelphia elicited a protest to the governor from some of the clergy and important people of the community, including Doctors Robert Jenny, William Smith, Francis Alison, and Messrs. John Ewing, and Jacob Duché. They held that lotteries encouraged a growing inclination among the people for "pleasure, luxury, gaming, and dissipation." Nevertheless, seven more schemes were initiated in 1762.

Hatred for the Proprietor and his school and the growing concern over the increasing number of drawings assisted the passage of an act on February 7, 1762, banning all lotteries not authorized by the legislature or by the British government. This time the old mistake was not repeated, and the law dealt only with lotteries. It assigned penalties of £500 for originating a lottery and £20 for advertising it or selling tickets, giving the fines to the Philadelphia hospital, an Assembly-sponsored institution. With this statute and its acceptance control finally passed from the governor to the legislature.

The less populous colonies were slower in taking action against unregulated lotteries, but even they were not exempt from the problems such lotteries raised. On May 4, 1751, because "many persons have lately, and do daily presume to set up lotterys under the denomination of sales of houses, lands, plate, jewels, goods, wares, merchandizes and other things," South Carolina fixed a penalty of £500, proclamation money, for such actions. The originators also were sentenced to the common jail for a year or until the fine was paid in full, and all participants had to forfeit five pounds. Yet this act failed to prove satisfactory, and upon its expiration in 1762 the penalties were increased to £1,000 with a year in jail for the instigators and a fine of £100 for each ticket bought. This must have daunted the most inveterate sponsors and gamblers.[34]

Owing to the sparsely settled condition of New Hampshire, it is doubtful whether there was much early lottery activity. There were enough private drawings by 1754, however, to attract the attention of the legislature, for at that time they were banned.[35] Likewise, the frontier settlement of Georgia found it desirable on February 29, 1764, to end the blissful existence of the "many idle, loose, disorderly persons" using lotteries as a means of supporting themselves "in a dishonest, dissolute course of life." Those setting up such raffles forfeited £500 and whatever was dangled as prizes. This act probably proved effective, for Governor James Wright reported in 1769 that the practice had never prevailed in Georgia.

In Virginia, however, the official attitude showed a marked unawareness of any problem concerning lotteries. In August 1736, within a year of the founding of the colony's first newspaper, advertisements of raffles appeared. Even in 1754, when the colonial government found it necessary to authorize a drawing for its own benefit, there was no attempt to curtail the competition from private schemes. Possibly the glitter of the "big names" which were often involved helped provide this immunity. Look, for example, at the distinguished roster of managers for raising 2,400 pieces of eight to build a church and market house at Belhaven in 1751: Colonel George William Fairfax, Major Lawrence Washington, Colonel William Fitzhugh, George Mason, and Major Augustine Washington.

The papers of George Washington, an indefatigable lottery patron, give some evidence of the numerous schemes in Virginia. He won a parcel of land with a £50 investment in the Colonel Byrd raffle,[36] put £5 10s. in an unidentified venture in 1760, gambled £5 in "Strother's" undertaking in 1763, and in 1766 recorded a gain of £16 in the "York Lottery." Two years later Washington signed the tickets for the Cumberland Mountain road scheme and in 1769 aided in "Col. Moore's" drawing. Finally, however, the number of such undertakings in Virginia and the abuses arising from their unregulated character led to the suppression of all unauthorized lotteries after November 1769.

Virginia's tolerance was duplicated by North Carolina's equal treatment of authorized and unauthorized ventures. The latter schemes evidently caused little trouble or attracted much attention. The earliest official notice concerning them is in a letter from Governor William Tryon to Lord Hillsborough, Secretary of State for the Colonies, March 30, 1770. Tryon wrote:

. . . as a difficulty arises to me in what manner I can check the practice in this province, tho' not very frequent, of selling of property by private lotteries without the parties troubling themselves about the form necessary to procure the sanction of the legislature, I must desire your Lordship will inform my judgement in this point that I may know how to regulate my conduct in these instances. I should be desirous to know if any Act of Parliament reaches this case, there being no law in this province that prevents such practices, and I have not the least hope that such a one can be obtained here.[37]

Apparently, Lord Hillsborough was unable to help.

The early lottery history of Delaware is unknown until her union with Pennsylvania in 1682. The settlement was an integral part of that colony until 1704, when the "Lower Counties" set up their own legislature with Penn's blessing. At the time of separation the Pennsylvania laws were re-enacted in Delaware, but there were none dealing with lotteries. Without the strong Quaker influence to appease, the Assembly followed a policy of laissez faire in regard to such schemes. Although the "Delaware State Lottery" was advertised in Pennsylvania newspapers in 1768, there is no evidence that it was an official drawing. As the number of drawings declined in other colonies, Delaware became the northern center for such activity. In 1771, for example, the "New Castle Lottery for Encouragement of the American China Manufacture" was held, and the next year William Alexander, Lord Sterling, disposed of his New York and New Jersey lands by a raffle. The same year George Washington recorded purchasing tickets in a "Delaware lottery." In March a Mr. Halsey and the president of New Jersey College (Princeton) were appointed to arrange a drawing at New Castle for the school.

This increasing business led the legislature to take control of all such projects in 1772. After the usual denunciations the act stated that, "Whereas lotteries for the disposal of private property at an over-rated value, for the sole benefit of the proprietors, and other selfish and illaudable purposes, have lately been set up and drawn in these Counties, and are become very frequent," a penalty of £500 was imposed on any originator, and buying, selling, or advertising chances would cost £10 for each offense. Parliamentary projects were excepted.[38]

Maryland had only private raffles until 1791, a liberality perhaps explained by the public nature of many of the drawings. In Annapolis in 1753–54, for example, a town clock was purchased and a public wharf built. In 1761 the First Presbyterian Church of Baltimore sought 300 pieces of eight to buy a lot, asking "the Generosity of our Fellow Christians to assist and encourage us in compleating a small lottery at a time when the Benevolence of our Countrymen is so well tried in this Way." [39]

The British attitude was still apparent, and as late as 1774 a New Jersey statute, fining all games in the nature of a lottery unless authorized by the General Assembly, was annulled on the ground that English ventures were not expressly exempted. This, although the colony's agent had explained that "The assembly of New Jersey probably take all lotteries Authorized by the Parliament of Great Britain to be State Lotteries . . ." [40] By the middle 1700's, however, colonial governments other than those in North Carolina and Maryland had succeeded in establishing the need for and their right to supervise these games. The drawings continued, but in slightly changed form. Whereas they had formerly been conducted at will, henceforth in these colonies they could be held only with the permission of the legislature and for goals more definitely in the public interest. Thus, as it had in other countries, the wheel turned again and another phase was begun.

Chapter III

Authorized Lotteries in
Colonial America

The silly man may buy a ticket
Perhaps 'twill open reason's wicket.
The lucky are accounted wise,
And so they are — in folly's eyes,
Who nought but fortune deifies.[1]

To understand why authorities began licensing lotteries rather than abolishing them altogether, it is necessary first to remember that the people as a whole wanted them, believing that the drawings could be kept honest. Most vocal opposition ceased with the assumption of government regulation; it was one's own affair if he risked his money in an honest lottery. Loyal citizens even were willing to circumvent the law, if need be, when a church or school was to benefit.

Second, and more important, all of the provinces needed funds to meet the high costs of wars against the French and Indians[2] and to perform other public services. Underlying this was the financial instability of the period. An unfavorable balance of trade with England drained specie from the colonies, and attempts to meet the need for a circulating medium by emitting bills of credit was scotched by the royal government. Caught between the desires of the indebted people for easy money and that of the crown for economic stability, the local authorities tried to appease both sides and failed completely. The net result was that the assemblies found themselves habitually short of funds, with the taxpayers resisting additional levies.

Lotteries seemed to offer an easy solution to these problems. Remembering the success of European countries with lotteries and observing the willingness of their own people to participate in them, it was inevitable that colonial officials should conclude that raffles offered a less painful method of raising cash than did imposing a new tax. Thus, schemes for the profit of one particular person were superseded by public ventures designed to aid governments, religious sects, schools, internal improvements, certain types of industries, and ill-fortuned individuals.

As a rule these undertakings followed a definite pattern. Generally some group of citizens would feel the need of an improvement that could not be readily financed by voluntary contributions. They then petitioned the General Assembly for permission to set up a lottery; the legislature, unwilling to levy new taxes, authorized it, and established the rules for the drawing.

Illustrative of this procedure is a Pennsylvania act of February 15, 1765. The preamble read:

Whereas it hath been represented to the assembly of this province by the church-wardens and vestrymen of the united congregations of Christ's Church and St. Peter's and by the trustees of St. Paul's Church, lately built in the City of Philadelphia, that notwithstanding the generous subscriptions heretofore made by the members of said churches toward raising a sum of money for the erecting and finishing thereof, there yet remains due upon the former the heavy debt of near fifteen hundred pounds and from the latter near the sum of five hundred pounds more than they have been able to procure for the completing their commendable and religious designs . . . We the representatives of the province of Pennsylvania, being desirous of aiding and encouraging such charitable and pious designs do pray that it may be enacted:
. . . That Henry Harris and Jacob Duchu, Esquires . . . shall be hereby nominated and appointed managers and directors of the lottery hereby instituted and directed to be drawn for the preparing and disposing of tickets and to oversee the drawing of the lots and to order and perform all such matters and things as are hereinafter directed . . .[3]

In accordance with this law, books were prepared with each page divided into three columns, with the innermost listing tickets numbered one to 13,350. The two outer columns were identical with the first, and the three tickets, in a horizontal row, were joined with oblique lines. Besides the year and number, each billet had printed on it: "This ticket entitles the bearer to such prize as may be drawn against its number if demanded in nine months after the drawing is finished, subject to such deductions as is mentioned in the scheme." The cost was thirty shillings each, and when sold, the tickets in the outer column were cut out of the books through the oblique lines, "indent-wise," signed by one of the managers, and handed to the purchaser. When all the chances in the outside column had been disposed of, the ones in the middle were clipped, rolled up, and "made fast with thread or silk," and put in a box marked "A." This container was then fastened with several seals by the managers. The tickets in the innermost column were left in the books for discovering any frauds or mistakes.

To determine the prizes the managers prepared other books containing two identical columns of 13,350 tickets each. Of these, 4,821 were "fortunate," and each had the prize it would bring printed across the face, the number of awards and the amounts being prescribed by the statute authorizing the lottery. In the present case these totaled £20,025, the sale value of all the tickets, from which the managers would deduct 15 per cent for the benefit of the churches before paying the winners. The "fortunates" and remaining "blanks" were cut from the outside column, rolled, tied, and sealed in box "B."

On the day of the drawing the managers were present at some public and convenient room at nine o'clock in the morning. There they had the two boxes opened and the tickets in each were carefully mixed in the presence of the participants. They then appointed "some one indifferent and fit person" to draw a number from box "A" and another person to select a ticket from box "B." Both slips were immediately unrolled and read aloud. If it were a prize ticket, the number and the reward were recorded and two of the managers signed as witnesses. The drawing continued until the billets were exhausted. The "fortunate" numbers and the amounts of each were published in the *Pennsylvania Gazette*. Each manager took an oath not to seek a prize for himself or any other person, to combat "any undue or sinister practice," and to deal justly with all adventurers. This particular act remained in force for twelve months.[4]

The above pattern, with minor modifications, prevailed in all colonies. The size of the scheme and the time allowed in which to draw it varied, as did the amount deducted and the proportion of rewards to blanks. Later, rotating drums, or "wheels," were substituted for the boxes and in some provinces the directors were required to give bond for honest behavior. The Massachusetts Faneuil Hall Lottery of 1762 illustrates the arrangement of prizes and a variation in which a certain sum was held back for the beneficiary and the remaining money divided as winnings instead of the usual practice of taking a percentage of the prizes. This plan, as reported in the Boston *Gazette*, November 1, 1762, provided the following awards:

1	prize of	1,000	is	1,000	dollars
1	" "	500	is	500	"
2	" "	200	are	400	"
12	" "	100	"	1,200	"
20	" "	50	"	1,000	"
20	" "	20	"	400	"
30	" "	10	"	300	"
200	" "	6	"	1,200	"
1200	" "	4	"	4,800	"

1486 Prizes   10,800
4514 Blanks

6000 Tickets at 2 dollars each is $12,000
       To be paid as prizes   10,800

Remains for the use of Faneuil Hall $ 1,200

With a proven technique at hand and public acceptance amply assured, the combined pressure of indebtedness and war expenditures led to the initial use of authorized lotteries. The first such in any colony was held in 1744 to raise £7,500 for the government of Massachusetts. The preamble of the enabling act justified it by the great expenses incurred in protecting the seacoast, the New England frontier, and the province of Nova Scotia against the French since the outbreak of King George's War. Since the inhabitants already were shouldering heavy poll and real estate taxes, and since a debt yet remained, it was desirable to clear it in the manner least burdensome to the people. An interesting feature of the lottery, illustrating the currency difficulties of the times, was the provision that chances could be bought by paying one-fifth in new tenor bills or in old tenor bills at the rate of four for one, and four-fifths either in like bills or in bills of credit of the other colonies whose issues were not prohibited by law. Since one-fifth of the value of all prizes was to go to the treasury, tickets worth £37,500 had to be sold. By a concurrent vote of the General Court, the directors were forbidden to sell billets to any Indian, Negro, or mulatto, since such action "might prove of mischievous consequence in many respects." [5]

The sponsorship of the government, the lure of a "good" cause, the "blue ribbon" roster of wealthy and socially prominent managers,[6] all united to make the Massachusetts undertaking a financial triumph. This success encouraged imitation, and once the gate had been opened, it was difficult to close it against other worthy needs.

Less than a year later the New York Assembly began debating the feasibility of raising £3,375 by lottery to fortify the approaches to New York City. An act was passed on February 27, 1746, necessitated, according to the preamble, by King George's War. The chances, priced at £1 10s., had a slow sale. On May 3 the treasurer of the colony was empowered to spend £1,000 for tickets and the time of drawing was postponed from June 1 to September 1. This expedient failed, and on July 15 that official was authorized to buy all the unsold billets, so the government ended by playing the game pretty much with itself.

The common fear of the French existed also in Pennsylvania. But although the danger was present, the funds with which to meet it were not. An authorized lottery was impossible because of Quaker opposition to both such schemes and war. Nevertheless, in 1746, with approval of the governor and the Philadelphia Council, 10,000 tickets at two pounds each were offered the public under the auspices of Benjamin Franklin and Edward Shippen: £3,000 was to erect batteries for the defense of Philadelphia and the remaining £17,000 to provide prizes. As encouragement the Council purchased 2,000 billets and turned back some of the prizes it won.

It is impossible to discover how much active opposition this undertaking encountered from the Friends. A statement by a staunch antilottery author writing almost a hundred years later suggested that it was considerable,[7] but probably more typical was the experience of Benjamin Franklin. In his *Autobiography* he told of proposing that his fire company spend £60 on tickets, but since twenty-two of the thirty members were Quakers, Franklin felt that the suggestion was likely to be rejected. On the night the vote was to be taken only one of the Quakers came to oppose the measure and eight others sent word of their willingness to come and support it if necessary, otherwise they preferred not to appear. Thus Franklin reasoned that twenty-one members favored the lottery to the extent of not being against it. He also added that his Quaker friend, James Logan, gave him £60 for chances but would accept no prizes. Accordingly, it would seem that while the Quakers did not openly identify themselves with the lottery for fortifying the city, they supported the measure by not denouncing it.

The popularity of this enterprise was shown in the notice issued February 2, 1747: "Preparations are making to begin the drawing of the Lottery on Monday next. The managers having no tickets left, and the demand still continuing, the Corporation continue to spare of the number they have bought, which may be had at the Post office till saturday next." [8] On March 1 the managers announced through the Philadelphia newspapers that most of the award money had been paid and that now they would turn to the construction of the batteries, inviting written comment from anyone knowing anything about the subject.

But the needs of war were not the only problems demanding a financial solution. Citing the shortage of public funds, badly depreciated paper currency, and the inability of the populace to pay additional taxes, the Rhode Island General Assembly on October 31, 1744, passed an act allowing lotteries to be "set up and put forth" with the consent of the legislature. This same body then appointed a committee of outstanding citizens to so raise £3,000 for a bridge across the Weybosset River at Providence. Not only was this sum raised, but since expenses were overestimated, the province netted £1,389 12s. 8p. In view of this and the successful conclusion of a £10,000 scheme to pave Newport streets three years later, it is not surprising that Rhode Island began an almost unbroken chain of grants.

Despite its earlier discouraging experiment, New York licensed another lottery in December 1746, the first of a series to raise funds for the founding of King's College, later known as Columbia University. This venture sought £2,250, and as Governor George Clinton explained to the Lords of Trade, was for "the advancement of learning, which is absolutely necessary, and much wanted in the Province." In April 1748 another grant was made for £1,800. According to a broadside issued at the time there were 8,000 tickets, at thirty shillings each, 1,304 of which carried prizes.[9] The lottery ran into difficulties, and once more the treasurer of the colony bought all unsold chances.

These repeated failures temporarily discouraged further New York authorizations but did not prevent wags from seeing the practical possibilities of the device. In 1747 a lady proposed a "Charitable Lottery" for the aid of distressed widows and deserving virgins. Since ordinary means had not secured husbands for them, she proposed that all such females between the ages of fifteen and fifty should be disposed of by lottery. Each unmarried male between the same ages would be required to buy one ticket at the cost of five pounds, the prizes being the said ladies ranked in order of desirability from "Beauties" down to "Saints of the First Magnitude."

In an undated letter to a trustee of Yale College, President Thomas Clap indicated how minds were working in Connecticut. He wrote that several colleges had had lotteries set up for them and, referring probably to King's College, added:

. . . it is probable, considering the Humour of Mankind, that Considerable Sums of Money will go out of this Government to build a college there. It is therefore tho't by Some, that it is best to take mankind in their own Humour and set up a lottery for building a College here. We want a new College [building] very much and the matter now lies before the Assembly, but considering the vast sums of Bills already emitted, it seems not likely that they will emit any more for Such a purpose. I have therefore had tho'ts that, if you & some other Trustees . . . think it convenient, and Some of the leading Members of the Assembly next week should advise to it, that then I would make a Motion to the Assembly for that purpose.[10]

President Clap undoubtedly secured his desired encouragement, for the first Connecticut license, in May 1747, favored Yale. The preamble stated that a new building was necessary to house half of the students. The face value of the drawing was set at £50,000, old tenor, with 15 per cent of the prizes going to the college. The project raised only £5,400, instead of the £7,500 expected, and the managers retained £200 for expenses. Because of the inflation and confusion of paper money at the time, the proceeds equaled only about £775 sterling.[11]

Rhode Island added a new dimension to the use of legal lotteries when in 1748 its third grant benefited an individual and illustrated one of the hazards of colonial life. According to this act, Joseph Fox,

"Scrivener of Newport," had been in jail for two years for a debt of £3,000. Having no way of supporting himself, his wife and several children, he could not pay the sum. Since the debt "ought in justice to be paid out of the estate of the late John Gridley, Esq.," a lottery for £32,000 was instituted with 8,000 tickets at four pounds each, one-eighth of the prizes to be deducted to free Fox from "these deplorable circumstances." Everyone apparently profited, for after payment of the debt, awards, and expenses, £406 14s. 8p. was cleared for the colony's treasury.

During the next three years, 1749–1751, a total of six lotteries were authorized — three by Massachusetts, two by Rhode Island, and one by Connecticut (see Table 1 at the end of this chapter). One aided a hard-luck case: in 1750 Rhode Island came to the assistance of Colonel Joseph Pendleton, who lost an uninsured vessel with a cargo of rum and molasses and could not pay his debts except by selling his real estate at a fair price. The market for land was poor, but luckily his land was admirably located and endowed for the site of a town. The Assembly therefore agreed to allow him to dispose of it by raffle. He divided the land into 124 lots for establishing a village and, as added inducements, offered cash prizes totaling £15,636. The result was payment of his debts, the beginning of "Lotteryville," and a surplus of £783 12s. for the provincial treasury.

Massachusetts, pressed by a large war debt the same year, moved to raise 26,700 milled dollars by lottery for the provincial government, on the basis that the changed circumstance of the settlements since the last evaluation made it impossible to levy a tax to pay off the debt with justice to all. The urgent need for funds caused the General Court to postpone redemption of the prizes, offering interest at 3 per cent instead. Despite the mortgaging of a tax of £8,010 to insure this payment, the tickets priced at three milled dollars each were not sold in the two months allotted by law. Two supplementary acts extended the time, allowed the purchase of chances in province bills and orders on the treasury, and raised the interest on unpaid awards to 6 per cent. Still sales dragged and finally the project was dropped. Officials blamed the failure on competition from outside the colony, complaining that "all the good laws made in Massachusetts against lotteries are rendered ineffectual by lotteries set up in the neighboring governments, and the sale of tickets in Massachusetts." A fine of £40 was placed upon receiving or buying "foreign" tickets, but complete indemnity from punishment was assured those turning state's evidence in such cases.

Apparently the surplus of authorized and private lotteries was general, for no new ones were sanctioned in 1752. The lull, however, was brief, and the next year brought four into the market. In New York on July 4, 1753, managers Peter Van Brugh Livingston and Jacobus Roosevelt were authorized to seek £1,125 for King's College. The act bore testimony to the growing feud between the Presbyterians, who opposed the school, and the Anglicans, who sponsored it. To keep the former from diverting the funds, an unusual clause in the statute declared that any representative who voted or consented to a diversion of this money would be ineligible to sit or vote in that or succeeding assemblies.[12] An identical scheme again was approved in the following December.

An interesting example of neighborliness was manifested that year when the six-year-old College of New Jersey (later Princeton), having been repeatedly refused a lottery by that colony, petitioned the Connecticut Assembly and was granted the right to hold a drawing in the town of Stamford. Oddly enough, it was allowed to raise a maximum of £2,000 "New York currency." It appears, however, that this undertaking was never completed.[13] Nor did Rhode Island have any better success with its 1753 lottery for four beneficiaries. The time of drawing was twice postponed before the legislature ordered the money refunded.

The year 1754 was destined to be an important one in America. Again history was unconsciously mirrored in the lottery grants of the day. In October, the Virginia legislature initiated a scheme to raise £6,000 to protect its citizens against the "insults and incroachments of the French." What went unsaid was that the trouble had resulted from the Virginia-backed Ohio Land Company's efforts to "incroach" upon the land claimed by France, and the final "insult" was the French defeat of young Colonel George Washington and Virginia troops the preceding July. Thus had begun the French and Indian War.

The enacting statute contained minutely detailed instructions, reflecting some of the experience gained from the numerous private lotteries active in the colony. The boxes holding the tickets were to be secured with seven different locks, each manager holding a key. The wheels, from which the prize numbers were chosen, were to be turned for fifteen minutes before the initial drawing and one-half minute between each selection. The directors were to receive one per cent of sales and vendors two pence for each ticket sold. Counterfeiting of chances became a felony.

The war, which was to serve as the direct or indirect excuse for numerous lotteries in the ensuing years, was slow to reach the North. The remainder of that year and the next saw drawings for four nonmilitary projects, but in 1756 only two of the five schemes legalized were for pacific purposes (see Table 1). In one, action was taken to restore harmony between the Anglicans and Presbyterians when the New York legislature gave half the funds raised for King's College to the City of New York for a jail and "Pest house" for persons with "contagious Distempers." Mindful of the penalty for such action, the legislators first had taken the precaution of repealing that section of the law of 1753.

The other three lotteries authorized in 1756 echoed the war. New York acts to arm the poor people of Richmond County and build a jail in New York City to house war prisoners were quickly passed. Rhode Island instigated a plan to raise funds to repair and arm the principal fortress of the colony, Fort George on Goat Island. (See Table 1.) Each drawing had 2,510 prizes, from ten to one hundred pounds each, and 7,490 blanks. In an interesting feature the Assembly protected the managers from all damages growing out of fire, attacks by the enemy, counterfeit bills, or any other extraordinary casualty. Whether through lack of money or patriotism, sales went so slowly that after two postponements the legislature agreed to take 500 tickets on its own account and "Risque." Even this boost was insufficient and the project was dropped.

The Connecticut Assembly announced in February 1757, "forasmuch as this Colony by past services for the protection and defence of his Majesty's just rights and dominions in North America against the common enemy is involved in debt and the public treasury much exhausted and supplies sufficient and seasonable for the next campaign cannot be obtained without great difficulty in the usual way . . ." citizens were asked to make free contributions to the government and to patronize a lottery to raise £8,000.

The year 1757 was also marked by two "firsts" in lottery history — a manufacturing firm was aided by Massachusetts and New Hampshire sanctioned her first lotteries (see Table 1). Governor Sir

Francis Bernard of Massachusetts told this story in a letter to the Lords of Trade on November 15, 1766: "In the year —— a manufactory for making glass bottles was set up at a Place called Germantown by Germans settled there, under English Taskmasters. In the year 1754, upon a petition that some of their buildings had been destroyed by fire or otherwise, the General Court granted them 1215£ to be raised by Lottery. The Bottle Manufactory is now quite at an End." [14]

Meanwhile, the early reverses suffered by the English in the French and Indian War brought the talented and energetic William Pitt into power as Secretary of State for the Southern Department, 1757–1761. He not only directed Britain's successful campaign for Canada, but also secured more financial cooperation from the colonies. Under his requisition system the assemblies voted money for recruiting, clothing, and paying the wages of the colonial troops. In 1758, to meet her share of the expenses in the projected drive on Canada, Massachusetts licensed a lottery to raise £30,000. The Council appointed Thomas Hutchinson and James Bowdoin, both future governors, as managers. The act provided that prizes would be paid in treasury notes to draw 6 per cent until the province was reimbursed by Parliament. A tax of £34,000 due in 1760 was mortgaged as security. Like the similar attempt in 1750 to pay off in I.O.U.'s, this project also failed and the money was ordered returned to ticket holders. Possibly as an adjunct to the war effort, £1,200 was sought to bridge the Saco and Pesumpscot rivers.

Elsewhere that year New York instigated a drawing for £1,125 to repay the city of Albany for expenses incurred in the conflict, and Rhode Island moved to aid a war casualty. Handley Chipman of Newport had bought a piece of land and built a "Still House, Soap House, Cooper's Shop, Ware House, Joiner's Shop, Chaise House and Stable," hoping for enough business to pay his debt. And he "probably should have done it, had not War come on, which has in a great Measure broke up the Business of Distilling and greatly injured almost every other trade." To clear himself he had outfitted a ship for trade, but he and his vessel had been captured by the enemy and all his present possessions lost. There was no way out except to sell his real estate and "no Person . . . will give any Thing near the Value of it." A lottery for £30,000 was assigned for his use.

The increased tempo of war put more and more financial pressure on both individuals and governments. Correspondingly, lottery schemes became more and more attractive and were granted with increasing frequency in the four remaining years of the conflict. No less than six governments, two for the first time, turned to this expedient in 1759, instigating ten different projects. North Carolina's governor explained her reason when he wrote to his English supervisors: "They . . . passed two small Bills, one for a Lottery for finishing the Churches of Wilmington and Brunswick, which I consented to as the like Bills are always passed in the Northern Provinces, and we can't get Vestries here that will lay on any Taxes to build Churches." [15] New Jersey made her initial move with three annual schemes of £600 each to repay the government for money advanced to quit Indian land claims. The managers stated their confidence that the drawings would prove popular "when it is rightfully considered how much Christian Blood this Purchase probably saved."

Elsewhere the franchises were varied. Connecticut approved schemes of £100 to recompense the owners of a house burned while occupied by English troops and to allow Matthew Stewart to dispose of four farms in order to recoup losses at sea. The latter perpetrated a fraud, for Stewart had secretly sold his holdings, and as late as 1770 the legislature was endeavoring to straighten out the affair.

The first lottery grant to a Masonic organization was given by Rhode Island in 1759. The "Society of Free and Accepted Masons" of Newport showed it knew the true way to a legislator's heart. Its petition was based on the grounds that the town had no building "sufficiently large and commodious for public entertainment, where the Governor and Council, or General Assembly may occasionally meet and dine; and where any of His Majesty's Governors, or other officers may be publicly entertained as they pass through this government." Thus the enabling act stipulated that the hall could be used for "celebrations of all publick Feasts and Entertainments" in which the governor and Assembly were "immediately concerned," but anyone else had to have the consent of the society.

All this activity and the grant of thirteen more lotteries in 1760 brought problems. New York, for example, had long been a market for large numbers of chances in schemes held outside its borders. The New York *Gazette* carried advertisements for most of the drawings, licensed and unlicensed, in the neighboring colonies. The March 5, 1753, issue noted the willingness of David Van Horn, Nathanial Hazard, and Daniel De Fore to sell tickets for a Pennsylvania venture to build a steeple on a Presbyterian church. The College of New Jersey announced its drawings on November 26. On April 22, 1754, the Reverend Henry Rapps, Lutheran minister in New York City, stated he had tickets to sell in the Germantown Lutheran Congregation Lottery; March 10, 1775, a church in New Jersey was represented; February and March 1756 saw appeals for the Academy Lottery of Philadelphia and for Robert Sloan of Connecticut; and so on and on it went. So common were these "foreign" billets that in December 1759 Lieutenant Governor James DeLancy pointed out to the Council "a Defect in the Act against private Lotteries, for though the law be sufficient to restrain them in this Government, yet it seems to fall short of the End proposed, as it leaves this [colony], a Mart for the Lotteries set on Foot in other Provinces." [16] A few days later an act was passed imposing a fine of six pounds upon persons selling tickets in out-of-state schemes.

By 1760 lotteries had become so important in Rhode Island's financial set-up as to warrant special attention in the courts. By a retroactive law of that date, directors of schemes instituted for public purposes were empowered to call special courts, consisting of three superior court judges, to hear suits over the collection of ticket money or payment of prizes.

Nor were all minds yet in agreement concerning the morals of the device. John Woolman, famous as an early opponent of slavery, wrote of a Quaker meeting for church discipline held in Newport on July 13, 1760:

. . . an Exercise revived on my mind in relation to lotteries which were common in those parts.

I had once moved it in a former setting of this meeting, when Arguments were Used in favor of Friends being held Excused who were only Concerned in such Lotteries as were agreeable to Law, and Now on moving it again, it was opposed as before. But the hearts of Some Solid Friends appeared to be united to discourage the practice amongst their Members, and the matter was Zealously handled by Some on both sides. In this debate it appeared very clear to me that the Spirit of Lotteries was a Spirit of Selfishness which tended to Confusion and darkness of understanding, and that pleading for it in our meetings set apart for the Lords work, was not right . . . At length a minute was made, a copy of which was agreed to be sent to their Several Quarterly Meetings, Inciting Friends to Labour to discourage the practice amongst all professing with us.[17]

But public opinion was more accurately reflected by the Reverend Samuel Seabury, father of Episcopal Bishop Samuel Seabury, when he recorded in his diary: "The ticket No. 5866 in the Light House and Public Lottery of New York, drew in my favor, by the blessing of Almighty God, 500 pounds sterling, of which I received 425 pounds, there being a deduction of fifteen per cent; for which I now record to my posterity my thanks and praise to Almighty God, the giver of all good gifts." [18]

With moral and public support generally assured, it is not surprising that legislators saw no necessity for curtailing their liberality. Of the thirteen lotteries granted in 1760 Massachusetts furnished six. One of these wrote a finish to a famous event in that state's financial history. In 1739–40 a land bank had been established by private individuals to issue paper money with land as security. But the interest on the notes accumulated faster than it could be paid, and on March 10, 1758, William Stoddard and his partners petitioned the General Court for relief. Finally an act of February 13–14, 1760, permitted them to hold a lottery, because, as the preamble stated, nearly one thousand pounds in paper had to be redeemed and this method was to be used to put a "final end to the perplexed affairs of that Company." The law provided for raising £3,500 sterling; any surplus after the bills were called in was to go to the provincial treasury. This scheme proved unpopular and after three postponements was finally abandoned.

The lottery franchises of 1761 were characterized primarily by the growing interest in water navigation, which accounted for almost half of them. At the same time there were schemes to finance paving city streets and building a meetinghouse for the "Baptist Society of the Ancient Order" in Rhode Island; repairs on buildings in New Jersey and on New York City's city hall. Earlier Boston's Faneuil Hall had been destroyed by fire. At a town meeting the Boston selectmen had been empowered to petition the General Court for help in rebuilding the hall on the grounds of a financial depression. A lottery was approved and the list of managers for the undertaking read like a Boston *Who's Who* of that period: Thomas Cushing, Samuel Hewes, John Scollay, Benjamin Austin, Samuel

Phillips Savage, Ezekiel Lewis, and Samuel Sewall. John Hancock's now-famous signature appeared on some of the tickets.[19] The directors announced that "the necessity of a large and convenient Hall in such a Town as this, upon all Public Occasions, Can't be disputed . . . and the Encouragement it will meet with from the Public, will, we doubt not, be in some Measure proportionable to its Importance."

This venture was successful but the cost of completing the hall proved greater than expected, and a second drawing was allowed in 1762, helping to run that year's total to the largest number of lotteries legalized before the Revolution. Of the eighteen lotteries originated, one allowed the trustees of Princeton College to seek £3,000, with the provision that no tickets be sold until previously sanctioned undertakings were concluded.[20] Rhode Island supplied twelve of this total for purposes which included constructing a workhouse for paupers in Kent County; repairing a steeple on the Anglican church at Providence; selling the goods of Captain Edward Wells, Jr., whose ships had been captured by the enemy and whose partner had gone bankrupt leaving him with the debts; removing Pawtucket Falls so that fish could go up the river; ransoming Samuel Dunn's mate, held hostage by the French in the West Indies in lieu of 1,000 pieces of eight demanded for his captured vessel (the ship and cargo were lost off North Carolina on the way home); and relieving a jailor who had gone into debt because so many of his prisoners had enlisted in the colonial army and gone away without paying their board bills.[21] Partial explanation of these ventures can be found in the jailor's plea that "money is so hard to be raised, that he cannot sell [his] Estate for but little more than Half the Value, which will not be sufficient to pay his just Debts." This situation may also explain why even the magic of a lottery was not always successful. The managers of the Johnston Baptist church venture (1761) reported to the Assembly that they had drawn the first class, after a "great Deal of Trouble and Pains," and though they had spent large sums of their own, "the present Scarcity of Money, together with the many lotteries now on Foot, render it impracticable for the Petitioners to proceed any further in the said Affair."

The year of the peace treaty, 1763, saw a change in England's attitude toward her colonies. Instead of viewing them as outlets for commerce, she also came to see them as sources of revenue. Colonial interests quickly felt the bind of the tightened controls. Few American colonists relished regulations of any kind; they were an independent and self-sufficient people. But until the restrictions upon their "rights" became more than the people could bear, the stringent British acts worked increasing hardships on the finances of the colonies.

Thus, the year 1763 saw only nine new lotteries, and the beginning of a sharp decline in the number of authorizations. Rhode Island again led with seven, three for bridges, two for streets, and one each for a wharf and a church group. The inhabitants of Little Compton, in petitioning for the wharf, said they would have constructed it, but that they were "very much reduced in their Estates by Reason of high Taxes, and their Crops of Corn and Hay falling short, there not being one Half of the Hay cut or Stock kept in former Years." The Presbyterians in Providence, desiring to build a parsonage and provide for a "settled Gospel minister," held out the hope that the greater part of their lottery tickets would be sold outside the colony.

But money was scarce everywhere, and Pontiac's Indian war and the growing friction with England diverted the attention of legislators. Only three grants, all made by Rhode Island, occurred during the year of the Sugar Act — 1764. The next year saw Massachusetts' final lottery of the colonial period. But at the same time Pennsylvania made its initial bow with a blanket bill to raise £3,003 15s. for seven Episcopal churches. Among this group was St. Peter's Church in Philadelphia. Its construction had plunged its members heavily into debt from which they had hoped to extract themselves without "recourse to Lotteries," but the "sudden rise of the price of materials and labour" made that impossible. A worse time for promoting the scheme could not have been chosen, for Parliament passed the Stamp Act in March, and Philadelphia merchants retaliated with a nonimportation agreement. Prices rose rapidly again, and the tickets failed to sell. After a postponement, the final day of the lottery (May 27, 1767) found 2,000 chances unsold. The final outcome is unknown, but quite likely nothing was realized.

Elsewhere the story was the same. The fate of a New Jersey scheme to raise £500 to straighten that colony's section of the road from New York to Philadelphia is seen from the New York *Journal's* announcement, December 18, 1766, that its postponement had been necessitated by "the troubled State of Affairs at that time, occasioned by the Stamp Act."

Meantime Harvard College was sorely pressed for student quarters and after long agitation was allowed by the Massachusetts General Court to seek £3,200. The preamble of the enabling act stated the great need for rooms, which would become worse when Stoughton Hall "shall be pulled down as by its present ruinous state it appears it soon must be." Since there were no building funds and because of the expense the government had borne in erecting Hollis Hall and repairing "Harvard College," it could not be expected that any further aid should come from that source. So there was "no other resort . . . left but to private Benefaction, which it is conceived, will be best excited by means of a Lottery."

In spite of this expectation, the project was destined to have a troubled future. Born amidst the clamor and confusion of the Stamp Act period, it suffered directorial trouble, including the death of the college president, Edward Holyoke, and the lack of sales appeal in the turbulent 1770's. In June 1771 the first set of managers refused to be prodded into action and resigned. Their successors had so much trouble disposing of the chances that they gave notice in 1775 that "unless the College would take off a number of the tickets," they, too, would quit. The school officials, feeling it their duty to prevent the "failure of so good a design," voted to take 2,000 tickets if so many remained unsold at the time of drawing. The outcome was noted in the college records: "N.B. The managers of the aforesaid Lottery afterw'd gave it up, the war breaking out."

These experiences should have given pause to the most enthusiastic of advocates. The only new activity in 1766 came when New Hampshire sought funds for a highway at Rye and the Council of West Florida allowed Nathaniel Thompson to raffle his house. But hope springs eternal and the following year Rhode Island renewed her efforts, seeking funds for three projects, including one allowing the Baptist congregation of Warren to finish their parsonage for the Reverend James Manning, who "hath now under his care several Pupils to be educated in the liberal Arts, who cannot be accommodated in the said House in its present condition." [22] A "Pier or Bason" at Gosport received New Hampshire's approval, only to be dropped later "by reason of the scarcity of money."

Maryland's nearest approach to an authorized lottery also came in 1767. A letter of Governor Horatio Sharpe to Hugh Hamersley on March 11 gives an interesting account of this development. Control of the Clerk of Council's salary had led to a dispute between Sharpe and the lower house. To substantiate their claim, the legislators sought money for an appeal to the crown. Of this, the governor recounted:

. . . they likewise Resolved [the lower house] to set a Lottery on foot for raising the Sum of £1,000 in Aid of the subscription & several of the Members undertook to act as Managers. You will see by the Scheme published in the inclosed Gazette what Arts they practize to draw peoples Money out of their Pocketts but I am told that the Managers would nevertheless have been greatly puzled to get off their Tickets had not the Pennsylvanians bought whole Books of them . . . They will however I suppose raise money enough by one means or another to prosecute the Affair.[23]

In June Governor Sharpe wrote that on the date set for conclusion of the scheme it still had not been drawn and the managers complained, despite its being known as the "Liberty Lottery," that the "People have not shewn such a liberal or patriotic Spirit as they expected would have been manifested on such an Occasion." [24] The final results are unknown, but there is evidence that the affair had not ended even by the next November.

The years 1768 and 1769 saw only nine new authorizations. Rhode Island accounted for five, Pennsylvania for three, and New Hampshire for one. Rhode Island's contribution consisted of schemes for street paving in Newport, the highway leading into Connecticut (after its inhabitants had promised not only to take a large number of tickets but also to have the road on their side repaired), a flood-damaged bridge, a workhouse in North Kingstown (which was "greatly burthened with poor People"), and a company which had suffered losses from fire and high tides in building Long Wharf at Newport.

The Pennsylvania legislature in February 1768 approved a project of £5,250 for purchasing a public landing and paving some streets in Philadelphia. In January 1769, weary of repeated requests, it resolved to receive no more petitions and recommended that succeeding sessions deny grants except for public purposes. This advice evidently did not apply to requests on hand since two were approved in February which aided a total of seven churches (see Table 1).

The year 1769 was more important for a near fatal blow dealt to lotteries by the British government. For a number of years royal authorities had viewed with growing concern the use being made of this device by the Americans. As early as April 21, 1761, following Massachusetts' passage of several lottery bills, the Lords of Trade pointed out in a letter that the acts provided for

temporary and inconsiderable Services of Ferries, Roads etc. by Lotteries, which is a mode of raising Money, that in Our Opinion ought never to be countenanced, and hardly be admitted into practice upon the most pressing Exigency of the State, more especially in the Colonies, where the forms of Government may not admit of those regulations and Checks, which are necessary to prevent fraud and abuse, in a matter so peculiarly liable to them.

The Lords of Trade not only objected to the use of lotteries upon general principle, but also opposed the "very unguarded and loose manner in which they are in general framed." In short, they would have recommended to the king that the laws be disallowed, except for the fact that they had probably already been carried out. However, "it is Our Duty to desire, that you will not for the future give your Assent to any Laws of the Like Nature." [25]

On May 8, 1761, Massachusetts' English agent wrote to clarify this action:

Lord Sandys having in his hand four acts for lotteries, he inveigh'd against them as mischievous in their nature, destructive to labor and industry, and introductive of the spirit of gaming, ever attended with many ill consequences. In excuse for these acts, I observed that the distress occasioned by the heavy expence of the war, of which the province had taken so large a part, had probably brought these lotteries into use; and the whole board having concurr'd with his lordship in declaring their evil nature, I told their lordships I wou'd take the first opportunity of acquainting the general Court with their sentiments thereupon.[26]

Evidently the General Court had acted in regard to the Faneuil Hall lottery (1761) before these letters were received. However, when the second drawing was approved the next year, Governor Bernard felt an explanation was desirable. On May 3, 1762, he wrote:

I take notice of this act only to declare that I am not unmindful of your Lordships orders concerning Lottery acts, from which I hope this act will not be considered as a departure altho it does make some addition to the

sum originally granted. Faneuil Hall the noblest public room in North
America was burnt down about a year and half ago. It belonged to the
town & should have been rebuilt by a general tax but the great losses by
fire which the inhabitants have suffered made that method to raise the
money impracticable.[27]

By acceding to this request the Lords of Trade unwittingly provided
the stage for the famous town meetings of the Revolution and justification for later raising £300 more for the Newbury bridge.

When friends of Harvard began their agitation, Governor Bernard postponed action until he could write to London. He explained,
October 20, 1762, that "irremidiable disorders" had broken out because the college was unable to bring all the students within its
walls and that it was impossible to ask the Assembly, after its "former ample beneficence," to contribute further. This being the case,
he felt no doubt that he should give his consent, but desired to
obtain from their Lordships a relaxation of their injunction or

rather a declaration that the rule of reasoning upon which your Lordships
disapproved of the raising the money by Lotterys for making bridges,
mend roads etc, matters due from the Community either of the County
or Townships, does not extend to this case. If there is any case wherein
a Lottery may be said to be lawfull & advisable, the providing for the
Education of youth in the higher path of learning, for which the general-
ity of the people are no ways obliged to contribute, is one upon this
principle.

Since he was under no injunction except theirs upon lottery bills of
"another kind," he begged their consent to this measure for the
benefit of a "Society well deserving your Lordship's favor, which is
neither like to be abused nor be repeated."[28] The permission was
granted, although on February 17, 1762, the Lords had objected to
North Carolina's usage of lotteries and advised her governor to dis-
sent in the future.

Ironically enough, the attention of the British government was attracted to New Jersey by that legislature's effort to straighten out
Peter Gordon's land raffle, an unapproved drawing held in 1757
outside New Jersey. An act was passed in 1762 to "relieve and secure
the Trustees and Managers of the said Lottery against any Action
that is or may be brought against them concerning the same." Noting
this action, the Lords of Trade informed the king on July 5, 1764,
that the law related to "a private Transaction, in which the Legisla-

ture of this Province has no Concern, nor ought in that Capacity to have interfered by an Act of Assembly in relation to it" and that it should not be confirmed. A short time later, in a letter to Governor William Franklin, the Lords condemned "the Practice, which has too much prevail'd in the Colony of New Jersey, of passing laws to empower people to set up private Lotteries." Even their use "for public Services is of very doubtfull policy, and is a measure seldom adopted except in cases of Public Exigency." Benjamin Franklin's son was able to answer that the statute in question preceded his term and that no law relative to lotteries had since been approved, "my Sentiments in that respect being entirely conformable to those of your Lordships." [29] But as we have seen, the "exigency" was not long in coming.

The Lords of Trade, in considering the act for paving Philadelphia streets and buying a landing (1768), called lotteries "a practice . . . obviously tending to disengage and mislead Adventurers therein from Industry and Attention to their proper callings and Occupations" and as introducing a spirit of "Dissipation prejudicial to the Fortunes of Individuals, and the Interest of the Public." [30] The license was allowed, however, but the Earl of Hillsborough, Secretary of State for the Colonies, in a letter on March 24, 1769, to the deputy-governor of Pennsylvania said it was "His Majesty's pleasure that you do not, upon any pretence whatever, give your Consent to any future Act of that Nature, without having previously received His Majesty's Permission for that purpose, upon a full representation . . . of the reasons and Necessity for enacting such Law." [31]

The climax came on June 30 when his Majesty's pleasure was made more emphatic. A circular letter to the governors of Massachusetts, New York, New Hampshire, New Jersey, Virginia, North Carolina, South Carolina, Georgia, and West Florida instructed them not to authorize any lottery without permission from the Crown. It read:

Whereas a Practice hath of late years prevailed in several of our colonies and plantations in America for passing laws for raising money by instituting public lotteries; and whereas it hath been represented to us that such practice doth tend to disengage those who become adventurers therein from that spirit of industry and attention to their proper callings and occupations on which the public welfare so greatly depends; and whereas it further appears that this practice of authorizing lotteries by acts of legislature hath been also extended to the enabling private persons to set up such lotteries, by means whereof great frauds and abuses have been committed; it is our will and pleasure that you do not give your assent to any act or acts for raising money by the institution of any public or private lotteries whatsoever until you shall have first transmitted unto us by one of our principal secretaries of state a draft . . . of such act or acts and shall receive our direction thereupon.[32]

Pennsylvania also fell under this ban because, although a proprietary province, she had to submit her laws to the king for approval within five years of passage. Delaware, whose claim of being a royal colony after her separation from Pennsylvania in 1704 was ignored by the British government, did not conform. Rhode Island, Connecticut, and Maryland, not being obliged by their charters to accept supervision, also continued to have lotteries until the Revolution.

The prohibition of colonial lotteries is difficult to explain in the light of the English authorities' actions at home. During the ten years preceding the proclamation there had been annual governmental lotteries, usually for £600,000. An even larger one, for £780,000 was held in 1769.[33] British hostility to overseas schemes probably arose from a conviction that the device had inherent evils which might be tolerated in a settled, stable economy but would probably prove ruinous under less favorable conditions. They seemed totally unaware that the frontier conditions gave added urgency to the need for lotteries. From the royal point of view, these drawings interfered with the development of trade and commerce — an intolerable situation — were degrading and subject to abuses, and competed with those ventures chartered by the home government. Officials also claimed that lottery speculation did not help stabilize the colonial financial structure, already demoralized by a superabundance of unsecured paper money. This proclamation was, of course, merely another aspect of the new colonial policy inaugurated after the French and Indian War whereby England tightened her hold on her overseas possessions and attempted to control more closely their economic life, thus ending the so-called period of "salutary neglect."

The scene of lottery activity now became more isolated. Maryland and Delaware, where no type of regulation existed, were now popular sources of origination. Rhode Island presented the only authorized schemes in 1770–71, a total of nine. Four were for bridges, two for churches — the "Sect called Baptist, whose Principles are contained in Hebrews, Chap. 6th and 1st, and 2d Verses" of Cranston and an Episcopal edifice in Providence — two for paving, and one for the Newport market house.

In 1772 Delaware's wide-open market was closed by the requirement of legislative authorization, but Rhode Island's projects were stepped up and Connecticut came back into the field.[34] Of the total of seventeen new grants, Rhode Island furnished thirteen. Six of these were for roads, streets, or bridges; four for religious groups; and one each for a wharf, a small pox hospital, and rebuilding the "Forge" in Coventry where a considerable part of the adjacent population was employed.

The year 1772 also apparently marked the first effort of any colonies coming under the royal ban to secure permissions for drawings. On August 19 New Jersey passed an act to raise £1,050 to repair the road leading through Bergen County to New York, with the proviso that no action would be taken until the King's consent had been given. That approval was not secured until 1774. George Washington was the prime mover of a bill in the Virginia House of Burgesses to secure money by lottery for "opening & extending the Navigation of Potowmach from the tide water to Fort Cumberland." Though the fate of this act is unknown, Governor John Murry, Earl of Dunmore, had been instructed in February 1771 to withhold his assent from any "private or public lotteries whatsoever." [35]

On November 25, 1772, the Reverend Doctor Eleazar Wheelock petitioned the New Hampshire legislature to be allowed to raise £5,000 for a "large house" at three-year-old Dartmouth College. The governor in a special message urged that the institution be helped, and the Assembly approached the new Secretary of State for the Colonies, the Earl of Dartmouth, for aid. The answer was apparently favorable, for Wheelock wrote on February 22, 1773, that he understood "it is likely the lottery will be granted." He proved overly optimistic, however, for nothing more was heard of the matter.[36]

After the large number of grants in 1772, it is not surprising that activity was curtailed the following year. Rhode Island's successful petitioners sought three, as did Connecticut's. Citizens of Colchester in the latter province held a lottery for £700 to replace a like sum lost when their tax collector absconded.

By this time a side effect of the royal proclamation of 1769 was being felt in the increasing numbers of unlawful drawings. As long as there had been abundant legal ventures, private undertakings held little appeal, for they could not offer the rich prizes or the same degree of protection to the purchaser. A New York act in 1772 provided not only for forfeiture of double the value of the illegal drawing, but also a fine of £10 on every chance sold and the confiscation of all prizes. By turning state's evidence persons who drew blanks could recover their money plus twice the cost of the law suit. To undermine the connivance between buyer and seller, the law permitted any manager who would testify for the government to keep his gains.

Connecticut faced this problem by placing a penalty of forty shillings upon each ticket sold in undertakings not authorized by the General Assembly. Although Pennsylvania took no new action, there were those who felt she should have. The Quaker yearly meeting of 1773 resolved: "It being observed that a number of lotteries have been set up for some time past, and desire of gain in this way being contrary to our religious professions and unjustifiable" and that some members had been "drawn to countenance and encourage this unjust and dishonorable practice," that the monthly meetings should labor against them. If any person, however, refused to condemn lotteries, "the testimony of Truth should be maintained against them." [37] In New Jersey a statute of March 1774 ordered forfeiture of the amount to be raised and a fine of three pounds per ticket for illegal raffles. The approach of war, however, must have solved her problem, for when the law was disallowed because it did not exempt English lotteries, no attempt was made to repass a modified version.[38]

Before the outbreak of hostilities, lottery supporters were to have one more fling. In 1774 Delaware apparently sanctioned its first drawing, a joint undertaking in favor of New Jersey College, the Presbyterian Church at Princeton, and the united congregations of New Castle and Christiana Bridge. The wide-scale interest is seen in the fact that the *Pennsylvania Journal and Weekly Advertiser*, June 15, 1774, carried a three-page supplement listing the prize-winning numbers. The announcement included a request that the "fortunate Adventurers . . . indulge the Managers with a few weeks time, to make the necessary collection in, as most of the Tickets were disposed of on credit, to persons at a considerable distance, and widely scattered through the different Provinces." [39]

There was also the Connecticut drawing for the church at Stonington, and in New York permission had been asked of the king to approve raffles of £12,000 for a "Province House" and a smaller amount to house the Church of England members in Brooklyn, where the Dutch Reformed congregation had the only existing church.[40] Rhode Island, liberal as usual, presented an assortment of ten lotteries for unusually appealing causes. Five were for individuals who had fallen upon hard times, two were for churches, one for a school, and another for building a gristmill dam. Prophetically, her last project, and what was probably the last in any colony before the war, was to outfit Jeremiah Hopkins as a gunsmith, because "Guns are much wanted at this Time when they cannot be imported from Great Britain."

Thus, a device considered too dangerous for individuals had become a common resort of debt-burdened governments. By 1775 all of the colonies had had experience with lotteries, either licensed, unlicensed, or both. In general the inhabitants had shown no disposition to disapprove of the practice, but on the contrary, had welcomed drawings, particularly when they benefited schools, churches, or the residents of specific areas. Not even the crown's heavy hand quenched the colonists' desire for such undertakings. The requests sent to London for royal permission, the resurgence of privately initiated schemes, and the scale on which lotteries were resumed after the Revolution indicate this. In fact, during the colonial period only the Quakers were convinced of the evil of the ventures, and they lost their lone point of control, the Pennsylvania Assembly, by the 1750's. The clergy, the only other group likely to oppose the custom, was effectively silenced by the rich rewards reaped by churches of all denominations. The one lesson learned (and this was not universal) was the necessity for governmental control. Abuses were recognized, but these were attributed not to lotteries *per se*, but to the excesses incident to unregulated schemes.

Undeniably lotteries made an important contribution to colonial finances, providing a means of collecting funds for projects too costly for the local governments or too large for private parties to handle unaided. Classed according to the object to be benefited, fifty-eight were for internal improvements, thirty-nine for cities and counties, twenty-seven for churches, nineteen for relief of individuals, thirteen for schools, ten for use of colonial governments, and

five for industries. It is impossible to estimate the number of unlicensed drawings held during this period. Many occurred before
newspapers were established, countless others were in small communities where gazettes did not exist, and many were so small as to
require nothing more than word-of-mouth advertising.

The lotteries with legal sanction are easier to tally. There were
158 licenses, not including those of "semilegal" status. All but thirty-
two of these were granted in New England, and Rhode Island, with
a population (in 1774) of only 54,460 whites, 25,117 of whom were
under sixteen years of age, originated some seventy-five in the span
of thirty years — a truly amazing record.[41] These figures, however,
are not clear representations of the scale of the ventures since very
often one scheme benefited a number of objects. This is particularly
true of the Pennsylvania licenses to churches when as many as four
commonly would be lumped into one enterprise. Also, the cases in
which the original amount later was increased or when more than
one drawing (or class) was held for the same beneficiary have been
treated as single lotteries in arriving at the total of 158.

Even more significant are the results of analyzing one year's lottery activity in a single state. Take the Rhode Island franchises of
1774, for example. These ten authorizations were intended to raise
approximately $16,000. If this sum represented the usual discount of
15 per cent, over $106,000's worth of tickets were offered for sale.
This fact is all the more impressive when one considers that none
of the projects of 1774 were large, that this was not Rhode Island's
most prolific year, and that at the time the colony's adult white
population was less than 30,000. With the ticket count enlarged by
the correct multiple and including fractional tickets, an almost un-
believable number of chances must have been pressed upon America's colonial forefathers.

TABLE 1

Authorized Lotteries in Colonial America

Colony	Year	Amount	Purpose
Connecticut	1747	£7,500 (old tenor)	Housing at Yale
	1751	unknown	Build the "Great Bridge" over the Shetucket River, Norwich
	1753	£2,000 (New York currency)	College of New Jersey (later Princeton)
	1754	£660	Wharf, New Haven
	1755	——	Dispose of property to pay debts of Robert Sloan
	1757	£8,000 (lawful)	Campaign against the French
	1759	£100	Pay owners of house burned while occupied by English troops
	1759	——	Dispose of four farms for Matthew Stewart
	1760	£300	Repair streets, Hartford
	1760	£500	Build a lighthouse, New London
	1761	£300	Clear and make navigable the "Ousatunnick" River
	1762	£250	Build a bridge, Windsor
	1772	£1,000	Extend Long Wharf, New Haven
	1772	£600	Build a bridge, Norwich
	1772	£337	Improve navigation of Connecticut River
	1773	£700	Replace money taken by tax collector, Colchester
	1773	£300	Landing, Hartford
	1773	£278	Complete bridge, Norwich
	1774	£400	Church, Stonington
Delaware	1774	unknown	Probably 3 churches and Princeton College
Maryland	1767	£1,000	To finance appeal to the Crown (originated by lower house)
Massachusetts	1744	£7,500	Government of Massachusetts
	1749	£2,500	Repairs on Miles' Bridge, Swansea
	1750	£1,200	Build a bridge, Newbury
	1750	$26,700	Government war expenses
	1755	£290	Bridge over "Teticut" River
	1756	£3,000	Repair damages to Boston Neck
	1757	£1,215	Glass bottle factory, Germantown
	1758	£1,200	Bridge over the Saco and Pesumpscot rivers

Colony	Year	Amount	Purpose
Massachusetts (*continued*)	1758	£ 30,000	Expense in Canadian expedition
	1759	£ 1,000	Paving Boston Neck
	1759	£ 1,666 13s. 4d.	Repair highways, Roxbury
	1759	£ 827	Rebuild bridge and causeway on the Sudbury River
	1760	£ 3,500 ster.	Land Bank
	1760	$1,800	Paving main street, Charlestown
	1760	£ 600	Bridge over Parker River, Newbury
	1760	£ 350	Remove rocks and shoals from Taunton Great River
	1760	£ 760	Paving, Roxbury
	1760	£ 400	Sudbury River Causeway
	1761	£ 2,000	Rebuild Faneuil Hall
	1762	£ 1,000	Additional for Faneuil Hall
	1763	£ 300	Complete bridge at Newbury
	1765	£ 3,200	Housing at Harvard College
New Hampshire	1757	£ 6,000	Joses Philbrook, to drain a pond and make a small harbor at Rye
	1757	£ 400	Bridge, New Castle to Ferry Point
	1759	£ 600	Paving, Portsmouth
	1760	£ 2,000	Bridge, Dover
	1760	£ 4,000	Bridge over the Exeter River
	1766	unknown	Highway at Rye
	1767	unknown	"Pier or Bason," Gosport
	1768	£ 1,000	Finish bridge over Exeter River
New Jersey	1759	£ 600	Three annual drawings of this amount to pay for Indian land claims
	1761	£ 1,000	St. Peter's Church
	1762	£ 1,000	St. Mary's Church
	1762	£ 400	Bound Brook Bridge over Raritan River
	1762	£ 3,000	Princeton College
	1765	£ 500	Straighten road from New York to Philadelphia
	1772	£ 1,050	Road to New York (not to become law until approved by King)
New York	1746	£ 3,375	Fortify City of New York
	1746	£ 2,250	Found King's College (later Columbia)
	1748	£ 1,800	King's College
	1753	£ 1,125	King's College (July)
	1753	£ 1,125	King's College (December)
	1754	£ 1,125	King's College
	1756	£ 150	Buy arms for poor people, Richmond County
	1756	(sell property)	Humphrey Avery

Colony	Year	Amount	Purpose
New York (*continued*)	1756	£1,125	Build jail for prisoners of war
	1758	£1,125	Repay Albany for expenses in French and Indian War
	1761	£3,000	Build lighthouse, Sandy Hook
	1761	£3,000	Repair New York City Hall
	1762	£3,000	To raise Sandy Hook lighthouse lottery to £6,000
	1763	£3,000	Provide bounty for hemp
	1774	£12,000	Build a "Province House"
North Carolina	1759	£450	Churches at Wilmington and Brunswick
	1761	unspecified	Navigation of New River
Pennsylvania	1765	£3,003 15s.	Episcopal churches at Reading, Chichester, Carlisle, York, Molatten, Concord, and Philadelphia (2)
	1767	£499 19s.	German Lutheran Church and school, Lancaster County
	1768	£5,250	Public landing and street paving, Philadelphia
	1769	£1,687 10s.	German Reformed [Presbyterian?] churches at Heidelburg, Lebanon, Yorktown, and German Lutheran at Yorktown
	1769	£3,099 12s.	1st, 2nd, and 3rd Presbyterian churches in Philadelphia and German Reformed church at Wooster
Rhode Island	1744	£3,000	Bridge across Weybosset River, Providence
	1747	£10,000	Paving, Newport
	1748	£3,000	Debts of Joseph Fox
	1749	£2,400	Repair bridge, Pawtucket Falls
	1750	£10,364	Debts of Col. Joseph Pendleton
	1753	£30,000 (scheme)	Complete Rent County Courthouse, build two bridges, and a fence and jail in Rent County
	1756	£10,000	Repair and arm Fort George, Goat Island
	1758	£30,000 (scheme)	Debts of Handley Chipman
	1759	$2,000	Rebuild colony house and library, Providence
	1759	$2,400	Masonic Hall, Newport
	1760	$1,200 (milled)	Library, Providence
	1760	$1,000	Land for Providence Courthouse
	1760	£24,000	Construct public granary and market house, Newport
	1761	£6,000	Paving, Newport
	1761	£6,000	Paving, Providence

Colony	Year	Amount	Purpose
Rhode Island (*continued*)	1761	unspecified	Meetinghouse, Baptist Society of the Ancient Order, Johnston
	1761	£6,000	Construction of artificial harbor, Charleston
	1762	£1,500	Remove Pawtucket Falls
	1762	$1,000	Repair Anglican Church, Providence
	1762	(sell property)	Pay debts of Captain Edward Wells, Jr.
	1762	unknown	Construct a poorhouse
	1762	£4,500	Ransom for Samuel Dunn's mate held hostage by the French
	1762	(sell property)	Relieve a jailor left with prisoners' unpaid board bills
	1762	£2,200	Repairs on highway, Providence
	1762	£6,000	Paving, North Providence
	1762	$4,500	Compensation for loss of merchandise by fire to W. & H. Wall
	1762	£2,000	Rebuild a bridge over Woonsocket Falls
	1762	£4,000	Repair road from Providence into Connecticut
	1762	unspecified	Construct a pond near New Shoreham
	1763	unspecified	Wharf, Little Compton
	1763	£560	Presbyterian group, Providence
	1763	£90	Drawbridge
	1763	£100	New street, Providence
	1763	£8,000	Paving, Newport
	1763	£400	Bridge at Furnace Unity, Cumberland County
	1763	£600	Bridge over Pawtucket River
	1764	£300	Repair and extend a wharf
	1764	£130	Build a workhouse
	1764	£106	Bridge, Warwick
	1767	$2,500	New steeple, church of Trinity Parish, Newport
	1767	£150	Finish Baptist parsonage, Warren
	1767	£225 (lawful)	Pave Mill Street, Newport
	1768	unlimited	Highway into Connecticut
	1768	$500	Pave King's Street, Newport
	1769	unspecified	Repair bridge, Warwick
	1769	£1,350	Succor for the company building Long Wharf, Newport
	1769	£120	Workhouse, North Kingston
	1770	$400	Repair Whipple's Bridge
	1770	$300	To aid a "Sect called Baptist"
	1771	unspecified	Market house, Newport
	1771	$400	Rebuild bridge, Warwick

Colony	Year	Amount	Purpose
Rhode Island (*continued*)	1771	unspecified	Paving and market house, Providence
	1771	unspecified	Complete Whipple's Bridge
	1771	£60	Repair North Providence Road
	1771	$600	Episcopal steeple and clock, Providence
	1771	$150	Bridge over Hunt's River
	1772	$350	Road in Gloucester
	1772	unspecified	King's Street, Newport
	1772	£40	Repair bridge at Furnace Unity
	1772	£165	Repair meetinghouse and roads, Barrington
	1772	$2,500	Rebuild forge destroyed by fire, Coventry
	1772	$500	Baptist meetinghouse, East Greenwich
	1772	$500	Rebuild wharf, Warwick
	1772	$1,500	East Greenwich Church
	1772	$400	Bridge and road, Gloucester
	1772	$500	Finish meetinghouse, Johnston
	1772	$1,000	Finish steeple and buy clock, King's Church, Providence
	1772	$500	Repair Wonscut road
	1772	unspecified	Build hospital, Coaster's Harbor
	1773	£700	Presbyterian tower and clock, Providence
	1773	(sell property)	Benjamin Wicham, Newport
	1773	$500	Baptist Church, Coventry
	1774	$500	Aid Abial Brown and family, South Kingston
	1774	$600	Lot and schoolhouse, East Greenwich
	1774	$500	Rebuild ironworks, Coventry
	1774	$600	Benjamin Greene
	1774	£300	Parsonage, Pautucket
	1774	£2,000	Baptist church, Providence
	1774	$1,200	Aid Gideon Almny, Tiverton
	1774	$600	Aid Nathaniel Stoddard, Tiverton
	1774	£50	Repair gristmill dam
	1774	$200	Buy tools for gunsmith
Virginia	1754	£6,000	Protection against French
West Florida	1766	(sell house)	Nathaniel Thompson (approved by Council of West Florida)

Chapter IV

War and Confederation Days

Before the lottery draws comes prayers, *after,* curses.[1]

The Revolution did more than free the colonies from English rule. Military operations were only one dimension of the years from 1775 to 1789 — the development and safeguard of personal rights and liberties was another. Self-government was inaugurated, along with the accompanying problem of determining the balance between liberty and security. This era was productive also in the arts, sciences, and letters, and in educational as well as political and social institutions. On the surface the stratified society of the colonies began disintegrating along with the old-world patterns of thought and behavior. Not all aspects changed, however; some practices carried over. The lottery was one such institution.

In colonial days lotteries had been particularly apt to appear during wartime when revenue was difficult to secure by other means. This was again the case in 1776 when the various states as well as the Continental Congress faced raising large sums for the war against England. There was no powerful central government, no uniformity of support for the revolutionary cause, and worse yet, there was no money. Altogether the amount of silver and gold in the colonies at the beginning of the Revolution did not exceed ten or twelve million dollars, and no small part of that was in the hands of English sympathizers.

Collection of taxes equal to the needs of the Revolution was impossible. Adequate power to collect, even, could not have created the means with which to pay. Thus the Revolution was financed by loans, requisitions on the states, state bills of credit, and the Continental currency issued by Congress. Continental bills to the value of almost $250,000,000 were circulated, with each state allocated a certain proportion to redeem. Instead, the states issued their own bills of credit, more than $210,000,000's worth. These successive emissions of paper money by both the nation and the various states flooded the country and pushed all prices rapidly upward. In 1780 the Continental currency was worth one-fortieth of its specie value, causing "new tenor" bills to be issued. When these yielded mostly worthless paper money in return, Congress was forced to take meat, rum, flour, and clothing from the states. Loans proved no more dependable, for domestic borrowing was influenced by the interest paid and the whims of the few who possessed money, and foreign loans were governed almost wholly by political factors. The financial situation was indeed acute.

One other system, however, was tried. It is ironical, considering English opposition to American lotteries, that the authority which superseded Parliament in the colonies immediately seized upon this device for aid in the fight for independence. Congress' dependence upon the states for funds — and the states' slow response, since they usually passed the responsibility down to local counties and towns — caused that body to turn desperately to lotteries, an action which probably also provided the opening wedge for their restoration by the states. On November 1, 1776, two months after the British defeat of General Washington at New York City and the subsequent loss of that town and its wealth for the duration of the war, the Board of the Treasury submitted a plan to raise $1,005,000 for the troops in the field. As finally approved it provided a complicated scheme involving 100,000 tickets. The drawing was in four classes, and prizes in each ran from $20 to $50,000. To realize as much ready cash as possible, all awards over $50 were to be paid in "treasury bank-notes," redeemable in five years with interest of 4 per cent. State loan-office commissioners would distribute the other prizes in their localities.

The project was activated immediately under direction of seven of Philadelphia's leading citizens. On January 11, 1777, the journals of that city carried notices of the first class of "The United States Lottery," which contained 42,317 prizes and 57,683 blanks, and

was set on foot . . . for the sole purpose of . . . carrying on the present just war, undertaken in defense of the rights and liberties of America . . . It is not doubted but every real friend of his country will most cheerfully become an adventurer, and that the sale of the tickets will be very rapid, especially as even the unsuccessful adventurer will have the pleasing reflection of having contributed in a degree to the great and glorious American cause.[2]

To insure the lottery's success, Congress requested the states to prevent forging or counterfeiting of the chances. At least four enacted such legislation. In March 1777 Rhode Island made the crime punishable by death without benefit of clergy plus confiscation by the local government of all real and personal property. North Carolina also imposed the death penalty. The latter state, however, in 1779, reduced the punishment for first offenders to standing in the pillory for three hours, having the right ear nailed to it and cut off, thirty-nine lashes, branding on the right cheek with the letter *M* (the iron being one by three-quarter inches), imprisonment not exceeding one year, and forfeiture of one-half of the culprit's goods! (Finally, in 1784, perhaps in a spirit of charity, the death penalty was restored.)

The early popularity of the United States lottery is seen in a letter from James Warren of Boston to John Adams on April 3, 1777. "Your tickets . . . were nearly all sold in a few days, and perhaps double the number would have sold. Whether patriotism or the hope of Gain has occasioned this rapid sale of 12. or 15.000 tickets in so short a time is a question that deserves the attention of the politician; but either of them will answer the present purpose."[3]

The later classes did not go so well. Chances were sent to the governors with the request that their states invest in them. North Carolina acknowledged receipt of 1,302. Massachusetts, by a resolution of October 14, 1777, agreed to purchase 900, but later released them for public sale to "oblige the people & promote the design of the Lottery." The people of Massachusetts were not enthusiastic, however, nor was the country as a whole. On May 2, 1778, Congress, now in exile from Philadelphia after that city's fall, postponed the second drawing until January 1, 1779, raised the interest rate to 6 per cent, and directed that the prize list be distributed to all postmasters and published by newspapers in weekly installments. The last three classes were never completely sold, and only after a number of delays were they finally drawn. Because of these deferments and the distances involved, accounts became so confused that Congress eventually decided in 1782 to accept the winning tickets as vouchers and to "certify the same as debts of the United States at and after the rate of one dollar in specie for every forty dollars for such prizes." [4] All in all, it is doubtful that in the long run the government made much on these lotteries, but the postponed prize payments did provide a temporary supply of seriously needed funds.

Throughout this period private lotteries were operated in competition with the authorized ones. Maryland was still the center of private raffles. In 1777, for example, Lower Marlboro Academy used this means to raise building funds. Things other than the war were more important, such as the lottery held by St. Paul's Parish (Episcopal) of Baltimore in 1780. It offered 12,000 tickets at forty dollars each and boasted of 3,837 prizes totaling $320,000. Small notice was paid to the 8,163 blanks, "there being but little more than two blanks to a prize." Advertisements reminded the public that "He who giveth to the poor lendeth to the Lord," and included the pious hope that "the good purposes expected from the sacred institution which carries to all the Divine blessing, independent of the advantageous terms offered to the adventurer, will be sufficient inducement for a speedy sale of the tickets." [5]

Military projects inspired only a small proportion of the state lotteries authorized during the Revolution. Americans were not a military people and few were willing to make personal sacrifices to support sustained warfare even for independence. Regular army service was unpopular; militia-type operations were more preferable, where each man could defend his neighboring territory but keep his crops up and his home-fires burning. Patriotism had not developed enough to put the young nation's welfare above the individual's.

A second explanation for the more numerous civilian lotteries might lie in the large drawings early initiated by the Continental Congress and by the taxes levied for support of the war effort. Armies simply could not wait for completion of the long lottery process to get money for food and supplies. Moreover, the chaotic conditions which existed during those martial years make it impossible to obtain complete records of the various governments. For example, the diary of the Reverend George Neisser, Moravian minister, noted that the "State Lottery" was drawn in York, Pennsylvania, in 1778,[6] but no official record of such a lottery exists. In all, records of five state-authorized lotteries to further the fight for American independence have been found (see Table 2).

TABLE 2

Lotteries for Military Purposes, 1777–1781

Year	Amount	State	Purpose
1776	$1,005,000	(Congress)	Troops in the field
1778	$750,000	Massachusetts	Reward enlistments
1779	$15,000	Vermont	Military defense fund
1779	£2,100	Rhode Island	Loyalist fund
1780	£20,400	Massachusetts	Clothe state's part of Continental Army
1781	£2,700	New York	Relief of Loyalist refugees

While Washington and his dwindling army of weak and ragged men suffered through the long winter at Valley Forge, petitions were being placed before legislatures for lotteries to finance schools and repair streets and bridges. The bulk of the licenses during the war years were for lotteries of this sort — to aid every-day living. A great many, however, were directly related to the war, such as the one for the Ulster County Courthouse in New York which was destroyed by the British and the many grants for road and bridge repairs. But even this destruction failed to arouse Americans to support their army, an army which was ill-fed, poorly clothed, and seldom paid. Cleaning up the havoc left by its retreat seemed more important. Lotteries to aid two schools, two industries, five county and municipal improvements, and eight internal improvements were authorized during the period of fighting, over half of these grants in 1780–81, the worst military years of the Revolution (see Table 3).

At the time that the German mercenaries were fighting the Americans, Virginia granted the first recorded state-approved lottery — for Hampden Sidney Academy. Despite the enthusiasm aroused by the Battle of Bennington, Massachusetts found it necessary in 1778 to issue its first lottery, one which would raise $750,000 to reward officers and men who would enlist in the army for three years. To keep as much of the money as long as possible prizes of fifty dollars or more were to be held until January 1, 1783, with 6 per cent interest. As a beginning, only $143,000 was to be raised in four classes. The first class involved 25,000 tickets at six dollars each, 6,374 of which were awards: one each of $4,000 and $2,000, two of $1,000,

TABLE 3

Lotteries for Civilian Purposes, 1775–1781

Year	Amount	State	Purpose
1777	unlimited	Virginia	Hampden Sidney Academy
1778	£1,500	Connecticut	Repair paper mill, Hartford
1778	£2,000	New York	Rebuild Ulster County Courthouse
1778	£300	Rhode Island	Repair Pawtucket bridge
1778	$2,000	New Hampshire	Bridge, New Castle
1779	£60,000	Massachusetts	Widening and "amending" streets, Charlestown
1779	$250,000	Massachusetts	Repair Long Wharf, Boston
1779	£4,500	Massachusetts	Bridge over "Housatonock" River
1779	£800	Rhode Island	Rebuild Pawtucket bridge
1780	unspecified	Connecticut	Recall old Continental currency
1780	£1,000	Connecticut	Bridge, New Haven
1780	£400	Connecticut	Bridge, Woodbury
1780	$200,000	Massachusetts	Road, Westfield to Great Barrington
1780	$40,000	Rhode Island	School, East Greenwich
1780	$30,000	Rhode Island	Pave Union Street, Providence
1780	unspecified	New York	Buy fire buckets
1781	£250	Connecticut	Bridge, Symsburry
1781	£200	Massachusetts	Bridge across Chekebee River
1781	unspecified	New Hampshire	Benefit glass factory, Temple

and so on, and 5,550 prizes of ten dollars. Advertisements strongly appealed to the buyers' patriotism.

The Directors flatter themselves they shall be able soon to compleat the First Class, when they consider the Money to be raised is to be applied to the benevolent Purpose of rewarding those Officers and Soldiers who have endured Want, Hardship and Toil, and Hazarded every Danger for the Safety of their Country, and who, when [the] Government, through a Series of unfortunate Events, was unable in some Instances to comply with its Promises for their Support and Comfort, nobly scorn'd to shrink from the Post of Danger, and, like their great Leader, resolved never to survive the Ruin and Desolation of their Country.[7]

On January 26, 1779, the managers began selling the 20,000 second-class tickets at ten dollars each, purchasable with the May

1777 or April 1778 issues of Continental currency. The third class, with chances at fifteen dollars each, started on March 11, and the last, patterned on the third which had "met with general approbation," began four months later, ending the following January at Faneuil Hall. By this time public ardor had cooled, and the lottery proved difficult to complete. On the whole, however, it was a successful series, surprising in view of the times, the large number of tickets, and the competition of the co-existing United States Lottery.

Vermont's introduction into the lottery picture came in 1779 with a law forbidding private drawings, along with one belatedly authorizing a $15,000 military defense fund. The colonial lottery stronghold, Rhode Island, was slow in picking up where she had left off at the outbreak of war. While Newport was under enemy control, the British Major General in March 1779 endorsed an undertaking for £2,100 sterling to enable the refugees and other Loyalists "to carry into execution such measures as may be necessary for the promotion of His Majesties service." There were 7,000 chances at forty shillings each, with 1,823 prizes and 5,177 blanks. An unique appeal to the Tory spirit was made by the managers:

> The hardened obstinacy of the factious leaders of the present rebellion — the vindictive and Malignant conduct of Congress, assemblies, etc., toward their countrymen, who honestly and faithfully fortold these evils and calamities which their sanguinary measures must ultimately lead to — the long abused lenity and indulgence of his Majesty toward his deluded revolted subjects, particularly in rejecting the benevolent overtures of the commissioners for restoring peace and all the blessings of the British Constitution to this once happy country, and thereby establishing the liberties of America upon the most equitable and prosperous basis, loudly conspire in the strongest manner to animate every loyal American and clearly point out the absolute necessity of carrying on the war in conjunction with the King's troops, with the most determined spirit and perseverance . . . And it is not doubted but every encouragement will be given . . .[8]

Evidently the people were insufficiently "loyal," for by August most of the tickets remained unsold and a new appeal asked that every "lover of his country . . . risque some share of his property" and enable the "much injured Loyalists" to avenge themselves. The English evacuation of the island on October 29, 1779, makes it doubtful, however, that the drawing was ever held. Only a few months after the launching of the Tory lottery, the "insurgents" undertook one of their own with no better success. On the grounds that the Pawtucket bridge had been built and always repaired by lottery, the General Assembly gave permission to raise £800 to rebuild that structure. The project soon failed, however, "by reason of rapid depreciation of the currency."

The enemy also played the game in New York, where in 1780 the British Commandant issued a license for a lottery to buy fire buckets. The next year a scheme was authorized for the relief of "poor refugees" — Loyalists who had sought safety with the king's forces. This lottery had a goal of $2,700, which was to be held in trusteeship by the Overseers of the Poor. An interesting postscript occurred in 1783 when the state of New York, reiterating the 1774 penalties against private lotteries, also pardoned all such offenses committed after July 4, 1776. This action was undoubtedly taken because the English had applied the regulation to patriotic undertakings.

Two of Connecticut's three schemes in 1780 were for bridges at New Haven and Woodbury, but the third is of special interest. In order to recall a required quota of the Continental Congress' old currency in preparation for a new issue, the legislature decided that the $3,000,000 in old bills could be brought in more speedily by lottery than by taxation. Prizes were to be paid off at the rate of one new note for forty old ones, with 10 per cent going to the state. It proved necessary to repeal this act in 1781, however, as the expected new money had not been issued. New Hampshire expressed the common sentiment of the time in denying permits for three lotteries for bridges on the grounds that they "would encourage others and lottery tickets would be as plentiful as continental money was in the highth of its flood and then possibly depreciate as fast." [9]

It is not surprising that a $200,000 lottery in 1780 to improve the road from Westfield to Great Barrington, Massachusetts, proved unpopular. The war was not going well for the Americans at this time. The British victory at Charleston and Benedict Arnold's treason shook the staunchest of patriots. Perhaps more telling, however, for the fate of the lottery was that 20 per cent of the prizes instead of the customary 15 was withheld. Then, too, the people were simply tired of lotteries. At least one petition was filed for repeal of the act, and three of the managers refused to serve, saying, "Lotteries are a Burden in the Community," and "Nothing but the most urgent necessity to effect a purpose of public utility can justify the raising of money by Lottery." [10] Either it was not considered an "urgent necessity" or something of this disgruntlement contributed to the failure of the lottery to clothe Massachusetts' part of the Continental Army that year, and the undertaking was later canceled for lack of public response.

The darkest months of the Revolution followed. Defeat piled on defeat. Despite the fact that the Articles of Confederation were finally ratified, Continental money was almost worthless, the states would not honor requisitions, and some of the militia mutinied for lack of pay and rations. But, even without the Americans realizing it, fortune had swung over to their side. By this time most of Europe was allied with the fighters for independence. On October 17, 1781, the British surrendered at Yorktown and stacked their arms while bands played "The World Turned Upside Down."

The Revolution had been the resultant explosion from the combination of new and old social forces in the colonies. This condition was under the surface for some years prior to 1775 but results were apparent soon after the fighting stopped. Many of the churches broke away from their old-world parent organizations, and all were affected by the sentiment favoring separation of church and state. Higher education expanded rapidly in the wake of the Revolution and pressure steadily increased for state support of popular education. Settlements were springing up on the western frontier of the country at the same time her statesmen were attempting to forge a bond of union. The war did not suddenly put the government into the hands of all the people, but it did give a larger number the right to vote. This was done when confiscated Tory property — the crown lands, the proprietors' large holdings, and the loyalists' estates — were broken up and sold for a few cents an acre. With the acquisition of fifty or more acres the least of citizens found himself a part of a society previously inaccessible to him.

This position brought responsibilities and problems, however, for the colonies were now states in a Union, in name if not in fact. The business of governing themselves as a nation proved to be a series of trials and rejections until 1790, with the states unwilling to relinquish to a central government much of their newly won freedom. In ruling themselves as individual states, however, they fared much better, some creating constitutions which lasted over fifty years and one serving into the twentieth century.

The most immediate problem, along with that of forming governments, was economic. After Yorktown the nation's financial position remained acute for many years and was one of the shoals upon which the Confederation was wrecked. The cost of the war in terms of gold has been estimated as between seventy-five and one hundred million dollars, but gold figures for the period are merely academic. The real indebtedness approximated a half billion dollars when measured in contemporary paper currency. That tremendous sum, as deflation began, rested in one way or another with crushing force upon the people, rich and poor alike. Shops and mills opened during the emergency closed, and available coin began once more to flow to England in an unfavorable balance of trade as long-established buying habits reasserted themselves.

Against such a background not only did the ravages of war have to be repaired, but also the material foundations laid for the youthful nation. Roads and bridges to open the back country; river channels and canals to transport market-bound produce; new industries to bolster the economy; churches and schools to tend the inner man — these made money essential. Taxation alone was still not adequate, and facilities to consolidate small individual contributions were lacking. Neither were there stock or bond issues,[11] and the lottery many times seemed the only resource. Thus, cupidity, not patriotism, often financed the new nation's future.

Peacetime brought a flood of drawings, both legalized and private. Maryland, the only state to countenance private raffles after North Carolina abolished them in 1780, had a tremendous variety and number. How many were held which were never recorded by memoirs or the press can only be surmised, but the following were advertised in one year in Baltimore alone: an Episcopal parsonage, £2,000; Pratt Street Wharf, £600; George Dowig's plate raffle, £1,400; street paving at Fell's Point, £6,500; a German Lutheran parsonage, £1,750; Engelhart Cruse's steam-operated grist mill, $2,000; Circulating Library, £2,727; Presbyterian Society of "Baltimore-Town," $2,780; Baltimore Canal, $965; and a set of bells for the German Reformed Presbyterian Church, $637. The relative success of all these is questionable, for the managers of the Fell's Point venture announced postponement until spring, and those directing the second class of the German Reformed and the Presbyterian raffles credited their delays to competition and the "extraordinary Sickness prevailing." The surplus of lotteries was emphasized by a newspaper contributor, "A Spectator," who, addressing himself to the "Honourable Representatives of Town & County of Baltimore," complained that in the past twelve months a total of $26,084.66 had been sought by different lotteries. To raise that amount required a ticket sale of approximately $100,000, making logical his conclusion that some drawings were luxuries and that all could not succeed "unless we possessed a greater surplus of circulating cash." It was his estimate that ticket sales had taken nearly £10,000 from Baltimore's pockets alone.[12]

Among the licenses granted during the Confederation, those for bridges, churches, and schools, each with seventeen lotteries apiece, were the most popular (see Table 4). Bridges held the spotlight the first few years, partly because of military destruction and partly because the expanding young country needed better means of communication. Most of these grants were made in New England, although one southern state, Virginia, did approve a project for a bridge over Shockoe Creek in 1782.

In Massachusetts between 1782 and 1784 six lotteries for bridges were instigated, while Connecticut held three and Rhode Island two. New Hampshire, where such structures had long been a favorite subject of petitions, issued no new franchises of any sort, probably because of currency difficulties. In March 1782 the managers for the Temple glass factory (1781) reported to the Assembly that "your petitioners . . . immediately proceeded to advertise the . . . Lottery, and print the Tickets, and began the sale thereof in Bills of the new-Emission, agreeable to the said Act. Soon after which your Petitioners were obliged to take back the Tickets, by reason of the failure of the paper Currency, and to give over the thoughts of drawing the same." [13]

New industries also drew attention in these early years; in Massachusetts three lotteries favored two mills and a glass factory, and in Vermont a lottery aided a paper mill (see Table 4). Rhode Island in 1782 granted a George Hazard Pechan the right to raffle off three lots to pay his debts and six years later gave him a grant to open a shop for making nails. Just what this particular individual's con-

TABLE 4

Lotteries of the Confederation Period, by State

State	Year	Amount	Purpose
Connecticut	1783	£ 300	Bridge, Derby
	1783	£ 400	Bridge, New Milford
	1783	£ 450	Bridge, Norwich
	1784	£ 1,000	Road repairs, Middletown
	1785	unknown	Meetinghouse, Stonington
	1789	unknown	Glass works, East Hartford
	1789	unknown	Levee on the Connecticut River
Delaware	unknown	unknown	"Wilmington Lottery" (date and purpose unknown, but an act of February 1787 provided for settling its accounts)
Georgia	1784	£ 350	Hospital for seamen, Savannah
	1785	£ 500	Hospital for seamen, Savannah
Maine District of Massachusetts	1784	£ 300	Remove log jam and falls from Saco River
Massachusetts	1782	£ 1,200	Paper mill, Milton
	1782	£ 1,500	Bridge over Parker River
	1782	£ 200	Bridge over Agawam River
	1783	£ 2,000	Bridge at Lancaster
	1783	£ 600	Bridge over Winchendon River
	1783	£ 330	Bridge over Westfield River
	1783	£ 3,000	Glass factory, Boston
	1783	£ 2,000	Rebuilding North Mills, Boston
	1784	£ 1,000	Bridge over Charles River, Watertown
	1785	£ 600	Leicester Academy
	1786	——	Massachusetts Land Lottery
	1788	£ 550	Harvard College
	1788	£ 1,200	Williamstown Free School
	1789	£ 1,000	Fortification of Marblehead
	1789	£ 10,000	For use of the state
New Hampshire	1784	£ 3,000	Dartmouth College
	1785	$1,600	Clear Merrimack River for logging
	1785	£ 300	Bridge over Sugar River, Claremont
	1786	£ 200	Bridge over Baker's River
	1787	£ 1,800	Dartmouth College
New Jersey	1786	unknown	Presbyterian Church, Elizabethtown
	1786	unknown	Presbyterian Church, New Brunswick
	1789	unknown	Union County Academy
North Carolina	1784	£ 500	Hillsborough Academy
	1784	unknown	Science Hall Academy
	1786	£ 700	Craven County poorhouse
	1787	unknown	Build "Avery's Trace"
	1787	£ 1,000	Warrenton Academy
Pennsylvania	1784	$42,000	Improve navigation of Schuylkill River and public roads west of Philadelphia

State	Year	Amount	Purpose
Pennsylvania (*continued*)	1785	unknown	German Lutherans, "Whitepain [sic] township"
	1785	unknown	Norristown meetinghouse
	1789	$10,000	Common hall, Philadelphia, $8,000; Dickinson College, $2,000
	1789	(sell property)	Settle estate of Robert Pine
Rhode Island	1782	(sell 3 lots)	Allow George H. Pechan to pay debts
	1783	£180	Whipple's bridge
	1783	$2,500	Baptist Church, Newport
	1784	£1,000	Bridge and market house, North Providence
	1784	$1,500	Congregational Church, Tiverton
	1784	$1,200	Congregational Church, Newport
	1784	$1,000	Episcopal Church, Bristol
	1785	$1,000	Navigation of Pawtucket River
	1785	(sell property)	To sell land and livestock of William West
	1785	$800	Episcopal Church, Providence
	1785	$600	Congregational Church, West Coventry
	1785	$1,250	Congregational Church, Newport
	1786	£500	Baptist Church, Gloucester
	1786	$400	Furnace Unity bridge, Pawtucket River
	1787	£600	United Congregational Society, Little Compton
	1787	£900	Bridge, Woonsocket Falls
	1787	£200	Furnace Unity bridge, Pawtucket River
	1788	£2,100	George Pechan, to build a shop for nail making
	1789	£400	Baptists, Hopkinton
South Carolina	1784	blanket	City of Charleston
Vermont	1783	£200	Paper mill
	1788	unspecified	Matthew Lyon's blast furnace
	1788	unspecified	Windsor Grammar School
	1789	£150	Roads, Chester County
	1789	£200	John Hubbard's brewery, Weatherfield
Virginia	1782	unlimited	Bridge over Shockoe Creek
	1784	£2,000	Grammar school, Williamsburg
	1785	£1,500	Free Masons, Richmond
	1785	£500	German Lutheran Church, Winchester
	1785	£700	Vestry, Elizabeth River
	1786	£500	Free Masons of Cabin Point Lodge, Surry County
	1786	£300	Washington Henry Academy
	1787	£500	Fredericksburg Academy
	1789	£1,000	Randolph Academy
	1789	£4,000	Fredericksburg Academy
	1789	£500	Fauquier Academy
	1789	£1,150	Pave Main streets, Alexandria

nections were is not clear, but it seems safe to assume that he at least succeeded in paying off his debts.

Others were probably not so successful, for in the year that the Peace of Versailles was signed and Great Britain recognized the independence of the United States, dark financial clouds hung over the country. North Carolina, in granting a lottery for a poorhouse in Craven County, had declared it "difficult from the variety of taxes now levied on the inhabitants to raise a sufficient sum by a tax." [14] Hopefully four thousand chances were offered in two classes of twenty- and thirty-shilling tickets. The managers gave $5,000 bond, receiving £50 in return for their services. A Rhode Island lottery sought $2,500 to rebuild a Baptist meetinghouse in Newport which had been used by the British and later by the French as a hospital. Records show that General Nathanael Greene bought sixteen two-dollar tickets and drew prizes totaling $120; General Thaddeus Kosciusko, the Polish hero, with one chance won $100.

Many other ex-soldiers had an opportunity to try for the lottery's riches during the first year of peace. Ten states made fourteen authorizations in 1784. Schools and churches provided half of the total this time, reflecting the growing desire for intangibles as well as the actual physical need for new buildings. North Carolina's act against private raffles in 1780 had specifically exempted lotteries established by public authority or for "the encouragement of any school," thus opening the way for its first legislative franchise, one in 1784 for Hillsborough and Science Hall academies. South Carolina made its only grant of the pre-Constitution period a blanket one permitting the Corporation of the City of Charleston to originate any lotteries "they may think necessary to establish for the use and benefit of the City." [15] That community evidently enjoyed this monopoly for a number of years, though no evidence of its use is available. Georgia, too, entered the picture for the first time by authorizing a scheme for a hospital near Savannah for sick seamen, increasing this from £350 to £500 the next year.

The first registered lottery act in Pennsylvania also came in 1784, to raise $42,000 to improve navigation of the Schuylkill River and the public roads into Philadelphia from the west. This is interesting evidence of the early desire to tap the trade of the back country. Such distinguished citizens as Benjamin Rittenhouse directed the government-operated raffle and tickets sold for four, six, eight, and ten dollars, respectively, in the four classes of 10,000 chances each, with $280,000 offered in prizes. The attempt met with small success, and six years later it was still in progress.

Congress again became involved in a lottery when John Adams, Minister to Holland, agreed to pay a bonus of 690,000 guilders for a 4 per cent loan of 2,000,000 guilders. This additional amount, made up of United States notes bearing the same interest rate, was distributed by lot among the Dutch subscribers. Though Adams feared the deal would discredit him, he wrote Benjamin Franklin that because of the tightness of the money market and the poor American credit the loan could not otherwise be negotiated.

Meanwhile in New Hampshire, President Eleazar Wheelock's personal appeal for Dartmouth College met with favor and the institution was allowed three years to clear not more than £3,000 in silver and gold for a new building of forty-eight rooms. The chances sold very slowly and the manager was finally directed in September 1785 to dispose of them for "money or produce, and to convert the produce into specie in the best manner he can." Sales still lagged, however, and the venture was reported a failure "from the great scarcity of cash."

Elsewhere in New England the few and scattered citizens of the Maine district of Massachusetts, under even more financial duress than their neighbors, were quick to petition the legislature for lottery favors. The settlers along the Saco River had requested a franchise to remove a log jam and falls from that stream. Consent was given March 15, 1784, to raise a sum not exceeding £300. The enabling act was detailed to an unusual degree: the town had to give a £600 bond against misappropriation of the proceeds; a counterfeiter of tickets had to sit on the gallows for one hour with a rope around his neck, pay a maximum fine of £100, be imprisoned up to twelve months, or be publicly whipped not more than thirty-nine lashes.

The next year, 1785, was a busy one. Of fifteen new lotteries eight were for churches. The purposes of the other seven were more varied. In a Virginia lottery to raise money for the Free Masons of Richmond, the trustees of Hampden Sidney Academy expressed gratitude for their earlier favor by buying a ticket, while four more were given them by friends.[16] Purchasers in Rhode Island were not so eager, according to the managers of a lottery to sell the land and livestock of William West. They reported that although the tickets "were principally sold upon Credit for the Paper Currency of this State," many who had drawn cash prizes "refuse or neglect to apply" for their awards. The answer to this curious situation probably lay in the rapidly depreciating value of the currency. Nevertheless, the legislature voted that unless such prizes were claimed after four months' notice in two state newspapers the money would be forfeited.

A unique lottery was originated by Massachusetts to dispose of fifty townships in the Maine region. The Massachusetts Land Lottery of 1786 offered the extremely popular inducement of containing no blanks. Twenty tickets were bought by the President and Fellows of Harvard College, who subsequently became possessors of 2,720 acres of wilderness. Another interested party was Hugh Orr of Bridgewater. In May 1787 he sent word to the General Court that two Scotsmen in his employ knew something of cotton-spinning machines. Since England would not allow export of this type of machinery, the Court, greatly interested, voted Orr and his men £200 and six chances in the land raffle to encourage their efforts. With the funds thus gained, according to historian John B. McMaster, the first stock-card and spinning jenny in the United States was made.[17]

But the general absence of manufacturing was but one of the problems. Transcendent and omnipresent was financial distress. Some states, such as Rhode Island, confounded the situation by issuing oceans of paper and forcing its acceptance at face value until merchants fled before would-be purchasers. Others, such as Massachusetts, increased taxes beyond the capacity of many to pay. One petitioner to that government spoke for many citizens when he wrote, "We beg leave to informe your Honours that unless something takes place more favourable to the people, in a little time att least, one half of our inhabitants in our oppinion will become banckerupt." State, county, town, and "class" taxes over the last five years, he wrote, were "equil to what our farms will rent for. Sirs, in this situation what have we to live on — no money to be had; our estates dayly posted and sold . . . [and] many of our good inhabitants are now confined in gole for det and for taxes."

The economic conditions which produced Shays' Rebellion in Massachusetts in 1786 were mirrored in the New Hampshire project for a bridge over Baker's River. The Assembly approved the unusual expedient of basing it upon wheat because it was the "produce of that part of the Country." The petitioners felt "if said Lottery should be bottomed on that article, it would be most likely, to answer the end proposed." [18] Such conditions greatly strengthened the hands of the advocates of a stronger central government, finally culminating in the formation of the Constitution. Little could they realize that they were also creating the weapon that would finally destroy the lottery system in the United States.

The general depression probably also influenced the decline in lottery grants for the next few years. One project did seek, however, to aid construction of a road called Avery's Trace from the south end of Clinch Mountain to Bean's Lick in the area later to become Tennessee, and the Board of Trustees of Dartmouth College carried "into effect a new scheme of lottery for raising country produce . . ." This last venture lagged with a second class finally being drawn four years later on the desk of the college chapel, "much to the scandal of some worthy people." Even this benediction helped bring the total yield only to about £360 out of an expected £1,800. Warrenton Academy in North Carolina also failed to raise £1,000 "as the Number of Tickets [2,500 at forty shillings each] contained therein could not be disposed of within the limited time" allowed. Perhaps they all should have followed the example of the Windsor, Vermont, Grammar School Lottery which sold its tickets for two bushels of wheat each, while prizes were in notes based on that same commodity.

The entrepreneurs of the £1,200 lottery for the Williamstown, Massachusetts, Free School did have the same inspiration. In coping with the currency problem they announced, "The extreme scarcity of cash has also induced . . . making sale of the remaining tickets on contracts for neat cattle . . ." This concession led to trouble in determining the cash value of the livestock, and some of the settlements dragged on for years. Finally anything from consolidated notes, new emission, old Continental money, to wheat or cattle was accepted as payment. Earlier, the managers had shifted the drawings to Boston in hopes of a better market, but they came into competition with the Charlestown lottery (approved 1779), whose cutthroat tactics soon compelled their withdrawal from the capital city. Still, with all these impediments the school cleared $3,449.09.

Prospects of a new federal government must have had a reassuring effect on the people of Massachusetts, for a second lottery was successful there in 1788. Harvard College, the recipient, avowed that the purpose was to "encourage the efforts of ingenuity" and the "advancement of Science and the public good" by raising £550 for an orrery (planetarium) built by Joseph Pope. The plan called for 3,000 two-dollar tickets with single prizes of $1,000, $300, and $200; two prizes of $100; three of $50; fifteen of $20; and 673 of $3 each. The undertaking was able not only to purchase the instrument and pay all expenses but also to clear £71 14s. 9p.[19]

Nationally, the year 1788 was devoted to the contest over ratification of the new Constitution. The crux of the matter was the division of powers between the states and the central government. Commercial and business interests, smarting from the depression and state interference, maintained that adoption was the only alternative to anarchy and chaos. Yet popular leaders such as Patrick Henry and Samuel Adams emphatically disapproved of the degree to which the proposed Constitution curtailed the powers of the states, and the absence of a formal guarantee of individual rights was deplored. Unquestionably, it would mean a new balance between liberty and order. State conventions were scenes of stormy debate and the issue was often in doubt, but before the year ended the necessary nine states had given their approval and the date was set for the selection of a President.

On this optimistic note, lottery activity experienced a small flurry. Fittingly enough Pennsylvania approved a joint $10,000 lottery: $2,000 for Dickinson College and $8,000 for a "common hall" in Philadelphia for public assemblies "such as the meetings of Congress." The use of a lottery for such a project was excused by announcing that the "taxes levied upon the inhabitants of said city (for state and city use) are exceedingly heavy and it would be improper at this time to lay any additional burden on them." [20]

Pennsylvania also assisted many "respectable" people who wished to retain in this country the collection of pictures and prints by Robert Pine, a London artist who had moved to America. The scheme provided for 1,100 chances at ten dollars each; in addition to the art work, several buildings and a lot also were to be awarded.

A Rhode Island lottery so illuminates the social history of the period that it is worthy of description. The state's lone permit in

1789 was for £400 for a Baptist church. This resulted from a plea by the citizens of Hopkinton that a considerable number of "Protestant Baptists" were to a great degree neglecting "the public Worship of the Supreme Being" for lack of a meeting place. The proposed edifice was to be used as follows: the "Sabbatarian or Seventh-Day Baptist" would have the right "to improve" the church every other Sabbath or "Seventh Day"; those called "Separates or New Light Baptist, that observe the Seventh Day as a Sabbath" would have the alternate Sabbaths; those called "First Day Baptists" would use the building on Sundays. Each group would be responsible for one-third of the repairs and expenses. How interesting it would be to know if this dangerous-sounding mixture worked.

As a fitting climax to an era, in Virginia a £1,150 lottery to pave the streets of Alexandria not only had the distinction of including among its managers Bushrod Washington, Charles Lee, and Richard Conway, but twenty tickets at six shillings each were purchased by George Washington, first President of the United States.

In the first thirteen years of independence, the fledgling nation initiated about one hundred lotteries,[21] with more than two-thirds of them furnished by New England. This rapid revival pointed out the system's deep roots in the past and strongly indicated what could be expected in the future. The lottery was believed to be necessary during this period of transition in which the states moved from a condition of decentralization toward the unity provided by the Constitution. In the new and economically embarrassed country, these schemes flourished and grew with the nation. To discard them as a financial crutch would not be easy.

Chapter V

A Period of Transmutation, 1790–1860

> The chance of gain is by every man more or less overvalued, and the chance of loss is by most men undervalued . . . That the chance of gain is naturally overvalued, we may learn from the universal success of lotteries. The world neither ever saw, nor ever will see a perfectly fair lottery; or one in which the whole gain compensated the whole loss; because the undertaker could make nothing by it . . . The more tickets you advance upon, the more likely you are to be a loser. Buy them all and you are sure to lose.
>
> — *Adam Smith*[1]

After 1789 the American lottery experienced its greatest period of popularity, followed by its eventual disgrace. This rise and fall is attributable to the people of the new United States. During the years between 1790 and 1860 a distinctive type of citizen developed, with characteristics that by the time of the Civil War were recognized as uniquely "American." By 1860 traits native to the mother countries were several generations old and had been melted and recast by the environments of the new world. The result was a national prototype who was a strong believer in hard work, equal opportunity, and individual rights. He had courage, ingenuity, and an abounding optimism; paradoxically, he loved comfort and adventure, and he covered his sense of insecurity by braggadocio and group activity. Being a man of action, he had little time for speculative thought and instead channeled his creative energy toward practical pursuits. His was an individualistic culture, able to absorb the streams of immigrants that poured into the United States from the old world. The stagnant social order of Europe of hereditary rank and position was replaced by the American measuring stick of material possessions, and any short-cut to the top was eagerly sought. Religion, education, artistic creativeness — all deferred to this cult of acquisition of wealth, until such time as their need was recognized.[2]

Some of these needs were slow indeed to be recognized. Life in the late eighteenth and early nineteenth centuries was relatively simple. The complexities and stimulations of urban living were known to little more than one-sixth of the nation, and the influences of a rural society continued strong until after the Civil War. Land was the basis of most wealth. George Washington, the wealthiest citizen of his day, was worth about $500,000, mainly in farms and various properties. The average citizen, a farmer, owned land worth $1,000 to $2,000 and had an annual cash income of about $100. The pioneer farmer still had much the same experiences as his colonial predecessor. His pleasures and problems were never far from his hearth and meetinghouse, no matter how often he moved them. And move them he did, many times. The same drive that had brought the colonists to America propelled him westward. This sense of personal discontent carried the United States through its greatest period of physical growth, a condition which exerted tremendous influence on its politics and economy and kept a constant raw edge on the culture of the country. Under the name of "progress" work became the creed, and acquisition the prime objective. Humble origin was no handicap in the national theory that with hard work and a little luck a man could rise to any position his capabilities would allow.

Politically, this period was one of adolescence in the nation. The fear of strong government and the particularism characteristic of the Confederation period weakened enough to permit the stronger bond of union in the Constitution, though how strong this bond was or how strong it should be was undecided. These two viewpoints were vitalized by political parties that developed during the first presidential administration. They were to undergo changes in names and objectives, but basically the Hamiltonian Federalist Party, dominated by the commercial interests, favored a strong national government, and the Jeffersonian Republicans, with their agrarian bias, supported states rights as a check on federal encroachment. The War of 1812 introduced a feeling of nationalism which made possible a revival of open advocation and use of such measures as a national bank and internal improvements at federal ex-

Medical Science Lottery, No. 3,

Will commence drawing in the city of New York, on or before July 1, 1817.

A SHARE of the HIGHEST PRIZE of Twenty-five thousand dollars was lately sold at ALLENS' to a patriotic soldier who had lost a leg in the service of his country.

FOR PRIZES go to ALLENS' $30,000 25,000 15,000

SCHEME.......PRIZES TO BE PAID IN GOLD.

1 Prize of	$25000	
1 —	10000	
1 —	10000	
1 —	5000	
1 —	3000	
1 —	2000	
17 —	1000	
20 —	500	
50 —	100	
9000 —	10	

FIRST DRAWN NUMBER — Day entitled to 1000 Dollars
1st, 3d, 5th, 7th, 9th, 11th, 13th, 15th, 17th, 19th, 21st, 23d, 25th, 27th, 32d, 35th, 37th, 30,10,000 40th, $25,000

Floating PRIZES.

—

ONE PRIZE OF $10000 5000 3000 2000

Only 26,000 Tickets....not two blanks to a Prize.

The first 6000 Blanks will be entitled to 10 dollars each. Prizes payable by the state 40 days after the drawing is ended.

Managers.—S. L. Mitchill, M. Kent, J. Johnson, Chas. D. Cooper, J. M'Lean.

Tickets, Halves, Quarters, and Eighths, for sale at

S. & M. ALLENS'
LUCKY LOTTERY OFFICES,

No. 122, Broadway, New-York; No. 449, S. Market-street, Albany; No. 158, Market-street, Baltimore; No. 24, Genesee-street, Utica.

Prize Tickets in other Lotteries, and most kinds of Foreign Bank Notes received at par for Tickets. Orders from the Country, (post paid,) promptly attended to.

S. & M. ALLEN had the pleasure of selling most of the *Rich Prizes* in the two classes that have been drawn of this popular Lottery, and they hope to furnish their customers with the *Brilliant Prizes* in this class.—Many of the prizes sold by them, were shared and sold to persons in indigent circumstances, namely,

One prize of thirty thousand dollars, sold in halves; one of twenty-five thousand dollars, sold in eighths; one of twenty thousand; one of fifteen thousand; two of ten thousand; four of five thousand; two of two thousand; and many of one thousand, &c. &c.

Medical Science lottery advertisement, 1817

Hope and Company lottery advertisement, *ca.* 1817

Harvard College lottery ticket, 1811

Faneuil Hall lottery ticket, 1765

Mountain Road lottery ticket, 1768

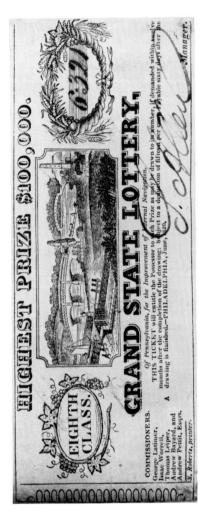

Grand State (Pennsylvania)
lottery ticket, 1820

National lottery ticket, 1821

pense. But the election of Andrew Jackson in 1828 reversed this trend, and many of the functions performed by the national government, such as internal improvements, again became responsibilities of the states. Nationalism also fostered western expansion, and the resultant rise of the slavery issue led to formation of a second Republican Party, heir to the Federalist philosophy of industrial interest and enemy of the expansion of slavery. Its victory in 1860 over the southern and agriculturally dominated Democratic Party (the descendant of the first Republican Party) led to a showdown between the forces of union and disunion in the Civil War.

Economically, the period opened with the United States in the continued throes of a depression, the result of the Revolution and the ineptness of the Confederation. Prosperity in general soon returned with the revival of American trade, made possible by the preoccupation of European competitors with the French Revolution. Though suffering set-backs during the Embargo and the War of 1812 and the panics of 1819 and 1837, the economy of the United States showed a persistent growth. Paralleling this was the increase in population from four million in 1790 to thirty-one million in 1860. With increased stability and maturity governments began recognizing their new responsibilities and expanding their functions to meet the challenges of a growing and potentially powerful nation. This development needed money. And more and more often the money was realized from a lottery.

The colonial and Confederation periods set the pattern for lotteries which would be followed with slight deviation for the next one hundred years. By 1790 lotteries were so strongly entrenched in the economy and habits of the American people that even if there had been strong opposition, state legislatures only reluctantly would have considered abolishing the schemes. However, opposition was not strong. Most people were willing to pay the cost for a chance to win the munificent prizes. Obvious evils were ascribed to misconduct on the part of the management, and the lottery's wide use by governments, schools, and churches probably brought many moral objectors to admit that the "devil's water was used to turn the Lord's mill." [3]

As the country grew, so did its lotteries. More ambitious plans for public improvements required more money, and the small, community projects of the earlier days gave way to drawings calculated to raise tens and hundreds of thousands of dollars. No longer was a single locality viewed as the market for tickets, but the wealth of a whole state and its neighbors was tapped. This evolution created new conditions and brought new problems.

A most important change was the introduction of ticket brokers and lottery contractors. These were men who saw the enormous possibilities in the lottery system and exploited them for their own personal gain. Also, they took over the functions formerly performed by unpaid managers and friends of the lottery beneficiaries. Specifically, the ticket brokers bought up large blocks of the tickets at a discount and sold them, originally as a side line and later exclusively, through their shops and branch offices throughout the country, thus relieving management of the task. By 1815 every town of 1,000 persons or more had its middlemen whose business was any and all transactions connected with selling lottery tickets. The contractors were a later development but just as inherent in the system. For a price, they assumed entire control and directed the lottery, using the brokers as outlets for the sale of tickets. Together, the contractors and brokers took the lottery to all corners of the nation. This was the genesis of American big business, for many of the promotional and organizational techniques originated by these groups later were used to advantage by all types of business concerns.

An important result was the lottery's role as one of the sires of the eminently respectable occupation of private banking and as a forerunner of the twentieth-century chain of stock brokerages. An historian of American banking has noted the connection between lotteries and modern economics and has pointed out that the lottery-ticket business "in a way stood for modern investment banking." Here was a method to gather small sums for conversion into real capital. At that time it was practically the only means by which the wealth of the little fellow could be tapped for permanent investment.[4]

The lottery-brokerage firm of S. & M. Allen provides an interesting study of the evolution of this phase of the business and its relationship to modern banking. In August 1808 Solomon Allen, son of a Presbyterian minister, began selling lottery tickets to supplement his earnings as a printer of the Albany (New York) *Register*. Shortly afterwards he set up "S. Allen's Lottery and Exchange Office" in

Albany, announcing that in addition to tickets he constantly had for sale other items such as *Dwight's Geography,* ink powder, sealing wax, slates and pencils, writing and wrapping paper, all kinds of legal blanks, "American" gun powder, and "Ladies Elegant Thread Cases." Of future importance was the note that "Eastern & Southern Bills [are] exchanged at a moderate discount or taken in payment for any of the above articles." This enterprise, by no means unique, proved so rewarding that in 1812 Allen left the *Register* to give full attention to the "Lottery, Exchange & Broking Business." Among tickets sold by him in 1812 were those of Union (New York) and Harvard colleges. He took promissory and all kinds of bank notes in payment, bought and sold bank shares, interests in "first-rate Privateers," and patent medicines. By 1815 he had established a branch office at Hudson, New York, and formed a partnership with his brother Moses in New York City called "Allen's Truly Lucky Office." The firm announced exchange at the usual rates of bills from any bank in ten specified states and the District of Columbia, liberal premiums for bank notes from Connecticut, Massachusetts, Rhode Island, and New Hampshire, and for gold and silver.

In 1816 the Allens branched out to Philadelphia, then to Baltimore. These offices, like most of the later ones, were called "S. & M. Allen & Co.," but consisted of the two brothers and a third local partner who became resident head of the partnership. Other offices rapidly appeared: Pittsburgh in 1818; Washington and Richmond in 1819; Charleston, South Carolina, in 1820; and Fayetteville, North Carolina, and Savannah, Georgia, in 1821. By 1827, in addition to the above, they also were advertising at Providence, Lynchburg, Boston, and Portland, Maine, and had contracts with firms in other places. All the offices engaged in a modified banking business, but up until 1827 the sale of lottery tickets was their primary interest.

Personal preference and the early stirrings of public opposition to lotteries caused the Allens to begin accenting the non-lottery aspects of their business. The New York house had practically discontinued ticket sales by 1823, turning them over to one of their former clerks. After 1827 the banking interest successively became dominant in the Allens' partnerships or their holdings were sold to the local partner. They began handling stocks and their far-flung connections made it natural also to engage in buying, selling, and collecting drafts, not only throughout the United States but also in England.[5]

The Allens were also interesting as the forerunners of other important private bankers. E. W. Clark & Company of Philadelphia, largest dealers in domestic exchange in the 1840's and 1850's, was established by Enoch W. Clark, a relative of the Allens, who learned the lottery and exchange business in the Allen concern. The Clark company in turn sired Jay Cooke and Company, the leading investment house of the Civil War period. Other banking firms with similar beginnings, to mention a few of the better known ones, include the several ventures of John Thompson. Thompson, the founder of the First National Bank of New York, began his career as a seller of lottery tickets and opened a Wall Street brokerage business in 1833. Later, he established the Chase National Bank. Jacob I. Cohen, Jr., and Brothers, private bankers of Baltimore, also originated as humbly. These businesses are noteworthy because of the typical pattern of their growth: money brokerage developed out of the lottery business. The ticket seller, in order to make sales, had to take the proffered medium of payment and then make a business out of handling whatever came to hand. The diversity of currency thus forced him to become a banker.

An even more interesting American personality identified with ticket selling was P. T. Barnum. Imbued with the lottery fever by the example of his grandfather, Phineas Taylor, who managed the Episcopal Society of Fairfield's lottery, Barnum obtained experience in his teens as a promoter of raffles. Upon opening a store in Bethel, Connecticut, about 1828, he began selling, on the advice of his grandfather, tickets on a 10 per cent commission along with his stock of fruit, confectionary, oysters, and toys. The ticket business proved so successful that he contacted Dudley S. Gregory, principal agent of Yates & McIntyre, concerning the possibility of opening an office in Pittsburgh. Dissuaded from that move, he turned down their agency for the whole state of Tennessee. He had learned, however, of the 25 to 30 per cent he could make if he bought his tickets directly from the managers. Thereafter he did just that, establishing his own subagents throughout the Connecticut area in such places as Danbury, Norwalk, Stamford, and Middletown. Orders were received by mail and sent out on commission by postriders and others. His sales soon rose from $500 to $2,000 per day. He maintained this profitable business until lotteries were abolished in Connecticut.[6]

The second innovation in the lottery field, contracting, brought in still another party to share the profits. As the schemes grew larger and more numerous, their direction became a full-time job and obviously too much to expect of even the philanthropically or patriotically inclined. Consequently, the practice grew of setting aside, often by law, about 5 to 15 per cent of the returns of a lottery for the managers. As more skill was needed the remuneration increased, and management of lotteries tended toward becoming a profession.

This new class of entrepreneurs quickly dominated the business. A promoter would approach an institution with a legislative franchise and convince its trustees that his contacts in other states and his knowledge of advertising would insure greater returns. He next had to get the franchise made assignable. This usually was easy since legislators were partial to local interests, particularly when it appeared that most of the money would come from outside the state, or a bit of bribery, perhaps, hastened the decision. Later the right of transfer was commonly included in the statutes of authorization. As the majority of schemes fell into the hands of big contractors, the remaining grantees found themselves woefully lacking the connections and facilities to compete successfully. So eagerly were these franchises sought that old grants, dormant for years, were revived and sold. In return, the contractor either paid a fixed sum each year, operated the lottery on a percentage basis, or worked for a fee.

The next move was to increase sales in other states. Prohibitory laws were already being evaded and so proved no great handicap. Some legislatures were politically corrupt and susceptible to bribery and for reciprocal reasons could be counted upon not to close loopholes.[7] Too harsh action against the tickets of a neighbor would bring retaliation. Smaller commonwealths, such as Rhode Island and Delaware, and the newly settled areas of the South, could hope for large sales only from outside markets. In many cases where proscriptive laws were in force, the small penalties were considered an annual tax by dealers. States like Pennsylvania which did not offer witnesses immunity from prosecution found them most reluctant to testify against the agents.

The tickets were distributed throughout the country to branch offices of the contractor, where they were disposed of either to salesmen employed on a commission basis or sold in bulk to ticket brokers who in turn sent out their vendors. A nation-wide campaign to ballyhoo the scheme followed. Thus, formerly quiet affairs, infrequently drawn and attracting little except local attention, lotteries now became the daily preoccupation of large segments of the population throughout the country.

A giant among the contractors was the firm of Yates & McIntyre of New York, composed of Archibald McIntyre, and Henry and J. B. Yates. McIntyre, born in Scotland, came to America at an early age. First a school teacher, he later went into a conveyance office and finally into the mercantile business. Entering politics, he became a member of the New York Assembly, 1798–1804; served as deputy secretary of state, 1801–1806; and was comptroller, 1806–1821. He won an enviable reputation for financial ability and incorruptibility, and as comptroller he had exercised supervision of all state-authorized lotteries. The other major partner, John Barentse Yates, a Phi Beta Kappa and a member of Congress, came from a distinguished New York family. One of his brothers was governor from 1823 to 1825 and another was a state senator.[8] By 1823 Yates & McIntyre had complete control of all New York grants.[9] They also bought numerous franchises in New Jersey, Pennsylvania, Rhode Island, Delaware, North Carolina, South Carolina, Maryland, Virginia, and the District of Columbia.

Phalen & Co., another large contractor, operated in Connecticut and Rhode Island and at different times held licenses in Delaware and Virginia as well. Gregory & Co., was headed by J. C. Gregory, a former mayor of Jersey City, New Jersey, who had as associates his brothers, B. P. and D. S. Gregory. The latter two occasionally bought grants in their own names. This partnership numbered among its clients concerns in Maryland, South Carolina, New Jersey, and Delaware. During its height it held at least two drawings daily and sold through established brokers in nearly all the middle Atlantic and eastern states. Beside these larger operators there were numerous small companies, such as Paine & Burgess of Rhode Island, who managed only one or two franchises.

Although considerable wealth could be made through contracting, the business also carried its risks, as Yates & McIntyre discovered. In 1823 they began selling tickets in their consolidated New York holdings. The firm charged their dealers a 15 per cent premium for tickets and in the first year sold approximately 99 per cent of all chances offered. But in 1825 sales began to drop, and just over 93 per cent of the tickets, worth a total of $2,994,500, were sold that year. This decline gathered momentum so rapidly that by April 1829 only 37 per cent of the chances offered were sold. As the number and amounts of the prizes could not be reduced accordingly, the contractor's only hope lay in the possibility of unsold tickets drawing most of the major awards.

Normally, however, contracting and ticket selling were extremely lucrative businesses, though highly competitive ones. It is not without significance that lottery men were among the first to see the potentialities of the new telegraph. The Magnetic Company, which opened a wire between New York and Philadelphia in 1846, derived much of its early revenue from this source. As more ticket agencies opened, methods of high-pressure salesmanship were developed to meet the competition. Standing accounts were opened for servants, apprentices, young clerks, and others, and prizes were credited and purchases debited monthly. Handbills of the "most insidious and seductive character" were scattered broadcast; street placards and newspaper advertisements with huge figures promised wealth to the gullible; and numbers were peddled to passers-by on the public streets. One account stated that if persuasion were not enough to induce a sale, the chances were physically thrust upon the reluctant customers.

Nearly every office claimed a monopoly on the affections of the fickle deity, proclaiming it in the establishment's name. Variations on the word "luck" or "fortune" were used, such as Allen's Truly Lucky, Gilbert and Dean's Real Fortunate, and Kidder's Lucky Lottery offices. Slogans and catchwords abounded: "Now is the time to fill your bags!"; "Nothing venture, nothing have!"; "Delays are Dangerous!"; "Now is the time to secure a chance for a handsome fortune at the low price of . . . !"; "Money made easy!"; and "Try your luck these hard times!"

A Newport dealer's advertisement in the *Rhode Island Republican*, January 1813, illustrates this approach:

HIGHLY IMPORTANT. — On Monday last, in Boston, No. 18,816, in the 7th class of Harvard College Lottery, came up a prize of $20,000 and was sold to George W. Martin, of this town, sometime after the commencement of the drawing of the Lottery by J. C. Shaw, at his *Truly Fortunate* Lottery Office, where have been sold in the short space of thirteen months, besides many other capital prizes, two tickets which have drawn the enormous sum of $35,000. Those in pursuit of an independent Fortune, will do well in the future to call . . . where the Goddess of Fortune has pledged herself to distribute favors with a liberal hand.

Next to patent-medicine advertisers, the ticket sellers apparently contributed most to the income of the press. A majority merely cited the available tickets and high prizes offered, but some showed real originality. A common pictorial device displayed Fortune blindfolded and balancing herself upon a lottery wheel or drum; in one hand she held a cornucopia from which coins poured into the hat of an improvident young person clothed only in modesty; in the other hand, the lady brandished a scroll bearing the inscription "$10,000." Other woodcuts showed a lottery drawing in process or pictured the beneficiary.

Whenever possible, motives other than mercenary ones were extolled. Feminine vanity and love of country were skillfully woven into this story from the *Columbian Centinel,* April 28, 1790:

Patriotism of the Ladies

The ladies of Massachusetts have ever been distinguished for their patriotism; and although their peculiar province is to soften the cares, and soothe the sorrows of life, yet they have never neglected any proper and decent opportunity of advancing public good: — When the Ladies found the Government had established a Lottery to ease the taxes of the people, they generally became adventurers, and it is pleasing to find that their patriotism has been in some measure rewarded, by *their sex* sharing the First *Capital Prize.*

Hope and Company, in the Philadelphia *Gazette,* September 7, 1808, invited the ladies who did not have to "consult their cautious plodding husbands" to buy tickets and gain the prizes awaiting "the claim of beauty."

Class and racial appeal underlay notices such as this one in the *Columbian Centinel,* June 5, 1790: "Two apprentices belonging to Mr. *Bemis,* Papermaker, in Watertown drew the 1000 prize in the Williamstown Lottery"; and in the Salem, Massachusetts, *Gazette,* May 10, 1791: "No. 17221, which drew 2000 dollars in the Semi-annual State Lottery, was paid on Friday last, by Messrs. Leach and Fosdick, in Boston. The proprietors were *four Africans* belonging to Newport."

The Harvard College lottery, 1807, incited greater originality. One newspaper advertised:

Revolutions of the Planets compared — The earth requires twenty-four hours to perform a revolution on its axis — To those who are not in the habit of studying Astronomy, the difference between this motion and that of another planet, must be a subject of interesting speculation. The Planet *Harvard College Lottery Wheels* turns completely on its axis in about sixteen seconds of time. An *Interesting Speculation* for Adventurers, who wish to be within the orbit of a planet so influential on the affairs of this world. More of these Astronomical Phenomena will be explained at GILBERT & DEAN's Observatory, no. 78, State-street.[10]

Under a view of the college building a broadside for a later class of the lottery carried the poem:

> Those who will not, when fortune offers,
> Hold to her hand their empty coffers;
> May well lament when others gain,
> What they've neglected to obtain.

Grand Harvard College Lottery. 33,000 Dollars and upwards, may be gained for the trifling sum of 500 cents!!! [11]

The school also shared the attention created by this offer in the Salem *Gazette*, March 24, 1807:

A New Dispensary!

Numerous are the instances that can be cited of a less, a much less, sum than *Twenty Thousand Dollars* having restored to their pristine vigor precarious circumstances, and of making the *poor become rich!* Let stubborn prejudices be laid aside, and an immediate resort made to that GRAND ANTIPOVERTY CORRECTIVE, CASH, which is now proffered as a sovereign remedy for all the complaints poverty is heir to: — in asserting the superior efficacy of this preventive of the evils attendant on a state of poverty, it is not intended to trespass on truth — let it be fairly tried, when [sic] the "Majesty of its own worth" will be manifest. The door is now open for the reception of such as would like to try the experiment: — There is the *Hatfield Bridge Lottery,* which commences drawing the 15th of next month; this affords a *potion* of EIGHT THOUSAND DOLLARS; if, after a fair trial here, the desired effect is not produced, then there is the *Harvard College Lottery,* which commences in May, which has the highly *balsamic cordial* of TWENTY THOUSAND DOLLARS, which will produce the most wonderful effects, by giving a *solid tone* to the regions of the pockets, and by enriching and invigorating the whole system as can be satisfactorily tested:– Twenty Thousand Dollars would "Cheer the heart, and make the spirits flow!" Perseverance is highly recommended, and if the wishes are not gratified by the attainment of the desired object, the consoling reflection will recur, that — *"there are not quite two blanks to a prize"* — which is more than can be said of quackery in general. Tickets and Quarters for sale by

JOHN RUSSELL

☞ To-Morrow the price of Tickets rise — purchasers can be accomodated until 9 o'clock this evening.

☞ A handsome Premium given for Essex County Money.

The same Salem, Massachusetts, dealer on another occasion depended upon an unusual arrangement of the type to attract the reader.

** If anybody Wants
*

TEN THOUSAND DOLLARS
they are requested to call

JOHN RUSSELL

who will, for a trifling consideration, put them in a
way to realize that, or another sum of less
magnitude, in the course of September
next, when the rich Wheels of Hatfield Bridge Lottery will begin
to move.

☞ Tickets will rise on the first of September to 5.50 — Prize Tickets exchanged.

A firm in Rhode Island praised themselves as they solicited business:

From a retrospective view of business, for four years, very pleasing and grateful sensations arise, and draw from them reflections of the most pure, rational and exalted kind. A recapitulation of our lottery business will convince all of the benefit of paying their devoirs in the temple of the fickle goddess of Fortune at their office. "The diamond receives its lustre from the labor bestowed on it"; and the many capital prizes sold by G & D are like so many lottery stars, which will be considered by the knowing ones of primary magnitude and brightness.[12]

Advertising in the Boston *Palladium,* June 9, 1807, one of the largest New England ticket agencies emphasized the small sum necessary to win a large prize and the advantages of "insurance":

20,000!! 5,000!! 1,000!!! Dollars

Who is there that would not give 6 dols. 50 for one of the above sums, or 1 dollar 75 cts. for a quarter of one of them. Chances to gain one are now selling at the above prices, at Kidder & Co's, *Lottery, Insurance on Tickets, and Intelligence* Office . . .

Tickets and quarters may be insured during the drawing of the lottery, which presents an excellent chance for saving the cost of Tickets!! Adventurers will do well to call!!!

The same firm took advantage of the excitement over foreign trade conditions by writing:

Lottery News!

Ye who on Fortune's golden sea appear,
Behold the chart, — there's no *Embargo* here.

It must give a confidence almost bordering on certainty to ALL who are in the habit of feeling that *tickling, pleasing*, painful sensation which always arises from having undrawn tickets in ones pockets; and to the "Lucky Ones," at least, it will be a matter of particular satisfaction to learn the following CAPITAL PRIZES have been sold at KIDDERS Established Lucky Lottery Office . . . in less than one year! [13]

The grandfather of the singing commercial appeared under a picture showing men and women in a boat trying to catch prizes represented as fish.

FORTUNE's ANGLERS: A New Lottery Song. Tune — "There are sweepers in high life as well as in low."

In the fish pond of fortune men angle always,
Some angle for titles, some angle for praise
Some angle for favor, some angle for wives,
And some angle for nought all the days of their lives:
Ye who'd angle for Wealth, *and would* Fortunes *obtain,*
Get your hooks baited by Kidder, Gilbert & Dean.[14]

The drawing for Harvard College in 1811 brought another series of ingenious advertisements. One in the Salem *Gazette,* May 17, read:

"Who Wants a Guinea?"

This Comedy by Coleman, has for some years past, been often read and justly admired; and the name now appears to have lost its novelty.

Something of greater magnitude is wished for; something which will furnish the possessor with more than a competency; which will assist the industrious and enterprising man, in accomplishing his laudable wishes.

This surely must be the true Philosopher's Stone, which wise men of all ages have sought for in vain. —This inestimable Gem, with some of the virtues usually ascribed to it will, after the Fifth Class Harvard College Lottery has completed drawing, belong to some person or persons who will now generously lend a hand to patronize this excellent institution.

Another notice burlesqued the common advertisements for instruction in the art of penmanship.

Writing
Taught in One Lesson!!

Persons of any age, sex, or capacity, *let their Chirography be never so bad,* may by *one* exercise *make* a VERY GOOD HAND *of it.* The means are found in the Scheme of Harvard College Lottery, which contains a most superb assortment of capital prizes. Persons desirous of securing the advantage of this *dispatchful* tuition will apply (wholes $5, quarters $1.38) to CUSHING & APPLETON . . .[15]

One seller used a new medical discovery as a soundingboard for his merchandise:

"Galvanism"

It has been found by Dr. NAUCHE, at Paris, that a person perfectly blind may be made to see very lively and numerous flashes of light, by bringing one extremity of the voltaic pile into communication with the hand or foot, and the other with the face, skin of head, or even the neck. In like manner, a person in the gloom of poverty may be made to perceive very lively and numerous flashes (say 20,000) of good fortune by bringing one extremity of a ragged bank bill into communication with the Book-Store and the other with the Lottery-Office, one door west of Central Building.

N.B. — Two grand piles are now offered to the public — Harvard College, where the process is now in active operation, and Plymouth Beach which is in a state of preparation.[16]

Churches were more dignified but no less enthusiastic in pushing their enterprises, as evidenced by the announcement in 1813 for the Second Baptist Church in Providence, Rhode Island:

"Public Worship Encouraged"

When the managers reflect that the above scheme is admirably well calculated to give adventurers a fair opportunity of obtaining a number of valuable prizes and that almost everyone in this enlightened land will feel a lively interest in the promotion of an undertaking so laudable and so important as that of establishing, at this alarming crisis of the affairs of our country [the War of 1812], a stated place for the promulgation of the blessed Gospel of Peace, which teaches the soldier to be content with such wages as he receives, Caesar to rule in the fear of God, and his constituents to render Him his due, and unto God the things which belong to Him, they cannot but anticipate a rapid sale of their tickets.[17]

One of the strangest of all lottery advertisements ran thus:

"The Historical Dictionary,"

By Ezra Sampson, author of the Beauties of the Bible, is one of the most useful little works of this nature which we have seen . . . Its subjects are Natural and Civil History, Geography, Zoology, Botany and Mineralogy . . . explained in such a neat and intelligible manner as to render it worthy of being (according to its design) a *Companion for Youth.* We select the following article as a specimen of the work.

LOTTERY

"A kind of public game at hazard, in order to raise money for the service of the state . . . [Here follows a description of the method of drawing.] Beside the consideration that this, as well as all other forms of gambling for money, tend to corrupt the public morals, it is also to be considered that the purchasers of the tickets are never permitted to play the game on fair and equal ground . . . [Here is quoted, without credit, the attack made by Adam Smith. See above, p. 79.]"

The above is surely a just account of the nature and principles of a Lottery; yet it does not destroy the fact that, distributed as the tickets always are among thousands, there must be some gainers, and that in spite of mathematics, there is a lucky number, which must draw the capital prize in the Plymouth Beach Lottery (without deduction) of 12,000 dollars. Both the *Historical Dictionary* and Lottery *Tickets* may be had at Cushing & Appleton's old stand.[18]

The occasional references to future advances in price illustrated the public's greed and excitement and another source of profit for the ticket seller. A notice in the New York *Daily Advertiser*, August 8, 1807, clearly demonstrates this: "If the capital prize of $10,000 remains in the wheel on the 45th day of drawing, tickets will then be advanced to 10 dollars each, and will continue advancing daily one dollar, as long as it remains in." The advancing prices were possible because the broker usually received chances from the managers at par value or less and retailed them on an increasing scale of profit ranging from fifty cents to twenty dollars, depending upon public interest and demand. S. & M. Allen advanced the prices on the fifth class of the Union Canal Lottery (1818) from twenty-five to sixty dollars per ticket. Brokers' earnings soon represented 20 to 25 per cent of the ticket price. Considering the by-products of the business as well, it would be no exaggeration to say that such men were the principal beneficiaries of the system!

The high cost of tickets might well have limited purchasers to the rich, at a time when few people had cash incomes and white-collar workers earned about $1,000 a year and laborers forty cents a day. But Lady Luck's salesmen had something for every pocket-book and every degree of cupidity. As a special come-on to the poor, chances were sold in halves, quarters, eighths, and even greater subdivisions, until the cost of a share might reach as little as twelve and one-half cents. The following case, reported in the *Massachusetts Gazette*, 1786, must have so increased the brokerage business:

Marblehead, April 3. The highest Prize in the State Lottery was drawn by a number of Females: About thirty were joint possessors of that fortunate number and five others: The highest share in them did not exceed one dollar, and the lowest was ninepence, expressive of the different abilities of the concerned; by which circumstance, the property of the prize is most agreeably divided: It has excited a smile in the cheek of poverty, nor diminshed the pleasure of those in easy circumstances.

The practice of selling fractional tickets was too great a temptation for unscrupulous brokers. Numerous accounts tell of vendors apprehended for selling more fractions than made up the whole. One man in New York sold nineteen-eighths of a lot. Unfortunately, it was awarded a prize of $400.[19]

Another trick commonly deplored was that of selling drawn numbers which the salesman knew to be blanks. Thus, many dealers specified that chances purchased in their offices were "warranted undrawn." This is amusingly illustrated by an advertisement of July 24, 1807:

Lottery Price Current. — In Boston Amoskeag Tickets, warranted undrawn, 6 dolls. In Salem, at Russel's 5.50 — at Cushing and Appleton's not warranted, 5.

Further Information. — The Amoskeag highest prize of Eight Thousand Dollars, is still undrawn, and the wheels are extraordinarily rich . . . Those who intend to purchase for the sake of a chance for the highest prize, are advised to do it *before* it is drawn out of the wheel . . . Those who purchase for the sake of a cheap ticket, would do well to wait till *afterwards*.[20]

Another inducement provided billets designed to be sold on an installment plan. One in a Pennsylvania venture read, "This ticket, on payment of four dollars, will entitle the bearer to such prizes as are drawn by this number . . ." A printed notation in one corner certified: "Paid 6 dollars; Due Four Dollars." It was not necessary even to own a share, for they could be rented. A ticket could be leased for a day at fifty cents or more, depending on how many tickets remained to be drawn. If that particular number came out on that day the prize went to the renter; if not, the ticket was returned to the office.

One of the most lucrative phases of the agent's business and the source of one of the most severe complaints against the lottery came from "insurance." No new phenomenon, it became widespread with the facilities provided by the many brokers. Benjamin Franklin recorded evidence of an earlier form when in his lottery of 1748 certain persons agreed, for a premium of 20 per cent, to make up any deficiency between the prize and the chance's cost. His Quaker friend, James Logan, thus protected his 125 tickets, but Franklin wrote, "I have not insured for anybody, so I shall neither lose nor gain that way." [21]

By the nineteenth century "insurance" or "policy" was widely practiced by those not having the price of a chance. Before development of the ternary combination system of lotteries, the physical act of drawing out the tickets consumed weeks and even months, depending on how many were drawn each day. On each day of drawing a certain portion of the lots were taken from the wheel, and any person could bet that a particular number would be drawn the next day, according to a ratio of increasing odds. If his guess, usually based on a dream or some omen, were correct, he did not receive a "prize" or "blank" but the amount for which it was "insured"; otherwise, he lost his bet. Literally, the agent gambled one pound against one shilling, or a like amount, that the speculator could not name when a number would be drawn. In another variation, wagers were taken on whether a billet would be an award or a blank. To aid the adventurers, offices carried libraries of dream books, and in New Orleans in the 1880's trained parakeets would select, for a price, the number to be played.

The ternary combination principle was introduced sometime during the 1820's to save time and put an end to "insurance." Under this plan each ticket carried a combination of three numbers. In a specific but common example the 78 numbers from 1 to 78 would produce a first combination of 1, 2, 3; a second of 1, 2, 4, and so on. In all, 76,076 different groups or tickets could be made. For a lottery of this size 78 ballots were prepared, numbered from 1 to 78. Twelve of these were drawn one at a time. The ticket bearing the first three numbers drawn in order of their appearance won the capital prize; the fourth, fifth, and sixth numbers drawn made the combination for the second prize, and so on, until the tenth, eleventh, and twelfth numbers drawn won the fourth prize. A combination of the second, third, and fourth numbers received the fifth award and so on. Those tickets with two drawn numbers won small prizes, as did those with only one. The 45,760 billets with none of the twelve drawn numbers were, of course, blanks and received nothing.[22]

A lottery of this description could be drawn in fifteen minutes. But it did not stop "insurance"; it merely changed the form. A gambler simply chose a "station" number and speculated on the order in which it would be drawn. To do this he customarily paid six cents and received $2.50 if he won, or proportions of these figures. "Watchers" took down the numbers at drawings and reported to the office by runners. An investigation by the New York legislature in 1819 showed that in three days one New York City office made $31,000 from "insurance" alone. Under both variations, "insurance" or "policy" salesmen generally were paid a commission of 12.5 per cent, and neither management nor the lottery's beneficiary received any part of this income.

In an advertisement for the "Baltimore Grand Lottery" in the New York *Daily Advertiser,* January 25, 1808, Waites Lottery Office listed its rates for "insurance."

		£o.	2s.	8d.
Sixth and Seventh days for	$10 [you pay]			
	50	0.	13	4
	100	1	6	8
	1000	12	5	8
Eighth and ninth days	10	0	2	10
	50	0	14	2
	100	1	8	4
	1000	14	3	4
Tenth and eleventh days	10	0	3	0
	***	**	**	***
	1000	15	0	0

The brisk competition between dealers and the lavish claims made by each enticing advertisement were all parts of a big business. The only possible shortage was that of purchasers. Agents undertook to sell chances not only in schemes licensed by their own states but also in ventures originating elsewhere. No state was able, if they seriously tried, to suppress entirely the sale of lots in out-of-state, or "foreign," projects. In view of the population of the country, the number of tickets which found takers is amazing. Even in the late eighteenth century when the inhabitants numbered about four million, a Pennsylvania scheme of 1782 offered 40,000 chances and the relatively small lottery for Harvard College in 1794 placed 25,000 billets on the market at five dollars each. It also was not uncommon for several similar ventures to be in operation in one state at the same time. At the height of the mania in the 1820's, when the population numbered about ten million, some of the larger undertakings ran into a dozen or more classes, involving 100,000 tickets. Many of these chances were sold in fractional parts, making the total number of customers even greater. With the substantial profit on each sale, not to mention the returns from "insurance" and similar practices, the stake of the retailers was enormous.

"Insurance" led to so many abuses that various states took remedial steps. New York in 1807 made it illegal to register numbers under a penalty of $250 or three months' imprisonment. It also became a misdemeanor to sell chances on tickets or publish any such proposal. In November 1809, Maryland declared that any person insuring or causing a number to be insured "for any purpose, or against any event," or selling any part of it by other than a complete and bona-fide sale, should pay $30 for every offense, one-half to go to the informer and the rest to the county in which the act had been committed. The statute also applied to sales for a day or other limited time, or any agreement other than outright transfer. Despite these and similar attempts, however, the profit and appeals of "insurance" were so great that it continued in varied forms as long as there were lotteries.

"Insurance" was not the only practice over which lottery men encountered the power of the state. The manager or contractor usually found a government official looking over his shoulder. During the colonial period most provinces had introduced "authorization" to assure "honest" lotteries; eventually it was required in all.

Experience soon proved, however, that licensing alone could not guarantee honest drawings. Additional rules and regulations were tried. One of the most common required substantial bonds of the managers. In the "Literature" and "Black River" lotteries in 1801, New York required a $10,000 bond from each manager and further required that as soon as ticket sales reached $5,000 the proceeds had to be placed in one of the state banks. An undertaking in 1803 carried the added stipulation that the directors post bonds of $12,000, but in turn gave them 10 per cent of the amount raised. In 1805 New York required monthly sales reports, forbade managers to buy tickets for their own use, and increased the rate of compensation to 14 per cent. The same year those in charge of the $80,000 Union College Lottery were each placed under $30,000 bond, with orders to deposit the receipts as soon as they amounted to $500. A series of scandals later brought supervision by the state comptroller of all managers and minute instructions on the mechanics of drawing, such as having the selector bare his arms, hold the ticket between his thumb and forefinger, and withdraw only one number at a time.

Other states found the problem equally difficult. In Connecticut three auditors were appointed to examine the accounts of all classes within thirty days of completion and report their findings to the Assembly. Rhode Island demanded bond equal to the amount sought and required that the secretary of state supervise all drawings. Maryland also had three commissioners to approve and supervise all lotteries. Most states, however, did not go beyond the requirement of surety and attempted to encourage honesty by prosecuting the dishonest and collecting forfeited bonds.

Contractors were also indirectly affected when the states started taxing the recipients of grants. In April 1824, Louisiana began requiring from 1.0 to 2.5 per cent of the funds obtained through sale of property by lotteries. Two years later the process was simplified so that those desiring to dispose of land or buildings in this manner had only to apply to the state treasurer for authorization, which would be granted automatically in return for 2.0 per cent of the property's assessed value. Maryland in 1817 started requisitioning 5.0 per cent of the proceeds of all schemes, and in 1832 she forced brokers and managers for outside ventures to pay $250 for each class drawn, or a total of not less than $5,000, and to hold a $15,000 drawing for the benefit of the state. Delaware taxed each class drawn

$50. Rhode Island and Tennessee in 1826 required managers to pay the general treasury 1.0 per cent of the value of each and every class and 0.5 per cent of the amount to be raised respectively.

Ticket sellers also felt the government's hand. Previously the only action that had affected them had been the ban on "foreign" ticket sales. Fines, regardless of their size, for sale of unauthorized chances had proven ineffective, so states began a system of licensing sellers. This could be used variously as a restraint, a revenue producer, and a factor to control the agents. Virginia in 1813 was perhaps the first state to impose a special license tax. In 1819 in New York all vendors had to have a $500 license and post $5,000 bonds in New York City and $100 and $1,000 bonds elsewhere. At the same time statutes subjected instigators of private lotteries to forfeiture of the sum sought, or $2,500 if this was in doubt, and a fine of $250 for each ticket sold. "Insuring" brought a possible penalty of $2,000.

During the same year Maryland required $500 permits and $200 bonds for ticket agents in Baltimore. Outside of that city the bond was set at $50. Louisiana in 1822 went to the extreme of assessing a $50,000 license on those dealing in chances of non-locally sanctioned lotteries and a fine of $2,000 on every sale without a permit. However, the $50,000 requirement was reduced to $5,000 in 1826. Connecticut followed in 1825 with a $100 fee for all ticket offices, and three years later assigned penalties for selling shares or charging above the fixed price. In 1826 Vermont placed a $500 tax on agents. Virginia abandoned its policy of excluding "foreign" tickets in 1828 and substituted a $300 annual fee on those who sold them, while charging only $60 for the privilege of selling state-authorized billets exclusively. Finally, in 1831 the tax on sellers for outside undertakings was set at $500, and a levy of 1.0 per cent on Virginia drawings.

Despite these restrictions, lotteries continued to thrive. Nothing better illustrated their exploitation than the rapid increase in the number of drawings and in shops handling the tickets. With a venture scheduled for virtually every day in the year, dealers operated on a full-time basis. Whereas formerly the sale of chances had been a sideline for a stationer or newspaper publisher, entire offices now specialized in the trade. Philadelphia, for example, had three stores for this purpose in 1809; four in 1810; sixty in 1827;[23] 177 in 1831; and over 200 in 1833. A citizens' committee estimated in 1831 that on an average these offices employed two persons, with perhaps an equal number of itinerant vendors. In 1826, according to a Massachusetts legislative report, a probable total of $1,127,575 was spent for tickets in Pennsylvania. Yates & McIntyre alone offered more than 200 classes there in 1831. The next year chances were sold in over 420 classes, 394 of which violated Pennsylvania laws, with prizes amounting to $53,136,930. The cost to the people of Philadelphia was placed at $30,000 a week.

These were not isolated conditions. The New York *Commercial Advertiser* stated in 1826 that there were upwards of 160 lottery establishments in that city. During the same period Boston had one hundred persons making their livelihood exclusively by this means. Portland, Maine, had twenty-five shops, besides numerous public houses where billets were sold. In that year the inhabitants of Rhode Island reputedly spent $1,350,000 on lottery chances; the people of New York $1,491,540; and the people of Massachusetts, $750,000. In 1839 Maryland had forty-three offices, of which forty were in Baltimore. The promoters were making good their boast to exploit such schemes to the utmost. Even by twentieth-century standards it was an important "big business." [24]

Chapter VI

The Lottery as an Aid to Government, 1790–1860

That none can "reap who never sow,"
Requires no argument to show;
Alike 'tis clear — none Prizes gain
Who never plough the Lottery main.

Then Madam: — Sir! — if no essay
You make in Fortune's mazy way,
"Who speedily waits to give great pelf,"
The blame rests only with yourself.[1]

In every lottery five basic groups were involved: the customers who bought the tickets; the ticket agents and brokers who sold them; the managers and contractors; the beneficiaries; and the state. Although the role of two or three of the groups was often played by one party, no single group combined the various functions to such an extent as did the several governments. They held the key position in all authorized lotteries, granting legal permission for them, establishing the rules, often supervising their over-all operation, occasionally purchasing tickets, and conducting inquiries when something went wrong. Some states, such as New York and Maryland, even acted as contractors for a while, and probably the majority on some occasion were the beneficiaries of their own schemes.[2]

During the colonial period provincial governments had authorized lotteries for themselves, in lieu of taxes, under the plea of "hard times." Why then did the return of general prosperity in the 1790's fail to end this practice? Because of the enduring unpopularity of taxes against the perpetual appeal of lotteries? Did the small fines and lottery taxes whet the state's appetite for the opulent returns of the managers, sellers, and beneficiaries? Possibly it all stemmed from the national urge to get things done as fast as possible and, in doing so, to make conditions better than they were originally. So, during the period before the Civil War, without revealing or perhaps even realizing their motives, municipal, state, and national authorities avidly competed with their citizens for a share of the lottery's wealth.

Some of the most interesting of such undertakings were held in connection with the federal government. When it was decided to construct a capital city on the Potomac, a series of financial problems arose. To meet these Congress passed an act in 1792 which gave the corporation governing the city authority to institute lotteries for important civic projects when ordinary revenues were insufficient. Needless to say, the day of insufficiency soon dawned as funds to erect public buildings quickly proved inadequate. In 1793 the Commissioners of the District of Columbia organized, "with previous approbation of the President," a lottery for "improvement of the Federal City," with Samuel Blodget[3] as construction supervisor and general lottery agent at an annual salary of £600. The plan involved 50,000 tickets at seven dollars each, 16,737 prizes, and 33,263 blanks. The grand award was "one superb hotel, with baths, outhouses, etc., to cost $50,000"; other prizes ran from $20,000 to $10 in cash.

The chances were sold throughout the country, finding purchasers as far west as the Michigan Territory.[4] President Washington showed his affection for the son of his secretary, Tobias Lear, by sending him a number, adding, "if it should be his fortune to draw the Hotel, it will add to the pleasure I feel in giving it." [5] The Commissioners reported tickets "taken up with avidity" and early sales highly successful. This happy situation did not long continue, however, for the large number of chances in this and other schemes soon clogged the market. Blodget might well have failed to meet his advertised time for drawing, September 1793, had not some residents of Georgetown combined to buy all remaining tickets.

The drawing proceeded so slowly, however, that rumors began to spread about the manner in which it was being conducted. One claimed that the Commissioners were in league with Blodget to delay the procedure so that awards could be bought at a great discount. Others suggested that the capital prizes had never been put into the wheel, and if they were in, they would not be paid. So universal were these opinions, that on September 20, 1793, the Commissioners obtained from Blodget and his associate, a Colonel Deakins, a statement absolving the Commissioners of all responsibility in the affair. Yet even before this phase was completed, Blodget announced he had begun selling tickets in a new class.

This action alarmed the city authorities, and on December 21, 1793, they carefully defined their position in a letter to him:

It may be that . . . most that you converse with, may be fond of another Lottery and may to you, approve the Manner of Conducting of the present, but the Majority of those who speak to us on this subject express very different sentiments . . . We certainly shall never give countenance to a Lottery further than mere naked consent, as was designed in the present, nor that, unless proper security is given before any tickets are disposed of. This is not from any suspicion of you but from a sense of propriety which ought to make the Rule universal.[6]

George Washington, too, was disturbed, and in a letter to Thomas Johnson, January 23, 1794, he predicted that the "worse detail in Mr. Blodget's conduct" had not yet been seen, for in spite of the Commissioners' admonition, he was determined on the second lottery and had actually sold tickets in it for Georgia land. In face of this defiance the President wrote that he had "directed the Secretary of State to inform him [Blodget] in explicit terms, that if he did not instantly suspend all further proceeding therein until the sanction of the Commissioners should be unequivocally obtained, I would cause the unauthorized mode in which he was acting to be announced to the public to guard it against imposition." [7]

To guarantee the payment of prizes in the first class, Blodget was forced on January 28, 1794, to hand over to two trustees a large piece of his personal property and 7,160 shares in the Insurance Company of America. The chief clerk in the Secretary of State's office and the auditor of the Treasury were put in charge of concluding the business. City officials, thinking their troubles over, wrote Edmund Randolph, Secretary of State, that they were relieved on the subject, and though it had caused much anxiety, were "satisfied on the whole [it had] been useful in bringing the City into general view and contemplation."

The grand prize was won by Robert S. Bickley of Philadelphia with a ticket which cost eleven dollars.[8] The hotel, though partially erected on the northwest corner of Seventh and E streets, N.W., was never finished, and in 1798 Bickley brought a damage suit for non-completion and received a money judgment from the Pennsylvania courts. He then carried the case into the District of Columbia to collect from Blodget's property held by the trustees. In 1801 the Supreme Court decided he was entitled to the hotel plus $21,500 to raise the total value to the stipulated $50,000. All of Blodget's holdings finally were sold in 1813 to satisfy the claim.

Meanwhile the sale of tickets in "Federal Lottery No. 2" had continued. To secure the "naked consent" of the Commissioners, thus making it appear under their auspices, Blodget declared this project was to build homes in the District. He offered $400,000 in prizes, the largest award being a $20,000 house plus $30,000 in cash, less 5 per cent for advertising. Others were less expensive dwellings and smaller sums of money. He announced that any surplus would become part of the fund for the proposed national university.

The authorities again forced Blodget to sign a statement that he "proceeded on the Sales at my own private risque under their express declaration that they would not be held responsible directly or Indirectly for this Business in any *event* or in any manner whatever." Evidently this precaution still did not prevent his trying to sail under false colors, since the Commissioners finally published their disavowal of the project in both the Philadelphia and Baltimore papers.

December 1794 had been set as the drawing date of the second class, but in June 1795 the public was told the ticket sales were too small because of competition with "three other respectable and similar institutions," i.e., the lotteries for piers at New Castle, Delaware; for the city of Paterson, New Jersey; and for Harvard College. The drawing, which finally began July 4, 1796, was handled in such a dilatory fashion as to make it the object of public scorn. The Washington *Gazette*, July 9, 1796, asserted that only a hundred stubs were drawn each week, making the life expectancy of the affair ten years; adventurers, therefore, would do well to mention their tickets in their wills. After a few weeks even this small amount of activity ceased for two and a half years.

William Cobbett, the transplanted English journalist, bitterly attacked the enterprise in his *Porcupine's Gazette*, August 25, 1797, in an article entitled, "American Lotteries: Advice to Those who Need It."

> Have you an itching propensity to use your wits to advantage? Make a lottery. A splendid scheme is a bait that cannot fail to catch the gulls. Be sure to spangle it with rich prizes: the fewer blanks — on paper — the better; for on winding up the business, you know, it is easy to make as many blanks as you please. Witness a late lottery on the Potowmack. The *Winding up*, however, is not absolutely necessary . . . The better way is to delay the drawing; or should it *ever begin*, there is no hurry about the *end*, or rather, let it have no end at all. If . . . discontented adventurers should happen to say hard things of you, show them that you despise their unmannerly insinuations, by humming the tune of *Yankee Doodle*. This may dumbfound them; but should they persist, there is a mode left that cannot fail to stop their mouths. The scheme of the lottery is your contract . . . : Produce this, and defy them to point out any breach of it on your part. *Entre nous;* I am supposing you discreet enough to avoid in your scheme anything that might look like a promise to commence the drawing on this or that particular day; or to finish at any given period.[9]

Cobbett continued that it was enough for the manager to promise to begin "when a sufficient number of tickets shall be sold." The director was, of course, to be sole judge, and as long as one chance remained unsold the venture need never be completed.

When the drawing was resumed in 1799 and proceeded in the same slow fashion, the newspapers once more assailed it. A writer in the Philadelphia *Aurora*, January 17, 1799, suggested that Blodget had misnamed his young son "John Adams" and should have called him "Washington Lottery Blodget." The same journal, February 4, said the scheme should be considered a perpetual annuity and a tax upon public credulity for the benefit of Mr. Blodget. With a lawsuit from the first lottery pending against him and only a fourth of the 50,000 tickets sold in the second, Blodget decided to drop the matter completely.

This experience so embittered the Commissioners that for a long time they resisted similar proposals. A petition to Congress in 1805 for a lottery for a university as a "permanent institution for the education of youth in the City of Washington" was quickly denied. However, the new municipal charter of 1812 again authorized such undertakings on condition that the President give permission and that not more than $10,000 be raised in any one year. It was considered necessary on November 23, 1812, to use this right to try to raise $10,000 to build and endow two public schools on the "Lancasterian system."

Less than two years later, on August 3, 1814, President Madison again approved a lottery for the maximum sum, this time for funds to build a federal penitentiary, and on May 10, 1815, consented to a like amount for a city hall. An additional $10,000 to help these three projects was approved by the President on May 4, 1816. Federal authorities continued annual use of this device to raise $10,000 until several major losses and immeasurable confusion caused them to abandon the lottery forever.

One such set-back had its origin in 1812 when Congress validated an act passed in 1795 by the Maryland legislature for a lottery to raise $52,500 in the city of Washington for a canal between Maryland and the District of Columbia. These powers were delegated to the Washington Canal Company on condition that they post bond for payment of prizes. The trouble began on January 21, 1820, when Virginia passed a law outlawing all chances unauthorized by herself. Promoters of the canal scheme, assuming that the act did not apply to congressional licenses, continued their sales in Virginia. On June 1, 1820, P. J. and M. J. Cohen disposed of two halves and four quarter tickets to William Jennings of Norfolk and were promptly fined $100. The case was finally appealed to the Supreme Court on a writ of error over the protest of the state of Virginia, which denied the court's jurisdiction. David B. Ogden and William Wirt represented the Cohens, and Philip P. Barbour and Alexander Smythe appeared for Virginia.

Virginia protested that acceptance of the appeal marked a great extension of federal power and an infraction of her sovereignty. On January 20, 1821, the state Assembly passed a resolution saying there was "no rightful authority under the Constitution to examine and correct the judgment for which the Commonwealth has been 'cited and admonished to be and appear at the Supreme Court of the United States,' and . . . hereby [they] enter their most solemn protest against the jurisdiction of that Court over the matter." [10]

The state's attorneys emphasized this view and also contended that Congress could not sanction sales where such were illegal. The Supreme Court under Chief Justice John Marshall, who as a member of the Virginia legislature had voted for many such lotteries, handed down a historic decision. On the first point it established a legal landmark: that in all criminal cases originating in state courts where a federal question was involved the Supreme Court's jurisdiction under the Constitution was undeniable and supreme. On the second point it declared the lottery ordinance "only coextensive with the city" and the Virginia court correct in its judgment. Congressional right to void state laws was not reviewed, but Marshall implied such a prerogative in affairs of a national nature. While Republicans looked upon this decision as a new peril in the continued encroachments on state sovereignty, the lottery supporters looked on Virginia's victory as a great check on improvements in the city of Washington.

As a result of this event and to avoid recurrences, the House of Representatives investigated the conduct of the District's lotteries on March 3, 1821, but found nothing amiss. On May 4, 1821, under a law of 1819 which allowed the franchise to be sold on a yearly basis, the next class of the national lottery was contracted by David Gillespie of New York for $10,000 payable in advance. During the course of this drawing, Gillespie defaulted on the $100,000 grand prize and several smaller ones. Chastein Clark, the major winner, brought suit against the city of Washington in the circuit court on March 31, 1823. The city held that it was not liable, and on losing, appealed to the Supreme Court. The question whether Gillespie was solely responsible or merely an agent was argued for the plaintiff by Daniel Webster, William Wirt, and Walter Jones against Thomas Swann, representing the municipality. The verdict, favoring Clark, in effect killed lotteries in the District of Columbia, for the judgments totaled $198,000.

While the case was in court the city blissfully continued dabbling in this suicidal activity. In 1825 President John Quincy Adams, on the advice of Attorney General William Wirt, refused to approve a quadruple lottery scheme for $40,000 but did sanction one for the usual $10,000. In 1826 and 1828 the schools, penitentiary, and city hall once more were beneficiaries. At this time the whirlwind was reaped and the city had to issue stock to pay Clark's and others claims against it. These warrants carried 5 per cent interest and were payable in ten years (a premium of almost $10,000 a year). It is ironical that if all the projects had yielded their legal limit, the city would have cleared only $120,000, yet this suit alone cost more

than $200,000! Needless to say, there were no more lotteries insti-
gated in the District of Columbia.

But the problem of dealing with other aspects of the business still
plagued the District. In 1823, for example, ticket vendors had to
be licensed, while four years later private ventures were forbidden
on penalty of $500 and the sale of chances not authorized by *some*
state was fined $50. By 1833 there were at least nine ticket agencies
in the city as shown by the license returns. Individual congressmen
varied in their reactions from serving as purchasers of chances for
themselves, their friends, and constituents, to denouncing the whole
lottery system. It was not until 1842, however, when the step had
already been taken by a number of states, that lotteries were entirely
prohibited in the District of Columbia.

In the states, grants for general governmental purposes, excluding
those for schools and internal improvements, numbered least among
the authorized schemes. This comparative infrequency makes them
of even more interest. Some of the objectives may not have been
considered state responsibilities in the early 1800's but would be so
defined in the twentieth century. The first such lottery after 1789
was caused by the failure of the federal Constitution to provide the
government with a meeting place. This situation was remedied temporarily by New York City's offer of its city hall and the subsequent
passage on February 18, 1790, of a franchise by the state allowing
a lottery of £13,000 to repair the building. New York's own capitol
building was helped in 1804 when the directors of the "Literature
Lottery" were ordered to raise an additional $12,000 for funds to-
ward construction of the state capitol. Likewise, in 1807 the directors
of the Union College drawing were required to hold four classes for
$5,000 each for the same purpose.

Construction of another statehouse caused creation of a lottery by
Connecticut. During the May 1793 session the legislature used this
tax substitute to raise £5,000 for a capitol at Hartford. The cautious
solons also provided that if any money were left after the building's
completion, it too would become state property. Managers were
placed under $50,000 bond, since approximately double the amount
to be raised was normally required there. However, competition or
an unattractive scheme caused poor results, and in May 1795 those
in charge of the lottery reported failure to sell even 7,000 tickets and

a loss of £2,784. As late as 1804 they could still show no profit, and presumably the undertaking was dropped.

In other commonwealths the denomination "for the state" was considered ample justification for licensing a lottery, often without any specific mention of the object to be benefited. Delaware used the term on three occasions, the first on January 29, 1791, for a £1,000 lottery for "fitting up and preparing chambers in the new courthouse in the town of Dover, for accommodation and reception of the General Assembly"; in 1835 a $100,000 project to benefit education included $25,000 for the general treasury; and on February 7, 1852, an additional $100,000 was sought for governmental needs. New Jersey used this same approach in 1812 and 1823 by requiring the managers for lotteries approved for Queens College (later Rutgers) to obtain an additional $5,000 for the state. Most ambitious in this respect was Louisiana, which sought $200,000 for the state treasury in 1822. Mention should also be made of the so-called "Georgia Land Lotteries" of the 1830's, which were not lotteries *per se* but the state's method of distributing land in the "gold region" and "Cherokee country." Every white male citizen over eighteen, widows, and orphans were entitled to participate, and the drawings determined only who would be allowed to purchase land.

Perhaps these state efforts, however, indicated the additional services being demanded. The nineteenth century was characterized by the rise and spread of humanitarian reform. Increasing population emphasized the need for reform, and growing contacts with Europe brought greater knowledge of what was being done in other parts of the world. The public evidenced progressive concern for the relief of the poor, the sick, and the handicapped of all types. It quickly became clear that the old tradition of private charity alone could not cope with the growing problem, and governments were forced to take a hand.

Early demonstrations of this incipient public conscience were seen in lotteries granted in states with the greater concentrations of people. In 1806 New York empowered its Board of Health to seek $25,000 for a hospital for persons with malignant diseases, and three years later authorized a drawing for $5,000 to aid the State Orphan Asylum. At the same time Maryland so financed the "preservation and distribution of Vaccine Matter," and the September 9 issue of the *Federal Gazette & Baltimore Daily Advertiser* carried notices for a $24,000 lottery to enlarge the Baltimore Hospital for the Insane (8,000 tickets at $20 each). In 1810 the "promotion of Medical Science" was furthered in New York by a drawing to obtain funds to buy the botanical gardens of Dr. David Hosack, while in May 1825 the directors and president of Connecticut's Retreat for the Insane were licensed to hold seven annual drawings for a total of $40,000 to establish a permanent endowment. Throughout this period six other lotteries also helped various municipal hospitals.

Just as the states were faced with increasing demands for additional services and expenditures, local governments also came under pressure, a pressure they had meager resources to relieve. Public buildings of almost every sort were badly showing the ravages of time or the fires which had devastated many communities during the war. The communities' new growth itself created problems: the Census of 1790 showed but six cities in the United States with a population exceeding 8,000 inhabitants, but by 1800 Philadelphia had 70,000; New York, 60,000; Boston, 25,000; Charleston, 18,000; and Baltimore, 13,000. By 1830 the population of New York alone exceeded 200,000. As the towns grew, the simple village attitudes and mores may have remained the same, but they were no longer adequate. The individual citizen could not manage such things as sewage arrangements and water supply without danger to the whole community. Streets were largely travesties of the term, receptacles for refuse of all sorts, and practically impassable after a heavy rain. Pigs and thousands of dogs roamed New York City streets as scavengers until the middle of the nineteenth century, a function performed by buzzards in the South. Fire was a constant hazard, since volunteer firemen with primitive equipment proved generally ineffective. All American cities obtained their water from wells, rain barrels, and cisterns, techniques which left much to be desired from the point of view of both quantity and purity.

Change came with frustrating slowness often because of public refusal to recognize these problems as mutual responsibilities and to assume financial liability for correcting them. City government by its very nature was often inefficient. It had been slow in developing, with Boston retaining its town-meeting form until 1822. Elsewhere, those who had property enough to vote elected aldermen, who in turn chose the mayor. The aldermen, often the largest property owners, were generally opposed to increased taxation. Then, too, after the Revolution effective action was hampered by greater control exercised by state legislatures and the consequent retardation of urban home rule.

Most cities were not as fortunate as Baltimore and Charleston, South Carolina. Possibly as a Christmas present (December 26, 1791), the commissioners of the former were empowered to raise not more than £3,500 annually by lottery, two-thirds to be used for deepening and cleaning the harbor and one-third for street paving. No other person or agency could hold unsanctioned drawings or sell tickets in Baltimore on penalty of £500. That metropolis made frequent, if not wise, usage of this grant until 1815 and, on occasion, interpreted its provisions rather loosely. For example, in March 1794 a capital prize of $10,000 was offered in a scheme of 10,000 tickets at five dollars each. Again in 1797 an ordinance sought $9,086, allowing the commissioners 5 per cent on ticket sales, but the project cleared only $3,153. A drawing authorized in 1798 seems never to have been carried into effect. In 1799 the purpose of a franchise was to defray expenses of conveying and distributing "pure and wholesome" water into the city. It netted $4,381.70 from an undertaking of 10,000 chances at eight dollars each, subject to a 12.5 per cent deduction. The year 1803 saw an effort to raise $12,000 for a "Town Clock and Alarm Bell"; the next year $15,000 was sought to build a market house in the western part of the city; and in 1809 the Baltimore Hospital for the Insane ($24,000) and a "Fire-Engine House" ($4,500) sought support. Probably the last effort made by Baltimore under this arrangement was a series of classes to net $100,000 for an arsenal in 1814.[11]

As early as 1784 the Corporation of Charleston had been empowered by the South Carolina legislature to draw any number of schemes for its benefit. One such use came with the ordinance of October 15, 1798, to raise $6,000 for work on East Bay Street. Either this project was a long time in completion or was the recipient of more than one grant, for the Charleston *Courier*, May 17, 1805, advertised the East Bay Street Lottery, to rebuild "Works" demolished by a storm. It consisted of 10,000 tickets at ten dollars each and was authorized by the city council. At the usual deduction this drawing alone should have raised twice as much as the figure set in 1798. The East Bay undertaking, however, has another claim to fame.

Denmark Vesey, Negro leader of the famous slave insurrection in 1822, used a $1,500 prize he won in this lottery to purchase his freedom.

A grant destined to enjoy a long life was made in 1809 to purchase a brigade parade ground in Charleston. Only a few classes had been drawn by 1827. It was dropped as a losing proposition only to have the right bought and drawings renewed in 1836 by Yates & McIntyre. In 1812 Charleston apparently also raised money for a bridge and turnpike. It is possible that other towns in the state enjoyed the same privilege, since there is lack of evidence of legislative sanction in several schemes openly advertised, such as that of Camden for building a steeple on the town hall in 1822.

Elsewhere, however, city fathers were restricted in their actions, faced with a resistance to increased taxation, and plagued by growing needs. They would have been less than human not to consider the use of lotteries. But even this solution had its difficulties. Long delays and uncertainty resulting from having to petition the legislature were complicated by the possibility that that body would hesitate to create competition for its own drawings in the areas containing the largest numbers of potential customers. Rural lawmakers might also be expected to be indifferent to specialized urban problems.

Compared to the number of lotteries granted for such things as schools and internal improvements, the total given for city needs was small, but then urban centers contained a minority of Americans. Towns were most successful in their applications for civic buildings, with street paving a close second. Interestingly, southern governments showed more willingness to approve such requests than their northern neighbors, indicating their greater lack of progress in accomplishing such things and perhaps their greater reluctance to levy taxes. Table 5 shows the distribution of the grants and extended period over which local governments were successful in obtaining lotteries for such establishments as courthouses, jails, market places, hospitals, and so forth.

The few grants to towns in New England did not mean that the region's municipalities were without needs or ambitions, as exemplified by New Hampshire's refusal of Portsmouth's petition in 1790 for £900 to build a market house. The few licenses granted were routine, such as West Greenwich's town house on "Noose Neck hill"

TABLE 5

Lotteries for County and Municipal Buildings, 1790–1839, by State

State	Year	Amount	Purpose
Alabama	1828	$5,000	Henry County courthouse
Delaware	1791	£1,000	Courthouse at Dover
	1795	$3,500	Courthouse and jail in Sussex County
	1812	$4,000 (split)	Newark market house
	1835	$10,000	Courthouse and jail in Sussex County
Georgia	1804	$20,000	Savannah poorhouse, hospital, and courthouse
	1815	$30,000	The same
	1825	$12,000 (split)	Brunswick courthouse and jail
	1826	$10,000	For poor in Burke County
	1830	unspecified	Scriven courthouse
Florida Territory	1828	$6,000	Duval County courthouse
Maryland	1796	$2,000	Debts on Georgetown market house
	1803	$12,000	Baltimore town clock and alarm bell
	1804	$15,000	Baltimore market house
	1809	$24,000	Enlarge Baltimore hospital for insane
	1814	$100,000	Baltimore arsenal
	1815	$30,000	"House of Industry" at Baltimore[a]
	1839	$150,000	Baltimore armory, town hall, and Hanover market place
New York	1790	£13,000	Renovate New York City Hall
	1795	£10,000	Poorhouse in New York City
	1823	unspecified	Yellow Fever Hospital in New York City
Pennsylvania	1806	unspecified	Philadelphia orphans' home and school
Rhode Island	1804	$2,500	Town house at West Greenwich
	1806	$3,000	Redwood Library in Newport
	1825	$6,000	Redwood Library in Newport
South Carolina	1794	£1,000	To buy lot and build poorhouse in Georgetown
Tennessee	1794	unspecified	Nashville "district gaol and stocks"
	1803	$2,000	Nashville jail
	1815	$4,000	Springfield courthouse
	1823	$10,000	Nashville hospital
	1824	$10,000	Nashville hospital
	1825	$2,000	Franklin town clock
	1826	$3,000	Lincoln jail
	1826	unspecified	Nashville library
	1827	$1,000	Nashville town clock
Vermont	1792	£160	Complete courthouse at Rutland

[a] Passed on February 1, 1815, this was to be a place where able-bodied paupers would be put to work according to the "Munich Plan." Although it was still in the public notice in 1820, little headway was made on the project. Blanch D. Coll, "The Baltimore Society for the Prevention of Pauperism, 1820–1822," *American Historical Review*, LXI (October 1955), 80.

and Rhode Island's scheme to buy books and repair the building of the Redwood Library in Newport. Not too uncommon was the fact, as in this latter case, that the sum approved often was not raised or proved insufficient, necessitating additional lotteries.

New York justified the construction of the poorhouse in New York City by this means because of the "expensive and necessary annual improvements in the said city since the war which have been borne by the inhabitants there with great cheerfulness [and] it would be too great a burden to raise the monies . . . by an immediate tax," and since the "city from its situation is necessarily the receptacle of a greater proportion of paupers than any other city or county within this State." In the last lottery granted for any purpose by that commonwealth (March 1823), the legislature proved less charitable. New York City was required to pay the state $40,000 for the privilege of holding drawings for the Yellow Fever hospital and was forbidden to sell any chances until all existing New York state lotteries had been completed — a period estimated to be about eleven and a half years in the future. Until then borrowed funds had to finance the building.

Perhaps because of their own stake in the enterprise, Delaware legislators were most cooperative in the venture to aid the Dover courthouse. Not only were the managers allowed 10 per cent of the net sum for their expenses, but also the state treasurer was instructed to buy one hundred tickets at the state's risk to encourage the scheme. Other beneficiaries were not so fortunate, the directors of the Sussex County courthouse and jail undertaking, for example, receiving only 5 per cent of the net sum and not sharing in the state's bounty. By contrast, Florida's one effort could boast only of its high-minded managers — all were church members and one a deacon.

Street paving, water systems, and fire equipment were other types of municipal improvements aided by lottery franchises. The need for paved streets should have been obvious to anyone who had plowed through the alternating mud and dust. Many towns had done no planning and their thoroughfares were narrow, crooked, and unfitted for the growing commerce. Yet only a few of the more ambitious communities tried to pave more than their principal routes. Paving was done ordinarily with gravel, graded from larger rocks on the bottom to sand on top, which was supposed to pack down to a smooth surface but usually did not. Flag stones, bricks, and wooden blocks were also tried. On the whole, the northern towns solved their street problems earlier and more often by local resources than did the southern communities. Table 6 shows the specific grants for street improvements made by the various states.

The Virginia lottery of 1790 for streets in Alexandria had an additional claim to fame: George Washington's records show that he paid a John Potts £4 4s. in part payment for twenty of its tickets.

TABLE 6

Lotteries for Streets, 1790–1834, by State

State	Year	Amount	Town
Alabama	1834	$10,000	Florence
Delaware	1812	$4,000 (split)	Newark
Georgia	1830	unspecified	Milledgeville
Maryland	1791	£3,500 annually: ⅓ for paving	Baltimore
	1803	unspecified	Annapolis
	1817	$7,000	Frederick
Pennsylvania	1797	$20,000	Lancaster
	1815	$1,000	Lancaster
Rhode Island	1791	£900	Providence
	1795	£400	Providence
	1795	$2,500	East Greenwich
	1815	$4,000	Providence
South Carolina	1798	$6,000	Charleston
Tennessee	1831	$17,000	Nashville
Virginia	1790	£5,000	Alexandria
	1791	£200	Winchester
	1796	$10,000	Norfolk
	1804	$15,000	Fredericksburg
	1804	$6,000 (split)	Harrisonburg
	1831	$20,000	Charlottesville
	1832	$50,000 (split)	Abingdon
	1832	$6,000	Fairfax
	1832	$12,000 (split)	Lexington
	1833	$10,000	Manchester
	1833	$10,000	Charleston

Apparently he had a standing account, for the balance was paid by the proceeds of prizes in earlier drawings. That these street ventures did not always enjoy smooth sailing, however, was evidenced by the fact that the Rhode Island managers of the 1791 scheme for paving in Providence reported four years later that the great number of lotteries then afloat prevented raising the £900 and therefore requested and received permission to seek an additional £400.

As was the case with most urban functions, supplying water was at first the responsibility of each home owner, but as the population grew, the towns and private water vendors began taking over the task. Until 1797 Philadelphia relied upon public pumps set up along the principal streets, but during the nineteenth century municipalities often found that additional or deeper wells were all too inadequate and had to resort to rivers and reservoirs for a constant supply. Even by 1860 most communities saw no problem except that of quantity. It was not until 1822 in Philadelphia that any city could have been said to have an important water works. The role played by lotteries in the matter of water supply is seen in Table 7.

One footnote to progress is seen in the fact that the franchise of 1805 for Charleston, Virginia, stated its purpose was to finance the

TABLE 7

Lotteries for Water Supplies, 1790–1838, by State

State	Year	Amount	Town
Georgia	1791	$1,350	Savannah
	1792	$1,800	Savannah
Kentucky	1838	$100,000 (split)	Frankfort
Maryland	1799	$10,000	Baltimore
	1803	unspecified	Taneytown
North Carolina	1811	$6,000	Fayetteville
Pennsylvania	1808	unspecified	Palmyra
Tennessee	1809	unspecified	Nashville
	1827	$5,000	Nashville
Virginia	1805	$8,000 (split)	Charleston
	1829	$30,000	Wheeling
	1832	$25,000 (split)	Leesburg
	1832	$12,000 (split)	Lexington

carrying of water "by pipes." The Leesburg lottery (1832) in the same state proved too large for local officials and was sold to Yates & McIntyre in 1834 for $1,000 a year for three years and a maximum of $2,500 a year thereafter until the $25,000 had been paid — meaning in effect operation of the lottery for at least twelve years. This was not an unusual type of contract, so it is easy to see how even a relatively small grant could go on interminably, especially if it were to the contractor's advantage. The Kentucky license of February 7, 1838, allowing half of a $100,000 lottery to be used for a water supply in Frankfort, was destined to exist for over forty years. Simmons & Dickerson, contractors, bought undrawn classes from the managers and organized it in 1877 as the "Kentucky State Lottery." Since most states had gone out of the lottery business by the time of the Civil War, this firm, with offices in New York and the principal cities, reaped a considerable fortune. Only repeal by the state legislature killed the grant in 1878.

Closely allied with the problem of a sufficient supply of water was its use for fire-fighting. Closely-packed houses of wooden construction, poorly built chimneys, and open fireplaces made the danger of fire ever present. After the 1790's protection from fire evolved from a private to a public function. By 1800 there were many types of American-made hand fire engines available, and by the 1830's some models adapted to steam were on the market. While some of this equipment was purchased by volunteer departments and insurance companies, more and more towns bought their own, sometimes with funds supplied by a lottery (see Table 8).

The actions of two territorial governments show that awareness of the threat of fire was not limited to the older communities. The grant in Missouri was its first lottery and despite its desirable objective proved unsuccessful. Detroit sought similar protection with a comparatively small raffle of 808 five-dollar tickets with eighty-four prizes. Despite the appeal of the March 26, 1819, *Gazette* to buy chances as soon as possible "to procure the means to lessen the danger from fire," the drawing was never held.

A variety of other local needs were recognized and aided by state-authorized lotteries. In 1790 Connecticut approved £200 to be raised for the town of Greenwich, but without specifying the use to which the money would be put. The following year Vermont approved an unspecified drawing for Shrewsbury, but New Hamp-

TABLE 8

Lotteries for Fire Equipment, 1803–1830, by State

State	Year	Amount	Type and Place
Georgia	1830	unspecified	Fire company, Augusta
Maryland	1803	unspecified	Fire equipment, Frederick
	1803	unspecified	Fire equipment, Easton
	1804	unspecified	Fire equipment, Annapolis
	1809	$4,500	Fire engine house, Baltimore
	1813	$2,000	Fire engine, Cumberland
	1815	$1,000	Fire engine, Sharpsburg
	1816	$10,000	Lot and fire station, Baltimore
Michigan Territory	1819	unspecified	Fire engine, Detroit
Missouri Territory	1817	$3,000	Fire engines, St. Louis
Virginia	1805	$8,000 (split)	Fire equipment, Charleston

shire was more cautious, even stipulating that if any surplus were left from an £800 grant for Hampton to erect a causeway against the river, it would become the property of the state. Pennsylvania legalized the "Aaronsburg Town Lottery" of 1795 without stating either the amount or purpose, and the next year Virginia empowered Bushrod Washington and Henry Lee, among others, to raise $25,000 to replace homes destroyed by fire in Lexington.

The nineteenth century saw still greater activity of this sort. In 1803 Connecticut used the establishment of the Middlesex turnpike as justification for a $3,000 lottery to pay assessed damages to the town of Haddam. During the next two years Virginia sought $5,000 to educate and maintain poor females in Fredericksburg, and one of the earliest acts of the Michigan territorial assembly set $20,000 as the goal for "improvement" of Detroit, the first official recognition of that town. In 1806 Virginia again used a novel means to aid her needy by legalizing a $4,000 lottery to build a toll bridge over the Cheat River, with part of the tolls to be used to support poor children in Monongalia County. The Georgia legislature in December 1807 moved to raise $6,000 to prevent the river from overflowing the town of St. Marys.

A Maryland municipal lottery is worthy of special attention because of its national significance and scope. This was a scheme to build a $100,000 monument to George Washington in Baltimore, the "Monument City." It resulted from a petition signed by hundreds of that city's citizens in the later part of 1809, just before the tenth anniversary of Washington's death. The lottery was authorized on January 6, 1810, and tickets were apparently sold throughout the country. The scheme attracted wide attention because of the richness of its prizes; Boston newspapers of 1811, for example, carried notices which boasted of single prizes of $50,000, $30,000, and $20,000, two prizes of $10,000, three of $5,000, and so on, with tickets at eleven dollars each. Not everyone approved of using raffles for financing the monument, and Timothy Pickering, Washington's Secretary of War and of State, writing a friend July 29, 1824, protested: "Above all, to effect this by a LOTTERY as at Baltimore, imports anything rather than affection, gratitude and respect. All dignity is excluded, and the monument rests on a mercenary basis laid in a game of chance." [12] Nevertheless, this scheme continued as a separate affair until 1823, when the state consolidated it with the other existing Maryland ventures under state supervision. From that time on the monument managers were paid the excess over $12,000 from the yearly receipts from the state lotteries until the memorial was completed.

Maryland again put a major entry into the field in 1816 with the approval of a $50,000 undertaking (later raised to $100,000) for deepening and walling up Jones' Falls in Baltimore where it was bordered by public thoroughfares. By 1820 Albany, New York, was deeply in debt, and on April 14 the Assembly allowed the mayor and aldermen to dispose of that community's public land by lottery for a return not to exceed $250,000, with the proviso that no tickets could be sold outside of Albany County. Similarly helpful, the Kentucky legislature allowed the town of Louisville in 1822 to seek $40,000 to drain some ponds.

Perhaps encouraged by the attention given the Baltimore monument lottery, two other states created similar schemes in 1826. Connecticut set four years as the time limit to raise $15,000 for a monument at Groton in honor of the men killed at Fort Griswold on September 6, 1781. Georgia fixed no bounds to the $35,000 venture to build a memorial in Savannah to General Nathanael Greene

and Count Casimir Pulaski, Revolutionary War heroes. The right
was sold and drawings continued as late as the 1840's. The propriety of the actions of these two states apparently went unchallenged.

Of the remaining miscellaneous franchises, three were granted
in 1827 to provide $2,000 to buy and destroy an unhealthful mill
pond at Paris, Tennessee; to authorize the proprietors of the town of
Clinton, Mississippi, to dispose of some lots; and to raise $4,000 to
help the inhabitants of Iberville Parish, Louisiana, pay the expense
of some canals probably for drainage use. Virginia furnished the
rest of the franchises, seeking $15,000 to improve the medical springs
at Bath and $50,000 to "wall in" the river at Wellsburg in 1829. The
next year provision was made to raise $40,000 for the "use of" Lynch-
burg and $4,500 to build public baths at Capon Springs. A license to
seek $75,000 to meet unspecified needs at Portsmouth was issued in
1831.

The absence of lotteries for local governmental services did not
imply a lack of desire by counties, towns, and cities to hold them.
Desire, as always, outran the willingness of the legislatures to gratify
it. But the approximately 130 separate lottery authorizations[13]
which were made for governmental functions between 1790 and
1860, exclusive of those for schools and internal improvements, are
conspicuous in that they show a gradual recognition of urban problems and the absence of normal methods of solution. These lotteries
were a contrivance to evade taxation for the most obvious civic
purposes. They were also striking proof of the absence of a widespread system of established public credit. Eventually, bond issues
became the approved mode of financing such improvements, but
this innovation was slow in developing, and repudiation of their
bonds, especially by southern states during times of depression, did
much to disparage this method of raising money. Regardless of
these facts, habit and a certain amount of moral lassitude must certainly share the responsibility for the regeneration of this type of
lottery after the establishment of the Constitution.

Chapter VII

Internal Improvements, 1790–1860

> It rarely happens that the object of a Lottery is interesting
> to the whole community. To save the *Metropolis of New-
> England* from declining in its commerce and consequence
> on the return of a general peace — to open its internal re-
> sources, to unite New-Hampshire & Vermont to Massachu-
> setts, by bonds of mutual benefits, as permanent as the
> rivers and canals, by which their intercourse will be carried
> on — to make Boston advance like New York, supported by
> a populous, extensive and productive back country, are
> *considerations* into which every reflecting man, every mer-
> chant, and every owner of real estate, must enter and must
> feel . . .[1]

One price of the rapid territorial growth that in seventy years
stretched the United States from a few scattered settlements west
of the Appalachian Mountains to the shores of the Pacific Ocean
was the creation of a gigantic transportation problem. The nation
had been blessed with a splendid natural endowment of rivers for
commerce and communication, but a mountain barrier separated the
Atlantic seaboard from the Mississippi basin, and navigable streams
did not penetrate every section of the country. Existing waterways,
therefore, had to be made passable and connected by canals and a
supplementary system of highways, which in turn had to be built.

At the close of the Revolution, America was mainly rural, and it
was hard to get back and forth between the cities. New York was
accessible from Boston, Baltimore, and Philadelphia over fair roads;
the main post road from Georgia to Maine took almost three weeks
to cover, if the weather was good. There were very few bridges. A
river was crossed by raft or by floating over in a wagon. Highway
construction and maintenance was generally in the hands of the local

authorities, who were not only uninterested in developing through routes but also lacked the capital to build them. At the turn of the century the demands for more than a cleared path through the trees brought on the introduction of privately financed turnpikes and plank roads. It was soon clear, however, that this type of investment was only for settled areas where a return might be expected; the needs of the frontier met with cold receptions from the various state legislatures and administrations. When state efforts failed, the national government seemed the only recourse.

One tangible result of federal aid to transportation was the Cumberland Road, reaching from Cumberland, Maryland, to the Ohio River. But the mild congressional and administrative enthusiasm that had inspired federal appropriations for roads and river and harbor improvements evaporated as sectionalism arose. The question of responsibility was settled for a time in 1830 when President Jackson with his Maysville Road veto definitely established internal improvements as the duty of local political units. Thus the local governments found themselves saddled not only with providing roads to span a continent but also with utilizing all possible water transportation facilities. Not by accident, therefore, did the states play an important role in the canal- and railroad-building eras in the years before the Civil War.

By far the largest and most spectacular lotteries, and in some states the most numerous, were those sanctioned for the purpose of making these internal improvements. The new systems of communication, carved from the wilderness, presented a cost greater than could be immediately borne by hard-pressed governments. Under such circumstances the tried-and-true — and relatively painless — lottery once more filled the gap. It would be interesting to know the number of bridges built, streams dredged, and miles of roads and canals constructed with funds raised by lottery. If all other records were destroyed, it would be possible from the lottery licenses alone to plot the curve of turnpike and canal "fever." Besides mirroring the efforts toward increased communications, the grants also provide interesting examples of interstate cooperation in projects too big for a single government to handle.

Historically, transportation followed this pattern of development: first, roads and bridges were built in settled areas; then turnpikes and toll roads were constructed; then canals; and finally, railroads.

Every New England state used lotteries for these purposes. Massachusetts was relatively sparing, however, authorizing only ten such projects, amounting to $110,000, between 1795 and 1818. These projects were the "Back-Cove" toll bridge, the South Hadley Canal, the Amoskeag Falls Canal,[2] the Hatfield Bridge, the Dixville Road, the Union Canal, the Springfield Bridge, Plymouth Beach, a bridge over the Kennebec, and a road from Ipswich to Gloucester. Builders of the South Hadley Canal, licensed to raise $20,000, boasted of having cut "through an entire mass of rocks for *three* miles." [3] Since the canal was on the Connecticut River, the state of Connecticut removed its ban against the tickets. The Amoskeag and Union canals and the Dixville Road, all ventures originating in New Hampshire, were given special legislative exemption from penalties in Massachusetts because of the benefit they would bring to Bay State trade. Massachusetts' largest venture was the $30,000 sought for the Springfield Bridge over the Connecticut River, but her most spectacular one was that in 1812 for $16,000 for repairs on Plymouth Beach. Scandal growing out of the Plymouth affair undoubtedly influenced the future rate of authorizations in Massachusetts. Something seemed out of order when after nine years of drawing the managers claimed the lottery was still incompleted, so a joint legislative committee investigated. It found that 118,000 tickets in eleven classes for total receipts of $886,439.75 had been sold, yet the entire sum received by the beneficiary was only $9,876.15. There is no doubt as to the committee's state of mind when it concluded its report, "that if the late disclosures . . . are insufficient to prove their [lotteries] pernicious tendency, nothing which [the committee] can say could be of any avail." [4] Nor is it surprising that in 1826 the General Court turned down a lottery petition to finance a canal from Boston to the Hudson River, despite the promoters' claim that it would prevent the annual loss of $250,000 being spent illegally on "foreign" lotteries.[5]

Rhode Island continued its colonial policy of granting lotteries to almost anyone who asked, and between 1790 and 1830 made thirty-one internal-improvement authorizations for a total of $126,800. The largest came in 1815 for $25,000 to enable the Rhode Island Bridge Company to rebuild its span. Other schemes were for funds to build or repair eighteen roads and eleven bridges, to deepen the channel of the Apponang River, to construct a stone pier on Block

Island, to erect a wharf at Church's Cove, and to make a breach between Charleston Pond and the ocean. Yates & McIntyre handled a number of these undertakings. State support of roads apparently held down private turnpike construction, for only one company, the Providence & Norwich Turnpike Society, was given any aid by lotteries. Although a ticket for the "Rhode Island State Lottery, Fifth Class," for the benefit of Buck Hill Road, claimed an "improved mode of drawing," [6] it was still the same old system doing the same old job.

Connecticut boosted eight local and two "foreign" internal improvement projects to the extent of $94,500 between 1790 and 1826. Typical was the experience of the Long Wharf managers in New Haven. In 1772 they had petitioned for £1,500 lawful money to extend the wharf and had received permission to raise £1,000. There is no record, but this endeavor was probably unsuccessful. In 1790 the managers once more received a license to seek £3,000. Permission to sell tickets in New York City was sought on the grounds that the wharf was "of vast importance to the trade and commerce of New York, as well as New Haven." The managers also pointed out that Connecticut citizens were daily adventurers in New York lotteries. Failure to secure this boon probably explains why nine years later a profit of only £98 2s. was reported.[7]

Bridges were favored most often in Connecticut, among them minor spans at Newfield and Stonington. In 1807 managers were placed under $50,000 bond to raise $40,000 for a bridge over the "Ousatonick" River, and in 1826 the Enfield Toll Bridge Company was allowed five years to raise $10,000 and expenses, with the proviso that no tickets could be sold before 1830. Two schemes sought to remove obstacles in the Connecticut River and make the Thames navigable between New London and Norwich. Two "foreign" ventures were exempted from prosecution, the South Hadley Canal project (Massachusetts) and clearing the Cuyahoga River (Ohio).

New Hampshire's internal improvement ventures based on lotteries were small but not uneventful. Four were for bridges, two for canals, and one each for the Dixville Road and a levee to protect Hampton. Three of these, the road and the two canals, were exempted from Massachusetts' penalties against "foreign" lotteries. Despite this cooperation, the trio had little success. The road issued tickets with a value of more than $240,000 in a scheme to raise

$32,104. But $6,000 was lost by the failure of some Boston vendors. This loss, with expenses and unsold chances, cut the net profit to less than $1,500. The Amoskeag Falls Canal on the Merrimack, empowered to seek $9,000 in 1799, returned only $5,000 and produced a bitter dispute between a Judge Blodgett, one of the leading promoters, and the lottery managers. The former charged mismanagement and the latter accused the judge of misappropriation of lottery money to build his handsome mansion. The Union Locks and Canal Company, also working on the Merrimack River, was granted a drawing for $20,000 on June 15, 1813. Before the undertaking could be completed, the company's charter expired. In 1820 the right was renewed for six years, but Massachusetts refused to extend its immunity. Since two other projects were active, each was allowed five months at a time to draw without competition. After six classes the Union Canal directors found the lottery was in debt $5,647.07! They tried to obtain an extension in 1827 and again in 1829, when their petition was postponed indefinitely.[8]

Vermont made nine authorizations between 1790 and 1804, all for small projects with a total of approximately $12,000. Of the twenty-four lotteries licensed during the entire history of the state, fourteen were for roads and bridges.[9] After 1790, seven schemes benefited small bridges; the largest of these grants was for $2,500. Other licenses provided for raising $2,500 to improve navigation on the Connecticut River and $500 for a road across the mountains at Manchester. The pressure on the legislature was reflected by the presentation of nine petitions for roads and bridges in 1794, only one of which was approved. Some of these small undertakings had hard-sledding, witnessed by a contemporary report that after two unsuccessful drawings one beneficiary sold his interest for $20![10]

Remote Maine also felt her transportation problems could be solved by lottery. While the territory was still a part of Massachusetts her citizens actively demanded and received help of this sort. On January 22, 1790, a petition for a £100 scheme was granted for a bridge over the "Whisgig" because by "the great exertions of your petitioners in the late war they are become deeply Indebt." Sectional feeling was revealed in the 1790 request from the freeholders of Lincoln asking for a road and bridge over the Eastern River. They pleaded with the Massachusetts General Court that "in very many Instances, prior to the late glorious Revolution, our western Brethren have been indulged by the Legislature with Lotteries for building Bridges, paving Cause-ways, making and amending Roads, and for various other public Purposes." This "paternal Indulgence" for the west had continued, but although their own war record had been equally as good, only one license had been granted the Maine district. Approval of a lottery, it was urged, would have no effect on current Massachusetts drawings since "there is seldom or never any superfluous Money found in the said County to send from thence for the Purchase of any other things than absolute Necessaries." In conclusion the people of Lincoln appealed to the "Impartiality, equal Love nourishing care and tender Regard of the Legislature." Needless to say, their plea was granted. They were allowed to raise £700 in two classes of 5,834 one-dollar tickets, with prizes subject to 20 per cent deduction. The act also changed the name of the river to "Sidney." [11]

On achieving statehood, Maine instituted three projects aimed at securing $79,000 between 1823 and 1826. These included $50,000 for the Cumberland & Oxford Canal Corporation, a $4,000 grant good for eight years for a bridge at Sullivan's Ferry, and $25,000 for Seward Porter of Bath to improve steam navigation between Maine and other ports. Both of the larger ventures were destined to cause trouble. In 1831, for example, the two schemes raised $5,524.24, but claimed expenses of $5,210.03.[12] Contending that the expenses had been padded, the legislature in 1832 forbade the canal corporation to make further sales on the grounds that they had raised their money. The next year, after an investigation by the governor, the stream navigation managers were also restrained from further activities. Upon their protest, a joint select committee reported on February 27, 1835, that the managers were asking $10,794.34 for their expenses out of a total of $16,126.55 gained in two hundred classes! The committee concluded that the state was saddled with a system "which the progress of Society had disabled from doing good, but not from doing harm." After that blast, the protest was dropped.[13]

The Middle Atlantic states also made frequent use of lotteries for internal improvements. In New York, between 1797 and 1817, thirteen authorizations were made for the benefit of sixteen projects, totaling $217,400. As might be expected, by far the largest amount, $106,800, was assigned six undertakings to improve navigation on

various sections of the Hudson River. Roads were next with six beneficiaries; in addition exemptions were granted a 1791 New Jersey
scheme for a toll bridge on the road between New York and Philadelphia and an 1817 Pennsylvania project for a road from Owego,
New York, to Milford, Pennsylvania. The latter was even allowed
to hold its drawings in New York City. Other licenses were for a
bridge over the Schoharie River, improvement of Sag Harbor to
encourage whale and cod fishing, and establishment of a ferry between Hudson and Athens. An Assembly committee, reporting on
the sums actually procured by New York lotteries of all types by
1819, listed $109,100 for roads, $108,000 for Hudson River improvement, and $5,000 for Sag Harbor, out of a grand total so far raised
of $584,847, leaving $561,791 still to be gained to complete all lottery commitments.[14]

New Jersey legalized six internal improvement projects for a total
of $186,200. Three of these came between 1791 and 1800 and pro-
vided for £27,000 for a toll bridge, $1,200 for a road in Morris
County, and for sale of tickets in the $12,500 Pennsylvania lottery
to erect a bridge over the Delaware River. The toll bridge project
was marked by rumors of misappropriation of funds, and both that
and the Delaware bridge venture seem to have been unsuccessful.
The last three licenses came in 1815 and 1816, one giving the Union
Turnpike Company three years to seek $7,500 for its debts and two
to raise $20,000 and $10,000 for investment by the state in the Milford and Owego and Paterson and Hamburg turnpike companies.

Pennsylvania ranked second among the states in the amount authorized for internal improvements, over $600,000 in sixteen grants.
Owing to the growth of private turnpike companies, Pennsylvania
gave little aid to roads, and only four were helped in this period.
The projects for these four were $20,000 to pave the link between
Philadelphia and the Susquehanna Turnpike, a like sum to pay the
debts of the Bustleton and Smithfield Turnpike Company (with the
proviso that this sum would be considered part of the purchase price
if the state later bought the road), $2,000 for the "great road" from
Catawissa to Reading, and finally the investment in the road from
Owego to Milford mentioned above. A miscellaneous grant in 1798
allowed $12,000 for levees on the Alleghany and Monongahela
rivers at Pittsburgh, and another in 1808 licensed $5,000 to finish a
meetinghouse and protect the river bank at Wilkes-Barre.

The number of streams and the expense of ferries had always made the state generous in providing lotteries for bridges. This policy was continued for approximately a decade after 1790, with six licenses for five spans issued during the period. The largest was in 1796 for $60,000, which, added to $32,000 set aside by the county commissioners, was to erect a stone bridge over the Schuylkill River at Reading. Later this act was repealed because of lack of interest. Nevertheless, the following year saw a goal of $20,000 set for a span over Perkinomen Creek. The remaining franchises included two for the Delaware bridge at Easton, and bridges at Jonestown and over Quemoning Creek.

The largest lotteries held in the state were those for river and canal navigation. Such ventures offered from 25,000 to 4,000,000 tickets each at a cost of $2.50 to $30.00 per chance. In 1798, $10,000 was sought to improve navigation of the Lehigh River. The Lehigh Navigation Company held several large classes and obviously obtained more than its grant. In a single drawing 50,000 tickets at $2.50 were sold; 15 per cent of the proceeds would have brought in $18,750. In 1805 a license for $20,000 was granted to remove obstructions in the Susquehanna and Juniata rivers. This was a state-operated venture with the treasurer of the commonwealth as its bursar. It offered classes totaling several millions of dollars and was known under a variety of names, such as the Susquehanna, the Pennsylvania State, the Internal Navigation, the Grand State Lottery, and so on. Its tickets sold throughout the United States, and it operated until 1827.

The largest lottery authorized at any time by Pennsylvania was a navigation license in 1795 for $400,000 to open canals and locks between the Schuylkill and Delaware rivers and the Schuylkill and Susquehanna, the first project to receive one-third of the funds and the second two-thirds. This effort to "connect the eastern and western waters of Pennsylvania" to the "great advantage and increase of the agriculture, trade and manufactures of the state at large" made slow progress. Despite several large classes, by 1811 only $60,000 had been raised; the illegal sale of "foreign" tickets in the state was blamed for the failure. That year the Union Canal Company was authorized to raise the remaining funds. Although a number of drawings of more than average size were conducted between 1811 and 1821, heavy investments left the company unable to pay dividends, expand the canals, and keep them in repair. In the belief that increased traffic would make the canals self-sustaining, thus alleviating the need for lotteries, the legislature extended the franchise for twenty-five years in order to raise funds which, added to the tolls, would allow 6 per cent annual interest on the stock. The franchise was operated from time to time by various contractors. Soloman Allen handled it from January 1817 to May 1821. It was then sold to Yates & McIntyre for $30,000 a year, without limit as to the number of classes.

The extension of the franchise precipitated a dispute which stirred all of Pennsylvania. It involved the question of whether the drawings were to be continued until $340,000 was raised or until the profits of the company returned 6 per cent. The company claimed the latter since it was slow to prosper. Drawings usually were held twice a month, yet a senate committee in 1832 reported a total of $124,072.54 still to be raised.[15] Up to December 31, 1833, the company had held about fifty different classes with prizes totaling more than $33,000,000. In 1832 alone premiums of $5,216,240 were offered. The project was finally ended only by the complete abolition of lotteries in the state.

Little Delaware made nine internal improvement authorizations between 1794 and 1835. Five of these benefited navigation and came after 1815. They sought a total of $36,000 for work on Mispillon (two grants) and Broad creeks, Little Creek Neck, and the Pokomoke River. The other four ventures were: £12,000 for new piers in the New Castle harbor, $1,000 for causeway repair near Frederica, $30,000 for the Gap & Newport Turnpike Company, and $700 for a bridge over Choptank River.

Maryland, on the other hand, attempted to gain approximately $300,000 from seventeen such authorizations between 1791 and 1846. Six bridges benefited, three by a single law, but roads were the most popular recipients. They included the post road through Allegany County, the road from Westminster to Georgetown, a turnpike from "Frederick-Town" to Harper's Ferry, a new highway from Western Port on George's Creek to the Savage River in Allegany County, repairs for the thoroughfare from Paul Hawk's Church to the Baltimore Road, and a turnpike from Westminster to the Pennsylvania line.

Rivers and canals were next in number, with the year 1795 alone witnessing licenses for two annual lotteries. One for $52,500 was for a canal between Maryland and the District of Columbia, and the other, for $50,000, was for navigation of the Susquehanna River. A later attempt by Congress to implement the canal project led to the famous judicial decision in Cohen v. Virginia discussed above. Two other schemes sought to improve the Pocomoke River and clear creeks leading to and from Upper Marlborough and Queen Anne. Harbors were also a concern, and in 1791 the commissioners of Baltimore were empowered to raise not more than £3,500 annually, with two-thirds of the amount to be spent on deepening and cleaning the city's harbor. In 1804 a lottery was undertaken to deepen Annapolis basin, and the construction of public wharves were financed by this means in Havre-de-Grace after 1795.

There apparently was no bottom to the well of optimism in Virginia. In both numbers and amounts of grants for internal improvements, this state led the nation. Between 1790 and 1833 no less than sixty-six such authorizations were made for a total of $1,503,000. During these forty-three years there were two periods totaling fifteen years when no lotteries of any sort were authorized, making the over-all total even more impressive. Many of the licenses were for multiple projects, raising the number of beneficiaries to nearly one hundred. For example, in an act of December 20, 1790, which authorized fourteen lotteries, two were for roads and one for a bridge. The most prolific years were 1832 with fourteen internal improvement undertakings for $372,500; 1831 with nine; and 1829 and 1833 with eight each.

Roads and bridges accounted for fifty-one licenses. Although the projects represented all sections of the state, the majority of them were for the western part. Before 1815 these lotteries were small; $10,000 to open a wagon road from Monroe to Greenbrier County was the largest. After 1815 the sums were uniformly larger, reaching a peak of $200,000 in 1831 for the Brooke Turnpike, but with six others of $50,000 or more. These latter projects included bridges across Goose Creek and the Shenandoah River, roads between the James and Kanawha rivers, between Stanton and the Little Kanawha, from Maryland to the Ohio River, from Moorefield to Harrisonburg, and from the Pennsylvania line to the North Western Turnpike. Among the turnpikes aided were the Alexandria, Fauquier, Stanton, Brooke, and Berryville.

The remaining fifteen grants, as might be expected, provided for phases of water transportation. While most of these came after 1815, they began in 1796 with £500 for clearing the Roanoke River and a combination grant of $4,000 for a stone bridge and a causeway at Petersburg. In 1805 the legislature authorized $10,000 for a canal on Quantico Creek. One of the largest projects provided $50,000 for the Dismal Swamp Canal. This lottery's tickets were sold as far west as Illinois. Between 1826 and 1829, two large and two small ventures were promoted to raise $50,000 each for docks at Richmond and levees at Wellsburg and a total of $9,000 for Quantico Creek. Between 1831 and 1833 the beneficiaries included communications between Back Bay and the Atlantic; $20,000 each for navigation of the Monongahela River and Craigs Creek; $50,000 and $10,000, respectively, for Holston River and Rappahannock Creek; $40,000 to join Back and Link Horn bays; and $50,000 each for wharves at Morgantown and Sistersville.

Incredible as it may seem, some pleas were turned down by the Assembly. One unsuccessful petition of especial interest was made in 1797 by Parson Mason L. Weems, biographer of George Washington and promoter of the cherry tree story. Calling the House of Delegates' attention to the delay in the mails and the great risk to travelers from the lack of bridges on the post road from Fredericksburg to Dumfries, Weems asked permission to sell his books by lottery and promised to contribute one thousand dollars from the proceeds for construction of said bridges.[16] Had Virginia seen fit to grant this request and the others like it, there is no calculating what the state's gamble for internal improvements would have been. As it was, in view of Virginia's population of less than 1,300,000, the amounts sought, and the competition from other state grants as well as outside ventures, it seems impossible that many, even a majority, of the authorized projects could have been successful.

North Carolina ranked fourth among the states in the number of internal improvement authorizations; it issued twenty-one licenses, five of these in 1811. Because of the state's relatively isolated position and sparse and unwealthy population, these grants, several for the same beneficiary, sought a total of only $120,050. Over half were for water transportation, with the largest license for $10,000. Between 1803 and 1833 the principal projects were the Neuse (three grants), Cape Fear (two grants), Catawba, Lumber, and Goshen rivers; Old Town and Cotentnea creeks; and canals connecting Lockwood's Folly and the Elizabeth River and waterways in Washington County. A number of these projects were undertaken in connection with established companies — the North Carolina Catawba, Deep and Haw River Navigation, Cape Fear Navigation, and Neuse River Navigation. Six bridges and a road were also aided. Symptomatic of changing times, the largest single internal improvement grant was for $50,000 to be raised in 1833 for investment in stock of the Cape Fear, Yadkin & Pee Dee Rail Road Company by the town of Fayetteville.

South Carolina made only five authorizations for internal improvements, but the smallest was for $5,000 for a canal from Back River to Chapel Bridge (1812). Beginning on December 17, 1794, the state empowered the directors and stockholders of the "company for inland navigation from Santee to Cooper river" to raise not more "than the neat sum of six thousand pounds." During the next two years the company held several fairly successful lotteries, but they did not relieve the stockholders of burdensome assessments. In 1795, £1,200 was approved to remove obstructions in the Savannah River between Vienna, Campbellton, and Augusta. The next year $10,000 was sought to make the Saluda navigable. The final license (1821) allowed the Cheraw Bridge Company to seek $30,000 for a bridge over the Pee Dee River. This right apparently was never exercised.

Between 1796 and 1831 Georgia approved ten internal improvement lotteries for more than $575,000. Eight of these boosted water transportation, beginning with an unspecified amount in 1796 to enable Augusta to build piers, and ending in 1817 with a plan to raise a permanent fund of $250,000 for improving river navigation. Before this last step was taken, individual schemes were sanctioned for the Altamaha, Oconee, Broad, Ogechee, and Canuchee rivers. The Oconee, running in a northwestwardly to southeastwardly manner approximately through the center of the state, was especially favored, and three licenses sought a total of $63,000 for its improvement. The remaining franchises were to aid the construction of levees at St. Marys, $250,000 for a turnpike from Athens to Augusta, and $2,000 for a bridge in Hall County.

Alabama sought $108,000 by eleven licenses between 1820 and 1832, $80,000 of this being earmarked for Buttahatchee River improvements, the Indian Creek Navigation Company, and the Mobile commissioners of navigation. The importance of these three projects is obvious when one considers the cotton economy of the state. The Buttahatchee joined northwest Alabama to the Tombigbee and thence to the great cotton port of Mobile. Indian Creek connected the Huntsville area with the Tennessee River. Three bridges, a turnpike from Mobile to Chickasaw Bouge Creek in west central Alabama, and three roads, connecting Butler and Baldwin counties and improving communications in the vicinities of Huntsville and Russellville, were contributed to the state's transportation network by lotteries.

Other states of the lower South showed more reluctance to finance internal improvements by means of lotteries. Only Mississippi and Louisiana established such lotteries, and these were few and comparatively small. One of the most interesting took place in the Mississippi Territory in 1811 when $3,000 "in cotton or money" was sought to build a levee on the Mississippi River at Warrington. Mississippi also used the device for improving "great Market Road" ($5,000), to build a highway in Amite and Wilkinson counties from Liberty to Fort Adams ($25,000), and for navigation of the Big Black River, joining the center of the state to the Mississippi River ($10,000). Louisiana made seven authorizations for approximately $60,000 between 1813 and 1828 — five for water transportation, mostly to improve bayous, one for a toll road from Springfield, and one for a highway at St. Francisville.

Among the South Central states, Kentucky made only four authorizations, two of which came in 1811. These were to provide $10,000 for navigation of the Kentucky River and $5,000 for a road between Maysville and the top of Limestone Hill. The former probably had only limited success, since its managers were forced to ask for several extensions. In 1822 a lottery was granted to open a road from Beaver Iron Works to Prestonburg. Part of the $100,000 Paducah grant in 1839 for education was shared with wharf construction.[17]

Tennessee, however, ranked third among the states with twenty-five internal improvement licenses and fourth in stipulated amounts, $347,700. Although beginning in 1794 with an unsuccessful scheme to open a wagon road into the Cumberland settlements,[18] the state made the overwhelming majority of its grants between 1823 and 1831. Better than half (thirteen) were for river navigation, designed to connect the larger cities and plantation areas with the commercial outlets furnished by the Mississippi, Tennessee, and Cumberland rivers. The largest single franchise was authorized in 1827 for $100,-000 for the Cumberland River. Other relatively large undertakings provided goals of $20,000 for the Holston and Tennessee rivers, $10,000 for the Sequatchee, $40,000 for the Hatchee, $30,000 for the Stones, and $10,000 for the Duck. The only canal so benefited connected the Hatchee and Mississippi rivers. Five bridges were recipients, with the largest lotteries providing spans over the Red River and $10,000 relief to the Nashville Bridge Company. Road building was assisted by six lotteries, the largest for $5,000.

Missouri's one internal improvement lottery provided sufficient scandal to rock the state. In 1833 a project was licensed to raise $15,000 for a mile-long railroad, later changed to a macadam or plank road, from New Franklin to the Missouri River.[19] This scheme became the basis for the Missouri State Lottery, a lottery that flourished into the 1870's. Permission was given originally to sell the contract and to continue drawing until the authorized amount had been raised. Despite repeal of the license in 1839, an 1842 act "abolishing all lotteries," the abandonment of New Franklin, and the caving into the river of most of the road, in 1842 the trustees transferred the rights to a Walter Gregory for a semiannual payment of $250 over a period of thirty years. Gregory, through his agents, did an enormous business throughout the United States. To evade Missouri officials the drawing in 1845 was even held at Windsor, Canada.[20] In 1855 Missouri fined several agents $1,000 for selling tickets, but their conviction was reversed by the state supreme court. Other attempts at prosecution were defeated by political influence. Only the prohibition of lotteries in the Missouri constitution of 1876 and action by the national government brought an end to the New Franklin lottery.

The Missouri Territory boasted a famous name and a curious lottery proposal. In 1816 Stephen F. Austin introduced Moses Austin's plan involving high finance and internal improvements to the legislature. This proposed a territorial lottery of ten years' duration which would be part of the territory's banking system. Ten thousand chances at ten dollars each would be marketed annually and from the government's 15 per cent, $25,000 would be used to purchase stock in a territorial bank and the rest to open a road and build bridges. Some prizes would be paid off in tickets in the next class to increase the government's return. This idea was rejected by the legislature, and the next year Austin unsuccessfully proposed a raffle for the sole benefit of public roads.[21]

Ohio undertook several ambitious internal improvement projects, but with only mixed success. In the 1806–1807 Assembly acts were passed forbidding private lotteries and authorizing three legal ones: a project to build a bridge across the mouth of the Muskingum, an undertaking to re-enforce the bank of the Scioto at Chillicothe, and an effort to raise $12,000 by the Cuyahoga and Muskingum Navigation Lottery for improving travel between Lake Erie and the Ohio River. The last, even though it was able to sell tickets in Connecticut and advertised the fact that prizes would be paid in Boston, Hartford, New York, and Albany, sold no more than a fourth of its chances. After many postponements, the project was abandoned.

A bill of January 10, 1810, provided for a bridge across the Great Miami River at Troy, but this venture too must have failed, since the license was repealed by the house in 1813, though not by the senate. The same year the senate appointed a committee to bring in a lottery bill to promote the navigation of the Cuyahoga and Muskingum rivers. This was passed by both houses. To aid these faltering undertakings an act of January 8, 1813, took the unprecedented step of making all previously issued lottery tickets negotiable.[22] There was little activity in lottery-backed internal improvements after that, but as late as January 1, 1829, the city of Cleveland petitioned for a scheme to raise funds to protect the city from Lake Erie. The Cleveland *Herald* editorialized that "the large sums now sent abroad for lottery tickets will be retained in the country, and be applied to an object of public utility."

The first General Assembly of Illinois in 1819 authorized two lottery projects — a two-year grant to raise $10,000 for navigation of the Big Wabash River and a scheme for $50,000 to improve health in the "American Bottoms" by draining its lakes and ponds. The latter was also the first health law in Illinois. Because of unfavorable financial conditions and the "impossibility of getting the materials for the lottery out from the East (which have been on the Ohio River for nearly two months)," the project was delayed nearly twenty years and still could claim only poor results.[23]

The citizens of Michigan proved more optimistic than their legislature and made numerous petitions for internal improvement lotteries, only two of which were actually granted. The first, in 1808, was for $6,000 for a road from Detroit to the foot of the rapids of the Maumee. This lottery probably failed, since the managers resigned a year later. The other, licensed in 1829 and known as the Michigan Lottery, was to raise $10,000 to eliminate the toll bridges on the road between Detroit and the village of Monroe.[24]

All in all, twenty-four states out of a total of thirty-three, representing every section but the far West, backed lotteries for internal improvements between 1790 and 1860. These governments together made at least 287 such authorizations[25] and sought more than $4,872,900. Consequently, schemes in excess of $32,486,000 must have been approved. As might be expected because of the large areas and relatively sparse population of the southern states, internal improvement lotteries were more common in the South than in any other section. If ranked on the basis of licenses, the top states would fall in this order: Virginia, Rhode Island, Tennessee, North Carolina, and Maryland. On the basis of the amounts sought, the top five would be: Virginia, Pennsylvania, Georgia, Tennessee, and Maryland.

There can be no question but that lotteries gave valuable aid in solving the problem of internal improvements in the new and frontierlike nation. More remarkable than the actual success of the lotteries in raising money for transportation and communication was the people's apparently unending faith in these schemes. Almost three hundred lotteries for internal improvements were approved, but all of the petitions, including those to governments which granted none for these purposes, would probably run to three times this number. And to some extent the people were right. Such improvements were vital to continued progress and expansion, and lotteries did provide funds to build the needed roads, bridges, and canals. Whether this success compensated for the infamous future of the system remained to be seen.

Chapter VIII

Churches and Schools, 1790–1860

> Among the Variety of Objects we are daily in pursuit of,
> the Attainment of Knowledge is certainly one of the most
> laudable; and it is to be hoped every well-directed Effort to
> facilitate so desirable an End will meet with due Encourage-
> ment from an enlightened Public.
>
> The genial Light of the Sun exhales the noxious Mists
> which would otherwise envelope the Face of Nature — the
> Rays of Literature, no less favorable to the Human Mind,
> dispel the Mists of Prejudice, and ripen forth to everlasting
> Bloom the sweetest Flowers of Thought.[1]

At the time of the Revolution a well-directed movement toward
separation of church and state existed which was mainly the result
of the dissatisfaction of non-English groups with religious domina-
tion by the Congregationalists in the North and the Anglicans in
the South. The orthodox of both these systems believed that not
only was it a church duty to support the state but also that it was the
patriotic obligation of civil authorities to support religion. Practical
application of this belief often found taxes going to maintain the
"established" church, while the authority of the church upheld political decisions. Thus, not only were non-church members penal-
ized, but Dutch Reformed congregations, Quakers, Lutherans, Men-
nonites, Presbyterians, and others often bore the double burden of
supporting their own religious organizations as well as the official
state church. In many colonies a citizen's political and even legal
rights were determined on the basis of church membership. Although four provinces (Rhode Island, New Jersey, Pennsylvania,
and Delaware) had no "established" church, religious freedom as it
later developed was generally unknown.

This revolution within the Revolution had far-reaching effects on education as well as religion. Until the revolutionary period the English idea that education was primarily a function of the church or of individual initiative, with its underlying corollary that education should be restricted to potential leaders, dominated American thought. Thus private and church schools provided most of the education before the nineteenth century, and colleges existed primarily to produce an educated ministry. Only in some areas of New England was there something akin to a primary school system, and it had been inaugurated by the Congregationalist-dominated governments.

As a result of the Revolution, the Anglican and Congregational churches not only lost their legally favored positions, but along with the other denominations, also suffered greatly from loss of physical equipment and property, manpower, and spiritual enthusiasm. Men were too busy with physical pursuits to tend properly their mental and spiritual beings. Church memberships also had quite often lost their clergy as well as their buildings. In some cases the ministers had been Tories and in others they had joined the patriotic army; after the war, many of those that were left succumbed to the lure of the West. Church schools felt these disruptive effects, and some closed their doors forever.

Educationally, the period at the turn of the century was a dark one. Much ground had been lost since colonial times. Indebtedness and poverty was common, and it was only the exceptional person who could read and write. The idea that education was for the minority still prevailed. Wherever free schools had been established, they were often regarded as charitable institutions and as inferior to the private schools which continued to set the pattern. But the spread of the concept of manhood suffrage and the growing importance of the common man led to a new evaluation of education. The dangers of universal suffrage coincident with universal ignorance were obvious. The revolutionary constitutions, by separating or laying the foundations for separation of church and state, had opened the way for free, tax-supported schools. The great battle for free education was fought in the second quarter of the nineteenth century, and by 1850 was won in the North and Northwest. In these sections education became a government project with the church falling into a secondary position. But the South, with its plantation and rural economy, caste system, and Negro slavery, remained true to the English tradition. Thus, two school systems continued, public and private, both requiring money whether in the form of taxes, church pledges, or benevolent gifts.

Meanwhile the churches, with their educational responsibilities reduced, began a period of steady growth and development. For a while the wounds of war were much in evidence. The wrecked buildings and trained leaders were hard to replace. This, together with the threat of European ideas of the Enlightenment, goaded the United States into a religious reawakening in the 1790's. The religious reassertion was probably inevitable in an intellectually confused and financially distressed period. Soon piety, or pseudo-piety, swept New England. As early as 1792 there were indications that the revivalism which had shaken the country in the Great Awakening in the 1730's might once more become a vital force. The middle and southern states also felt the religious impulse. In the South the principal supporters were the smaller farmers, and the Baptists, Methodists, and the evangelical wing of the Presbyterians gained much strength. For some time after 1800 the great revival swept like wildfire through the West, and the pioneer people attended the camp meetings by the tens of thousands. Claiming that God did not require an educated ministry to do His work, the young denominations rapidly filled their pulpits to meet the demands and new meetinghouses moved westward with the frontier. By the 1830's religious freedom had become a fact, and though the line between the temporal and the spiritual had been closely defined and would be carefully guarded, the church had regained its place in American life.

Although the church, especially that of Calvin, had made its peace with capitalism, adjustments still had to be made between the two. A corollary to the feeling that the "end justifies the means" is the American, perhaps universal, interpretation that taint can be taken off peccant money by devoting part of the proceeds to "good" causes. The robber barons of the nineteenth century won public approval by endowment of colleges, educational funds, and elaborate gifts to churches. Twentieth-century foundations may well be touched with the same latent impulse. Hence, it is not surprising to find their predecessors feeling that lottery proceeds could be so destigmatized. The Reverend William Bentley of Salem, Massachusetts, commented on this feeling in his diary in 1794, "This liberty for building Colleges, & meeting Houses seems a public license to the clergy for speculation, which many of them chearfully [*sic*] embrace." In some states, after lotteries were no longer held for other objects, churches and schools continued to find franchises readily available, and these became the most numerous types of grants made. In the United States from 1790 to the Civil War, forty-seven colleges, approximately three hundred lower schools,[2] and two hundred church groups were made recipients of lotteries.

Churches were heavy beneficiaries of the philosophy that the ends justify the means, seen in the fact that during this seventy-year period fourteen states[3] granted lotteries for their religious groups. It is significant that those states (Pennsylvania, Rhode Island, and Maryland) with a history of the greatest degree of religious tolerance, hence a larger variety of sects, were most liberal with this type of grant. Worthy of note, also, is that with the exception of the Quakers every major denomination and most of the minor groups drank from this fount. Among the latter groups were the Pacific Congregational; Universalist Society; Free Will, "New Connexion," Six Principle, First Day, and Catholic Baptists; English Episcopal; German Presbyterian; German Reformed Calvinist; Hebrew; Church for All Denominations; German Religious Society of Roman Catholics; High German Reformed Presbyterian; English Presbyterian; French Evangelical Church Society; and Dutch Presbyterian Protestants. Nor did the white churches enjoy a monopoly, for the Asbury African Church of New York and the African Episcopal Church of St. Thomas of Philadelphia were recipients of four grants at various times.

By far the most liberal state with church lotteries was Pennsylvania, which licensed lotteries to benefit ninety-eight church groups. Sixty of these licenses fell in the period from 1790 to 1833, when that commonwealth abolished all lotteries. These later franchises breakdown thus: fourteen Lutheran (eight Dutch and six German), ten Presbyterian, seven Episcopal, seven Reformed, five Calvinist, three Roman Catholic, two Hebrew, one Baptist, two Universalist, and nine for use by unspecified denominations. These were usually drawings of a single class with 5,000 to 15,000 tickets, yet they placed on the market in the neighborhood of a half million chances and awarded some three million dollars in prizes. Most of them were licensed prior to 1810, which date is probably indicative of stiffening church opinion.

Next in generosity was Rhode Island with forty-two religious recipients between 1790 and 1831. Though lotteries were used in the state after 1831, no grants were made to churches. These authorizations sought a total of $126,825, and on the basis of the customary 15 per cent deduction must have offered tickets valuing $845,500. The individual ventures were small and probably similar to the schemes issued by the Second Baptist Society of Coventry in 1824. It offered 2,222 tickets at three dollars each, a top prize of $700 out of 797 awards worth $6,666, subject to a 15 per cent deduction, and 1,425 blanks. As might be expected, Baptists and Congregationalists requested and received the bulk of the licenses given churches in Rhode Island.

Maryland occupied third position with thirty-two franchises between 1791 and 1817.[4] Numerically the most favored sects were the Episcopalians, Presbyterians, Lutherans, Catholics, Reformed, and Baptists. Some of the undertakings were relatively larger than those in other states. One of the largest was a lottery for the Catholic Cathedral in Baltimore. A single class offered the munificent sum of $210,000 in prizes, subject to the customary deduction, and the list of distinguished managers was headed by the Right Reverend John Carroll. In October 1803 its sponsors announced that the tickets were going very rapidly, "the demand for them from various parts of the *United States,* as well as from *foreign countries* being of late very considerable . . . ," but two years later its advertisements were still being carried by the newspapers.[5] When in 1819 a tax of 5 per cent was placed on the gross of lottery prizes, most religious groups were able either to get special exemption or a deduction in the amount, usually to one per cent.

Connecticut passed thirteen acts for the benefit of twenty-two churches between 1800 and 1820. These were to bring in a total of $63,100 for the various congregations involved. A survey of Connecticut newspapers for the year 1801 indicates the nature of these schemes. The three most commonly advertised were the Danbury Episcopal Society lottery with 6,000 tickets at two dollars each, the Goshen Meeting House lottery with 4,800 tickets at three dollars each (12.5 per cent deduction), and the second class of the lottery for the Norwich Presbyterian Meeting House with 4,800 tickets at two dollars each, with the same discount.[6] In 1820 by far the largest such undertaking, and a rather unusual one, was authorized for the trustees of the "Bishop's Fund" of the Episcopal Church in Connecticut to raise the net sum of $15,000 within six years. The legislature further resolved that no other lottery should be granted before 1825, a pledge that was honored.

In the remaining states forty-seven other church lotteries were distributed as follows: nine each in Virginia and South Carolina, seven in New Jersey, six each in Louisiana and Delaware, five in North Carolina, two each in Georgia and Kentucky, and one each in New York and Mississippi. Such requests were justified by the need to pay debts, to defray ministers' salaries, to build steeples, to add bells, to provide graveyards, and to repair damages because "the Dispersion of the Society during the late War [Revolution], occasioned their church to go very much to Decay." Lack of population and money did not shake the conviction that God would provide, as seen in the prospectus of the Dutch Presbyterian Protestant congregation of Lexington, Kentucky, in 1793. To raise $500.00 it offered 1,000 tickets at one dollar each, a prize of $50.00 and one of $25.00, two of $10.00, ten of $4.00, twenty of $2.00, and 325 of $1.00.[7]

It might be expected that a religious lottery would be assured of a loyal following and hence of success, especially since church "raffles," even after complete lottery prohibition, continued to have popular support. The records show, however, that this was not the case. Petitions for time extensions or for new franchises were numerous, for small church projects found themselves ill-matched in competing with the lottery giants of the day. One such sad story occurred in 1799 when Pennsylvania authorized the Roman Catholic Church of St. Augustine, Philadelphia, to raise $10,000. On April 30, Father T. M. Carr wrote Bishop John Carroll of Baltimore: "The Lottery Bill has passed for the new church. I fear to proceed with it. I foresee the great attention and laborious exertions it requires; nor can I hope for much assistance from any of the managers. I w^d be thankful to Your Lordship for informing me what prospects of disposing tickets I may look to in Baltimore. For unless we can vend a considerable portion of them in the principal cities of the union, it were folly to embark on the business." [8] This plea was all the more remarkable in view of Maryland's prohibition of "foreign" tickets in 1792. Despite sales to some of the sister churches in Pennsylvania, the venture itself apparently drew a blank.

The African Episcopal church of Philadelphia reported to the Pennsylvania legislature in 1809 that it had been able to secure only $2,500 of the $8,000 originally approved five years earlier. St. John's of Baltimore ran into an unusual hurdle when the mayor of that city refused to allow its lottery tickets sold there. Even after overcoming that obstacle, the drawing was stopped after the first hundred numbers had been drawn because 985 of the 8,000 tickets offered were unsold. The management explained that the contest would not continue until this number had been reduced by half. In 1808 Delaware sanctioned St. Peter's Catholic Church, New Castle, to seek $2,000, yet seven years later the legislature reproved its managers for inactivity and gave them four months to begin drawing. Even the Connecticut "Bishop's Fund," with its monopoly, had hard sledding. In 1826 Frederick Lee, who had bought the right, was reported unable to make anything because of losses and "misfortunes."

But enough of the grants were successful and a sufficient number of churches and ministers had reason for gratitude toward the lottery to insure the temporary stifling of any stirrings of conscience. The drop in the number of church schemes after the mid-1820's probably indicated a lessening dependence upon this source of revenue and a slowly rising concern over the moral issues involved. Decline in the use of lotteries made it possible for religious leaders to disassociate themselves from the device and to line up with, and occasionally lead, the attacks that occurred with increasing frequency after the second decade of the nineteenth century. Besides the perpetual Quaker protest, by 1823 a letter in the *American Baptist Magazine* criticized lotteries. This was followed shortly by statements in other religious journals, such as the *Religious Intelligencer* and the *Christian Spectator*, and by such important church leaders as the Reverend Lyman Beecher of Massachusetts. But on the whole, it was not religious condemnation that sparked the drive against the lottery.

The schools benefited as greatly as did the churches from the lottery's treasure trove. It would be difficult to overestimate the lottery's value in the development of the American educational system. A study of the grants — more than 300 in less than seventy years

— is not only a clue to school financing before the Civil War but also to the changing pattern of the primary and secondary educational structures, from academies — "Lancasterian," "monitorial," "pauper," "free," "female" — to public schools. State-supported universities developed during this period, and many states befittingly used lotteries to aid their struggling institutions of higher learning, since colleges had been favored beneficiaries before 1790.

Harvard, already familiar with this device, turned to it again in 1794. The new grant renewed the 1772 franchise, which had failed during the war, and allowed four years to raise £8,000 for a new building. An interesting feature of the act was a ban against selling fractional tickets at advanced prices. The school-appointed managers, including the historian George Richards Minot, offered four classes, the first three consisting of 25,000 tickets at five dollars apiece, with 8,358 awards subject to 12.5 per cent deduction, and a first prize of $10,000. It was "*positively*" to commence drawing on November 13, in the Representatives Chamber, and was to be "*completed* with all *possible dispatch*," with prizes to be paid "*on demand*." These assurances must have made the scheme attractive to the pious as well as the prudent, for the Reverend Gideon Hawley, missionary to the Mashpee Indians (at an annual salary of $175), wrote the Treasurer of Harvard College, "You will . . . please pay my son $50 . . . and he will return you five dolls., the price of the ticket in the Lottery which I wrote you [to] buy me and deposit with Doctor Thatcher. When James knows its number he may inquire further about it . . . My son James has commenced a preacher of the Gospel to good acceptance . . ."

The first three classes seem to have been easily concluded. A fourth class with ten-dollar tickets and double prizes, however, also doubled Harvard's troubles. The drawing was postponed three times because "it appeared that the number [of unsold tickets] was so great as to render it inexpedient for the college to take the risque . . ." The project ended in a squabble between the grand award winner, the bankrupt managers, and the school authorities. After compromising with the unhappy parties, Harvard cleared about $11,435, which was added to other funds to build Stoughton Hall.[9]

By the time this structure was completed the college again needed funds, and either having forgotten its tribulations or despairing of getting the money in any other fashion, sought a new lottery. In 1806 it was allowed to raise $30,000 to pay a debt on Stoughton, to construct a new building, and to repair Massachusetts Hall. The first class enjoyed a rapid sale and the supply failed to meet the demand. To remedy this, the second class consisted of 25,000 tickets at five dollars each with no deductions, but with only $108,120 returned as prizes. For novelty, six dollars was given to each of the first 3,000 blanks selected.[10] In all, seven classes were held with a par value of $805,000. During the six-year run, over $608,000 was paid out as awards, with the cost of operations, commissions, publicity, and so on, approximately $90,000. Including the premiums charged by the agents, the total amount involved was not less than $1,250,000 and brought the school a net of $29,000, which helped erect Holsworthy Hall.

Massachusetts' only other aid to education allowed Dartmouth College lottery tickets to be sold in the state. Eight hundred chances in the fourth class were peddled in Boston alone. This lottery was authorized by New Hampshire on December 31, 1795, for $15,000 and expenses, to be raised within a five-year period. Seven drawings were held between 1796 and 1800, with net proceeds of about $4,000. A man in southern New Hampshire attracted state-wide attention by tearing down the advertisements, asserting "that it was an infamous thing, that they pretended the college was in debt, but really the money would be put in their pockets . . ." Investigation proved that he was a disgruntled undergraduate engaged in smearing tactics. New Hampshire turned down three later requests for lotteries by the college, but reciprocated Massachusetts' kindness by exempting Harvard's tickets from the law barring "foreign" projects.[11] Secondary schools had little better luck in New Hampshire. Charlestown Academy received a lottery for £500 in 1791, but a joint petition for £3,000 for four other academies was turned down by the legislature in 1792, despite a favorable committee report. Only two other schools were successful, Chesterfield and Haverhill academies, which were allowed $5,000 and $3,000 respectively in 1808.

Brown University also owes a debt of gratitude to the lottery. In 1795 a committee from Rhode Island College (later Brown) petitioned to raise $25,000. For "cogent reasons" the legislature acted favorably in 1796, and tickets were placed on sale at six dollars each.

But times were not propitious, and the project moved slowly. Even the president of the school attempted to sell 303 chances but could dispose of only 168. A final report on November 8, 1800, showed a gross of $33,548.50, with a net return of $8,000.[12] The next effort was more modest and probably relatively more successful. In October 1811 the college was given a license for $2,000 to build a house for the steward and "generally promote various objects of the institution."

Among the New England states Rhode Island most often used lotteries to finance her common schools. From 1795 to 1825 eleven separate schools so benefited, some on more than one occasion. All of the grants were small, with the largest for $5,000 and the smallest for $600. Even so, some were not successful. The managers for the Smithfield Academy lottery, having received permission in 1812 to raise $2,220, three years later reported a net loss of $78.15. The smallness and infrequency of these licenses question the assertion by the historian of Rhode Island education that some petitions for academy charters were merely preliminary to requests for lottery franchises.[13]

Indirect aid, however, came in many forms: a lottery in 1795 for $25,000 to rebuild Long Wharf and construct a hotel in Newport gave the rents and profits from the latter to support the town's public schools. The Newport school system was the direct beneficiary of a scheme for $10,000 in 1825. A lottery license of 1837 let the Rhode Island Historical Society hold drawings for two years with no monetary limit, provided that $4,000 went into the state public school fund. An act of 1826 gave the general treasury one per cent of all classes drawn and of the sale of "foreign" tickets. Two years later dealers had to have state licenses costing $100. By the act of January 1828 "to establish Public Schools" all license money from lottery dealers and auctioneers became a school fund to be distributed according to each town's number of children under sixteen years of age. A report to the legislature in October 1830 showed that a total of $43,516.69 had been so raised in three years — $39,033.60 from managers; $1,783.09 from the sale of "foreign" tickets; and $2,700 from dealers' licenses.

Beginning in 1831, Rhode Island moved to monopolize lottery revenue by generally restricting future franchises to use of the school fund. A series of licenses, normally for fifty-two classes, or one a week, were farmed out to professionals for $10,000 each. From 1826 to 1844 lotteries provided Rhode Island's school fund with over $200,000. At one time or another most of the big contractors took part in these ventures: William Dinneford, Yates & McIntyre, John L. Clark, Paine & Burgess, and Philip Case, among others.

In comparison with such big-business techniques, the efforts of the rest of the New England states look amateurish. Connecticut granted only one school lottery — $15,000 for Episcopal Academy at Cheshire for a library and apparatus in 1802. The committee on education of the General Assembly of Vermont reported October 28, 1825, in favor of a state lottery for schools, holding the "good derivable is apparently more than commensurate with the evils to be feared." Since most of the evils were already present in the form of tickets from outside the state, the committee held it to be the "prevailing dictate of wisdom and sound policy, to endeavor to participate in the benefits of lotteries, as a defensive measure, and to count upon this resource for a share of the advantages which are realized, by diverting the course of these thousand little streams which flow away from us, and by pouring them into the bosom of our own benevolent and public institutions." Since there were offers of five thousand dollars or more a year for the franchise from four contractors, the temptation must have been great. Nevertheless, prudence prevailed and the bill was dismissed.

New York held the biggest and probably the most troublesome lottery for a school. From an innocent beginning in 1805 it eventually involved the state, the college, and one of the biggest lottery brokerage firms in the United States, and ended in a hassle that went far toward killing the whole lottery movement in New York. On March 30 Union College was allowed a lottery of four classes to raise $80,000, to be divided as follows: $35,000 for buildings, $35,000 for endowment, $5,000 for a library, and $5,000 to pay expenses of needy students. The state-supervised drawings were a limited success, however, and only $55,000 was cleared.

To remedy this partial failure was probably one of the reasons for the seemingly innocuous step taken by the legislature on April 13, 1814, when what turned out to be the last of New York's large lotteries was established. The preamble of the act recognized that "well regulated seminaries of learning are of immense importance to every country, and tend especially, by the diffusion of science and the promotion of morals, to defend and perpetuate the liberties of a free state." It provided for raising $200,000 for Union College ($100,000 for buildings, $30,000 for debts, $20,000 for the library, and $50,000 for the charity fund), $40,000 for Hamilton College, $30,000 for the College of Physicians and Surgeons of New York City, and $4,000 for the Asbury African Church of New York City. Credit for the bill's passage was given to the "unwearied exertions of the able and eloquent president of Union College," the Reverend Eliphalet Nott. Few bills created a greater commotion than this one. Columbia heatedly objected to the partiality to Union College, and to ease the situation, the Hosack Botanical Gardens, which had been purchased by lottery from Dr. David Hosack in 1810 "for the promotion of Medical Science," was given by the state to Columbia as a new home. If not at first, this gift should have later been consoling indeed, for the property developed into valuable real estate and became the basis of Columbia's eventual wealth.[14]

In the meantime the lottery was proceeding. The course of this financial juggernaut was anything but smooth. By 1822 none of the institutions had received a penny, the returns being consumed by the expenses of the state-appointed officials. In April 1822, at the instigation of the beneficiaries, the legislature turned control over to them in order to secure "less delay, hazard and . . . greater economy." As of that time the various institutions were due $322,-256.81, including interest, so they were allowed until April 1843, or the sale of $4,492,800's worth of tickets, to finish their grants.

Soon afterwards, Union College, the major party involved, purchased the rights of the others and contracted the whole affair to Yates & McIntyre for $276,090.14, incidentally giving that firm a monopoly on all drawings in the state. For services rendered, Dr. Nott was personally to receive 2.25 per cent of the gross amount of each class drawn. Business between the contractors and the college became so snarled that it is impossible to estimate the total received by the college, but evidence indicates it lost money. Dr. Nott brought suit against Yates & McIntyre, and as late as 1850 the legislature was still attempting to straighten out the affair.[15]

Other types of education, however, had not been overlooked in the zeal to aid colleges. New York in 1801 optimistically sought $100,000 in four classes for the "promotion of literature." Of this, $12,500 was ear-marked for the academies of the state and the residue for common schools. How much actually was netted is in doubt, since the defalcation of one of the managers, Philip Ten Eyck, lost the state $41,059.78 in 1809.

Nevertheless, the system was not yet discredited, and in 1810 the managers of the Medical Science (Hosack Gardens) Lottery were given the extra responsibility of raising an additional $5,000 for Fairfield Academy. The fact that this venture, too, produced a scandal must have given pause for thought. The regulatory act of 1819 required, among other provisions, all vendors to have licenses and equally allotted those collected in New York City ($250 each per annum) between the Institution for Instruction of the Deaf and Dumb and the Free School Society. In 1832 the latter gave its share to the deaf and dumb institution because of the society's disapproval of lotteries,[16] a true sacrifice for in 1827 the society had received $3,875 as its share. The legislature's final act for secondary education required the mayor of Troy to turn over his city's license fees to establish the Lansingburgh Monitorial School to train teachers for common schools. By now public opinion had turned against the schemes and in 1833 they were abolished by the state.

In comparison to her neighbors, New Jersey might be termed miserly in respect to lottery aid for schools. Only two grants for secondary schools were passed, and both came early: in 1793, $4,000 was authorized for Newark Academy, and in 1794 a blanket enactment favored seven academies for a total of £3,250. Very reasonable and modest, also, were the grants made by New Jersey to Queen's College (later Rutgers) in 1812 and 1823. A January 16, 1812, act which empowered the school to seek $25,000 during a three-year period — $5,000 of which was to go to the state — was preceded by considerable legislative bickering. One legislator went so far as to propose an amendment changing the title of the bill to "an Act to promote gambling," a motion which secured one-third of the thirty-six votes cast. The citizens of New Brunswick sent in a petition bearing 221 names asserting that a raffle was the only way to preserve the institution and "the charities of thousands of citizens of New Jersey." After all this, less than $10,000 was raised from the numerous drawings of the Queen's College project, and the expenses were not cleared up until 1819.

To an appeal on the grounds that the goal had been unobtainable in the time allowed, the college was given a three-year extension, still with the requirement that the state receive its unpaid $5,000. This time the trustees farmed out the drawings to Yates & McIntyre. An investigation in 1825 by the state attorney general showed that $336,997 had been taken in, of which the school received 5 per cent or nearly $17,000. It is doubtful that more was gained, for in 1826 the trustees asked that the $5,000 given the state be returned since the grant had been withdrawn before realization of the authorized amount.[17]

Pennsylvania did not renew her colonial practice of giving grants to colleges. However, great use continued to be made of lotteries for lower education, a practice begun in 1755–1762 for the city academy, college, and charitable school of Philadelphia. They were usually small affairs of only one class with moderate prizes, and tickets were sold by interested people in the community. Yet altogether they placed about 250,000 chances on the market with prizes of about $1,000,000. The first education lotteries after the Confederation period occurred in 1798 with one for $5,500 for a schoolhouse in New Hanover and a Presbyterian church at Harrisburg, and another of $5,004 for Lower Dublin Academy. Churches monopolized the franchises until 1803, when Bustleton Academy was allowed $5,000 for a building fund. One of the best years for schools was 1805, when out of a total of nine acts, five schools benefited. These schemes ranged from $1,500 for erecting Zion Church and two school buildings in Womelsdorf to $6,000 for "English Worship" and an "English" schoolhouse at Reading. A slack season followed with only a drawing for the Orphans School and Home of Philadelphia in 1806 and $2,000 for the Northampton German Lutheran church and school in 1807. Thirteen grants were made in 1808 for twelve churches and four schools, each of the latter for $2,000 or less. By this time the state obviously was oversupplied with lotteries of all kinds and a temporary halt was called. The single exception and the last lottery that might be termed educational in purpose was held in 1809 for the encouragement of "Useful Arts," a project that Maryland also boosted by allowing 5,000 of the tickets to be sold in that state.

About the time Pennsylvania dropped lotteries for schools, Delaware began increasing their use. In 1810 the trustees of Dover Academy were permitted to seek $10,000 to buy land and erect buildings. Two years later $4,000 was authorized for paving and for repair of the schoolhouse and market in the village of Newark and $1,000 for the Glasgow Grammar School. The next permit was in 1816 for an unnamed school. In 1818 Newark Academy was allowed to raise $50,000 to expand into a college, and three years later Trap School, Newcastle County, was the beneficiary. Middletown Academy received licenses to raise $6,000 for a building in 1824 and $4,000 for an endowment in 1825, when these two grants were sold to Yates & McIntyre for $10,000. The Georgetown Academy was aided in 1827, marking a halt until 1835, when a new departure was made. This was a scheme for $100,000 created to provide among other things $25,000 for "establishing schools in the State of Delaware." This project was bolstered in 1841 by requiring ten dollars for the school fund from every lottery class drawn in the state.

Delaware was also generous to her institutions of higher learning. Grants in 1805 and 1811 for the College of Wilmington are of interest only because of the requirement in the later year that the managers post bond of $50,000 to raise $10,000 and the fact that the school probably closed before the lottery was drawn. As we have seen, seven years later the trustees of Newark Academy were empowered to seek $50,000 to erect and establish a college. Four of the twelve managers appointed were ministers. In 1835 the same institution was the joint beneficiary of the $100,000 lottery mentioned above. Fifty thousand dollars was for the college, $25,000 for the state school fund, and $25,000 for use by the general treasury. Public opinion had undergone a change since 1818, however, and the president of the college, the Reverend E. W. Gilbert, believing such money to be tainted, resigned rather than accept it. The scheme went into effect, but five years later the trustees asked Gilbert to return. He agreed only on condition "that the lottery . . . should be given up, or that the legislature should make an appropriation of the same amount as had been raised by lottery, so as to assist the institution in a less objectionable way." A special act in 1841 provided that returns from the lottery should be paid into the state treasury and an equal amount paid out to the school. Two years later the state took over control from the contractors "for the more speedily and effectually raising and securing the payment of the balance of the money." [18]

In Maryland, after a slow start, lotteries became one of the chief sources of revenue for education. After the requirement of legislative sanction in 1792, the first school given a license was "Baltimore College" in 1804. The March 31, 1806, issue of the *Federal Gazette & Baltimore Daily Advertiser* carried an advertisement of a $30,000 scheme for St. Mary's College of Baltimore for the "Encouragement of Literature." Since there is no trace of a license in this name, it is probably the Baltimore College grant. The school was again favored in 1808 and apparently raised approximately $30,000. This undertaking inspired its supporters to the following use of verse:

> Thanks to the state for every favor past
> And this indulgence, greater than the last;
> The richest wheel e'er offered to your view
> The Prizes many, and the Blanks but few;
> Here Faith and Hope may run an equal race,
> And leave the Office with a better grace.
> Just the design, where learning is the cause,
> To teach each youth to read his country's laws,
> And draw an early duty from each page,
> In childhood planted, and rever'd in age;
> And prove, in every station he is plac'd,
> That public bounty is not public waste.[19]

In 1807 the College of Medicine of Maryland was permitted to raise $40,000, and the University of Maryland was the object of lottery franchises in 1808, 1811, 1813, 1816, 1819, 1820, and 1827. The largest single authorization for the university was that of 1816 for $100,000, bringing the total to $140,000, to be used to pay debts, build and furnish buildings, and buy scientific apparatus. In 1818 the state began conducting drawings for the benefit of the general treasury and found that the Washington Monument and University schemes gave serious competition. Therefore, management of these was taken over by the state, and $5,000 a year was paid the school until its grant expired.[20]

Smaller institutions were not overlooked, and in 1815 a $50,000 license was given to the "Surgical Institution" of Baltimore. Two years later Washington College was allowed to seek $30,000, and in 1824 this amount was raised to $80,000 and the contract sold to a New York firm. In 1821 St. John's College received a license for $80,000, but only one-fourth of that sum was realized. The last lottery of this type is interesting only by being so typical in its genesis. In 1769 the people of Frederick County had been allowed to raise $900 for the Frederick County School by lottery; in 1801 another lottery of $3,500 was sanctioned to enlarge the building and provide a library for the now-called academy. In 1830 the school became Frederick College, and two years later raised $2,500 by lottery.[21]

This transition was a common occurrence and was also typical of Maryland's attitude in helping the lower schools. The trustees of Charlotte-Hall Academy were authorized in November 1801 to lay out Charlotte's-Ville and dispose of the plots by lottery. This right was restated and enlarged by an act of 1803.[22] Fifteen years later a $40,000 undertaking was sanctioned. The *Federal Gazette & Baltimore Daily Advertiser*, May 9, 1804, under a woodcut of a teacher, announced a drawing for benefit of an "Impartial Free School" for the education of orphans of every denomination. In January 1817 the legislature approved $5,000 for the "Impartial Academy" of "Taney-Town." The German Evangelical Reformed congregation of Baltimore held drawings in 1807 for a parsonage, schoolhouse, and church. In 1812, $1,800 was the goal for buying a lot for a school and meetinghouse in "Coxe's-Town." Grants ranged in 1816 from $800 for a school at Ballenger's Creek Mills to $20,000 for West Nottingham Academy. The next year, which had franchises totaling $130,000 for colleges, was marked by undertakings of $1,200 to finish the school and buy church bells at Boonsborough; $10,000 and $20,000, respectively, for Blandensburg and Cecilton academies; and $20,000 for the Philomanthanean Society of Upper Marlborough for a school and library. An act of February 5, 1817, might be used to mark the development of Maryland's public education system. It provided for lotteries to raise $50,000 a year for five years for the state school fund. After this the state virtually took over the lottery system, both as to supervision of drawings and the returns. In 1818 more drawings were instituted for the sole benefit of the general treasury, and it seems likely that some of these proceeds found their way to the schools.[23]

Between 1790 and 1834 at least thirty-seven Virginia secondary schools were aided by state-approved raffles. These projects were all quite similar. About the only distinguishing feature was their optimism; one project was for as much as $50,000, and sums of $20,000, $10,000, and $5,000 were not uncommon. Otherwise, only a few are worthy of special notice. One act alone on December 20,

1790, established fourteen lotteries; three of these were for schools — including one for Transylvania in Kentucky. Among the statutes of December 1, 1791, was one which incorporated "Scottsville Lodge Academy" under the Free Masons and provided a drawing of £1,000. So many lotteries were passed in these two years that no others were granted until 1796, when among eight licenses two were for schools. Then came another hiatus until 1803; from that year through 1806 ten educational institutions benefited from lottery grants. One for a library for Rumford Academy boasted as managers John and Spencer Roane, Virginia congressman and jurist respectively; another, in 1804, was to educate poor females in Fredericksburg.

On February 12, 1811, the legislature empowered the president and directors of the Literary Fund to raise $30,000 annually by lottery for a period of seven years. The results reported by the managers in 1821 showed that only $334 had been cleared. But of this, $300 had been lost on tickets in the Prince Edward Female Academy scheme, leaving only $34 actual profit.[24] In 1812 Governor James Barbour had suggested the establishment of a State Lottery Commission, under the Assembly's direction, to conduct drawings for benefit of schools. He pointed to the success of this plan in other states and to the fact that despite laws to the contrary large sums were expended by Virginia citizens in lotteries of other states. This view found no support, and the legislature continued its practice of making individual grants until 1834, when the state stopped giving lottery licenses. Two of the last franchises continued for a long time — much longer than intended. In the 1847–48 session a special committee of the House of Delegates reported the Monongalia Academy scheme (1829) had been sold to Yates & McIntyre and could not be suppressed until 1852. The same firm was drawing for Leesburg Academy (1832), but would complete this three years earlier.[25]

The only higher education grant in Virginia was for William and Mary "University" on January 9, 1804, with St. George Tucker, Littleton W. Tazewell, James Semple, and its president, the Reverend James Madison, among the managers appointed to raise $20,000. In spite of this array of talent the scheme had difficulties, and on June 2, 1804, Madison, the chairman, apologized for postponing the drawing. The directors had been overly sanguine concerning ticket sales and found it difficult to discover just how many had been sold. He promised an early start and offered chances on ninety days' credit with security or with the purchase of ten billets. Even so, six months later he again had to plead with the agents to make a report so the affair might proceed.[26]

On May 5, 1817, the Visitors of Central College (later the University of Virginia), consisting of Thomas Jefferson, James Monroe, James Madison, and J. H. Cocke, voted to put into effect a lottery they had inherited from Albemarle Academy. This apparently was never done, for when the university was established in 1818 an annual appropriation was authorized which may well have made the raffle unnecessary.[27]

The University of North Carolina, the first active state university (1795), early turned to lotteries. In 1801 to complete its main building the trustees obtained a grant from the legislature to raise not more than £2,000. This they attempted in two drawings: the first of 1,500 tickets at five dollars each, the second with 2,800 tickets at the same price. Their efforts had the support of leading citizens — the judge of the United States District Court, the president of the state bank, and the governor, among others. The managers were confident of success, "however, illy [sic] it may comport with the wealth and dignity of the State." There was, nevertheless, such great delay in payments by delinquent ticket agents that the college treasurer asked authority to publish their names, for "if neither sense of shame nor regard to propriety can actuate them I must try what incessant importunity will do." When the returns were finally in, the first class netted $2,215.45 and the second, $2,865.36.[28]

Perhaps memories of this lottery and of the more than fifty academies and schools given such support between 1796 and 1825 caused the president of the university, Joseph Caldwell, to declare in 1832 that any proposal to establish a southern school system supported solely by taxation was doomed to failure at the hands of public opinion. Almost all of the academy undertakings had been small, the largest for $10,000 and the average about $2,000. Aside from the number of grants, the most impressive fact was the way education was virtually able to monopolize the lottery franchises in North Carolina. Many a year educational institutions received the only grants; in others, the vast preponderance. In 1809, for example, out of the eight schemes chartered, five were for academies.

Out of eleven in 1810, seven were for schools; ten schools made a complete sweep in 1818–19. As was true in other southern states, it was also obvious that academies dominated North Carolina's educational system, for, aside from the university, only one other type of school was aided, the "Free School" of Wayne County, and it apparently never followed up the grant.

With so many lotteries clamoring for attention, it is not surprising that the records indicate many failed completely. The more fortunate ones were able to sell their rights to contractors. Between 1825 and 1827 the North Carolina Lottery for benefit of the Oxford Academy was managed by Yates & McIntyre, and from 1834 to 1837 the firm also held drawings for Salisbury Academy (authorized in 1814). In 1837, alone, the firm drew about twenty-six classes for Salisbury Academy.

As early as December 1825 an effort was made to secure legislative sanction for creation of a school fund by means of a lottery. In the next session a senate resolution asked for a study of the expediency of so raising $630,000 for distribution in $10,000 portions to each county for a public school. Although this plan was not accepted, the Assembly did approve a drawing for $50,000 for the Literary Fund, with a proviso that as much as $25,000 must be given to aid A. D. Murphey in completing his history of North Carolina. After being refused by all the principal contractors, the directors of the fund reported on January 3, 1828, that they themselves did not want to assume the risk. Though the governor suggested making the grant more attractive by giving the contractor a monopoly in the state, no action was taken by the Assembly. As late as 1852 a joint legislative committee was studying the possibility of raising funds for schools and internal improvements by lottery, but the plan seems to have gone no further.[29]

To the south the states were active, though not on so grand a scale as North Carolina. South Carolina licensed twelve lower-school ventures between 1792 and 1823, eleven of them for academies and all averaging about $5,000 each. The two college lotteries came early, and presumably both failed. In 1791 Charleston College was allowed no more than two drawings to raise £3,000 sterling. Its first effort, consisting of 4,500 tickets at twenty dollars each, failed completely. After another fiasco, the trustees tried unsuccessfully to sell the right.[30] By an act of 1792 the second grant went to Cambridge College, in the District of Ninety-Six, and probably was also unsuccessful in getting the stipulated £500.

One student of Georgia education found thirty-one lotteries for county academies in that state between 1795 and 1855.[31] Aside from the long duration of such approvals, Georgia's attitude was marked by a couple of variations — on at least two occasions counties were specifically empowered to invest $1,000 or more in academy tickets and in 1821 the law assessing a $100 penalty on each unauthorized ticket delegated these fines to the free school fund. Human frailty justified a grant favoring the University of Georgia in November 1806. The school was permitted to seek $3,000 for a library on the grounds that President Josiah Meigs had overspent the institution's funds for scientific apparatus. There is no evidence, however, that this license was ever used. If it were not for the numerous other lotteries spawned by the state, the answer might lie in the fact that the college debating society later voted negatively on the question of the desirability of lotteries.[32]

Mississippi colleges succeeded little better than their sister institutions in the lower South, although they were favored by a generous legislature. While Mississippi was still a territory, the authorities established a college in 1802, named in honor of President Thomas Jefferson, and authorized its trustees to raise $10,000 by lottery. But after two years the effort was given up and the money refunded. This lack of funds kept the college from opening and Washington Academy was established on the grounds. In 1811 the Jefferson trustees reorganized and took over the academy and a lottery it had in operation, only to find the ticket money had already been spent and thus was unreturnable. Even though all the tickets could not be sold, they were forced to hold the drawing. Ruin was avoided only because the larger prizes providentially were drawn to unsold billets! [33] After these experiences it is not surprising that eleven years passed without another college license, then only two small ones were issued. These came in 1821 and provided $10,000 for Jefferson and $4,000 for Hancock colleges.

Between 1809 and 1827 Mississippi approved but eight lotteries for pre-college education, for a total of over $41,000, of which $25,000 was for Mississippi Academy. A unique law in 1829 pro-

vided for admission of Louisiana lottery tickets for literary, charitable, and religious institutions provided that Louisiana reciprocated
for similar schemes originating in Mississippi.

There is no evidence, however, that such an agreement was
worked out, though Louisiana, between 1819 and 1828, authorized
raising $126,000 for six school groups, the largest grant being
$40,000 for the regents of New Orleans schools. Also, as in Missis-
sippi, the territorial legislature of Louisiana (1805) tried to establish a college by means of annual lotteries to produce $50,000. In
1807 the act was repealed and the managers repaid $711 they had
spent in preparation for a drawing. Then, with the actual establishment of the College of Orleans, the franchise was reissued in 1813.
During the school's fifteen years of life it secured $125,000 by this
means, although its license was frequently revoked and renewed.
Another source of unpredictable support came from six gambling
houses licensed at $5,000 each. The year 1819 was a big one for
colleges with drawings sanctioned for Hancock, Rapides ($20,000),
and Orleans ($25,000). The last prewar scheme came in 1827 for
$40,000 for the College of Louisiana.[34]

The remaining Gulf states supported no colleges by lotteries but
did use them for their schools and academies. Alabama sanctioned
eighteen between 1812 and 1854 for a total of $152,500. Sixteen of
these were for academies and were quite modest, except for $50,000
for the Tuscaloosa Female Academy (1831) and $25,000 for the
Southern Military Academy (1854). The non-academy grants were
for $25,000 for the Mobile County school commissioners and $2,500
to enable Huntsville officials to establish a free school on the Lancasterian plan. Even the Territory of Florida, with a population of
only 34,000, permitted the mayor and aldermen of St. Augustine to
raise $10,000 to establish a free school in 1834 and Quincy Academy
to seek $1,200. The Texas Republic also toyed with this lure. A bill
to obtain $300,000 by lottery for promotion of public schools was
introduced on December 31, 1838, and passed two readings before
the legislature decided to substitute a land grant instead, which
became the present-day basis for that school system's wealth.

In Kentucky lottery schemes to aid education might be said to
have begun in 1791 with the Virginia license for Transylvania
"Seminary" to erect an academy. The December 22, 1792, issue of
the Lexington *Kentucky Gazette* gave notice of the Assembly's con-

sent to a project for Salem Academy. By far the most important legislation, however, came in 1798 with passage of a law giving every academy the right to hold a lottery to raise a maximum of $1,000. It is almost impossible at this date to ascertain how many took advantage of the prerogative, but presumably many did, for no other school lotteries were licensed until 1833. On February 7 of that year the town of Frankfort was empowered to raise $100,000 for a city school and water supply. As we noted above, this undertaking operated until 1879. In 1839 Paducah was allowed to seek $100,000 to build and furnish two seminaries. This grant was also purchased by Simmons and Dickinson, who, with illegal offices in New York and other cities, and drawings on the first and fifteenth of every month, had many years of rich harvest before being restrained by the courts.

Kentucky did not forget its institutions of higher learning, either. Four licenses were issued, the first in July 1804 for a medical school for Transylvania University. Eighteen years later $25,000 was sought to build a medical school at Lexington. Shelby College was authorized to raise $100,000 in 1837, and an attempt to revoke this privilege twenty years later was held unconstitutional by the circuit court. The last such undertaking was sanctioned in December 1850, for $50,000 for Henry Academy and Henry Female College.[35]

In the remaining states the lotteries were generally smaller and fewer in number. Tennessee authorized seventeen ventures to raise $90,200 for twenty secondary schools, but only two colleges were benefited. In the first (1810), the managers of a drawing for East Tennessee College asked Thomas Jefferson to be one of their agents and were refused.[36] In the second in 1826 the legislature authorized Cumberland College to seek $200,000! In Ohio in 1807 and 1809, Cincinnati University lured dollars by combing appeals to cupidity and love of learning. Ohio University was granted a lottery in 1817 but never used it.[37] The first General Assembly (1806) of the Indiana Territory incorporated "Vincennes University" and allowed it to seek $20,000. The grant was not completed and was claimed by the trustees as late as 1883, when the United States Supreme Court ruled there could be no vested interest in a lottery.[38] One of the early acts of the Michigan territorial legislature was on September 5, 1805, to raise $20,000 by four classes for "promotion of literature" in Detroit. Another in 1817 sought to establish a university and provide support by four successive lotteries. Since the territory had less than 7,000 inhabitants and the school existed only on paper for twenty years, it seems safe to assume the drawings were unsuccessful or, more likely, never held.[39] While still a territory, Missouri held a $4,000 lottery for Potasi Academy, but despite support of citizens such as Moses Austin, who acted as an agent, the venture failed. One of Ohio's few lottery statutes provided for $2,000 for books and equipment for an academy in Trumbull County in 1809.

By way of summary, twenty-three states authorized educational lotteries between 1790 and 1860. It is significant that eight of the top ten in number of licenses were southern states, Rhode Island and Delaware being the exceptions in seventh and ninth places respectively. This also goes far to account for academies being the favorite beneficiaries. North Carolina's leadership in southern postwar education was foreshadowed by the fact that that state led the nation with fifty-two school-lottery franchises after 1790.

Thus, by 1860 many of the religious and educational wounds of the Revolution had healed over, and the new systems were often more vital and vigorous than their colonial predecessors. Frequently the cure had been greatly speeded by funds from the many lotteries established for schools and churches during this period. Taken one at a time, the individual drawings were rarely significant, but collectively they meant nourishment for another phase of the "American way of life." Just as the physical expansion of the United States had been supported and propelled by a timely drawing — so had the spiritual and intellectual institutions been revived and revitalized.

Chapter IX

Private and Semi-Private Lotteries, 1790–1860

> She seems to give to all who ask
> Without imposing labour's task
> The idle as the busy bask
> Alike i' the sunshine of her mask.[1]

The earliest lotteries were those for personal use. The first in America were also those instigated by individuals, and it was these spontaneous efforts which were first restrained by the early governments. But, in the shadow of the large number of lotteries to aid transportation, schools, and other public projects, there always existed a small group of licenses for private societies and persons. These grants were a minor multiple of the many requests put before the legislatures. Thus the drawings that were authorized and the causes they benefited mirrored so well the personal dreams and despairs of the new American.

The years before the Civil War brought many changes in American attitudes. While Europeans watched the tentative steps of the young Republic with mixed opinions, America in general felt it was getting off to a good start. During the colonial period there had been acceptance of its cultural immaturity and the fact that most of its civilization was derivative. After 1790 the United States had both the chance and the desire to develop a more characteristic way of its own. While the Revolution was the time of physical fighting for independence, so were the decades following the war a search for cultural freedom. National pride urged the cause on, and eventually Americans became convinced at last that theirs was a unique culture, equal to Europe's.

Before this ideal was attained, however, much had to be done. Old World institutions had to be changed to serve New World democracy. For example, the Masonic order, introduced from England in the 1730's and boasting such well-known members as George Washington, Andrew Jackson, and Henry Clay, had to be purged of its aristocratic stigma before it was accepted as "American." Theoretically, education no longer was the privilege of the few, and its primary distributor, the printed word, was made more accessible to all. Libraries, formerly the sole possession of individuals or colleges, were commonly public by the second decade of the nineteenth century. Native literature and authors, in turn, found encouragement and recognition. There was also a gradual maturing in the American attitude toward wealth. Making money remained of paramount importance, but stinginess did not always follow its acquisition. Charity became a more meaningful institution in this land of opportunity. Once the sole responsibility of churches and individuals, it slowly came to be viewed as a community obligation in the great reform drives of the 1820's and 1830's. Its spirit included the unsuccessful, and whereas in Europe bankruptcy meant a degrading termination of a career, in the United States it was merely an unfortunate part of a man's business education. He was expected to start over again and as often as necessary. There were always new fields waiting for him to try.

But all of these new concepts depended a great deal upon America's economic self-sufficiency. England had discouraged the development of colonial manufacturing, a lack that was dramatized by experiences of the war and Confederation period. At first there was disagreement on how this independence should best be accomplished. Thomas Jefferson, visualizing a nation of hardy, self-reliant farmers, wrote concerning manufacturing in his *Notes on the State of Virginia* (1781), "It is better to carry provisions and materials there [Europe], than bring them [Europeans] to the provisions and materials, and with them their manners and principles. The loss by the transportation of commodities across the Atlantic will be made up in happiness and permanence of government." [2] But the critical shortages produced by the Embargo and the War of 1812 overcame even Jefferson's antipathy to manufacturing, and the United States was shortly on its way to becoming an industrial power.

Symptomatic of this changing attitude was Massachusetts' lone use of the lottery for private benefit after 1790. In 1791 the General Court tried the curious experiment of making the proprietors of the "Cotton Manufactory" at Beverly a gift of 700 tickets in the next two classes of the Massachusetts Semi-Annual State Lottery. This action proved unpopular, for many thought it lessened their own chances of winning. The *Salem Gazette,* March 8, 1791, editorialized, "Some people, out-doors murmur at this as an ill-judged liberality; but perhaps they are not acquainted with the argument which induced the grant. The disposition of Government to foster our infant manufactures is certainly laudable." Nevertheless, when 25,000 chances in the next drawing were not sold, the gift to Beverly was used as an excuse.[3]

Rhode Island, which ranked second highest among all the states with twenty-four private authorizations, used the device for some very curious purposes between 1791 and 1837. The first of these allowed Nicholas Easton's land to be sold by lottery to pay his debts and clear something for his minor heirs. This venture failed, for in 1794 the managers reported to the legislature they had been unable to dispose of all the tickets. Another grant in 1791 gave John Robinson the means of extending his wharf at Point Judith, and the next year a potential new industry benefited when Pardon Allen of Exeter was empowered to raise $250 in specie to erect a nail factory. A 1795 act sought $4,000 for completing and furnishing an "exchange or coffee house" in Providence.

Private societies in Rhode Island got their share of attention. In 1803 and 1825 two groups of the Masonic order at Newport and Wickford received licenses to help construct their halls. Two licenses (1806, 1825) allowed the Redwood Library of Newport $6,000 for repairs and increasing its supply of books, and in 1825 and 1830 the Providence Franklin Society was granted lotteries for a total of $13,000. In the latter year the Providence Bar Library was also assisted, and the Rhode Island Historical Society was empowered to raise $5,000 "to aid them in objects for which they were incorporated." Seven years later the society was given permission to hold drawings for two years, without limit as to the number of classes, upon payment of $4,000 to the school fund. This was canceled by mutual consent in 1839.

Other lotteries were of wider public interest. The Rhode Island Society for the Encouragement of Domestic Industry sought $20,000 under grants made in 1820 and 1822. A license in 1829 for $2,000 was to aid James Stevens of Newport in publishing a map of the state. The Newport Artillery Company was the subject of three lotteries to erect an armory. Under the first authorization, in 1830, the company could raise $800. The next year they were allowed to increase this to $1,200 and to sell the right. Finally in 1833 they were permitted to hold not more than fifty-two classes in return for paying $10,000 of the proceeds into the state treasury.

The most interesting of the Rhode Island grants came between 1808 and 1812 when five licenses were issued in hopes of aiding the discovery of coal in the state. The first, for $1,000, went to an unnamed party; the second for a like amount was for Benjamin W. Case to explore the island of Rhode Island. In 1812, three undertakings, for a total of $82,000, were approved. The first of $30,000 was for the Aquidneck Coal Company, which was required to obtain New York's permission to sell tickets there[4] and to spend $20,000 in Rhode Island from the proceeds. The second, for $12,000, was to enable four individuals to dig and explore for coal in Cumberland. Finally, the Rhode Island Coal Company was given a $40,000 scheme, but for some unstated reason this amount was reduced to $30,000 the next year.

Of the remaining New England states only Connecticut and Vermont established private lotteries. Connecticut's one grant was issued in 1791 for £3,200 "for the encouragement of a manufactory of Woolen, Worsted, and cotton, in this state, under the superintendance of William M'Intosh, (late of London) a Gentleman of information and Experience in the construction and use of the new invented machines for that Purpose, a Number of which being completed he hath now in use." An advertisement in the Hartford *Connecticut Courant*, May 16, 1794, indicated that the lottery got off to a slow start.

Vermont's five authorizations were made between 1792 and 1802. Anthony Haswell, Vermont postmaster general and editor of the *Herald of Vermont*, was empowered to raise £200 to cover the loss of his plant by fire. Jabez Roger (1792) and Horatio Knight (1802) were favored with licenses for £1,200 and $1,000, respectively, for unspecified reasons. The remaining grants carry real speculator appeal. The first, of $2,000, was for a Joseph Hawkins, who had lost his sight during a voyage. This "Philanthropic Lottery" in two classes was to send the "unfortunate Mr. Hawkins" to Europe for medical care. Tickets were sold as far south as Rhode Island and one drawing, at least, was held in Boston. The other (1797), for $500, was to repay John Wood for what he had spent in preventing a massacre at Westminster in 1775.

Only three private authorizations were made by New York, one of which assisted a Pennsylvania lottery in 1820 to dispose of books, maps, plates, prints, and so on, by allowing it to sell 2,666 tickets there. An omnibus act in 1803 included a $15,000 provision for the Society for the Relief of Poor Widows in New York City. Eleven years later the Historical Society of the City of New York was the beneficiary of a $12,000 lottery to buy manuscripts. This right was sold to Union College and in turn to Yates & McIntyre.

New Jersey issued only one license, but it was of unusual interest because of its size, purpose, and connection with Alexander Hamilton. Among the Hamilton manuscripts in the Library of Congress are two hand-written sheets entitled "Ideas for a Lottery." According to him a successful lottery scheme had to have the following ingredients: simplicity, so as to be understood and so the purchaser could see "fewer obstacles between *hope* and *gratification*"; low-priced tickets, to bring them in reach of greater numbers — "Everybody, almost, can and will be willing to hazard a trifling sum for the chance of considerable gain"; a small number of large and many medium prizes, for "adventurers would as lieve lose altogether as acquire trifling prizes and would prefer a small chance of winning a *great deal* to a great chance of winning little — Hope is apt to supply the place of probability — and the Imagination to be struck with glittering though precarious prospects."

On further thought Hamilton decided that moderate prizes were best for this country, since they would appear munificent to most adventurers and a large number of winners would, in turn, be good advertising. To raise $30,000 he suggested the sale of 50,000 tickets at four dollars each, with a top prize of $20,000 and lesser prizes ranging down to 400 of $100 each. An alternate plan would have one prize each of $50,000 and $20,000, five awards of $10,000, and fifty of $1,000. Ticket offices should be opened on the borders of New York and Pennsylvania giving New York City and Philadelphia as markets. This last is an interesting proposal in view of the proscription of "foreign" sales in both states. He concluded that he "should not think [$]30000 likely to be beyond the reach of pretty easy accomplishment."

The reason for this note was probably a New Jersey act of November 1791, incorporating the Society for Establishing Useful Manufactures with a lottery clause to raise $100,000. Hamilton, a member of the society, probably was asked for advice. If so, his suggestions were unfortunately ignored. The first class for $40,000, announced January 1, 1794, consisted of 38,000 tickets at seven dollars each, with 14,000 of the 14,539 prizes being for twenty dollars or less. The project had rough sledding from the beginning. The Pennsylvania Assembly denounced it on the ground that the society could undersell small private manufacturers. New York refused to license its sales, and despite the facts that tickets were sent as far north as Boston and agents were allowed 2.5 per cent of their sales, the project failed. A second class in 1795 sought only $6,667.50 and probably yielded little more than expenses.[5] Nevertheless, in 1844 the lottery was still active.[6]

Pennsylvania issued only four private licenses, three of them in 1806 and 1807. These included aid for the Bohemian Library, for "useful arts" (this project was allowed to sell 5,000 tickets in Maryland), and for the "Vine growing Association." This last act stated that since the association had bought ground and vines but had not received the needed support from subscriptions, it was permitted to raise $7,000 by lottery. In 1820 the firm of Murry, Fairman & Company, engravers of Philadelphia, was allowed to sell 8,000 tickets at $12.50 each in a lottery with prizes consisting of books, maps, plates, and prints. It listed awards consisting, among other things, of 550 sets of "Dr. Rees's Cyclopaedia," 250 sets of engravings, and 300 atlases. As previously noted, New York permitted sale of these chances.

Delaware was more active than Pennsylvania, making six authorizations for private lotteries between 1797 and 1827. Four of these benefited branches of the Masonic order in Wilmington, Milford, New Castle, and Georgetown. The latter two ventures were joint affairs, one assisting St. John's Lodge No. 2 and the New Castle Library Company, and the other an academy and the Masonic hall in Georgetown. The largest Masonic grant (Wilmington, 1812) was for $15,000. The two non-Masonic private ventures benefited individual entrepreneurs. In 1797 the sum of $4,000 was sought to enable Jacob Broom to re-establish a "cotton manufactory" destroyed by fire; the governor was required to approve the scheme and Broom to furnish $24,000 bond. In 1825 Abel Jeans was allowed to raise $2,000 to pay the cost of exploring his farm for coal.

Thirteen private licenses between 1796 and 1827 rank Maryland in sixth place among the other states. The greater bulk of the authorizations came in the last fifteen years of the period. Early franchises included $2,000 to pay the debts on a market house at Georgetown (1796). In 1807 not only were lotteries approved for the Society for Promotion of Agriculture and Domestic Manufacturing and the Charitable Marine Society for Widows and Orphans, but also Pennsylvania was allowed to sell tickets in her undertaking for encouragement of "useful arts." An interesting act in 1812 provided for raising $15,000 to build a "Carpenter's Hall" in Baltimore. The Fell's Point and Elkton Masons were aided in 1816 and 1817, respectively. Two other private groups raising money in this manner were the Library Company of Baltimore (1815), which sought $30,000 for a lot and building, and the Philomanthanean Society of Upper Marlborough (1817).

The remaining warrants went to four individuals, two of whom hoped to dispose of books. In 1820 Hezekiah Niles was allowed to raffle a stock of works, including bound sets of *Niles' Weekly Register*. A curious proposal was sanctioned on March 12, 1827. Eliakim Littell, who wished to publish a "large collection of the standard works of literature and science" and to establish a thousand public libraries in states that assisted him, was authorized to sell the books by lottery *after* he contributed a tenth of the number of volumes he proposed to give in each scheme. No book could be raffled unless approved by the governor and council! Other permissions for drawings were to Zephaniah Water to establish a fulling mill with carding and spinning machinery and to Thomas Jefferson, who could sell chances in Maryland on his property if his drawing were not connected with a proposed national Washington City lottery.[7]

In Virginia's twelve authorizations of private undertakings, all issued before 1833, the majority might be called in the public interest. The first, in 1790, was for the Amicable Society of Richmond for £1,000. During the next year Masonic lodges at Scottsville and in Charlotte County were helped, and licenses were granted for £300 to erect a paper mill near Staunton and $4,000 to repair Smyth

Tandy's bleaching mill in the same town. The infant labor movement was probably encouraged by franchises of $10,000 in 1830 for the Petersburg Benevolent Mechanics Association's building and $30,000 in 1832 for the Mechanical Benevolent Society of Norfolk. The last was still drawing five years later. The promotion of learning was the beneficiary on three occasions. The most obvious was $20,000 for the Literary Society of Romney in 1832. Nevertheless, a scholar might cast wishful eyes at the £2,000 granted for Nathaniel Twining's geographical research (1790) and £4,000 for William Tatham to complete a similar book (1791).

Humanity must have inspired two of the licenses. In 1796 Bushrod Washington and Henry Lee, among others, served as managers of a $25,000 lottery to rebuild homes destroyed by fire in Lexington. The other, in 1826, involving Thomas Jefferson, wrote a sad obituary to that great life and mirrored public opinion and manners of the day. The story of how the eighty-three-year-old Jefferson was eaten out of home and estate and into a debt of more than $80,000 by his admirers is a familiar one. On February 17, 1826, he wrote James Madison, "You will have seen in the newspapers some proceedings in the legislature, that cost me much mortification." He explained that because of his heavy liabilities and the low price of land he determined to try to dispose of his acreage for a fair price by lottery, a practice "often resorted to before the Revolution to effect large sales, and still in constant usage in every State for individual as well as corporation purposes." If allowed to do so, "my lands here alone, with the mills, etc., will pay everything, and leave me Monticello and a farm free." [8] His plea to the legislature was the most eloquent ever recorded in behalf of such schemes and was all the more remarkable considering his earlier hostility to them.

> . . . If we consider games of chance immoral, then every pursuit of human industry is immoral; for there is not a single one that is not subject to chance, not one wherein you do not risk a loss for the chance of some gain . . . But the greatest of all gamblers is the farmer . . . Yet so far from being immoral, they are indispensable to the existence of man . . . Almost all these pursuits of chance produce something useful to society. But there are some which produce nothing, and endanger the well-being of the individuals engaged in them, or of others depending on them. Such are games with cards, dice, billiards, etc. . . . . There are some other games of chance, useful on certain occasions, and injurious only when carried beyond their useful bounds. Such are insurance, lotteries, raffles, etc.

These they do not suppress, but take their regulation under their own direction . . . Money is wanting for a useful undertaking, as a school, etc., for which a direct tax would be disapproved. It is raised therefore by a lottery . . . An article of property, insusceptable of division at all, or not without great diminution of its worth, is sometimes of so large a value as that no purchaser can be found . . . The lottery is here a salutary instrument for disposing of it . . .

Jefferson then listed the specific occasions on which Virginia had used lotteries for benefit of the state, schools, rivers, roads, towns, religious congregations, private societies and individuals.

. . . Between the years 1782 and 1820, a space of thirty-eight years only, we have observed seventy cases, where the permission of them has been found useful, by the legislature . . . These cases relate to the emolument of the whole State . . . and of individuals under particular circumstances which may claim indulgence or favor. The latter is the case now submitted to the legislature, and the question is whether the individual soliciting their attention, or his situation, may merit that degree of consideration which will justify the legislature in permitting him to avail himself of the mode of selling by lottery, for the purpose of paying his debts.

That a fair price cannot be obtained by sale in the ordinary way, and in the present depressed state of agricultural industry, is well known . . . To be protected against this sacrifice is the object of the present application, and whether the applicant has any particular claim to this protection is the present question.

Here the answer must be left to others. [Jefferson then listed the offices he had held and the services he had rendered the government.]

. . . My request is, only to be permitted to sell my own property freely to pay my own debts . . . To sell it in a way which will offend no moral principle, and expose none to risk but the willing, and those wishing to be permitted to take the chance of gain. To give me, in short, that permission which you often allow to others for purposes not more moral.

Will it be objected, that although not evil in itself, it may, as a precedent lead to evil? But let those who shall quote the precedent bring their case within the same measure. Have they, as in this case, devoted threescore years and one of their lives, uninterruptedly, to the service of their country? . . . Have the stations of their trial been of equal importance? . . . If all these circumstances, which characterize the present case, have taken place in theirs also, then follow the precedent . . . And should it occur . . . it will not impoverish your treasury, as it takes nothing from that, and asks but a simple permission, by an act of natural right, to do one of moral justice.[9]

His petition was granted in February 1826 over strenuous opposition, both by his enemies and by those who did not want him exposed to what they considered degrading circumstances. Jefferson's gratitude was almost pathetic. The management of the lottery was turned over to Yates & McIntyre and states as widely separated as Maryland and Louisiana moved to give the project legal immunity. Had the lottery been started immediately, it seems almost certain to have been successful. As it was, the outcome was explained by his friend and neighbor, James Madison, in a letter to General Lafayette:

The general sensation produced by the resort to a lottery, and by the occasion for it, unfortunately led some of his most enthusiastic admirers to check the progress of the measure by attempting to substitute patriotic subscriptions, which they were sanguine as to rely on, till the sad event on the 4th of July [Jefferson's death] benumbed . . . the generous experiment; with like effect . . . on the lottery itself. And it is now found that the subscriptions do not exceed ten or twelve thousand dollars, and the tickets but a very inconsiderable number, while the debts are not much short of one hundred thousand dollars.

The postponement of ticket sales had been requested by Mayor Philip Hone of New York and a group of Jefferson's friends, who raised $16,500 as a gift. Hone also had attempted to start a movement to purchase the lottery and publicly destroy the tickets, but Jefferson's death ended that. On July 29, 1826, Yates & McIntyre revitalized the lottery, announcing a scheme of only three prizes — Monticello, Shadwell Mills, and the Albemarle estate — 11,480 tickets at ten dollars each, to be drawn the following October. But on February 20, 1828, Madison wrote, "the lottery, owing to several causes, has entirely failed." [10]

North Carolina, on the basis of sixteen authorizations between 1790 and 1826, ranked fourth among the states in assisting private causes by lottery. Most numerous were those aiding directly or indirectly some business. In December 1790 a license permitted Henry Emanuel Lutterloh of Fayetteville to raise $6,000 annually for five years to bring in "many useful artisans who may be greatly conducive to the promotion of the population and manufactures of North Carolina." [11] Six years later Christopher Tayler of Halifax was allowed $5,000 for a cotton mill. To assist the infant printing business an unusual law in 1802 gave manufacturers and printers of books general permission to dispose of them by raffles. How many

availed themselves of this right is unknown. Salt production benefited by grants in 1805 and 1808, when William Eaton and J. W.
Bryan were allowed £25,000 and $4,000 respectively for this pur-
pose. Among the eleven licenses of 1810, Alex Smith received $1,500
to aid in manufacturing steel and nails.

Societies and individuals were next in order. The Masons, including St. John's Lodge Number 3, Eagle Lodge Number 71, and
Golden Fleece Lodge Number 74, were recipients of four acts averaging about $3,000 each. In 1814 the Cape Fear Agricultural Society
was given a scheme for $20,000. The grants to individuals showed
varied excuses. The period opened with the "unfortunate" William
Porter being permitted to raise $1,000 and Alexander M'Call being
allowed to sell his property by lottery for $3,000 to pay his debts. A
bit of forethought is seen in the law of 1810 empowering George
Cloud, sheriff of Stokes County, to raise an amount equal to the
public money stolen from him in 1806. Prizes were to consist of his
property.

Two acts in 1825 and 1826, for benefit of Archibald D. Murphey,
were interesting. By the first Murphey was allowed three drawings
to seek $15,000 to complete a historical and scientific survey of
North Carolina, "as the publication of such a work is much desired,
and would be useful and creditable to the State." The next year he
was offered up to $25,000 of the proposed $50,000 to be raised by
lottery for the Literary Fund in return for relinquishing his franchise. But this did not end his problems. Charles Fisher of Salisbury
wrote Murphey, May 5, 1827, that the only chance for the venture
was to sell it to a broker. "Failing this, I think it would be worse
than useless to attempt any thing in the way of Small Schemes. The
truth is, the habits, and persuits [sic] of the people of No. Ca. will
not afford encouragement to lotteries, and in addition to this, the
hardness of the times is peculiarly unfavorable to them." Fisher was
not alone in this opinion, for in January 1828 the directors of the
Literary Fund reported that the principal brokers in the United
States had been contacted without success so the board had decided
to do nothing. Left unassisted, Murphey renewed his petition in
1831, asking for a $50,000 franchise. He wanted funds to go to
England to copy records which would complete more than twenty
folio volumes, and he calculated that a lottery of this size would

bring him $15,000 or $20,000 from northern brokers if the time and number of classes were not limited. This project was refused on the basis of previous failures.[12]

South Carolina ranked just below her northern neighbor with fourteen private authorizations after 1790. The vast majority were for societies, with the Masons most often helped. Seven lodges benefited by six acts, the largest of which provided $50,000 to be raised for halls at Columbia and Charleston in 1815 and a like sum for the Grand Lodge of Ancient Free Masons in Charleston in 1828. Other licenses were for the Indigo Society of Georgetown, the Camden Orphan Society, the Botanick [sic] Society of South Carolina, the Savannah River Literary Society, the South Carolina Academy of Fine Arts, and the Literary and Philosophical Society of South Carolina. One of the three remaining franchises was to raise £800 for "promotion of useful manufactures," with £400 to be paid to William M'Clure if he would build a cotton factory and constantly employ and instruct seven white people for seven years. The sum of $10,000 was set as a goal in 1816 to succor the victims of the Pickensville fire. A lottery limited to $150,000's worth of tickets was approved in 1836 to replace a cotton and woolen factory at Laurens destroyed by fire. In 1839 the right was sold to D. & J. Gregory & Company for $20,000 to be paid in installments. But by 1844 only $11,000 had been collected, and so it ran for years.

Six of Georgia's eleven licenses for private causes were for the Masons of Augusta, Brunswick, Milledgeville, Macon, and Monroe. The remaining acts allowed Joseph Rice to raise $10,000 by raffle of plate, jewelry, watches, and so forth, on a $200 payment to the state; $10,000 for the Agricultural Society of Georgia; $7,000 to establish a woolen factory; $10,000 for the poor in Burke County; and aid for the Independent Fire Company of Augusta. An annual license of $1,000 was required in 1858 for lotteries profiting individuals, but there is no record of any being paid.

Despite the Florida Legislative Council's failure in 1837 to approve an undertaking for a Masonic hall, the next year a $10,000 lottery was allowed the Tropical Plant Company of Florida for funds to buy a scientific library, tools and machinery, unusual seed, and so on, in their efforts to acclimate tropical plants, fruits, and flowers.

With two minor exceptions, Alabama's private authorizations

were monopolized by the Masons, who received eight grants totaling $97,000. Many members of the order also benefited because of a curious law of 1821 which provided that the "worshipful master and officers of every lodge of ancient free-masons in the state of Alabama, shall have the privilege of raising by lottery the sum of three thousand dollars for the use and benefit of their lodges respectively . . ." The two other specified lotteries were for $1,000 for the Pikesville Library Company in 1827 and $500 for the Sommerville Phylomathian Society in 1828.

Undoubtedly Louisiana led all other states in the use of personal lotteries, although it ranked only third numerically, with twenty-two licenses. The explanation of this seeming contradiction lies in the fact that for a period the state viewed certain schemes of this type as a means of revenue. An act of April 1826 formalized a previous policy of allowing anyone to raffle his property after the state treasurer appraised it, and 2 per cent of the appraised value was paid into the treasury. Thomas Jefferson, alone, was exempted from this requirement. How many made use of the act before it was abolished in 1841 is unknown, but the local presses recorded some of the more spectacular cases. For example, the July 16, 1830, issue of the New Orleans *Courier* advertised the "lottery of a Negress." In the depression year of 1839 a large building, Bank's Arcade in New Orleans, valued at $700,000, was offered as first prize in a property lottery. Other awards were a city hotel, valued at $500,000, and 598 parcels of real estate and blocks of bank and gas company stock. The whole thing turned out to be a gigantic swindle when the promoters decamped before the drawing.[13]

In addition to those who held lotteries under the blanket authorization of 1826, thirteen people were given specific licenses. Typical were the acts permitting Pierre Roche to sell a library worth $10,000 upon payment of 2.5 per cent of the proceeds to the state; Louis Guerlain to raffle thirty-two lots of land over a ten-month period; Louis Bourgeois to raffle six slaves, with a 2 per cent tax on the proceeds; and Symphorien Verrette a year to dispose of a plantation, with 2 per cent of his gains going to the state.

It is surprising to find only one license for the Masons, $35,000 for the New Orleans Grand Lodge of Louisiana. Other societies were more successful. Among them were the St. Francisville Library Company ($2,000 a year for ten annual drawings) and the New

Orleans Library Society ($2,000). A probable successor of the latter, the New Orleans Library Association, received a grant in 1825 for a $25,000 lottery. In 1819 the St. Charles Medical Society was licensed to raise $15,000, and in 1828 St. Charles Lyceum and the French Evangelical Society of New Orleans sought licenses for $20,000 and $30,000 respectively. The significant lack of industrial interest is reflected in the fact that only one lottery to further industry was undertaken, in 1828 for $6,000 to develop the steam engine of Henry Lainhart.

Kentucky made at least ten authorizations for private ventures, the last in 1858 and the majority in 1822. Seven were for Masonic lodges and one for the Lexington Light Artillery Company. Another for the Athenaeum caused the Lexington *Kentucky Gazette*, January 15, 1819, to announce that "the friends of Science and all who have a regard for the literary reputation of Kentucky, will doubtless be prompt to aid and to build up this infant establishment." An unusual act in 1858 "for the encouragement of the Fine Arts" provided that it be lawful for "that class of artists called painters, to dispose of pictures the entire creation of their pencil and individual art, in shares" and then to determine "by lot, to what shareholder in a picture the same shall belong." None but "citizen artists, residents of this commonwealth" could enjoy the benefits of the act.

If Louisiana's blanket authorization for property sales is ignored, Tennessee led the nation with twenty-nine private authorizations between 1790 and 1834, the date the state abolished lotteries. There may have been many others without official sanction, since it was not until 1809 that unauthorized lotteries were forbidden on penalty of double-the-scheme value. One that may have gotten in just under the wire was reported in the May 25, 1809, issue of the Carthage *Gazette*. William Moore, tired of sending long distances for paper, decided to dispose of some property by raffle and build a paper mill in Tennessee. His last drawing was announced on June 8, 1810, and on March 8, 1811, Moore informed his neighbors that his mill was in operation and he was buying rags.[14]

Thirteen, almost half, of Tennessee's acts aided the Masons; these schemes totaled $74,500, and the largest single grant was for $10,000 for the Knoxville lodge. Most of them concerned funds for buildings or repairs, but in December 1827, $5,000 was set as a goal for a clock for Columbia Lodge No. 31. With the exception of the Nashville

Library, the Masons were the only societies so honored. Sale of personal property received the next greatest number of licenses, twelve, benefiting eleven individuals. The last lottery sanctioned by Tennessee was of this type, seeking $6,000 to pay Colonel R. H. Dyer's debts to the state. Three laws helped infant industries: in 1819, $10,000 to erect an iron-works on Yellow Creek, and in 1826, $1,500 to encourage the making of salt in Bedford County and $30,000 to increase "Domestic manufacturing" of cotton goods in White County.

Missouri created only two private lotteries. The first, in 1817, was for $8,000 for a Masonic hall in St. Louis. In February 1833 the Sisters of Charity Hospital of St. Louis was given a license for $10,000, with permission to sell the franchise. The newspapers subsequently charged that the contractor was growing rich while the hospital received practically nothing. A committee appointed to study the case cleared the broker, however. The scheme was probably successful, and the tickets "got good play," even in Illinois.

The remaining states of Ohio and Indiana together made three authorizations. Ohio's two grants were in support of infant industries. In 1824 the sum of $25,000 was sought to rebuild the burned "steam mill" of Oliver Ormsby at Cincinnati, and in 1828 a $6,000 lottery to help Elisha Barret overcome fire-damage to his woolen factory was authorized. According to the Cleveland *Herald*, on November 27, 1828, the Barret drawing was postponed for lack of sales. On June 25, 1829, the completion of the first class was announced, and on November 12 the second class was abandoned and money refunded.

Governor William Henry Harrison of the Indiana Territory signed a bill on November 23, 1810, licensing the Vincennes Library to seek $1,000 by lottery and requiring each director to give $200 bond. This right seemingly was not exercised until 1815, when the "Vincennes Library Company" held a raffle in which books and clocks were offered as prizes.[15]

California was no stranger to the system, although her schemes could not be classified as authorized lotteries. For example, the San Francisco *Californian* of November 11, 1847, carried two notices, one in English and one in Spanish, that since no one would pay its value, a house in Monterey would be raffled in the presence of the alcalde of Monterey. The 270 tickets at thirty dollars each were for sale in most of the surrounding towns — San Francisco, Los Angeles, Santa Barbara, and so on. The 1849 California constitution prohibited lotteries, yet despite this and an act of 1851 calling for a fine of not less than $500 and forfeiture of all prizes to the state, the practice died slowly. In fact, the promoters were so brash that in the June 29, 1853, issue of the San Francisco *Herald* more than six columns of lottery advertisements appeared. These featured a "Monster Gold Ingot," a "Monster Gold Bar," and numerous awards of furniture and jewels as prizes, all to be had for about one dollar a chance. Along with "Randolph's Third Diamond Raffle," the papers for July 13 announced the "Grand Real Estate Lottery," offering a ranch of 1,000,000 acres worth $150,000 as bait, with tickets at five dollars each.[16]

Twenty-one states gave 186 licenses for "private," or at least "semi-private," lotteries, and this figure does not include lotteries held under Louisiana's blanket act. It is significant that, as in the case of lotteries authorized for internal improvements during the years after 1790, the bulk of the 186 authorizations for private projects[17] were southern in origin. On the basis of this number, nine of the top ten states issuing private licenses were slave states, emphasizing their rural nature, the absence of organized systems of public assistance, and the favored position of the Masonic order. It is also noteworthy that one of the oldest forms of lotteries was among the last to die in the United States. Wisely the various state governments sprinkled their numerous authorizations with a few for personal benefit. It seems certain that the continuation of this type of grant let many people continue identifying their personal interest with the lottery system at a time when it had become a big business of national scope.

Chapter X

The Shift in Public Opinion, 1790–1830

> Run Neighbors run, the Lottery's expiring,
> When FORTUNE's merry wheel, it will never turn more;
> She now supplies all *Numbers* you're desiring,
> ALL PRIZES, NO BLANKS, AND TWENTY THOUSAND FOUR.[1]

Public opinion — the inconstant, unorganized way by which the people promulgate what they want and think, the voice of command to the politicians — played a great part in the rise and fall of the American lottery. There were always faint voices of opposition to the system even in the periods of its greatest activity. Strengthened by the reform movement which swept the United States in the 1830's, critics soon were lamenting its abuses and frauds. Eventually the majority of the people found little to praise in the lottery and much to condemn.

Newspapers in the 1790's and early 1800's gave little evidence of the lottery's future disgrace, however. In fact, the historian John Bach McMaster concluded that there was a lottery wheel in "every city and town large enough to boast a court-house and a jail . . . The State of the Wheel became as regular an item in the papers as the ship news or prices current." [2] Though the first statement might have been poetic license, there was no exaggeration in the latter. The extent of the mania was discussed in a letter of March 23, 1790, from the Reverend Jeremy Belknap of Boston to his friend, Ebenezer Hazard, a Philadelphia businessman:

You could scarcely imagine what a rage we have here for lotteries. 8,000 tickets sold in four days, in the Marblehead lottery . . . I wonder Secretary [of the Treasury] Hamilton does not hit upon a lottery. It would be more popular than laying a duty on *salt,* which, if he does will greatly injure our fisheries.

Hazard replied on April 14, 1791:

Your *mania* reached this city. Jonas and I sold 500 of the semi-annual [Massachusetts] lottery tickets; and, had we had them, I suppose we could have sold 1,000. Their punctuality in drawing at the time appointed has given your managers great reputation here. We think it will be worth their while to send us a parcel in the next lottery, to dispose of on the same commission as they allow to others.[3]

By a single act on December 20, 1790, Virginia approved fourteen separate raffles. The *Pennsylvania Mercury,* August 24, 1790, commented, "The lottery mania appears to rage with uncommon violence. It is said there are nearly twenty lotteries on foot in the different States. The sale of tickets has been uncommonly rapid. Lotteries have been formed, published, and the tickets sold and drawn in the course of ten or fifteen days." Since, despite laws to the contrary, "foreign" and unauthorized chances were brazenly advertised in every state the situation was compounded beyond the approved offerings. In 1799 a single Rhode Island merchant advertised tickets in the Harvard College, Connecticut Manufactory, Hartford Court House, and Vermont Philanthropic lotteries.[4] The Boston *Columbian Centinel,* January 22, 1791, summed up the situation succinctly — "Every part of the United States abounds in lotteries."

The lottery had its ups and downs, however, and the diary of the Reverend William Bentley of Salem, Massachusetts, showed a cycle of its popularity. On February 1, 1790, he recorded numerous lottery petitions and noted that the "desire for adventuring is so great . . . that Brokers, &c. have speculated upon the purchase of Tickets, a speculation before unknown in America." Two months later he wrote that a "Gazette extraordinary" was printed in Salem just to announce the winners in the first class of the Marblehead lottery. "The effects are already visable, the poorest people are spending their time & interest to purchase Tickets, and already the number of Lotteries are sufficient with their schemes to fill a Gazette. The State, Charlestown, Williamstown, Lancaster, Marblehead Lotteries are in this day's print and all to draw within a month." These represented schemes totaling $39,000, and such ventures were "but at the commencement of their Career, according to appearances." Ticket sales were "amazing rapid, hundreds sell at a time for speculation, & there is hardly a person who is not an adventurer & sometimes large parties buy conjointly so as to pay themselves their money again."

On July 29, 1790, Bentley reported that his friend Isaac White had won $500, and that "such success has increased the disposition toward adventuring, & this is the Subject of general conversation. Schemes are every day projecting in warm imaginations for the money when it comes." The following January, "the rage for Lotteries increases every day." On March 17, mentioning the beginning of the Semi-annual State Lottery, the largest Massachusetts venture to that time (25,000 chances at five dollars each), he stated that the sum had proven too much. "The smaller lotteries by their speedy sale of tickets left the rage unbounded, but this has measured the full extent . . . Not a ticket scarcely is asked for at this time so near drawing, so thoroughly are the people glutted." On the last day of the drawing he commented, perhaps sadly, that "the balance against this town will probably be great." On May 7, his prophecy was ful-filled, "Of the last Semi annual Lottery it is said that Boston lost $25,000, & Salem, above $3,000." Two more entries concluded the story. "The Governor," Bentley wrote on June 6, "has expressed his disapprobation of Lotteries in a very concise but pertinent manner," and on March 27, 1792: "The Gazette abounds with invectives against Tontine, Lotteries, &c." [5]

Many states temporarily lost their taste for lotteries at this time, as the fall in ticket purchases revealed. In Connecticut the McIntosh grant (1791) for a textile mill had to ask for an extension of time in 1794 and the statehouse lottery reported in 1795 that it had lost £2,784 on the first class. In Rhode Island the managers for Nicholas Easton asked the legislature in February 1794 to cancel their bond and permit refunding the tickets they had succeeded in selling, and in January 1795 the directors for the Providence Street project re-ported failure.

This plethora of lotteries in the last decade of the eighteenth cen-tury undoubtedly caused some of their warmest advocates to wonder whether there could be too much of a good thing. It is interesting that as early as June 1790 the need was felt to defend the use of lotteries. On June 29, the Salem, Massachusetts, *Gazette* defended the government's licensing the schemes on the grounds that the legislature had been careful to approve only those in which the good of the project outweighed the evil of the means. Also, "monies raised by lotteries cannot impoverish the community — as they are not sent abroad, but only taken out of one pocket and put into another." Although the majority of citizens apparently agreed, a Major Benjamin Russell facetiously inquired of a member "of an important body" whether he thought the General Court would grant a drawing to support a missionary and supply each person in the eastern part of the state with a Bible. When the story got out, a correspondent of the *Columbian Centinel* commented on February 26, 1791, "Let not the serious reader frown, as that member did; for if there is nothing contained in that sacred book which can be thought opposed to this method of gambling, neither the one nor the other can give a substantial reason why, in the present rage for lotteries, the people should not be indulged in raising money in the way most agreeable to their humour." Major Russell reattacked a month later in the same paper.

The *National* and *State Legislatures* being in recess, there is a "Plentiful Scarcity" of domestick occurences . . . This is locally remedied by the Lottery, which seems to arrest the attention of all ranks of citizens. — To describe the symptoms of the *disease* is impossible — all are fascinated — all expect to be the favored children of Fortune. — The rich court her smiles, as eagerly as the poor — and whilst, O! fickle Goddess, the *young* pour forth their supplication for thy favors . . . The delusion is general — and general must the mortification be.

This prophecy was fulfilled, and as the Reverend Bentley noted, general disenchantment swept Massachusetts early in 1791. In a public address on May 26, Governor John Hancock characterized lotteries as a species of gambling calculated to ensnare and injure citizens otherwise guiltless of the vice in its common forms. While many would not have agreed with this characterization in its entirety, no new licenses were issued until 1794. Upon an appeal from Harvard College the General Court decided to take another chance and granted a lottery for the school.

This action provoked a new outburst of protests. Joel Barlow's denunciation of lotteries before the National Convention of France was reprinted in the newspapers,[6] the late Governor Hancock's stand was widely quoted, and Bentley recorded on February 25, 1794, "The idea of Lotteries are reprobated seriously by some people."

In spite of the protests, the legislature was vindicated when the lottery proved successful. Perhaps a circumstance noted by Bentley in July had helped: that many of the clergy were supporting the venture.[7] At least one, the Reverend Gideon Hawley, expressed himself when on offering to buy a half ticket, he wrote, "having never been successful in Lotteries I should not have made the proposal had not this been in favor of the course of literature."[8]

If the leaders of the religious denominations felt they were in a compromising situation, few gave any indication of it. Even during this period of the lottery's temporary disfavor, censure for not opposing lotteries was rare; on the contrary, such ventures were urged for the benefit of churches. Schools, too, felt they had a rightful claim on clerical support, and some, such as Leicester Academy (Massachusetts, 1790) did not hesitate to ask for it. "As the design of this lottery is for promoting Piety, Virtue, and such of the liberal Arts and Sciences as may qualify the Youth to become useful members of society, the Managers wish for and expect the aid of the Gentlemen Trustees of the Academy, the Reverend Clergy, and all persons who have a taste for encouraging said Seminary of Learning."[9]

In most cases individual congregations continued to hold their drawings in competition with secular institutions. There was no hesitancy in connecting the furtherance of God's work with such enterprises, as is evidenced by their advertisements. Some went as far as the James Street Methodist Church of New York, whose records show a speculative purchase: "1790, March 1, cash paid for a ticket in the Lottery, £2–0–0."[10]

Most ecclesiastical governing bodies took evasive action or no stand at all on the question of the morality of such enterprises. One of the rare occasions of a vote of censure came in October 1792, when a large meeting of the Baptists of Dover Association in Virginia resolved that the purchase of tickets was a species of gambling not to be tolerated in members of their churches.[11] The Quakers continued their opposition. The "Rules of Discipline of the Yearly Meeting held on Rhode Island, for New England," in 1809 reiterated: "It is advised that a watchful care be exercised over our youth to prevent their . . . being concerned in lotteries, wagering, or other species of gaming. And if any of our members fall into . . . these practices . . . and if they be not reclaimed by further labor, proceed to testify our disunity with them." The yearly meeting for the State of New York and "parts Adjacent" for 1810 condemned them in almost identical terms, and if erring Friends resisted "tender labour in the spirit of restoring love," they were to be separated from the Society.[12]

More typical was the action of the Synod of the Presbyterian Church which met at Fair Forest in western North Carolina on October 4, 1810. When confronted with the question, "Are lotteries even for religious purposes, such as building churches, &c., consistent with the morality of the Gospel?" it bypassed the issue and took the unusual step of referring it to the Assembly.[13] At the General Conference of the Methodist Church in New York City in 1812, the Reverend John Sale, member of the western, later Ohio, conference, offered a resolution to forbid preachers and private members from buying or holding lottery tickets, or having anything to do with the system whatsoever. The group's sentiment was divided, and the motion was deferred to the next meeting in May 1816.[14] The "test by fire" was applied in a meeting of the Missionary Society of New York in 1813 when a roguish individual dropped a Union College lottery chance into the contribution box. A long discussion ensued on the propriety of retaining it before the practical decision was agreed upon to withhold a decision until *after* the drawing![15] These isolated cases of "searching of consciences" were an indication of things to come, but for the moment they had little influence.

An important economic and social expediency such as lotteries could not miss being included in the literature of the period. The great majority of journals and newspapers approved them, at least to the extent of ignoring them or publishing the profitable advertisements furnished by the lotteries. But by 1805 some of the numerous small magazines were commenting unfavorably upon them. One of the earliest was in 1804 when the *Massachusetts Missionary Magazine* called for complete abolition of lotteries as being irreligious and "really tempting God" by making Him determine the winner.[16] The *Companion and Weekly Miscellany*, January 12, 1805, published one of the first morality stories on such speculation. In it a young farmer after winning £20,000 so lost his head that in less than seven years he had alienated his wife and come to the end of his life and fortune.[17]

A reputedly true account of lottery degradation appeared in the *Evening Fireside*, which reprinted a young businessman's account of how his infatuation for the schemes had caused him to desert his friends and work. After he had lost most of his money and endangered his health, a clergyman happily had shown him the error of his ways.[18] Possibly with such testimony in mind, a writer in the *Monthly Anthology*, 1806, made an unusually strong attack upon lotteries as injurious to public morals. They were the "meanest way a legislature ever pursues of laying a tax"; and a state might as well imitate France and license other vices also.[19]

With few exceptions these early flare-ups were one-shot affairs. Obadiah Optic, editor of the *Eye*, a Philadelphia publication, however, was more persistent or convinced of the lottery's dangers and on February 25, 1808, began printing a series of blasts. "Nothing," he wrote on his front page in May, "at this moment, more anxiously calls on the moralist, the divine, and every man anxious to promote moral rectitude, for a union of their influence, and a full and free expression of their thought, than LOTTERIES." As long as they remained unsanctioned, they lacked the power of doing much evil, but when they were reduced to a regular system, so that all civic improvements had to be made in that manner, then "the many must be impoverished that the few may be enriched." If the government alone favored such schemes, there still would have been the church to "save us from a total depravity of morals"; but now "even the *clergy* . . . have forsaken us, like DEMAS, in love with the present world." Though some ministers admitted the questionability of the system, "nevertheless they have permitted *the ends to sanctify the means*, and *flourishing churches* have been raised by iniquitous lotteries . . ." All faiths except the Society of Friends were guilty. "All blame them, yet all use them."[20]

On the other side, a long article by "Priscus" in the March 1811 issue of the *Connecticut Evangelical Magazine and Religious Intelligencer* strongly favored the undertakings. His justification was that they were not morally unlawful, but had been ordained by God Himself. In sanctioning a lottery the legislature usually had a good end in view, so the adventurer with the same objective might "honestly pray for success." On covetousness, he claimed that "This principal is dominant and essential in our fallen nature." Lotteries were the best form of taxation because they were "voluntary and all cause of complaint by those participating is prevented." A direct tax would be preferable, but it could not "be exercised with safety to the State" for fear of causing uprisings, for the people would bear no more taxes even for good things.[21] Since "Priscus" was not answered, either the magazine had a very limited circulation or his readers must have agreed.

The purveyors of homespun common sense, the almanacs, on at least one occasion commented on the lottery. Robert Bailey Thomas, in the 1813 edition of his famous *Old Farmer's Almanack*, wrote on the page devoted to January:

I have often imagined that I had hit upon the path where happiness had passed along, and fancied I should very soon be saluted with the brightness of her countenance. *Here-here!* cried I to neighbor Simpkins, *here is the way.* See — every guide board *points in this direction.* "Ah, Zuckins," cries neighbor Simpkins, "You will soon find yourself mistaken. Your path leads down to the gloomy pits of ruin. Your charming enticer is in reality a haggard hobgoblin — look out neighbor, look out!" I was putting my hand in my pocket book to take out a bill to purchase a ticket in the lottery, but my neighbor's caution prevented my throwing away my money in this manner. "Here," said I to my boy, "here, Tom, take this *five dollar* bill to the widow Lonesome; tell her, it is at her disposal; then hasten back to your school." [22]

The earliest attack in book form appeared in 1814, when Samuel Wood, proprietor of the Juvenile Book Store in New York, republished the *Wonderful Advantages of Adventuring in the Lottery*. In his preface he acknowledged that the story was first printed in England and though fiction, it presented so natural a picture of the demoralizing effects of such schemes as to be useful in the United States. Although it was intended primarily for the young, he hoped their elders would also read it and be induced to stop setting such a bad example by participation in this "licensed mode of gambling." Wood expressed amazement that Christian legislatures could sanction lotteries; if morality meant nothing, they should consider the loss to the state in time, cost of tickets, and insurance. "Covetousness being the foundation of such works, it cannot be reasonably expected that a blessing will attend."

The tale concerned a merchant's trusted servant, John, who decided to try his luck in a lottery despite his wife's pleas that God was the best judge of their needs and that if so much could be gained by the tickets why did not the agents keep them for themselves.

John invested in six numbers, insuring them for the first day of drawing. Dreaming of prospective wealth, he neglected his job and became gloomy and short-tempered with his family and master. On the fateful day he was shocked by the presence at the drawing of a "number of drunken, ragged, blaspheming wretches." While awaiting the appearance of his numbers, he lost his money gambling on which number would come out next and pawned some silver stolen from his master. While drinking to drown his anxiety, he agreed to aid in a highway robbery to replenish his purse. In the holdup the victim was slain, John was captured, and was sentenced to death. The grief killed his wife. The judge concluded the trial and story by advising all to shun these schemes as a "plague, which will destroy domestic happiness and inward peace, and bring . . . every kind of distress." [23]

The War of 1812 indirectly contributed to one of the most unusual bits of literature dealing with the subject, *The Lottery, A Poem*, by St. Denis Le Cadet, published in Baltimore in 1815. After the first fifteen pages of invocation to the muse, the poet unfolded fifty-two more on the saga of a simple-minded hero, Edward, who pawned his watch and snuff box to buy a lottery ticket. The shock of winning nearly killed him, but he recovered to invest his winnings successfully in privateering. Although the poem was not written as antilottery propaganda, the author warned:

> Should you or I such bus'ness try,
> And distant chance for ready buy;
> Chance 'tis we should have cause to sigh.

But these moralists were voices crying in the wilderness. The cycle was beginning its upward swing once more. The self-styled victory over England in the War of 1812 had imbued Americans with new confidence in themselves and in their country. They saw it growing in size and strength and many of its citizens of low birth attaining social and political heights impossible in Europe. America was the land of opportunity, and everyone felt compelled to better himself. Ignorant of other paths to distinction and superiority, many turned to money-getting. The get-rich-quick ideal spread. John J. Abert, an advisor to the War Department, wrote concerning this phenomenon, "The desire to grow rich, and to grow rich rapidly, are the besetting sins of our country." Noting that in the United States there were no marks of distinction "but such as are awarded by the common consent of the community," he decided that with a commercial people the distinction took the form of wealth. "Even ambition, therefore, high tone, high minded ambition sees in wealth so important an auxiliary that all its efforts are lost without its aid . . . and therefore with the many, if one is only successful, the means of acquiring it are not looked into, and if not too glaringly dishonest are rarely condemned. Look around you in the world and see what a crime it is to be poor." [24]

This spirit and its effect on lotteries was well defined in 1840 by Professor W. G. Goddard of Brown University:

Lotteries . . . are rendered especially mischievous in this country by the nature of our institutions, and by the spirit of the times. Here, the path of eminence being open to everyone — but too many are morbidly anxious to improve their condition; and by means, too, which in the wisdom of Providence were never intended to command success. A mad desire for wealth pervades all classes . . . It generates a spirit of reckless speculation; it corrupts the simplicity of our tastes; and . . . it impairs not infrequently . . . the obligations of common honesty. Upon these elements of our social condition and character, the Lottery system operates with malignant efficacy . . .[25]

The early decades of the nineteenth century saw the lottery spiral reach its zenith. Throughout this period of great lottery speculation, however, the disenchanted kept up their cries. A new charitable organization created in 1817 was the Society for the Prevention of Pauperism in the City of New York. On February 4, 1818, it bore out Goddard's statement with a report on the principal causes of poverty. Drink, lotteries, pawnbrokers, and the many charitable institutions in the city were listed in that order. The Baltimore branch of the organization, in its own list three years later, merely replaced the pawnbrokers with prostitution. Both reports attacked lotteries on the basis of the anxiety, disappointment, depression, and time wasted in following the drawings; the practice of "insurance"; and popularizing the belief that "there does exist a dispensation different from that imposed by his adorable Creator — that in the sweat of his face he shall eat his bread — that property may be gained, that wealth may be acquired without labour." [26]

Each state had its problems with lotteries, and each handled them in its own way. There was no nationally directed antilottery drive before the Civil War; state abolitionists were self-initiated and directed with only occasional glances elsewhere for examples. Many states, in hope of heading off a lottery fiasco, began as Maryland did with regulatory legislation. In 1809 laws against "insurance" were passed in Maryland, and the system was taken over by the state for all intents and purposes in 1817, when a 5 per cent tax was placed on all schemes, three commissioners were appointed to supervise the drawings, and lotteries for the direct benefit of the state were begun. These steps were taken after the legislature heard arguments that it was useless to try to suppress lotteries as long as they flourished next door.

Aside from the common problems of unauthorized ventures and "insurance," New York had little to criticize until its state-appointed managers began giving trouble. In 1809 the state lost $41,059.78 because of the defalcation of Philip Ten Eyck, a director for the Literature Lottery, and the sum was paid from the treasury. This called attention to the general problem of supervision, and a comprehensive law of regulation was passed in 1813. In addition to a high bond, managers were required to take an oath not to sell tickets in which they were personally interested or buy any on their own account. In 1818, however, there occurred an event which shook the lottery system to its roots in New York, and by undermining public confidence in the effectiveness of close government regulation and supervision, caused reverberations throughout the country.

This event was the famous Baldwin libel case.[27] On September 16, 1818, Charles N. Baldwin, editor of the *Republican Chronicle*, shattered the calm of lottery "business as usual" with an editorial blast:

CITIZENS, LOOK OUT

It is a fact that in this present Lottery . . . there is SWINDLING in the management. A certain gentleman in town received intimation last week that a number *named* would be drawn on Friday last! And it was *drawn that day!* The number was insured *high* in several different places. A similar thing had happened once before in *this same lottery:* and on examining the manager's files, the number appeared *soiled* as if it had been in the pocket several days! If this be true, *and we vouch for it,* it may be previously known who shall have the 100,000 dollars in this lottery. It deserves immediate investigation by our magistrates.

The next day Baldwin printed further revelations, and on September 18 stated he would make no retraction. He added that "the practice of dropping numbers on the floor, picking them up, and throwing them back into the wheel, and the still more *dangerous* practice of the boy in drawing several numbers at a time, and throwing them into the lap of a *Sub-Manager*, is reprobated, and may open a door to most pernicious SWINDLING! We have no doubt this lottery will be fairly conducted *now!*"

Four days later he amplified his accusations: the morning of the fifth day of the Medical Science Lottery, ticket number 3,865 had been heavily insured. It was a winner, causing large losses to the insurers, but there was no suspicion of foul play. On the seventh and ninth days like fates occurred to numbers 30 and 15,468. In the case of the latter, the youth pulled out three billets, dropped them into the lap of John H. Sickles, the acting manager, who then announced still a fourth, 15,468. Investigation had revealed that all three of the suspected numbers were soiled. Insurance agents also found that a man named Thorne had wagered most of the money on 15,468, claiming he had dreamed it would win.

The directors of the lottery then made, for them, the unfortunate mistake of hailing Baldwin into court on a libel charge, thus furnishing a sounding board for the most famous case in the history of lotteries. Through the resulting publicity the public learned for the first time of many hidden frauds and the carelessness with which these affairs were conducted. Hearings were held by Mayor Cadwallader Colden and two New York City aldermen on November 11, 12, and 13. By a new law, truth of statements could be admitted as a defense in such arraignments. The question was whether there was proof of collusion or other circumstances implying malpractice.

Baldwin's attorneys singled out Sickles as responsible for the chicanery. They proved that he had informed two people that certain low numbers in a previous class would not be drawn and that in the Owego Lottery he had been personally interested in the ticket which had won $35,000. On still another occasion Sickles, as acting manager, had shown a Mr. Burtus four billets, claiming to have found them under the wheel and also claiming that he had discovered ten more in a crack under the carpet, none of which he had reported. He also admitted having bought, jointly with five other speculators, 20,000 tickets in another drawing under his supervision, for which he had a key that gave him access to the tickets at any time. In this case it was charged that the managers had seen Sickles take the boy's place and draw the lots, a handful at a time, putting them into his lap or back into the wheel.

All opportunities for deception were introduced as evidence to the court, and thereby to the public. In one instance it was found that the lad doing the drawing had concealed a number on instruction from his master; in another, bribed by insurance agents, he had hidden a billet with heavy bets upon it. The custom of giving large sums to the first-drawn lot on particular days made it easy for the boy to palm his choice and pretend to have picked it in a normal manner. This, plus much more testimony, made it obvious that fraud was not only possible but probable, and in the Baldwin case, a proven fact. The court took only fifteen minutes to decide on acquittal.

Following this suit a special committee under the chairmanship of John Pintard, a public-spirited merchant prince, was appointed by the Society for the Prevention of Pauperism to find a solution for these ills. Pintard wrote his daughter, November 16, 1818, that corruption was apparent, but its prevention was beyond his comprehension as any plan had to be workable "for men & not for angels." A letter written twelve days later alleged that the public had lost faith in the managers and favored abolition of lotteries, but that the state was committed by its licenses.[28] In December the group recommended stricter control of lotteries and their discontinuance as soon as practical. The report calculated that in order to raise $30,000 by lottery an expenditure of $170,500 was necessary. Although the number of ticket offices in the city had greatly diminished from the one hundred before the Baldwin affair, two partners still had cleared $100,000 in the course of a single class. There was no solution which would eradicate the evils entirely: "So long as the cause remains, the effect will be felt." [29]

A New York legislative committee next made a thorough inspection. Its printed conclusion, running to 149 pages, not only damned Sickles but also placed the whole lottery system in a sorry light. It hammered hard at "insurance" as a malignant phase of the business — one shop alone had received $31,000 in premiums from three classes of a scheme. Salesmen were paid 12.5 per cent of the ticket price to entice women, children, apprentices, servants, Negroes, and

the poorest and most ignorant into speculation. Furthermore, loss to
the state through failure and defalcation by directors had amounted
to over $109,000. The only commendation the committee could give
for raising money by lotteries was "the cheerfulness with which it
is paid." [30]

This report was followed by a very detailed act on April 13, 1819,
which among other things subjected unauthorized lotteries to forfeiture of the sum sought and a fine of $250 for each ticket sold; set
a $2,000 penalty for "insurance"; required licenses up to $500 each
for all ticket sellers; and described in detail the mechanics to be
followed in drawing. For example, the arm of the person drawing
had to be bare, the lot held between the thumb and forefinger, and
only one number withdrawn at a time. Later, Article VII, section
11, of New York's constitution of 1820 provided that "no lottery
shall hereafter be authorized in this state." While this was the first
actual prohibition of lotteries, it failed to apply to those already in
operation. What is more, on at least two occasions it was evaded.
Also, in April 1822, a statute transferred control from the state-appointed overseers to the institutions holding the licenses in order to
speed operation and save money for the government. As we have
seen, this enabled Yates & McIntyre to take control of the lotteries
in process.

Public memory was short, and by 1825 a contemporary New
Yorker could write: "If the city did not appear like a huge lottery
office, with innumerable departments, it was because the citizens
were too excited by the rage for money making to see it as it really
was." [31] Another person quoted the New York *Commercial Advertiser* in 1826 to the effect that there were "upwards of one hundred
and sixty lottery offices in that city." [32] Yates & McIntyre reaped their
share of profits, reporting in 1826 that since taking over the grants
they had sold tickets worth $2,743,793.38. Another local paper an-
nounced in 1827 that visitors to New York City received the impres-
sion that "one-half of the citizens get their living by affording the
opportunity to gamble to the rest." Successful abolition had to await
another cause célèbre in New York.

Sparked by the Baldwin case in New York, however, American
public opinion began reflecting more doubts over the wisdom of
perpetuating lottery legalizations. In 1818 the New York *Evening
Post* had had the courage to take a strong stand, even though it

meant a severe financial loss since lotteries furnished almost one-fifteenth of its advertising. William Coleman, the editor, wrote: "Look at the crowd of poor, ragged wretches that beset the office-keeper's doors the morning after the day's drawing is over, waiting with their little slips in their hands, to hear their fate, and the yester-day's earnings ready to be given to the harpies that stand gaping for the pittance." [33] The next year the *North American Review* raised its voice. Quoting from a British member of Parliament, T. F. Buxton, the *Review* flayed American governments for sponsoring vice for the sake of revenue.[34]

About the only English work on lotteries widely quoted in this country was the study of prison discipline by Buxton in which he pointed out the relationship between lotteries and crime.[35] Contemporary movements in Europe toward prohibition of lotteries had surprisingly little influence on the fight in the United States. Contrary to the case in many parallel reforms, there was apparently no correspondence between the leaders in Britain and the United States, even though the opening struggles took place almost simultaneously. This may well have been because there was no nationally recognized head of the American movement. Instead, there was a large number of scattered, local protagonists, who, in general, were not conspicuous in other reforms then being advocated in the United States. Also, enough "home-grown" illustrations of the system's evils flourished in both nations to make unnecessary their exchange.

To some extent, however, England's determination to end lotteries did reinforce American opposition. As early as 1818 John Bristed, British by birth and education but a naturalized American, lamented:

There are . . . drawbacks upon the high elements of national greatness . . . to be found in some of our political and social institutions . . . *Lotteries* pervade the middle, southern and western States, and spread a horribly-increasing mass of idleness, fraud, theft, falsehood, and profligacy throughout all the classes of our labouring population. The crying iniquity and evil of this system are compelling the British parliament to abolish it altogether in that country. Our state legislatures never assemble without augmenting the number of lotteries! [36]

Only a few Europeans who traveled in the United States left a record of their impressions regarding such ventures. One of the first, Fortescue Cuming, 1807–1809, reported that lotteries reached the frontiers almost as soon as the settlers. He was surprised to find that Somerset, Pennsylvania, had requested permission to raise $3,000 for a church when the town consisted of only seventy houses and that the backwoods settlement of Chillicothe, Ohio, had a drawing on foot to raise funds to shore up its river banks. William Faux noted in 1820 that George Washington did not have a proper tomb and would not until a "national grave is made by lottery. Graves and Cathedrals are raised, in this country, by means of lotteries!" The same year Adlard Welby reported lotteries as frequent as in Britain — "schemes are forever publishing, and without any other difference than the substitution of dollars for pounds . . ." [37]

Even after England's abolition of lotteries in 1826, Englishmen made little mention of America's failure to follow suit, C. D. Arfwedson being one of the few exceptions.[38] Nevertheless, American publicists were not quiet. In 1826 Theodore Sedgwick asked his countrymen what British statesmen could say for "the innocence of the young republic" as long as the United States tolerated such undertakings. A number of other writers pointed to lotteries as evidence of the United States' failure to progress as rapidly as the mother country. France, on the other hand, which retained the system, was more than once pictured as a depraved country and a bad international influence.[39]

Meanwhile, problems mounted in the United States. In 1821 Pennsylvania was still wrestling with the sale of "foreign" tickets. Despite heavy penalties the practice had become so excessive that at least fifteen prohibited drawings were announced in Philadelphia annually, "quite as a matter of course." "Transgressors had so long enjoyed impunity that they almost claimed it by prescription." [40] The same problem, perhaps to a lesser degree, existed in nearly every other state.

Events in Massachusetts fanned the abolition flame still higher. In January 1821 a senate committee under Peter Chardon Brooks was appointed to examine lottery affairs in that state. It reported on three schemes: the Union Canal, the Springfield Bridge, and the Plymouth Beach. Conditions in the last were so bad that examination by a joint committee of both houses was recommended. This was done with Brooks again as chairman. The report stated that "beyond the admission of a doubt" the approved amount had been obtained, and that as early as May 1814 the three then completed installments, even after deduction of all charges allowed by the enacting law, had cleared $22,718.97, an excess of $7,718.97. The investigators were "at a loss to conjecture" why the undertaking had not closed at that time! Notwithstanding, the managers had drawn eight more classes and still had not paid the city its lawful share. The exposure of this fraud dealt the death blow to such grants in Massachusetts, although the system was not to pass away without a struggle.[41]

Two events followed in 1822 which showed the running of the tide. In February a request to Massachusetts from the District of Columbia to sell tickets in projects sanctioned by Congress was refused by a joint committee, which resolved that lotteries however carefully guarded "must produce great evil." Also during the year *The Lottery Ticket: An American Tale,* a book undoubtedly written as antilottery propaganda, was published in Cambridge. In the story, Mr. Meriam, a young, enterprising, and respected farmer of New Hampshire, during a period of illness was pressed by a hardhearted money-lender for payment of his mortgage. Half of a lottery ticket was offered by the landlord as a chance to secure the funds. Despite his good wife's protests and fears, he won $1,000. Her rebuke, that if he had gained this at a billard table in Boston he would have considered it the "wages of iniquity," only brought his retort that billiards were illegal and raffles were not. Inflamed with desire, Meriam began his downward slide to debtor's prison, finally to be rescued by his good wife and her Bible. When this tale was reissued in 1827 at Hartford, a second story, "The Destructive Consequences of Dissipation and Luxury," was added, another riches to rags account.[42]

In January 1823 the *American Baptist Magazine* of Boston, published by the Baptist General Convention, carried a letter on the "Immorality of Lotteries," which opened with the statement: "Public gaming by Lotteries so far from being less criminal than other species of that vice, is the worst of them all; for it abets and sanctions, as far as example and concurrence can do it, a practice which opens the door to every species of fraud and villainy; which is pregnant with the most extensive evils to the community and individuals." [43] That it was not speaking for all Baptists was evident from the occasion as well as from the curious notation made by

Jonah Titus on the back of his chance in the Second Baptist Society's Lottery (Rhode Island, 1824): "I purchased this ticket very much against my views of interest but like him who gambles in any thing else hope to gain by it." [44]

In Frederick, Maryland, the Lutheran church passed several resolutions in 1825 which were pertinent to the times. The first read:

Whereas the discipline of our church enjoins the members of the Council to lead an exemplary life; and as we consider the encouraging and attendance of horse-racing, cock-fighting, unlawful gaming and public balls to be inconsistent with such conduct:

Therefore Resolved, That it is the decided opinion of this Council that any member of the Council attending such places renders himself liable to expulsion.

Its next action was the adoption of a motion proposed by the pastor: "Resolved, That we highly appreciate the zealous and repeated exertions of Samuel Barnes, Esq., for his endeavors to promote the pecuniary interest of this congregation by introducing, maturing and advocating in the house of delegates at their recent session the bill intended to grant a lottery for its benefit." [45] This device had been used by the congregation several previous times and these resolutions reveal the inconsistencies to which a church could be led in its definition of morality, especially when legal sanctions cloaked the method of raising such needed money. But the pastor, the Reverend David F. Shaffer, showed himself of short memory or the beneficiary of rapid conversion, for the next year he began striking at lotteries in a paper which he published. Later articles were on "Immorality in Maryland," which listed the drawings as an evil, and an essay entitled "Lottery Riches have Wings." [46] His doubts and those of others were reflected in an unsuccessfully proposed amendment to the Maryland constitution in 1834 to forbid such schemes.

The District of Columbia also was nearing the end of its lottery days when in 1825 the Supreme Court included in its decision in Brent v. Davis its views on lotteries: "However questionable may be the policy of tolerating lotteries, there can be no question respecting the policy of removing, as far as possible, from those who are concerned in them, all temptation to fraud." Another case, Clarke v. City of Washington (1827) required the city to pay $150,000 in defaulted prizes and virtually ended lotteries in the District, in practice at least, if not by law. [47]

The next few years found the system coming under fire on widely separated fronts in the United States. Charles A. Hill and his colleagues were able to defeat on moral grounds bills for lotteries for educational purposes in the North Carolina legislature in 1825 and 1827.[48] The latter occasion brought on a lively discussion of morality. Hill, who had successfully led earlier fights against such franchises, had a starring role in this one. A Mr. Leake, sponsor of a drawing for Richmond Academy, said that he could vote for such a useful purpose with as little reproach of conscience as he would enter into a "cotton or other speculation where there was a chance (as is always the case) of involving his family in ruin." Hill replied that as anxious as he was for cultivation of the human mind and the spread of the benefits of education, he could not promote these aims by a lottery, since he was not convinced that the "utility of the end, sanctified the impurity of the means," and he would never approve any measure that "savored of the damning influence of gambling."

In rebuttal it was argued that the legislature should promote the best interest of its people and that the school could not be saved in any other fashion. Among other things, Hill's policy would merely drive the practice underground. After all, lottery speculation was no different from buying a land warrant or insuring the safe arrival of a cargo. Other states had not suffered the predicted terrible fates, or the system would not have flourished so long. Besides, this measure would eventually create a hostility to gambling by annually turning out a large number of well-educated youths. Hill answered that he would remind them of only one of many instances — that of Jonas Frost, who, "perhaps, had managed his lottery as judiciously as any one ever did." After selling the tickets, he pocketed the money and fled without drawing it! When the bill came to a vote, it passed the upper house thirty-seven to twenty-two but was later killed in the lower.[49]

Niles' Weekly Register for September 23, 1826, denounced lotteries as "always objectionable," a "fraud upon the oppression of the poor and unreflecting," concluding that "whoever purchases a ticket in them encounters an odds against himself equal to about forty percent." The Concord, Massachusetts, *Yeoman's Gazette*, was quoted as having said on December 23, 1826, that its editor had heard a lottery broker boasting of defrauding prize winners; that spurious tickets, chances numbered higher than any legally issued, and several of the same number were "often" sold — one vendor was detected selling nineteen quarters of a billet.[50] The same writer stated that there were one hundred persons in Boston at that time who got their living exclusively by selling tickets to people who were spending $750,000 for them despite the law forbidding all unauthorized sales.

In May 1826 the New Haven County West Association of Connecticut proposed for discussion at its next meeting, "Is it the duty of ministers & churches to do anything for the discouragement & suppression of lotteries: & if anything what?" [51] The loudest voice in Connecticut raised against lotteries was the *Religious Intelligencer* of New Haven, which only fifteen years earlier had printed the "Priscus" article in their support. In October 1826 it enumerated some of the evils of the system, and again on November 11 and 18 the editor presented very strong articles, declaring lotteries had had their origin in Connecticut because the legislature feared to be thought illiberal. Three more articles appeared in March and April of the next year, gleefully pointing out that the United States Supreme Court had recently held that lotteries were "gaming," and hailing the new and stricter licensing system in New York. Connecticut had laws against nine-pins but authorized lotteries — "Surely this is straining at a gnat, and swallowing a camel." [52]

Joining the attack was the *Christian Spectator*, "conducted by an Association of Gentlemen" and published in New Haven. In April 1826 it printed a letter telling how England had found that the lottery augmented her poor rates faster than it swelled her treasury, emphasizing the great sum invested in a single scheme, and pointing out that the legislatures would not act until public opinion had been aroused. Next month the editor compared the system to the sale of "ardent spirits" and found it similar in results. Such ventures, he stated, multiplied so fast it seemed as though the assemblies met for no other reason than to approve them. The following January, referring to the use of lotteries for building monuments, the editor wrote, "It would seem . . . that our wise legislators deem it more important to celebrate the virtues of the dead than to preserve the morals of the living." A long article on "The Morality and Public Tendency of Lotteries" was contributed by "A H E" to the February and March issues. It stressed the waste of capital and labor, the creation of extravagant hopes and desires, the neutralization of charity, and the taking from the many and giving to the few. Eventually, the author expected to see wasted villages with a church at one end for the support of religion and a lottery office at the other for support of the minister. Succeeding essays followed the same lines of reasoning.[53]

After these blasts it was not surprising that the Connecticut legislature rejected almost unanimously that year a petition by Middleton Military Academy to hold a lottery for $20,000, on the grounds the practice was "highly injurious to the morals and best interest of the community," and in 1828 and again in 1830 stiffened penalties on unauthorized lotteries.

The rest of New England was also becoming self-conscious about this situation. An attempt to get permission for a lottery to construct a canal from Boston to the Hudson River made the schemes, along with Jacksonianism, liquor sales, and the question of free bridges, a main issue in the Massachusetts election of 1827. The sponsors of the water-way argued that the illegal sale of tickets showed that the people did not want government interference or restraint, and "since an unabateable evil does exist, let it be converted to the best possible purposes." The Boston *Daily Advertiser* said this argument was a libel on the state, and since Massachusetts was becoming a thriving manufacturing center, the reintroduction of lotteries would jeopardize this interest.[54]

One of the most important results of the controversy in Massachusetts was the organization of the Hanover Association of Young Men in January 1827 by Lyman Beecher, pastor of the Hanover Street Church, to assert the position of orthodox Christians in politics. An early meeting produced a report on lotteries so well drawn that it was later embodied in the Massachusetts law on the subject. Within the year three or four similar groups were established. Beecher proudly claimed that they were instrumental in stirring up public opinion against raffles, liquor booths on the Boston Common on holidays, and steamboat riding to Nahant on Sundays. The popularity of the movement is seen in his comment that on one occasion he addressed some 1,200 members in a meeting at the Tremont Theater.[55] Undoubtedly their activity greatly influenced the legislature's decision to disapprove the canal company's request.

In January 1828 an unsuccessful attempt was made to change the

Massachusetts law so as to allow licensing of ticket agencies, and in 1830 an effort to obtain sanction for a series of drawings to complete Bunker Hill Monument stirred the embers. Beecher and his cohorts once more stripped for battle. James White, a member of the Hanover Association, related how Beecher "stamped indelibly the brand of infamy on lotteries." Preceding the Monday on which the vote was to be taken, Beecher prepared a special opposition sermon and invited the members of the General Court to attend. The packed house gave careful attention as the orator pointed out the public and private effects of the system "with simplicity and honesty of description, but with startling and terrific coloring." Just how terrific was this coloring is best seen in the words of the author:

Youth, morals, business interest, social order, widowed mothers and orphaned children, the wreck of homes and character, the blight, the ruin, the remorse of conscience and the woes of the lost in hell through the direct or indirect influence of lotteries, were worked up with marvellous vividness and power from the first stroke of the master's pencil to the close. There was an intensity of momentum that was almost painful till the matchless climax came. Then the passionate preacher stopped . . . suddenly . . . His spectacles were taken off. His manner became subdued and solemn. Leaning over the pulpit, with his right hand and index finger thrown sharply forward, with a fiery penetration of eye, and a marvelous inflection of voice, with a most adroit assumption of the personal character of the petitioners themselves . . . he exclaimed: "Gentlemen and honorable members of the General Court of Massachusetts assembled, *all these things will we do for you if you will vote for our bill to-morrow! And we will finish Bunker Hill Monument in the bargain! Will you do it?* WILL YOU DO IT?"

He stood waiting as if in anxious silence for an answer. And there seemed to go up a long-drawn, silent vote of relief. "NO MORE LOTTERIES!" It must have been registered in heaven.[56]

It was at least confirmed the next day when the monument proposal was overwhelmingly rejected. Perhaps equally strong was the opposition of the women of the state who agreed to pay for the completion of the memorial rather than have it finished by lottery.

Lotteries were also an issue in Vermont at this time. On October 28, 1825, a committee on education had reported favorably to the legislature on a state lottery for schools, arguing that it was the "prevailing dictate of wisdom and sound policy" to divert the "thousand little streams that flow away from us" and direct them "into the bosom of our own benevolent and public institutions."

Nevertheless, on November 14, the bill was rejected. Because of agitation to reintroduce the matter at the 1826 session, the governor declared in his message that for more than "twenty years past, the Legislature . . . has uniformly manifested its disapprobation of raising money by lotteries for any purpose whatsoever," and that he believed the "great body" of citizens were opposed. "Indeed the principles of morality in Vermont must suffer a sad decline, before this species of gambling will be sanctioned by the government, or approved by the people." He admitted that there had been a large sale of chances during the past year and that there should be an investigation of why the old grants were continuing, seemingly undiminished, year after year. Legislative concurrence came in the rejection of a lottery bill by a vote of 194 to 7 and the enactment of a $500 vendor's license to curtail sales. In 1827 the Brattleboro *Messenger* began a series of attacks on the system for moral reasons. The same year the governor asked for a stricter statute since the existing one was not a sufficient handicap. The money received, "although expended for the best of purposes," would never repay the community for the "various species of immorality" that had received encouragement. A prohibitive charge of $1,000 for a vendor's license was enacted and a penalty of $2,000 set on violators. Apparently the active opposition of the government, the high price of doing business, and the vigorous enforcement of the laws succeeded in ending lotteries for all practical intents in Vermont, though they were still not legally proscribed.[57]

Maine, only six years a state, was in the throes of the system in 1826 with two large lotteries sanctioned that year. Nevertheless, opposition was appearing. A clear picture of events was presented in 1827 by "Civis" (F. O. J. Smith), who evidently considered the subject touchy, for he did not sign his name to his *Dissertation on the Nature and Effects of Lottery Systems,* and he also mentioned the possibility of stirring up hatred and that a Kentuckian was killed for injuring an agent's feelings. He reported that Portland alone had over twenty-five shops, besides the public houses, where tickets could be bought. In fact, chances were so easily obtained, "or as easily made," that there was no pecuniary limit to how many persons could enter the business. He had seen "bastard" numbers being sold that "looked truly solemn." They were signed in a red ink that completely faded away after purchase. The people of Maine, he avowed, were too poor to stand the drain of such events as the third class of the Cumberland and Oxford Canal lottery, which cost the public over $6,390 to raise $3,510, the difference going to the managers and agents.[58] Experience was to prove him correct, but until a later day the lottery continued undiminished in Maine.

At the same time in New Hampshire Governor Benjamin Pierce's plea that something be done about the sale of "foreign" tickets led to increased fines for all unauthorized undertakings. The Assembly also showed its attitude by refusing three petitions for new ventures on the grounds that they were "inexpedient." One last attempt in that state came in 1829 when the New Hampshire Canal and Steam-Boat Company vainly requested permission to hold a $100,000 lottery.

Meanwhile, in New York, Yates & McIntyre were having their troubles. Correspondence between them and their colleague, the Reverend Eliphalet Nott, Union College president, revealed the maneuvering of the lottery lobby in the state legislature. Henry Yates wrote Nott early in 1827 that the sales had been good outside New York during the past year and would be good there if the state would exclude "foreign" chances, especially those of Rhode Island and some of the other New England states that undersold theirs. Their lobbyists were working for this and also to keep down the talk of abolition, which was proving disastrous. In February 1827 the company was faced with an adverse legislative report by a committee under Samuel Starkweather, who, Henry Yates claimed, was influenced by Francis Granger and John Canfield Spencer.[59] On February 21, J. B. Yates wrote this committee that, if legally required, he could prove that from

this laborious, perplexing and perilous business, pursued by us with unremitting assiduity, for some years, under our contract, we have not yet realized a single dollar of profit; and but for the avails of more advantageous contracts, made in other states, and for the timely assistance received from the institution [Union College], and from personal friends in this state, we must, with all our *supposed extravagant gains*, before this, have been involved in irretrievable ruin.

Since by their agreement 8.75 per cent of the ticket sales went to the college, it is not surprising that an equally wry picture was constantly portrayed to Nott, with dark overtones of unsold tickets and bad debts.[60]

In the meantime other events were affecting the system's future in New York. Early in 1827 the influential *Evening Post,* under the editorship of William Cullen Bryant, once more came out with a strong blast against lotteries, and in August announced it would no longer accept their advertisements.[61] Israel Corse, a Hicksite Quaker, actively entered the fight and widely publicized his views.[62] The same year the Public School Society of New York, which received a considerable part of its income from its half-share of dealers' license fees, advocated a strong law to curtail if not prohibit lotteries and presented a memorial to that effect to the Assembly.[63] On January 2, 1828, Oliver G. Kane, secretary of the National Marine Company, killed himself, leaving a note saying his was the "Tragedy of the Gamester." His accounts were short $140,000, mainly lost through lotteries.[64] Adding fuel to the flames was George Brewster, Jay Street Academy teacher. His published speech, *An Oration on the Evils of Lotteries,* subtitled "Advice to Those Who Would Make Haste to be Rich" and citing the text, "The love of money is the Root of All Evil," contained the usual arguments of managerial frauds, abuse of the poor, and encouragement of crime.[65]

The results of these blows showed up in Yates & McIntyre's sales. They had begun drawing the "Literature Lottery" on May 20, 1823, at bimonthly intervals and the first year sold approximately 99 per cent of all tickets. In 1825 a slow decline set in, but up to 1826 over 93 per cent was sold. Conditions began becoming worse, however. In June and December 1828 the rate of ticket sales fell to 66.6 and 61.3 per cent respectively. On January 13, 1829, the company lamented that they could seldom form a scheme that would sell half its chances and that sales in the larger classes would not reach even one-third. The April report on the literature lottery bore them out — only 37.5 per cent of the tickets had been sold. The seriousness of the situation from the company's viewpoint was obvious.[66] The handwriting was on the wall for all to see.

New York public opinion, now thoroughly aroused, became impatient of delay. This was reflected by the verdict of a legislative committee, appointed to investigate the feasibility of repealing all lotteries, that it was "no longer a question but what lotteries are bad, but how soon can they be stopped." All authorizations made previous to 1814 had been drawn, but Yates & McIntyre owed Union College $143,516.58. Despite the "pernicious" effects of the system, the group felt that the state should neither break faith by annulling its grants nor try to terminate them through purchase by the state treasury. A way out was found when the brokers agreed to conclude their operations in 1834 if they were not the subject of any proceedings prior to 1835, "inasmuch as every attack upon our rights has proved a serious injury." This solution was approved by a joint resolution of both houses. Nevertheless, the firm complained to Nott on April 21, 1830, that all they were getting was the "filthy abuse and painful odium attached to the lottery business."

Concurrent with this battle was one in Pennsylvania where the press was baying increasingly at the heels of the promoters. Typical was the November 10, 1827, issue of the *Rural Repository*, describing the drawing of the thirty-second class of the Pennsylvania Union Canal Lottery. Among the sordid crowd of lottery patrons "there was the miserable besotted drunkard, dreaming upon oceans of gin twist and brandy, which he foolishly supposed would flow before him from the fraction of a ticket which he held in his drink-enfeebled hand. There too . . . was the poor, dejected, almost helpless widow . . ." *Niles' Register* rejoined the fight on June 14, 1828, and the *Christian Spectator* gleefully reported a memorial to the legislature, signed by the mayor and other citizens of Philadelphia, asking for abolition. The *Spectator* from time to time in 1828 denounced the absurdity of a tax that cost about "225%" to collect, the fact that it had cost the people $3,000,533 to raise $150,000 for the canal. Through a contributor the journal called upon the holders of grants to give them up for the sake of mankind because the states could not abolish them because of commitments. "God Almighty will blow upon that institution" which did not relinquish them.[67]

Petitions descended upon the Pennsylvania Assembly from all parts of the state. In February 1828 a legislative committee investigated the expediency of repealing the franchises and further restricting "foreign" billets. It reported that Yates & McIntyre's contract for the Union Canal scheme ran until December 31, 1829, and that since some $64,000 was still due, nothing could be done until that time, but recommended that the scheme be ended then. Out-of-state tickets were difficult to suppress as long as legal lotteries existed, since they afforded facilities "to evade the laws, superadded by the temptation to do so." [68]

The question was injected into the Pennsylvania political campaign of 1828. The new Working Men's Party denounced lotteries as one of the four chief evils facing the laborer. They came out against the system each year until their newspaper, the *Mechanic's Free Press,* was discontinued in 1831. Upon the decision of the government to renew the Union Canal contract on the basis that the obligation of 1821 had not been fulfilled, the *Press* in 1829 attacked the lottery as one of six means "whereby the labourer has been defrauded of the work of his hands." The next year the party in its city and county conventions denounced raffles, and their legislative candidates were pledged to utmost efforts to end them — whether "instituted for the building of churches or the cutting of canals." Their conventions viewed lotteries as "an appendage, if not a component part of chartered monopolies." They bitterly avowed there were approximately two hundred ticket offices in Philadelphia and an even greater number of persons engaged in hawking chances. The itinerant vendor "assails the poor man at his labour, enters the abode of the needy, and by holding out false promises of wealth, induces him to hazard his little all on the demoralizing system." [69]

In 1830 Joseph Hemphill introduced a resolution in the legislature of Pennsylvania favoring congressional action to deprive all states and territories of the right to authorize lotteries after February 22, 1837. It was evidentially tabled.[70] The time for a definite stand by Pennsylvania or for positive abolition of all lotteries by any state had not yet arrived.

Chapter XI

The Fight for Abolition, 1830–1860

Tis the last day of drawing, now dawns to our view
And we breathe to the Lott'ry a final adieu;
All its gay splendid Prizes, will soon be no more,
And Fate puts her seal, upon Fortune's chief store.
I'll not leave thee, old friend, tho' death claims thee now.
At thine own well-known shrine, for the last time I'll bow;
Thy glory still burns, though thy frame's growing cold,
And thou sett'st like the sun, in an Ocean of gold.[1]

By 1830 the lottery reform movement was taking definite shape and making itself felt in most states. This was the beginning of a period characterized by Ralph Waldo Emerson as leading to the greatest scope for the doctrine of reform that the history of the world had ever seen. It seemed to him in 1841 that every human institution was being questioned, and not a "town, statute, rite, calling, man, or woman, but is threatened by the new spirit."

Literally, it was a time when slavery, intemperance, war, prisons, and other evidences of social maladjustment were under close scrutiny by skeptical Americans. Inevitably lotteries had to face the test. The pattern of lottery abolition generally coincided with that of other reforms. (1) The antilottery drive was in line with the prevailing concept that man could and should better his condition. (2) Although the drive was not the result of a national crisis, the Panic of 1837 probably hastened action in some states. (3) The speed of the movement decreased with latitude, the South being slowest to react. (4) In all cases, however, abolition action by a state always preceded that of the federal government. (5) And though lacking the usual international connections, (6) abolition could claim a religious motivation.[2]

Generally, as shown by the taunts of reformers, organized religions, with the exception of the Quakers, were slow to take an active stand in opposition to lotteries, although religious arguments had been used against them from the beginning. It was not until the trend of public opinion became more obvious that church leaders acted boldly and supported positions previously held by scattered clergymen, religious periodicals, and congregations. For example, the Presbyterian General Assembly of 1830 declared that even though lotteries were sanctioned by legislative acts, they could be regarded in no other light than "legalized gambling." [3] More typical, however, was what occurred at the General Conference of the Methodist Church meeting at Philadelphia on May 1, 1832. A decision on the morality of lotteries had been postponed in 1812 and not mentioned since. At the 1832 session Henry G. Leigh, of the Virginia Conference, seconded by Nathan Bangs of New York, moved that the second section of the second chapter of the Discipline be amended to read, "indulging sinful tempers, words, buying or selling lottery tickets, or disobedience to the order and discipline of the church, etc.," would be grounds for a dismissal. The motion was tabled, however, and never came to a vote.[4]

This seeming unwillingness to take a positive stand can possibly be explained by facts related to the separation of church and state, after which the churches had not been in a position to dictate policies of government — and probably they felt some reticence even to make suggestions. Then, too, it must be remembered that the churches, with the constant exception of the Quakers, had used lotteries for their own benefit. A denunciation of the system, therefore, could be viewed as biting the hand that had fed them, or an admission of moral error with the church a partner in immoral actions.

Undoubtedly, the major factors leading to the abolition of lotteries were the social effects and the frauds, which occurred at every level from the ticket vendors up through the contractors. Outstanding examples of abuse usually acted as catalysts for public opinion, and people began to realize that even the most careful supervision was ineffective. Backed by concrete examples, the enemies of the lottery changed their tactics from debating the issue of biblical legality to strongly denouncing the vice accompanying the lottery's use. General knowledge that less and less money was going to the intended beneficiary and more and more into the pockets of others made it urgent not only to interdict new schemes but also to terminate quickly those in legal operation. The struggle was to be a long one.

The mounting wave of criticism was also evident in the states' efforts to enforce old lottery laws and to write new ones aimed at making the system as acceptable as possible short of outright abolition. Connecticut's answer in 1830 was a joint committee of the legislature to study the problem. Its findings were incorporated in a comprehensive statute covering practically all phases of the lottery, with special emphasis upon those that had been most condemned or most subject to abuse. A year later the state required an immediate balance sheet from the institutions holding grants, showing total gains and losses, and an annual report thereafter. At the same time Vermont cracked down on H. F. Saunders for issuing tickets from Jersey City, New Jersey, in a bogus project entitled "The Green Mountain Lottery of Vermont, for the benefit of the Green Mountain Turnpike Association." According to the Boston *Evening Transcript*, February 19, 1831, Saunders was fined the whole amount of the scheme, or $402,660.

Indicative of the growing concern about lotteries was the report published in 1831 in the staid *Journal of the Franklin Institute* of Pennsylvania of James K. Casey's patent for "an improvement in the mode of Instituting and Drawing Lotteries." Casey's mode was to be marked by the absence of "those excitements and appeals which are now so constantly resorted to, and which are alike injurious to the public morals and to the condition of the poorer classes of society, who should be assiduously excluded from all modes of enterprise inconsistent with their means and their duties." Though the device's "chief glory" was its death blow to "schemes of morbid excitement, and of complicated fraud and treachery," it would attract those who wasted their "time, money, and morals, at Faro-tables, or other places of unlicensed, improper, and unfair adventure."[5] Unfortunately for lottery promoters, Casey was born too late.

In New York, Yates & McIntyre thought they had obtained at least a temporary respite from legal attack, but their troubles were far from over. In 1830 a grand jury of the City of New York returned a stinging indictment of lotteries as "an evil of the most alarming nature, both in a moral and pecuniary point of view." It found that about fifty-two classes had been drawn each year, offering 1,857,000 tickets and about $9,270,000 in prizes. Since there was "much apparent mystery" in Yates & McIntyre's operation, the jury was unable to state accurately the expense and profits.[6] Yates & McIntyre reacted to this "old slang" by prophesying that nothing would come of it unless "our *virtuous* corporation [the City of New York] takes the matter up, and present it to the consideration of our *virtuous* legislature." Nevertheless, they requested their old friend, President Nott of Union College, to write an article in defense of lotteries.[7]

The tempo of the attack against these contractors was also increasing in Pennsylvania. In 1831 Governor George Wolf questioned the franchise of the Union Canal Company and said that laws against "foreign" tickets would fail unless that license was voided. He suggested that with the expiration two years hence of the company's contract with Yates & McIntyre all such undertakings cease.[8] An investigation by the Ways and Means Committee on this portion of the governor's speech whitewashed both parties to the contract and suggested that the state buy it by paying the remaining sum to be raised.[9]

Meanwhile two more publications had joined the Pennsylvania fight. Daniel B. Shrieves, editor of the *Independent Expositor and National Philanthropist*, devoted five issues in 1831 to exposing the abuses of the Union Canal Lottery. But undoubtedly the most persistent foe was the Quaker weekly, *The Friend*, published in Philadelphia. From 1829 to 1895 scarcely an issue failed to comment adversely upon the existence of lotteries somewhere in the United States. On February 21, 1829, it quoted at length the speech of Philadelphia's John Sergeant before Congress — how because of improvements in speedy drawing, the lottery had become the "most rapid and powerful kind of gambling now existing"; how "in a thousand cases" it had urged men to acts that had "brought them to a jail, if not to the gallows"; and how only those venture "who ought not to buy them; who are in no circumstance to do so." With the question a pressing one in Pennsylvania, the *Friend* urged citizens to stop bearing "patiently, or, perhaps, more properly speaking, pusillanimously," this evil and to form a society to combat it.[10]

On December 10, 1831, the *Friend* announced that a citizen's group had been formed to study the matter and had called a town meeting to petition the legislature for abolition. It enjoined all Quakers to attend since it was "one of those occasions on which our civil and Christian duties coalesce." [11] The first meeting of record was held on December 12 in the state supreme court room with B. W. Richards as chairman and George Toland as secretary. George M. Stroud outlined conditions in the state, and W. M. Meredith read a memorial for presentation to the Assembly. Ten thousand copies of Stroud's report were ordered, and the appeal to the government was published in the daily press. The petition made not only the usual generic accusations, but also attacked the canal franchise on the grounds that the original grant had been fulfilled, possibly as early as 1830.[12]

At the opening of the Assembly in 1832 Governor Wolf re-emphasized the need for immediate action against lotteries since Yates & McIntyre's agreement would expire the next year. On February 10, a house committee condemned lotteries in the strongest terms. It declared that the canal company was demanding more rights, yet its agents paid no more for classes involving millions than it had for ones consisting of thousands of dollars. The classes had grown from $318,300 in 1824 to $5,216,220 in 1831. Why should the broker howl? His "contract for enormous gains was but a lottery, and if he has this time drawn a blank, he cannot complain with any propriety when he reflects how many blanks he has sold to others." Yates & McIntyre had already overdrawn $65,000, and this should be a lesson to the legislature on the danger of trusting any system based upon immoral foundations.[13]

Ten days later Archibald McIntyre petitioned the legislature to spare his privilege because he was losing money. After all, the undertaking had been recommended to him by that body as a public-spirited measure, and three lawyers, John Sergeant, Horace Binney, and James C. Biddle, had assured him the law was on his side.[14] Next day a report of a senate committee apparently agreed with him, for it stated that the canal company was entitled to raise $124,-072.54 more before their franchise would be completed. They did recommend, however, that when the contract with Yates & McIntyre expired, the right should be bought by the state.[15] To the reformers, this was not a popular verdict and part of the dissension over this interpretation was voiced by the pamphlet, *Let Not the Faith, Nor the Laws of the Commonwealth, Be Violated.*[16] At this distance in time, however, it is impossible to determine whether the license was legally in force or not, for each side drew conflicting conclusions from the same law and could quote statistics to support its view.

The seriousness of the situation was evident, nevertheless. From the three ticket offices in Philadelphia in 1809, the number had grown to sixty in 1827, 177 in 1831 (an increase of 117 in four years), and would be over 200 in 1833. In 1831 Yates & McIntyre alone drew 450 classes. In 1832 the various Philadelphia offices sold tickets in 420 different drawings with prizes amounting to $53,136,-930.[17] Obviously, despite the 1791 law that prohibited sale of "foreign" tickets in Pennsylvania, all of these schemes did not originate in the state. Public opinion, in general, had been so unconcerned and law enforcement so lax that Philadelphians reportedly spent $1,500,-000 a year on tickets, the greater part of which left the state or benefited the agents. The small fine against the sale of foreign tickets was paid regularly by many offices as a sort of tax. Altogether, it was the usual picture of a law's being circumvented by public opinion.

Despite the conflicting reports of the house and senate committees, an administration bill for the abolition of all lotteries was introduced in 1832. A state-wide organization publicized the issue by circulating a petition favoring adoption of the measure. In March, the measure passed the house seventy-six to six but met defeat in the senate.[18] The antilottery forces, however, continued to press for immediate passage in 1833. Memorials reflecting this view poured in.

At another public meeting in Philadelphia on January 12, 1833, Job R. Tyson, a prominent Philadelphia lawyer and Quaker, read an essay on the "history, extent, and pernicious consequences of that species of gambling [lotteries]," and 5,000 copies were printed for gratuitous distribution throughout the United States.[19] Well bolstered with facts, the work was by far the most important to come out of the movement. It undoubtedly speeded final abolition in Pennsylvania and was used virtually as a handbook by antilottery fighters throughout the country. Tyson cited well-documented cases of fraud and numerous occasions when crimes had been committed to get money for speculation. One was the case of Clew, a porter for the Bank of the United States, who after many smaller thefts was apprehended stealing $2,000 to pay his debts for tickets. He had had on hand 2,327 chances, which after being drawn produced less than twenty dollars. Tyson related, also, that in 1832 of the 420 classes with tickets for sale in Pennsylvania, all but twenty-six were illegal under the law against "foreign" tickets — a law that "ever since its enactment has been constantly infringed with scarcely an attempt at concealment."

Probably Tyson's most telling evidence was a certified list of debtors taken from the records of the Insolvent Court for the City and County of Philadelphia. Included were such petitions as that of a young man who had begun speculating in the lottery and in six months had lost all he had and owed upwards of $3,300. In some cases the debts owed ticket agents were as high as $30,000. Tyson's list was by no means complete, for many who lost money in lotteries did not disclose the fact in their petitions and others were yet to be driven into the court by their creditors. But for the years 1830–1833 Tyson found fifty-five cases in this single court.

On February 2, 1833, the *Friend* happily announced passage of an antilottery bill by the senate; by March 1 the measure had been accepted by both houses and the governor. It declared that after December 31 "all and every lottery and device in the nature of lotteries shall be entirely abolished, and are declared thenceforth unauthorized and unlawful." Any person aiding in the sale of tickets, or connected with the managing or drawing of such an undertaking, would either forfeit a sum from $100 to $1,000 for each offense or be imprisoned for not more than six months at the discretion of the court.

From 1747 to 1833 records have been found of the existence of 176 separate Pennsylvania-authorized lotteries. Since several of these were operated jointly, they benefited 187 institutions or groups. Thus, before abolition more than 8,000,000 tickets were placed on the market and prizes of about $50,000,000 were offered.

On April 3, 1833, at the insistence of George Toland,[20] the legislature instructed the governor to transmit copies of the abolition statute to executives of each state, who in turn were to ask their assemblies to cooperate with Pennsylvania in putting an end to lotteries. It was also to be requested of the President of the United States to suggest that Congress halt lotteries in the District of Columbia. But still the crusaders were not satisfied. The *Friend* urged its readers to "conjure our fellow members in religious professions every where to be continually on the alert, to improve every opening . . . for effecting the total eradication of a system so corrupt in its origin, and demoralizing in its operation." [21] In November a new edition of Tyson's pamphlet was ordered printed and sent throughout the states still holding lotteries.

But Pennsylvania barely beat several other states under the wire for the honor of being the first to outlaw such schemes completely. In Massachusetts public opinion had spoken decisively against new authorizations in 1828, but the evasion of the law against "foreign" chances aroused little comment until an occurrence in February 1833 electrified the state. An outstanding young man named Ackers, thirty-five years old and for the past ten years bookkeeper and treasurer of a large Boston mercantile house, committed suicide. He had gambled away his property and $18,000 of the company's funds in lottery speculation. The General Court was then in session, and Joseph T. Buckingham of the house of representatives, learning the facts of the case, successfully moved for a committee to inquire into the lottery situation. The next day, February 12, Governor Levi Lincoln sent to the legislature a memorial for total abolition throughout the United States, signed by such worthy citizens as William Sullivan, James Read, Charles Tappan, Abbott Lawrence, Stephen Fairbanks, Gustavus Tuckerman, William Sturgis, and Charles Sprague, representing an association of citizens "who with commendable zeal" were trying to arrest these frauds. The governor condemned the high-handed manner in which the lottery laws were being violated by open sale of "foreign" and fictitious tickets, the debauching and cheating of the poor, and the encouragement of violations of trust and heinous crimes.[22]

The legislative group, under Buckingham, found among other things that in the February term of the municipal court of Boston the grand jury had brought seventy-six indictments for violations of the lottery laws. Large numbers of "spurious" tickets were being manufactured and sold in the state, and the yearly traffic in chances in Boston alone amounted to more than $1,000,000. They recommended that the General Court take advantage of the "temporary excitement, to effect a permanent good" and that other governments be asked to cooperate in the fight for total abolition.[23]

Massachusetts had her Tyson in the person of George W. Gordon. His *Lecture on Lotteries*, delivered before the Boston Young Men's Society on March 12, 1833, and widely circulated in pamphlet form, was favorably reviewed in a number of magazines.[24] In addition to the usual complaints of fraud and enticement of the poor, he asserted that this illegal business in Boston was highly organized, with vendors appointed to each district to visit the taverns, barrooms, cellars, arriving ships, homes, and places of business. Appearing probably a short time afterwards was an anonymous tract, *Candid Remarks Addressed to Christians on the Subject of Their Having Concern in Lotteries,* which contained mainly a rehash of the old question of biblical sanction.[25]

These combined pressures led to the law of March 23, 1833, which marked the legal end of such schemes in Massachusetts. By this statute any person that "shall make, sell, or offer for sale or shall have in his possession with intent to sell," or be concerned in any drawing, was to be fined not less than $100 or more than $2,000. The second offense was made subject to the same fine and from three to twelve months in jail. People advertising tickets, a lottery where chances could be bought, or in any manner enticing others to adventure, were to forfeit from $30 to $100 for each offense. The punishment for making or selling billets in fictitious lotteries was from one to three years confinement in the state prison, and anyone bringing such offenders to court was to receive $50 from the state treasury for each conviction. All prize money was to be confiscated by the commonwealth.

The rest of New England's conscience suddenly awakened. In Maine the two big lotteries in operation, the Cumberland and Oxford Canal and the "steam navigation" scheme, came under fire. In 1832 the legislature decided that the former had raised its money and forbade further sales. The governor, upon looking into the affairs of the navigation company in March 1833 concluded that it too should stop drawing. While this action legally ended lotteries in Maine for all intents and purposes, the echoes continued. The managers of the navigation scheme took their case to court, where it was still pending in 1835. A joint select committee of both houses of the legislature revealed on February 27, 1835, that the directors were asking $10,794.34 for expenses out of a total of $16,126.55 gained from 200 classes. The next year a senate group concluded that the state was saddled with a system "which the progress of Society had disabled from doing good, but not from doing harm." When the Assembly agreed that the contract was voided since those in charge had violated their trust, the company dropped the matter and the last local authorization was terminated.[26]

New Hampshire, with no local grant outstanding, nevertheless was troubled by lotteries originating in other states. A correspondent wrote J. R. Tyson in 1833 that "until recently foreign tickets were sold in almost every bookseller's shop in the state in open defiance of the law . . . when on account of the great disgust against the whole lottery system among the greater part of the community, their sale, has nearly . . . ceased." Nevertheless, even after imprisonment had been added to the 1828 fine of $50 to $100, illegal markets were flourishing in 1834.[27]

Vermont had not chartered a lottery since 1804 and had passed a law setting licenses at $1,000 each and a penalty of $2,000 for violations. The fact that the former figure was prohibitive in this area of small sales and that the law was rigorously enforced probably accounts for Tyson's statement in 1833 that such schemes were dead in that state.[28]

The same year Connecticut's governor unsuccessfully recommended an antilottery bill to his Assembly, and Rhode Island's contribution was the publication of one of the most readable opposition works to come out of the campaign. This book by "Sui Generis: Alias, Thomas Man" was entitled *Picture of a Factory Village to Which Are Annexed, Remarks on Lotteries*. The latter portion was a biting satire written as if a broker, Sharker, were telling the truth to his patrons and giving away the tricks of the trade. When asked why he sold tickets, he replied: "The Profit, equal to 29 1/6 per cent . . . Who would not sell tickets at this rate?" He advertised:

> Come, ye Fortune Seekers, to our Office, and buy *Three Tickets;* you are sure of *One Prize,* and may draw *Four.*
> *At the Junction of Folly and Indiscretion-streets,*
> No. 1000—"Don't Forget the Number"
> "Broadway leads directly to our office."
> "THE GOLD MINE"
> "Ever True to its Motto."
> FORTUNE'S HOME FOREVER

☞ Where have been, or will be paid to Fortune's Favorites, to the amount of more than *One Million of Money, in Gold.* A *Few Blanks* in the last Grand State Lottery, drawn in this town, at the State House, for sale (if called for soon) . . . at a liberal discount. The chance of success to the purchaser of one of these, will be about the same, as a new Ticket in the next class.

Man was most bitter in his description, saying, "The Broker's wealth is the Heart and Soul of the Beggar's Wallet — the accumulated Mites of the Widow and Orphans — the sigh and tear of Disappointment and Distress." The tax on the country of "all the *Billiard Tables* and every other species of Gaming" was nothing compared to the lottery. Then why did it flourish? "It is the effect of 'that Little Flippant Thing' called *Fashion,* at whose Shrine are offered daily sacrifices, from the Crowned Monarch, down to the Hatless Vagrant." Then, too, as "*Mammon is the God of this World,* and money the Ruling Passion of most men,*" this appeared the shortest method of obtaining it.[29]

In New York, meanwhile, Yates & McIntyre's troubles had been mounting. A new thorn in the person of Palmer Canfield, a reformed lottery dealer, was irritating them. Canfield argued that their contract for the Union College scheme had been voided by their selling more chances than authorized. On June 29, 1831, McIntyre wrote President Nott:

You have probably seen the malignant attack on permutation [ternary] lotteries, by that meanest and worst of all men, xxxx, as also the unadvised and ill-natured remarks of the editors of various journals, which xxxx, by his importunities, induced them to publish. — Had the original slander been confined to the filthy Lottery Argus, we should think it unworthy of notice; but as other journals have been deceived, and published slanders founded on Canfield's, we think we are compelled to notice these attacks.[30]

A break in the working relationship between Yates & McIntyre and President Nott, however, occurred in 1832 when the firm claimed to have fulfilled its contract. Dr. Nott brought suit, and as late as 1849 the matter was unsettled. Although it is impossible to determine the exact sum the school obtained, it was doubtless less than the $272,000, plus interest, originally named, since the largest figure ever given for the receipts was $225,773.14.[31]

Canfield's claims were supported by a grand jury's report in 1832, but the attorney general ruled that the law permitted the drawings to continue until April 21, 1834. In 1833 Canfield petitioned the state senate to take action, alleging 245 classes totaling $40,000,000 had been finished. Yates & McIntyre generally ignored these charges, ascribing them to a "demonical malignity . . . laboring for years without a known cause, to do them injury by misrepresentation." The Assembly appointed a special committee to confer with Yates & McIntyre and a compromise was reached whereby the contractors agreed to give up their right as of December 31, 1833. An act of April 30, 1833, made this official.

Yates & McIntyre thereupon inaugurated an intensive campaign to make the most of the waning year. C. D. Arfwedson, a British traveler, described the scene in 1833:

In no place have I seen so many Lottery Offices as in the City of New York. They are numberless in Broadway. Their puffing exceeds all belief. Each collector called heaven and earth to witness that he was the luckiest among his worthy colleagues. One of them went so far as to affirm, that he had paid prizes to a larger amount than would liquidate all the debts of bankrupts in the United States.

Following the serious cholera epidemic he reported agents used the newspapers to congratulate the people on the plague's disappearance and to invite them to make a speedy investment in the "lucky wheel." [32] Drawings continued up to the very last moment.

With the close of Yates & McIntyre's operation of the Union College franchise, local New York schemes ended. But there still remained the problem of "foreign" tickets. A new law, resulting from a senate committee's report in February 1834, provided for a fine of $150 or three months imprisonment for persons involved in any such sale.

In other states 1833 was a fruitful year for antilottery forces. Public opinion in New Jersey forced abandonment of a plan to charter a lottery to build a penitentiary, and the North Carolina lottery business was reported in the doldrums because of suspended schemes and lack of ticket offices. In March, Virginia started the long and tedious road toward abolition when the House of Delegates voted 97 to 2 to cease all lottery franchises on a date to be determined. The bill was adopted by both houses, but a senate amendment sent it back to the house on the last day of the term, leaving no time to act on it. [33] After a glut of drawings, Louisiana revoked in April all lottery privileges as of January 1, 1834; anyone drawing or selling tickets after that date was liable to fines of from $1,000 to $5,000 and three to twelve months in jail. In 1838 the state made it clear that this law applied equally to enterprises drawn outside the state.

By the end of 1833 lottery abolition was well launched, but all voices had not yet joined the chorus. With the exceptions noted, newspapers championed the system or kept silent. As the *Friend* complained, "The influence of the lottery brokers, as advertising customers has completely silenced that Cerberus, the daily press." The position of Horace Greeley, a man well known later for philanthropic zeal, was indicative of the state of affairs during this period. In 1833, the last year of drawings in New York, he and Francis V. Story issued a triweekly, the *Constitutionalist*, which in spite of its dignified title was the avowed organ of lotteries. Its columns contained a card stating that "Greeley & Story . . . respectfully solicit the patronage of the public to their business of letter-press printing, particularly lottery-printing, such as schemes, periodicals, and so forth, which will be executed on favorable terms." The *Gentleman's Magazine* was able to spin a tale concerning one of these schemes without moralizing. The *Ladies Companion,* also, translated a French story in which the proponent of lotteries got the best of the argument by declaring, "Every time I give my five franc piece for a quarter of a ticket, I receive more satisfaction than if I had spent it at the Restaurateur, for I purchase the privilege of raising air castles for the next twenty-four hours." As late as 1839 Greeley's *New Yorker* and the *Corsair* published identical stories in which the hero after winning a lottery lived happily ever after.[34]

But the year 1834 saw the abolition fight renewed on two fronts — to kill the projects in additional states and to make sure they stayed dead in those where such action had already been taken. The latter was necessary because the system was not dying quietly. Reformers soon learned that passing laws was not enough. Drawings were merely shifted to friendly communities, while the brokers complained through their lobbies that the legal measures against them were violations of their civil or charter rights.

In Massachusetts, after the "famous Ackers' suicide," a legislative investigation probed continued ticket sales and a private society was created to prevent and punish violations of the statute. In New York the *Mercury* was quoted as saying that there was underground lottery activity in that state in 1834 and that the dealers were still keeping up their old signs. A report by a New York senate committee studying the sale of "foreign" tickets led not only to a new and more detailed law on the subject, but also to formation of a citizens' group to aid the government in stamping out infractions.

In Pennsylvania, the *Friend* believed that Philadelphia, too, was still the scene of covert sales — "witness the large letters in flaring red and other dazzling colours, to be seen in some windows" — and demanded that the "mischief" be driven out of its hiding place. On August 9, 1834, Hazard's *Register of Pennsylvania* reported the formation on June 6 of the Pennsylvania Society for the Suppression of Lotteries. Alexander Henry was a prime mover, Thomas C. James was president, and J. R. Tyson one of the counselors.[35] This group took the whole nation for its battleground. Offenders of the Pennsylvania law were warned of the penalties through the newspapers, and those that persisted were haled into court by the society. Tyson wrote a new pamphlet, *Address to the People of Pennsylvania and the United States by the Pennsylvania Society for the Suppression of Lotteries* (Philadelphia, 1834) charting the progress made by the various states. This, along with copies of the Pennsylvania and Massachusetts laws on the subject, was sent throughout the country. When the Pennsylvania constitutional convention of 1837 met, lottery opponents, fearing that a future legislature might repeal the law of 1833, led a state-wide movement similar to that of 1831–1833 to get a prohibition inserted into the bill of rights. Despite numerous petitions, they failed.

Undoubtedly influenced by the success in other New England states, Rhode Island antilotterites made a strong fight in 1834 against the authorization of further school-fund lotteries. In May, Elisha R. Potter of South Kingston moved that the prevailing system be studied and compared to other governments' action, with a view to ending such ventures. The committee reported in June favoring abolition, with a resolution ordering the attorney general to draft such an act. But their findings were tabled, and a new lottery bill was introduced the same day. Opposition to this grant was led by Daniel G. Harris of Smithfield and the support by Christopher Allen of North Kingston. Harris succeeded in delaying the proposal for a time, but Allen argued that if it were not soon passed, the legislature would be forced to resort to a bank or land tax to supply the treasury. When Harris declared his belief that the people would prefer this resort, he was personally attacked by Allen, who claimed abolition was a "hobby" of Harris' and that he wished members would leave their pet ideas at home. He, Allen, on the other hand, was there free to act for the good of the state. How could they get along without the money?

At this point, James Allen, also of North Kingston, spoke characterizing lotteries as gambling and no less evil because of legal sanction. He cited figures to prove that the amount gained was a mere fraction of that sent from the state and advised immediate suppression. Despite Harris and Potter's enumeration of the hardships caused by the system, two days later Christopher Allen called up the bill again. Another debate ensued, with J. L. Tillinghast of Providence leading the compromise group. He admitted that popular feeling was against a renewal, but argued that the Assembly had not made the evil but merely turned it to a general good, that of educating their children. He feared the free school plan would fail if this revenue were stopped. After a speech in favor of the lottery by Jonah Titus of Scituate (an interesting fact in view of the notation on his ticket in 1824), the bill was passed and the license granted Yates & McIntyre.[36] Rhode Island was destined to have still another decade of such schemes.

The opposition was more successful elsewhere, however. In Connecticut in May 1834 a law ordered no lottery or class drawn under pretense of previous law except those made or published before June 3, 1834. Violations involved a fine up to $300 and/or maximum imprisonment of ninety days. The same penalty applied to selling or advertising *any* tickets. In Virginia a proposal for abolition passed the lower house without a dissenting vote in January, and was confirmed by the senate in February. The measure provided that after January 1, 1837, all such undertakings would be illegal and subject to heavy fines. Typically, however, this did not mark the end of lotteries in that state.

The Tennessee constitutional convention of 1834 saw a successful fight led by Chairman West H. Humphreys. A committee reported that the right of lottery franchise was "a power which they [the legislature] should not have, and that a prohibition to that effect should be part of our fundamental law." The majority agreed, and Article X, Section 5, of the constitution not only took away the power of making such grants but also required passage of laws to prohibit the sale of tickets. The latter requirement was complied

with on March 1, 1835, by an act repealing all such licenses and setting fines for violations.[37]

The farther south, the less spectacular were the results of lottery
opponents. In Maryland the 1834 battle was marked by unsuccessful
efforts to amend the constitution to forbid lotteries and to pass a
joint resolution of the legislature favoring abolition as soon as the
active grants were fulfilled. In line with their "wish . . . that the
lottery system shall expire at as early a day as practicable," all such
privileges were ordered transferred the next year to the state commissioners.[38] Despite this action, schemes still flourished. Consequently, in 1836 the house adopted a resolution unanimously denouncing the system, and a bill to confirm the 1834 action for abolition after the expiration of the grants was passed 62–7. This was
reinforced by a constitutional amendment in 1836 prohibiting sanctioning of schemes or sale of tickets after the end of current franchises. Once more, however, this failed to end the trouble.[39] In 1840
another Maryland constitutional amendment placed an immediate
ban on all state lotteries except those for institutions. These, known
as the "consolidated lotteries," had been sold to D. S. Gregory &
Company for $15,000 a year. The government had received in 1839
more than $25,000 from the system, of which approximately $10,000
was from license fees from the forty-three ticket agencies. In 1840
the rate of the contract was increased to $17,500.[40]

During 1834, also, South Carolina turned down a bill to end the
system as "inexpedient at the time." Slight tremors of conscience
nevertheless continued to ruffle the scene — for instance, the denunciation by the Charleston Union Presbytery on November 11,
1839, of a proposed lottery. This "splendid scheme" would prove
only a "lure to draw money from the thoughtless and inconsiderate."
The demoralizing tendency of this "species of gambling" was perhaps greater than any other as it was "more widely extended, em-
bracing almost every description of people" and was the "stepping
stone to most other games of hazard." [41] In several states where the
issue was not before the legislatures, other groups spoke out. The
Bethel Association of Alabama Baptists labeled raffles a "species of
gambling." [42] About the same time, as mentioned earlier, a formal
debate at the University of Georgia found the opponents of the
system successful, though it is not clear whether they won on speech
techniques or on moral grounds.[43]

In Arkansas, where no lottery had ever been licensed and private schemes had been outlawed in 1820, a fight took place in the constitutional convention of 1836. Victory went to the antilottery forces and Article VII is a model of brevity — "no lottery shall be authorized by this State, nor shall the sale of lottery tickets be allowed." [44] The 1838 Indiana Yearly Meeting of the Society of Friends reiterated their stand against lotteries or any other kind of gaming, "it being abundantly obvious, that those practices have a tendency to alienate the mind from the council of divine wisdom — and to foster those impure dispositions which lead to debauchery and wickedness." [45]

Something of the tactics used by lottery supporters is seen in Missouri's contradictory actions in 1835. At that time a law provided that after January 1, 1836, "all and every lottery . . . shall be utterly and entirely abolished" on pain of $500 to $10,000 in fines or six months in jail. Nevertheless, another paragraph in the same law stated that the "foregoing provision shall not be construed to extend to any lottery . . . now authorized by any law of this state." The franchise of the New Franklin lottery was repealed in 1839, but this action succeeded only in driving it from the state.

At least two other states felt the force of the agitation during the same period. Although Ohio had not authorized a lottery since 1828, "foreign" tickets continued to be advertised openly as late as 1845. The Cleveland *Herald*, January 4, 1834, carried an announcement by two Pennsylvania dealers that they were establishing offices outside that state. Such activities probably were one of the reasons for the formation of an Anti-Gambling Society at a public meeting in Cleveland on October 3, 1835. While the main motive was to combat a newly opened race track, its avowed aim was to end all gambling in the state.[46] The fight in Michigan was ended with the adoption of the constitution of 1835, Article XII, section 6, which forbade authorization of lotteries and sale of tickets.

The decade of the 1830's was one of almost universal change. It was as if mankind were rushing to found a new social order, repudiating the old as it went. Many innovations were made, but even more impressive was the demolition of old concepts. England passed the Reform Bill and abolished slavery in the British colonies; France outlawed the Loterie royale; Spain ended the Inquisition. And the United States kept pace. This period saw the dominance of Jacksonianism with all it meant to the common man, the rise of the American Anti-Slavery Society and the United States Temperance Union. The American Peace Society flourished, and organized labor, as well as countless other reform movements, had their spokesmen. The New England literary renaissance was well launched, and the anti-lottery crusade showed tangible results. It was a busy and fertile ten years; Americans could well afford to look back with satisfaction.

In regard to lotteries, the reform drive had produced prohibitory laws in twelve states by 1840, and in most of the other fourteen states the system seemed to be dying. Their very success made the lottery fighters most vulnerable; the remaining lotteries seemed small cause for alarm. It was easy to be sidetracked by economic problems growing out of the Panic of 1837 and be absorbed by the seemingly more pressing issues of slavery, territorial expansion, sectional disputes, threatened hostilities with England, and war with Mexico. Thus in the 1840's and 1850's the concerted drive against lotteries degenerated into limited skirmishes and spasmodic attacks led by the dedicated or the locally involved citizenry.

New England, one of the first regions to turn against the system, still had its troubles. Mrs. J. Thayer wrote in the *Boston Weekly Magazine* that although lotteries had been abolished in Massachusetts, there should be no rest until the offices had been "razed from our land." Consequently, to do her bit in exposing the "folly and vice," she contributed a story of the fall of a struggling young lawyer through such speculation. It was true that Boston was not guiltless, for during the early part of 1841 fourteen indictments were found against inhabitants for violations of state lottery laws.[47]

The last New England stronghold of the lottery, Rhode Island, underwent a new attack in 1840 led by Professor William Goddard of Brown University and other respected citizens. They petitioned the Assembly to end such projects and save the state the "enduring reproach" of being the last to do so. Their petition summarized customary charges that by this time had become standardized: (1) lotteries were liable to the strongest objections that could be cited against gambling and were more dangerous than most forms because they were less offensive to decorum and less alarming to the conscience; (2) they presented the strongest temptations to fraud on the part of all concerned either in the drawing or sale of tickets; (3) they acted as a tax upon the community — a tax paid mainly by those who could least afford it; (4) they were the parents of much of the pauperism of the land; (5) success was hardly less fatal than failure, since the fortunate adventurer was never satisfied; and (6) they were especially mischievous in America because of the nature of its institutions and the prevalence of the get-rich-quick mania. The memorial concluded with the opinion that the majority of the people in the state, regardless of party, favored abolition.[48]

Rowland G. Hazard, woolen manufacturer and well-known author on philosophical, political, and economic questions, contributed a pamphlet, *Lecture on the Causes and Decline of Political and National Morality* (Providence, 1841), in which he stressed the role played by lotteries. The legislature concurred and resolved that no future lottery should be granted and effective laws should be passed to prevent the sale of "foreign" tickets. Part of this was confirmed by a prohibition of future schemes in the constitution of 1842.

This action should have meant conclusion of Rhode Island lotteries with the expiration of Philip Case's contract in 1844. The only difficulty was that the constitution was interpreted as applying only to lotteries of the domestic variety. So it turned out that Rhode Island, and the firm of Daniel Paine, remained the center for lottery supplies for other states and a market for their wares. As a result Professor Goddard and his cohorts presented another memorial to the Assembly in 1844, accusing it of breaking faith if sales were allowed to continue. Repeated public protests resulted in the act of 1846 forbidding all dealings with lotteries in the state.[49] Thus was brought to an end a device that had dominated Rhode Island in several ways besides financial for approximately one hundred years.

The Delaware legislature declared in February 1841 that since "drawings of lotteries now under contract, and authorized by acts of the Legislature of this State, cannot at present be prohibited," they should be more closely regulated and those schemes not in the process of being drawn were declared null and void. Two years later it took over the Delaware College Lottery "for the more speedily and effectually raising and securing the payment of the balance of the money."

Congress belatedly fell in with the antilottery procession by banning all ticket sales in the District of Columbia after 1842. During the same year in neighboring Maryland an applicant for church membership felt called upon to repent his having sold lottery tickets and promised he would never again engage in the business "even to the smallest extent." [50] Missouri came up with an act in 1842 "abolishing all lotteries." However, the managers of the New Franklin Lottery, disregarding this law and the fact that its privilege had been repealed in 1839, transferred the right to Walter Gregory for payment of $250 semi-annually over a thirty-year period. The venture, known as the Missouri State Lottery, reached such proportions by 1853 as to announce "two schemes drawn daily." In 1855 reformers succeeded in having several agents prosecuted and fined $1,000 for selling tickets, only to have the decision reversed by the state supreme court. The fight continued, but political influence kept the company in business until after the Civil War.[51]

In 1843 Alabama rescinded all of her licenses as of May 1 and placed a penalty of $100 to $500 on unauthorized chances. Nevertheless, ten years later the state fell from grace and sanctioned a $25,000 scheme for the Southern Military Academy of Chambers County. A contemporary observer related that the contract went to a "sharp man" who inflamed the state with prospects of riches until the "country, in many portions, was impoverished of money." [52]

All was not quiet to the north, either. Pennsylvania was disturbed by reports in the Philadelphia *North American* that about $3,000 had been raised to lobby for legalized lotteries to liquidate the state debt. The *Lottery Exterminator* published in New York by a civil engineer, J. A. Powers, boasted that it contained "an Exposition of the Enormous frauds incident to the modern system of Lottery Gaming; with simple methods of Detecting them; Frauds and artifices of managers and venders; etc." Published monthly at fifty cents a year, free copies were sent to ministers, congressmen, and state legislators. A single issue (April 1842), besides offering articles on "Lottery Gaming Exposed," "Challenge to Managers and Venders," "Fallacy of Lotteries as a Means of Revenue," and the "Remote Chance of Drawing the Capital Prize," made the following claims: not less than $12,000,000 was spent annually on tickets; there was an average of six drawings per day throughout the United States; three hundred vendors in New York alone were selling tickets on the sabbath; "insurance" still continued in New York and would be ended only by imprisonment of offenders; and New Jersey was the "hot-bed" of lottery activity. Not to be outdone, Jonathan H. Green, writing as a "warning to the youthful and inexperienced," included a chapter in his book, *An Exposure of the Arts and Miseries of Gambling* (Philadelphia, 1843), on the frauds and swindling in lotteries and "insurance."

New Jersey, perhaps tired of being a "hot-bed," moved into the opposition column in 1844. When J. G. Gregory, contractor for the lottery to benefit the Society for the Establishment of Useful Manufactures (1791), gave evidence of prolonging that scheme indefinitely, many petitions and several bills for abolition were unsuccessfully introduced in the legislature. The question carried over into the election and constitutional convention of 1844. Joseph C. Hornblower, lawyer, professor, and chief justice; W. R. Allen, farmer and strong opponent of slavery; Ellis Ogden, lawyer and bank president; Martin Ryerson, lawyer and strong temperance and antislavery man; and Bernard Connolly, newspaper editor, were leaders in the fight for prohibition of lotteries. They succeeded to the extent that the new constitution forbade further authorizations and vending or purchasing of any tickets not sanctioned by the state.[53]

Gregory & Company agreed that the Useful Manufactures undertaking could be concluded by the end of 1846, and in order to quiet opposition they decided to concentrate on "foreign" sales. Daniel M'Intyre, an associate of the firm, wrote Gregory about keeping agents out of Camden, his headquarters, because they "would get up an excitement against the business. Very few know we have an office here and nobody cares, it would be otherwise if tickets were sold by retail." The policy would be continued so that the office might remain there after the grant was concluded. He also added the enlightening statement — "we ought not to sell any more prizes, we can't afford it." On December 31, 1846, he wrote Gregory: "This day closes our career as Lottery Managers! Well, upon the whole we have no reason to complain, it is true we have had a good deal to contend with in one way and another, but then I trust we have all a competency and resign the business into other hands without regret." [54]

Before its death, however, the company made its influence felt elsewhere. T. H. James, an Englishman traveling in the United States in 1845, noted:

. . . though New York has kicked out the nuisance with contempt, and made it penal for any person to deal in lottery tickets, yet they are purchased in various public places of the city as easily as cigars, and the first thing that strikes the eye of the stranger when he crosses the Ferry from New York to New Jersey is a large board with "State Lottery Office" written up; and a capital business it appears to be . . .[55]

The truth of this statement is seen in M'Intyre's reports on October 21, 1845, and April 16, 1846, that sales were good in New York and that the New Jersey lottery was preferred to that of Delaware.

In conjunction with other contractors Gregory worked behind the scenes in Pennsylvania. In a letter written November 17, 1845, M'Intyre frankly admitted bribing members of the state legislature. Reasons for this activity were made clear on January 28, 1846, when he wrote Gregory that the grand jury was about to destroy the business by attacking brokers and customers. M'Intyre's letters of February 4 and 10 told of the efforts of his office through lobbyists to kill the Pennsylvania law suppressing the sale of tickets. Three days later he wrote that they were trying to reintroduce lotteries by tacking on a rider to another bill. He noted that the western and southern counties would disapprove because they were "puritanical in their notions," but the middle and northern counties did not care "where the money comes from as long as they are not taxed." On February 16 he believed the move would succeed if the "anti-lottery people will keep quiet." Advocates were using the argument that as long as lotteries existed anywhere, the state might as well benefit. M'Intyre, however, promised that he would "not put out much without prospect of success." On May 6 he gleefully reported that the bill "for more effectual suppression of lotteries" had passed the senate but failed in the house. The final word in regard to lotteries in Pennsylvania was contained in his letter of July 21, 1846, stating that the Camden, New Jersey, office was supplying tickets to agents in Pittsburgh.

But the tide of public opinion swept slowly and relentlessly on. In 1845 Texas entered the Union under a constitution that forbade lottery authorizations, and Louisiana's constitutional convention reaffirmed without debate its previous stand. During the next year Iowa, whose defeated constitution of 1844 had contained a like provision, ratified another with the same prohibition, also without apparent opposition. The South Carolina legislature decided in 1846 that D. & J. Gregory's interest in one of its franchises had expired, and after taking the matter to court terminated this, its last scheme.[56] Illinois repealed all of her previous licenses in 1847 and proscribed any new ones in the constitution adopted in 1848. Wisconsin featured a like restriction in the struggle for ratification of its 1847 constitution, but when this was voted down because of its radical stand on banking and the rights of married women, the same lottery prohibition was reinstated in the constitution adopted the following year.[57]

The influence of the antilottery forces reached California by 1849. In the organizational convention of that year much time and discussion was given to the fate of such enterprises. It was argued that Californians were gambling people, and it was better for the state to get the revenue from lotteries and exercise control over them. The money would help establish the government, since, as one delegate phrased it, the population was of a floating character and could not be found for purposes of taxation. Another member stated that he had had no instructions on prescribing the particular kinds of amusements at which his constituents should pass their time, nor as to when they should go to bed or get up, but that he was in favor of the "broad and general principles of religious freedom." An advocate of prohibition answered that he failed to see how permitting lotteries came under this heading, but it "might be contended that gambling was a sort of liberty, as it took the largest possible liberties known in any community where religion existed." New York's difficulties with Yates & McIntyre were discussed, and, after much argument, a ban on lottery authorizations became a part of the constitution.[58]

This ban was complemented in 1851 by placing fines of $500 to $5,000 and/or six months imprisonment on originators, forfeiting prizes to the state, and making the sale of tickets a misdemeanor. But the system continued to flourish under another name, as is seen in the numerous California newspaper accounts of raffles of a "Mammoth Gold Ingot," "Monster Gold Bar," ranches, furniture, and so on. In 1854 another act attempted to clarify that of 1851 so as to cover such projects. Finally, on April 10, 1855, a new law made it illegal to dispose of money, goods, personal property, real estate, and other valuables by lottery, raffles, gift enterprises, and so forth. Nevertheless, seventeen days later the legislature specifically exempted the "distribution of property known as 'Hock Farm' called the 'Relief Fund of General John A. Sutter.'" This was not, moreover, the last exception to be made.

The year 1850 also saw the final blow by three other states. As late as March 1846 Maryland had licensed the raising of $60,000 for a turnpike and in 1847 had interdicted sale of "foreign" tickets and increased the penalties on "insurance." On January 18, 1848, the *Friend* reported the "disgraceful" news that Maryland through such means had netted $68,000 during the last three years.[59] The constitutional convention of December 1850 brought the struggle to a head. Eventual agreement to end lotteries led to an argument over the terminal date, which was finally set as April 1, 1859. Another provision forbade sale of tickets after that date. That others were interested in this outcome was seen in an abolition petition from some New York citizens which was received by the convention at the time. The lottery forces claimed it an "impertinent interference" and said that it came from dealers wishing to curtail competition. The prohibitionists saw it as proof that the undertakings did evil not only in their home state but also in others.[60]

When a special committee of the Virginia legislature found in 1847 that all grants, including Yates & McIntyre's claim, could be concluded by January 1, 1852, the constitution of 1850 set that date as the deadline, and banned future authorizations and sale of chances. An additional act in May 1852 set a minimum fine of $500 and a maximum term of one year in jail for those selling or transferring any lottery tickets. The Indiana convention voted in 1850, 41 to 27, to proscribe all such activity in that state.[61]

The remaining years prior to the Civil War saw similar action in still other states. In 1852 North Carolina briefly considered a plan to create a state lottery for common schools and internal improvements, but took no action. This may have been a factor in causing the twenty-seven churches of the Broad River Baptist Association, meeting at Shelby, North Carolina, in 1855, to answer the question of its Cedar Springs affiliate, "Can we fellowship members of the Baptist church who engage in buying or selling lottery tickets?" with a blunt "No." [62] Kansas was so determined to outlaw lotteries that provisions to do so were included in the Topeka (1855), Lecompton (1858), and Wyandotte (1859) constitutions. Minnesota and Oregon placed like prohibitions in their charters adopted in 1857.[63]

Georgia, on the other hand, had more difficulty in making up its mind. The monument lottery (1837) was renewed in 1852, two new schemes were created for schools in 1855, and the Fort Gaines Academy scheme (1831) was revitalized in 1857. Nevertheless, support for measures of this type was waning, and on December 11, 1858, all laws permitting drawings and sale of tickets were repealed as of June 1, 1860. In 1860 Alabama, which had not licensed a lottery since 1853, set fines from $100 to $2,000 for each unauthorized ticket sold. Pennsylvania also finally got more effective legislation with a maximum fine of $1,000 and imprisonment for two years in solitary confinement at hard labor for managing a lottery or selling or advertising tickets.

Opposition in Delaware never became effective before the Civil War. Local citizens put up a struggle, but every attempt was beaten down by the interests of the three large brokerage firms, Gregory & Company, Phalen & Company, and Paine & Company. On May 11, 1846, just before he closed his offices in Delaware, Daniel M'Intyre wrote J. G. Gregory that a Judge Hall had written a pamphlet against lotteries, and with a "leading Quaker," was circulating a petition against them to send to the legislature. "As nearly everyone is signing our successors will . . . have an early opportunity to try their hand in managing Legislative bodies." Four days later he wrote that a newspaper called "The Blue Hen's Chickens" was leading the fight in Wilmington and that Paine & Company had been responsible for stirring up the trouble. On May 20, M'Intyre referred to Judge Hall's "Lottery Killer" as "nothing more than cold Kale warmed over again." [64]

Hall and his companions lost this round, but in January 1849 the Assembly jointly resolved that thereafter no new privileges should be granted. It was assumed lotteries would end with the termination of the last grant in 1861. Despite this, a bill to sell a ten-year franchise for $50,000 was narrowly defeated after a meeting of outraged citizens in Wilmington in February 1852. In 1855 opponents were again successful. But advocates of such schemes persisted, and in February 1859, after turning down an offer of $612,000 for a seventeen-year license by Wood, Eddy & Company, of Wilmington, the legislature gave Richard French of Baltimore a twenty-year monopoly for payment of $750,000. The bill passed by a majority of one vote in each house. French defaulted on the first payment, and the act was repealed in 1862, although drawings continued after that date. [65]

By this time only two other states, Missouri and Kentucky, had been unsuccessful in ending lotteries. In Kentucky an effort to write an abolition clause into the constitution of 1850 failed, and a statute of 1857 voiding all previous franchises had been held illegal.[66] It should be pointed out that there were no lotteries in Mormon Utah, perhaps because of the stand taken against them by the church leaders. Brigham Young declared raffling to be a modified name for gambling and advised women against it. President Lorenzo Snow also disapproved, and laws against gambling were quite strict.[67]

Fittingly the voice that had spoken the longest and most bitterly against lotteries summarized the cumulative results, when the editor of the *Friend*, on March 24, 1860, expressed gratification over the way public opinion had changed in the past twenty years. Once openly patronized, lotteries were now carried on only in secret. The demoralizing consequences had become so obvious that there were "only one or two states that don't now prohibit them . . . It is a great disgrace to Delaware, and an injustice to its neighboring States, through which its lottery schemes are covertly circulated, that it should persist in legalizing this nefarious business." [68] Well might the editor look with pride on past accomplishments, but little could he realize that the lottery was to blossom forth once more and was yet to have its most lucrative, if not its brightest day.

Chapter XII

The Civil War and the Postwar Revival

"Cash gifts to the amount of $500,000.
Every ticket Draws a Prize!" [1]

The Civil War had a paradoxical effect on the lottery. First, it presented tailor-made excuses for reviving old grants and inaugurating new ones. This very renaissance, however, brought the schemes to the attention of the federal government. The emergence of Washington as a lottery policeman was significant, for its subsequent actions led eventually to the lottery's banishment from American shores.

Meantime, the state governments struggled gamely with the problem. Radial centers of the trouble were three states which had yet to outlaw the system. Delaware in 1861 placed new penalties on unauthorized tickets, which competed with its own lotteries, and required yearly vending licenses of $300. Of Kentucky, an English traveler, Edward Dicey, wrote in 1862 that he "saw lottery offices in every street." In St. Louis, Missouri, he noted:

The town . . . is crowded, like a Bavarian or Papal one, with the offices of the State Lottery. It shows the practical working of the American Constitution, when you consider that the United States Government has no more power to hinder every State in the Union from establishing lotteries than we have to require Belgium to suppress the gaming tables at Spa; and it shows, too, the wise actions of the State Governments, that in only three out of the thirty-six States, and these all Border Slave States — Kentucky, Delaware, and Missouri — are lotteries permitted by local laws.

Dicey failed to realize, however, that this situation would change in short order, with lotteries restored by new authorizations or even by new constitutions, in some cases. He found the American lottery system more "iniquitous for the player than the Papal one, a thing which beforehand I thought impossible." Based upon the ternary method, drawings were held twice a day. From the number of offices Dicey concluded that it must be a thriving business, perhaps accounting for the light taxes and also the poverty in Missouri.[2] Although sometimes inaccurate in his facts, he was probably nearer the mark than his fellow-countryman, James D. Burn, who wrote three years later that ticket offices were open to adventurers in all the principal towns in the country and that this speculation had a great hold upon the people.[3]

Despite Louisiana's constitutional prohibitions in 1845 and 1852, the war emergency was the nominal excuse for the New Orleans undertaking in the fall of 1861 to benefit Confederate soldiers. According to the *Daily Picayune* the venture had 2,442 prizes donated by prominent citizens and yielded a profit of $59,789.38.[4] The war probably also accounted for the flaunting of Missouri's law in 1863 by the sale of a St. Joseph tavern, the Patee House, by lottery. The property's value was $140,000 and tickets cost two dollars each. The sum of $25,000 was ear-marked for cities and towns in ratio to their ticket sales.[5] To the reformer the war period was saved from complete negation by West Virginia's and Nevada's forbidding all such transactions in their first constitutions.

A slight aura of respectability was given the system on June 30, 1864, when Congress placed two taxes upon lotteries. One required $100 yearly licenses of ticket dealers and the other assessed a levy of 5 per cent of the gross receipts of the business. As part of a general revenue bill, it was opposed by Congressman John V. L. Pruyn of New York on the ground that "we ought not in any way to recognize the legality of lotteries." Justin S. Morrill, of Vermont, speaking for the measure, answered that the law did not recognize lotteries but proposed "to tax them where they are recognized to be legal." When Iowa's A. W. Hubbard wanted the tax increased, Morrill argued that then it would fail to bring in revenue. The bill was passed after acceptance of a motion by Charles Upson, of Michigan, to include a statement that the act did not legalize any lottery. Nevertheless, those for charitable purposes, especially the Sanitary Commission which looked after disabled soldiers and their dependents, could be exempted from the tax. The returns from these levies between 1865 and 1868, inclusive, are highly indicative. Licenses amounted to $245,603, with $77,686 in 1867 the highest single return. The gross receipts brought a total of $246,932, the greatest amount being $78,072 in 1866. This would indicate an average annual gross of about a million and a quarter dollars.[6]

Obvious in these tax returns was an upsurge of speculation, a not incongruous development in the light of the generally low moral standards of the post-bellum period and its fixation with the importance of money. With the wartime opportunities for quick wealth largely gone, many new lotteries, legal and otherwise, appeared, together with a new market for tickets from Cuba, Mexico, and Spain. Even the old ventures found new vitality. In Missouri, for example, even when the 1865 constitution forbade lotteries, the New Franklin scheme continued to function, despite the additional facts that the town had disappeared and the railroad the scheme was supposed to benefit had caved into the river. Nevertheless, the drawings were held with much formality and witnessed by distinguished citizens during the 1870's. Finally, in the face of losing revenue, a crusade by the state newspapers, particularly the St. Louis *Republican,* killed the venture. A series of articles exposed the false pretenses under which the managers were operating, with the result that the state supreme court, which had formerly upheld the contract, declared it void.[7] The final blow came after a bitter fight when the proscription was reaffirmed in the constitution of 1876.

In Kentucky old grants were revived to give that state its period of greatest exploitation. In 1877, the 1838–39 licenses to Frankfort and Paducah were sold to the firm of Simmons & Dickinson and became the Kentucky State Lottery. Although the legislature repealed all lottery franchises on April 30, 1878, the Kentucky State scheme continued a golden, though illegal, harvest. With offices in New York and other principal cities, it held drawings on the first and fifteenth of each month, making its influence nation-wide. Zachariah Simmons, the "insurance" or "Policy king" of New York, based his games on these drawings and after becoming a member of the contracting firm was alleged to have manipulated the drawings to his own advantage. Other states faced the constant danger of such embarrassing resurrections, exemplified by Indiana's Vincennes University's claim of a vested right in its grant of 1806. The school did not, however, attempt to hold drawings, and in 1883 the United States Supreme Court denied it the privilege.[8]

New authorizations were confined to the South and West. Youthful governments and transient populations made the West vulnerable, while in the South the postwar poverty made lotteries seem desirable to both the people and their graft-minded legislators or officials. Chaos growing out of the political instability of the defeated states, the ignorance and susceptibility of the newly enfranchised Negro, the disdain for prewar laws and customs, and the rash of new constitutions, all made the South a happy hunting ground for lottery advocates.

On February 3, 1866, Alabama incorporated for twenty-five years the Tuscaloosa Scientific and Art Association to encourage art, replace the war-destroyed state university library, and establish a scientific museum. The charter empowered the organization to sell "certificates of subscription, which shall entitle the holder thereof to any articles that may be awarded them; and the distribution of awards shall be fairly made in public . . . by the casting of lots . . ." The articles awarded were books, paintings, statues, scientific instruments, or any other useful or ornamental property. Even this worthy objective did not make the measure entirely palatable, however, and a leading Methodist bishop stated in a sermon that it would be better that the university's walls should never rise from their ashes, "better its foundations were sowed with salt and plowed up, than that by such a means, it should be helped . . ." [9] But this was not yet the common sentiment, and on October 10, 1868, Alabama enacted a law "to establish a Mutual Aid Association and to raise funds for the common school system of Alabama." This venture was of the same nature as that for the university. The association had to pay $2,000 to the school fund annually for twenty years and offer prizes for the best essays, works of art, and useful inventions produced by Alabamians. An act of December 31 provided for a state commissioner of lotteries and a one per cent tax on all authorized lotteries.

Other states followed Alabama. In 1866 Georgia established the Masonic Orphans' Home for indigent widows and orphans, and a committee of six women and a man was empowered to hold a series of lotteries to purchase land and erect buildings. The Mississippi carpetbagger legislature of 1867 created the Mississippi Agricultural, Educational, and Manufacturing Aid Society and gave it a twenty-five-year lottery monopoly in return for $5,000 down and an annual payment to the state college of $1,000 plus 0.5 per cent of the gross returns. This action apparently met opposition for the constitution adopted the next year stated: "The Legislature shall never authorize any lottery, nor shall the sale of lottery tickets be allowed, nor shall any lottery heretofore authorized be permitted to be drawn or ticket therein be sold." On July 16, 1870, the legislature passed a law to implement this restriction. But in March 1874 the state attorney general was forced to file an information in the nature of a *quo warrento* against the society. It admitted holding a lottery but claimed justification under its charter. Finally, in 1879, the case reached the United States Supreme Court on the grounds that there had been a breach of contract. Chief Justice M. R. Waite handed down the decision that such enterprises fell within the police power of the state, extending to all matters affecting public health and morals, and that the legislature could not enter an agreement which bartered away this power. Contracts protected by the federal Constitution were property, not governmental rights.[10] This decision effectively killed the project.

Only one more authorization was made in the South, aside from the fabulous Louisiana Lottery. On March 16, 1871, the incorporation of the Public Library of Kentucky allowed certain persons "to give not to exceed five in number, public library, musical, or dramatic entertainments, at which they may distribute, by lot, to the patrons of the entertainments, a portion of the proceeds arising from the sale of tickets of admission for the benefit of the library mentioned." The Louisiana Lottery, chartered in 1868, will be discussed in the following chapter.

The West had two new lotteries in this period. California re-entered the field when the Democratic-controlled Assembly passed a bill on February 19, 1870, to aid the debt-ridded Mercantile Library of San Francisco by allowing it to hold not more than three public entertainments or concerts at which personal property, real estate, or other valuables could be raffled. This scheme was approved by the governor, though it was obviously contrary to the constitution. The Republicans made much of this fact in the 1871 election, and upon coming into power, immediately repealed the act in January 1872, although the purpose had already been accomplished. According to a California historian, the raffle raised $500,000 in three days. The second instance occurred seven years later, when John C.

Fremont, as governor of the Arizona Territory, was the moving force behind a bill to "aid in the construction of capital buildings and for the support of the Public Schools . . ." By this law the Arizona Development Company was given a twenty-year lottery franchise. The governor or his successor was to act as commissioner and receive $100 per drawing for his supervision. Ten per cent of the money collected was to go into the territorial treasury and the first two years be applied toward capital buildings and afterwards to education. Unfortunately for Fremont, the measure was disallowed by federal authorities and repealed in 1881.[11]

Most of the illegal enterprises of the postwar period took the form of "gift companies" which evaded the law under the pretense of straight merchandise sales and were active in practically all states. Typical was the Empire Gift Company conducted by Stewart, Hall & Company of New York. It advertised for its fourth annual "distribution" in 1869 not only five cash "gifts" of $20,000 each, ten of $10,000 each, etc., but also 50 rosewood pianos, 75 rosewood melodeons, 350 sewing machines, 500 gold watches, silverware, etc., to a value of $1,000,000! A customer buying a chance for twenty-five cents received a sealed ticket describing his "purchase." For an additional dollar this "gift" would be delivered.[12] Oil stock, in particular, was a favorite "gift," but the stock so bought was usually fake and the "gold" watches were plated and without works. Illinois was host to the North American Prize Concert, the International Musical and Gift Concert, and the Union National Gift Concert, each offering tickets at a dollar each. In 1867 Crosby's Opera House of Chicago was rescued from financial distress by the Opera House Association, which sold 210,000 billets throughout the country.[13] The more successful the attacks on lotteries *per se,* the more this type of evasion flourished.

This revival of lottery activity throughout the country, legal and otherwise, was quickly mirrored in public opinion. In the Thirty-ninth Congress (1865) it was suggested that the Postmaster General step in and deny use of the mails. The Solicitor of the Post Office Department decided that his agency had the right to refuse to deliver mail to any name known to be a part of a system to defraud the public, but that additional laws were needed to bolster this moral right. Congress, however, failed to pass the necessary legislation.[14]

The *Boston Review*, a religious journal and old lottery critic, spoke out once more in its January 1866 issue to condemn the use of lotteries in raising money for churches. The editor quoted a statement from the *Daily Evening Traveler*, December 20, 1865: "NOTICE TO UNITARIANS. Fairs are becoming unpopular. Why? Because they have features of questionable propriety. Among those are *lotteries, raffles, grabs,* and other *sales by chance.*" In the October 1866 number the Reverend William Barrows of Reading, Massachusetts, wrote that raffles were merely polite names for lotteries and were therefore illegal. He pointed to the experiences of England and France — "Even the morality of France could not bear lotteries and raffles." (He seemed singularly unaware of the existence of legal American schemes.) Those countries still using this device, he averred, were "intensely Roman Catholic countries, whose religious and moral code teaches them that the end justifies the means." Finally, he warned that God avenged the "prostitution of the lot" by dwarfed industry, pauperism, and misery, and in immoralities.[15]

That the tendency to erase this nice distinction between raffles and lotteries was becoming more prevalent was evidenced by a short novel published ten years later. The story opened in New York City with a Mrs. Limber berating her maid for planning to marry a man who had won $3,000 in a lottery and predicting dire results from such a match. In defense, the servant pointed out that her mistress at that very moment was engaged in running a raffle for her church. Mrs. Limber was horror-stricken to hear "our innocent little raffle for the best of causes, compared to a vulgar lottery," and promptly called in her husband. He, in turn, appealed to the minister, who answered that some lotteries could be considered pious. A lawyer, however, took the stand that both were one and the same and were alike evil, morally and legally. He reminded them that the prohibition was not only by statute but also in the New York constitution and that the most "advanced communities" were unanimous in this attitude. He cited case after case where raffles had been held to be lotteries by the courts and so convinced Mr. Limber that, at his instigation, all participants in the raffle were hauled into court, thus convincing both the church and the city of the evils and dangers of raffles.[16]

State governments were not oblivious to these trends. In 1866 Nebraska entered the Union under a constitution which forbade lotteries. The Georgia convention of 1867–68 was the scene of a fight over such ventures. James L. Dunning early offered an unsuccessful resolution against lotteries, and C. C. Richardson's proposal met a similar fate. Yet in the final document, Article I, section 13, forbade authorizations or sale of tickets in games of chance. A law of October 9, 1868, provided a penalty of from $100 to $500 for first offenses of this nature, but these actions were not considered retroactive with regard to the Masonic grant then in operation. Also during the same year constitutional interdictions were set forth or reaffirmed in South Carolina, Florida, and Arkansas.

Significantly, it was at this time that the federal government took what might be interpreted as the first step toward curbing lotteries on a national scale. On July 27, 1868, Congress declared it unlawful to deposit in a post office to be sent by mail any letters or circulars concerning lotteries, gift concerts, or any similar enterprise "offering prizes of any kind under any pretext whatever." Part of a general act to amend the postal laws, this section attracted little debate or attention. The only issue grew out of a Senate amendment which sought to authorize postmasters to remove from the mails any letters or circulars which they "suspected" of containing lottery material. The House refused to accept this, feeling that it would not be wise to delegate "this extraordinary power to be exercised upon a mere suspicion." [17] Lottery advocates probably felt that this act was of slight danger to them, and as shall be seen, the measure failed to accomplish its purpose.

A new law on June 8, 1872, revising, consolidating, and amending the statutes relating to the Post Office Department, inserted without debate the word "illegal" before the word "lotteries" making it unlawful to convey by mail or to deposit in a post office materials concerning "illegal lotteries, so-called gift concerts," or "schemes devised and intended to deceive and defraud the public for purposes of obtaining money under false pretense." It provided a maximum penalty of $500, which proved so small that many companies paid it as a sort of tax on their business. Postmasters could not act as lottery agents and the Postmaster General, on satisfactory evidence, might refuse payment of money orders to fraudulent concerns and return registered letters. He was specifically forbidden, however, to open any mail. Although these restrictions proved ineffective, they nevertheless were tested on the grounds that they violated freedom of the press. In *Ex parte* Jackson (96 U.S. 727) the authority of Congress was sustained on the grounds that its right to "establish post-offices and post-roads" carried power to exclude anything deemed injurious to public morals.[18]

During the same year (1872) state governments were meeting the problems in their own fashion. Alabama required licenses from promoters and the posting of from $10,000 to $50,000 in bonds as protection for ticket purchasers. The constitution of the Territory of New Mexico moved in the opposite direction by forbidding establishment of such schemes or the sale of their chances.

The next few years saw other heavy blows struck at the lottery system. The Episcopal Church in its council of 1874 passed a resolution declaring "any participation in lotteries, gift enterprises, gift concerts and raffling, to be inconsistent with the profession of a Christian, and that it [is] improper for any church or church institution to be aided by money made by such means."[19] Alabama took the final step and outlawed such undertakings by constitutional provision in 1875. Georgia brought an end to her participation by repealing the Masonic Orphan's Home grant, effective December 20, 1876. Colorado joined the procession, indicting such drawings and sales with Article XVIII, section 2, of her constitution of 1876.

About the same time, however, the assistant attorney general of New York reported that lottery companies and ticket vending were still flourishing. There were, he asserted, thirty-three agencies in the City of New York alone, receiving an average of 7,661 ordinary and 1,993 registered letters weekly. He estimated that millions of dollars annually were flowing into their tills, making them "financial vampires" sucking the life-blood of legitimate business and "inflicting upon society a species of distempered mental leprosy, which will require years to remove."[20]

Since this situation could be duplicated in nearly every city of any size, it probably explains the stand by the national convention of the Prohibition Party at Cleveland in May 1876. The fourth plank of its platform called for the "suppression by law of lotteries and gambling in gold, stocks, produce, and every form of money and property, and the penal inhibition of the use of the public mails for advertising schemes of gambling and lotteries."[21]

This pronouncement, together with the obvious failure of existing regulations and the fact that a depression was prevalent, probably led to the new federal law of July 12, 1876, dropping the term "illegal" in the previous act and making it unlawful to carry in the mail letters concerning any sort of lottery, licensed or otherwise. The bill was reported unanimously by the House Committee on the Post Office and Post Roads, which explained that there was matter mailable in some states that was not mailable in others because some had legalized lotteries. The purpose of the amendment was to secure uniformity and prohibit lottery material of any kind from passing through the mails. The act passed the House without difficulty but was strongly challenged in the Senate.

Public attitude caused even Senate opponents of the measure to state quickly that they personally did not favor lotteries. Senator William P. Whyte of Maryland claimed that the bill would do an injustice in certain sections of the country where lotteries were legal by making it impossible to send such materials even within the state itself. It was therefore an infringement of rights in states where lotteries were not criminal or improper. Hannibal Hamlin of Maine, chairman of the sponsoring committee, answered that all lotteries were regarded, "when legalized, as legalized gambling; and in that view the Committee on Post-Offices and Post-Roads, with concurrence of the [Post Office] Department, deem it wise and just for the best interest of the country to strike out the word 'illegal' and to prohibit any matter relating to lotteries." The Post Office Department had had difficulty in the past determining what were and what were not legal undertakings, since a great many schemes had been created "apparently with the form of law, but yet of doubtful legal force."

Senator J. Rodman West of Louisiana felt that if a state chose to legalize a lottery yet the United States would not lend the machinery of the post office to carry it on, "there [was] no end whatever to the jurisdiction of Congress over the morals of the people in their State enactments." He argued that Congress had no right to close the mails to such matters as were legalized by the states. After speeches by John A. Logan of Illinois, Justin Morrill of Vermont, and Samuel B. Maxey of Texas denouncing the immorality of lotteries, the ineffectuality of state prohibitory laws as long as one state chose to sanction them, and the duty of Congress to protect all the American people, Whyte retorted, "I am delighted that our friends on the other side, the Senator from Illinois and other gentlemen, have suddenly become moralized . . . They were not so very moral when they could make money out of lotteries during the war." Morrill justified the act of 1864 as an obstruction to lotteries, while Whyte now proposed to aid them. After more verbal fireworks, a motion to strike out the amendment was defeated by voice vote, the bill was passed, and was signed into law by the President.

The Postmaster General thereupon instructed postmasters to refuse to receive or deliver letters addressed to lottery companies or their agents, on the assumption that such mail "concerned" a lottery. This statute was tested and upheld in Commerford *v.* Thompson (1880), when the Louisville, Kentucky, postmaster refused to deliver mail addressed to the Commonwealth Distribution Company and returned it to the Dead-Letter Office.[22]

Even this was not a fatal blow. The Louisiana Lottery in open violation of state laws was advertising in the New York *Daily Graphic,* December 8, 1877, "LET NOT A MOMENT ESCAPE YOU OR YOU MAY BE TOO LATE," and the Kentucky State Lottery was reactivated under the grant of 1838 by a New York firm. The gift companies prospered to such an extent that on January 9, 1881, the Postmaster General listed 137 persons and firms running bogus lotteries or gift companies. Among them were the Arizona Lottery, the Commonwealth Distribution Company (Kentucky), the Great Western Distribution Company (Wyoming), the Texas Gift Concert (one of the most successful, bringing in about $100,000 profit annually), the Denver Land Company (offering house lots for one dollar each), the Cheyenne Lottery Company, and several Canadian firms.[23]

In New York City in 1889 about a million and a half tickets were seized from the following schemes: the Original Little Louisiana Company of San Diego, California; Supplement to the Louisiana Lottery, Kansas City and New York; the Oakland Little Louisiana Company of Oakland, California; and the Original Little Louisiana Company of San Francisco. In 1890 postal authorities broke up the Denver State Lottery with the arrest of its promoters, Arthur C. Johnston and Jerome H. Boyd. The Cheyenne, Laramie City, and the Wyoming lotteries, operated by the "Pattee gang" of New York, were perhaps the biggest frauds of all, for drawings were not even held. Prosecution finally forced the Pattee organization to move its headquarters from New York City to Canada.[24]

But slowly, but surely, antilottery forces were snuffing out these mavericks. State and local authorities applied increasing pressure. The Kentucky Lottery was held illegal by that state's supreme court and all such grants were repealed by the legislature on April 30, 1878. The Alabama license had likewise been revoked, leaving the Louisiana Lottery to boast: "This is the only lottery in any State ever voted on and endorsed by its people." Its competitors were without a shred of legal existence. Thus the Louisiana enterprise enjoyed a virtual, and profitable, monopoly even in areas where surreptitious operation was necessary. The sole survivor of a once-great system, it was a giant worthy of its antecedents. Its story, then, became the lottery story.

Chapter XIII

The Louisiana Lottery

Conrad! Conrad! Conrad!
In accepting the Presidency of the Honduras National Lottery Company (Louisiana State Lottery Company) I shall not surrender the Presidency of the Gulf Coast Ice and Manufacturing Company, of Bay St. Louis, Miss.
* Therefore address all proposals for supplies, machinery, etc., as well as all business communications to

PAUL CONRAD, Puerto Cortez, Honduras, Care Central America Express Port Tampa City, Florida, U.S.A.[1]

The lottery destined to be the most famous, or infamous, in the history of such ventures had its genesis on April 6, 1864. The Louisiana constitutional convention went against the precedents of 1845 and 1857 and granted legislative power "to license the selling of lottery tickets and the keeping of gambling houses," with lottery licenses at not less than $10,000 a year. The legislature soon moved to use its new power when on January 23, 1866, Charles E. Fenner (later a justice of the Louisiana supreme court) introduced a measure to license sale of tickets, allotting the first $50,000 of the revenue to the New Orleans Charity Hospital and the remainder to the general state fund. Section 11 of the bill specified that it did not authorize the establishment of a lottery within the state. With almost no opposition it passed the house by 46 to 25 and the senate, 20 to 6. The New Orleans *Times* justified the measure on the grounds of financial necessity, as a deterrent on the corrupting influence of illegal gambling on officials, and as a healthy tax upon extravagances of the citizenry. Altogether these licenses to sell tickets returned $36,000 in 1866 and 1867 and $28,000 in 1868.[2]

The Louisiana constitutional privilege was just the foothold needed by a New York gambling syndicate which had been formed in 1863 by Benjamin Wood, Charles H. Murray, Zachariah Simmons, John A. Morris, and John Morrissey, among others. Through their agent, Charles T. Howard, the group set up operations in New Orleans in 1865.[3] Howard, the front man, had been the New Orleans representative of the Alabama State Lottery before the war, returning to Louisiana in 1865 as agent for the Kentucky State Lottery (self-styled at that time as the only legal lottery in the United States), a position he "filled with remarkable success." By 1866 he was announcing ticket sales from six branch offices in New Orleans and also that he represented the revived Alabama State Lottery. The next year the Georgia State Lottery was added to his list of clients. Although in 1867 Alfred Bourges of Orleans was unsuccessful in his legislative bid to give "C. T. Howard and his associates" a ten-year franchise for charitable lotteries on payment of $200,000, it was evident that Howard was becoming a power in the state and that the New York syndicate had chosen wisely.[4]

The introduction of carpetbag government in Louisiana made Howard's task easier, and a new lottery bill was presented under the Warmouth Republican administration. The bill's sponsors claimed it was justified by the state's need for revenue and to keep gambling funds from being lost to other states. The New Orleans *Daily Picayune*, August 4, 1868, reported the objections raised by the minority reports of the house committee as including charges that lotteries were immoral and corruptive influences; that the company would be a monopoly, yet by terms of its contract would not be financially sound; and that its stock and capital would be exempt from taxation, leaving the industrious and honest citizens the burden of supporting the resultant poverty and crime. But as later revealed in testimony by the officers and incorporators in a fight over the profits, the issue was not left to stand or fall on its own merits, for the syndicate had liberally bribed carpetbagger and Negro legislators. Consequently, Act No. 25 of 1868, introduced by B. C. Wren of Bossier became law on August 11 without the governor's signature and in spite of considerable opposition.

The bill had been cleverly drawn and skillfully managed in the legislature. Howard's name appeared nowhere in the act. The monopoly feature was played down and the measure was entitled "to increase the revenues of the State and authorize the incorporation of the Louisiana Lottery Company." The first section prohibited sale of "foreign" tickets, as "many millions of dollars have been withdrawn from and lost to this State by the sale of Havana, Kentucky, Madrid, and other lottery tickets, thereby impoverishing our people." Under the articles of incorporation, the company allegedly met the following objectives: protection of the state against losses in outside schemes; establishment of a solvent home institution with assurance of fairness; and provision of funds for educational and charitable purposes. After January 1, 1869, the company would pay the state $40,000 annually for twenty-five years but would be exempt from all other taxes. It was also empowered to sell real estate by raffles.

Such a rich plum was not bestowed without contest, and a rival, Dave C. Johnson, reported that five members of the senate offered him the franchise for $40,000, but he did not have the money. He also charged that a total of $100,000 in stock was given to members of the legislature, the board of directors, and Howard.

Most of the money to get the bill passed and the company into operation reputedly was put up by Murray and Morris of the New York group. The directors named in the act were apparently straw men from the beginning; nine days after passage of the law, they transferred their rights to the New York syndicate, and Howard became president of the new lottery firm.[5] He lost no time. The newspapers announced public drawings daily at 4:00 P.M., beginning on January 2, 1869, with the two wheels under supervision of Adam Griffen, former state treasurer. Rapidly branching out, the firm held the "Grand Real Estate Lottery" in July with prizes of $1,264,000 in property. The primary award was the St. Louis Hotel (valued at $750,000); second, its furniture; and third, the Old Citizen's Bank. Tickets were ten dollars each.[6] Later, to add more of an aura of respectability and honesty to the proceedings, two former Confederate generals, P. G. T. Beauregard and Jubal A. Early, were hired to "supervise" the actual drawings.

The company was not able, however, to stifle all criticism. The Methodist *Christian Advocate* and the *Daily Picayune*, edited by R. B. Rhett, Jr., constantly attacked the company. The *Advocate* stated on March 20, 1869, that "it would seem the mouth of hell had been opened by law" and, on May 8, that by "looking into the public gambling saloons of St. Charles street one may see the tail of the dragon of which the present government of Louisiana is the head." The *Picayune* was so troublesome that finally in 1872 Howard sued Rhett for $20,000 in damages resulting from attacks upon the lottery.[7] The same year a grand jury in Orleans Parish reported that lotteries were *"contra bonos mores."*

Nevertheless, the company's power vastly increased during the Reconstruction period. Their jealously guarded monopoly was protected by a successful suit in 1869 against an agent of the Alabama Mutual Aid Association. Enormous sums were spent in bribing legislators to prevent other companies from being chartered and to retain its own franchise. A desperate attempt was made in 1874 to license a rival, the New Orleans Lottery Company, in hopes thereby of breaking Howard's power. Charges of unconstitutionality and bribery flew back and forth before the bill finally was killed by repeated postponements after its third reading. Then to secure more strongly its position, Howard's company obtained the enactment of two laws that increased the penalties for selling or drawing illegal tickets. The ease with which these measures were passed seem to justify the repeated claim that the company controlled every Louisiana legislature from 1868 to 1892.

But enforcement of the new laws was another story and led to many legal battles; in one instance it almost caused calling out the state militia. The local police, said to be under Howard's control, were kept busy. A number of citizens were jailed without benefit of habeas corpus when unable to pay their fines. Public opinion was so opposed to these high-handed methods that in one case (the Agusti trial) four justices of the supreme court sat with the trial judge to give dignity to the proceedings. This failing, a threat was made by the judge that the militia would be used.[8]

The legislature of 1876 found itself confronted with three bills that variously proposed to repeal the company's charter, repeal the acts of 1874, and investigate the alleged bribery in 1868 by the Howard forces. Though these led to a public airing of much of the lottery's dirty linen, serious damage was prevented, and the firm was able to play a commanding role in the disputed state election of 1876. In that contest the Democrats won clear majorities, but the Republican state board of canvassers revised the results to achieve a Republican victory. Dual governments resulted, and there is strong evidence that the lottery company came to the rescue of the impoverished Democratic Nicholls regime, supplying it with funds to undermine the loyalty of supporters of Stephen B. Packard.

While Francis R. T. Nicholls' own personal feelings on the subject were not clear, it is significant that after its final victory over the carpetbaggers, his administration did not attack this relic of their handiwork. Later, in an attempt to explain and justify this tolerance, a *Daily Picayune* editorial of February 1, 1879, summarized a state senator, also a member of the Democratic Committee of Safety in 1877, as saying that an offer had been made to the committee to render "material service" in establishing the Nicholls government if the legislature would pledge not to repeal the lottery charter. The desperate needs of the hour and a desire not to alienate one of the large corporations led to a "tacit understanding." Not only was the bill for repeal tabled in 1877, but also when the matter came up again in 1878 the administration acquiesced in the company's insistence that its immunity applied to both sessions.[9]

By 1878, with demands by many Democratic leaders for a constitutional convention to replace the carpetbag document of 1868, the lottery inevitably came into the question and the struggle extended beyond the legislative halls. When a meeting of the Real Estate Owners' and Taxpayers' Union of New Orleans attempted to discuss the matter, it was broken up by rowdies, a disturbance blamed on the company. The firm was also accused of bribing legislators to prevent a convention. Such charges furnished fuel for attacks by the press in all sections of the state. While the principal argument in favor of continuing the license was financial, chief points of condemnation were its political activities, that it was a creature of Reconstruction, that it had muzzled the press, and in the words of the *People's Vindicator* of Natchitoches, it was "a nuisance stinking in the nostrils of all good men." The New Orleans *Democrat* asserted that if old Methusaleh had bought a daily ticket all of his life he would have spent about $250,000 to win $2,678.85. Nevertheless, the move to call a convention and also an effort to submit to the people a constitutional amendment ending the lottery were defeated.

But the attacks continued. The daily drawings were criticized, as was the lottery's claim of fair practice. The odds were too high, and the prices so low they encouraged those who could not afford the luxury of gambling. The company was further accused of not having a just proportion between the prices of its tickets and the prizes. Also the awards were smaller than those in Italy, France, Austria, or Bavaria, where, as the *Democrat* pointed out, all but 15 per cent of the amount paid in was returned, against the Louisiana schemes' almost 48 per cent.

To meet these charges the syndicate brought up its big guns in the form of the revered generals, Beauregard and Early. These two, on the eve of the semi-annual "Extraordinary Drawing" of June 5, 1877, issued a public statement attesting to the fairness of their procedures. A year later, on June 13, they again used the newspapers, declaring this time that if it had happened that the large prizes had been drawn by the company itself, it was because not half of the chances had been sold. To those who complained of the monopoly feature, the old warriors had an ingenious reply: they felt this desirable, for if "lotteries are all great evils, then it is better that they should exist as monopolies than that the right to conduct them should be general." Also during this period, suits totaling $90,000 were filed against Albert C. Janin, editor of the *Democrat*, for his expression, "Howard and his brother thieves," and for suggesting that some morning would find the company's "imposing palace of vice" torn down and Howard and his cohorts "treated to a short shift and long rope." [10]

After the company beat down this rebellion on the home front, trouble broke out in another quarter. The New Orleans headquarters began receiving reports from the Washington office that a new effort was being made to exclude lottery material from the mails. The immediate threat was seizure of the firm's mail at New Orleans, New York, St. Louis, Cincinnati, Memphis, and other vital points. The management decided to test the legality of the federal law of 1876. Ben Butler, stormy petrel of the Civil War, postwar political king-pin, and the brother-in-law of the Secretary of the Treasury, headed a corps of nine lawyers to press the fight. Howard reportedly hurried to Washington for personal interviews with President Rutherford B. Hayes and Secretary of the Treasury John Sherman, a move interpreted by northern newspapers as an attempt to inject the lottery into national politics. Despite numerous indications that the lottery was unpopular, the Attorney General handed down a decision which was berated by lottery foes as sustaining the law of

1876 but at the same time preventing its enforcement. Thus, it was generally agreed that the company had won the battle of Washington as well as that of Baton Rouge. At least, temporarily.

On the third day of its session in 1879, the newly elected Louisiana legislature was confronted by a bill to repeal all pro-lottery laws in the state, including the company's charter, and provide heavy penalties for all such activity after March 31, 1879. Feelings mounted and again the state rang with rumors of attempted bribes and threats. Nevertheless, the act passed the house, 64 to 20, the senate, 19 to 17, and was signed by the governor on March 27, 1879.

The company refused to die easily and applied for an injunction from the United States Circuit Court. It was issued by Judge Edward Billings, despite the fact that the Supreme Court had sustained the right of repeal in a similar case, Boyd v. Alabama (1877). When the state attorney general refused to recognize Judge Billings' ruling, the police chief was enjoined from carrying out the law.

Before the case could reach a higher court, the company decided its best chance lay with influencing the constitutional convention which was then meeting, since its principal attorney and thirty-nine other Reconstruction friends were members. There, with almost every delegate having his say, the issue consumed eight days of debate. Intense excitement over the huge state debt, a legacy from Reconstruction days, probably won the balance of power for the pro-lottery forces. Article CLXVII was a compromise which tolerated lotteries until 1894 but revoked the previous monopoly. Henceforth a tax of $40,000 a year was to be paid into the treasury by the Louisiana Lottery Company for the use of the New Orleans Charity Hospital. When this constitution was ratified in December, lottery supporters cited it as evidence of popular approval for lotteries; the opponents, as merely a good instrument except for that provision.[11]

To celebrate its "lawful renaissance," the company made an especially big event of the drawing on December 17, 1879. The affair was held in the Grand Opera House, with General Early calling the numbers and General Beauregard the prizes. Afterwards, the public was treated to a free concert. Well might the firm celebrate, for it was entering what was probably its most profitable decade — an unprovable statement since before this time its returns had been a carefully guarded secret. But several things lead to this conclusion:

the size of the later schemes was greater, sales were national and thus larger, and old rivals were operating on a small scale or had been forced out of business. The Kentucky Lottery had been held illegal by the Kentucky supreme court and all such grants in that state were repealed by the legislature on April 30, 1878. The Georgia and Alabama franchises had likewise been revoked, leaving the Louisiana enterprise to boast, "This is the only lottery in any State ever voted on and endorsed by its people."

Many people, especially in Louisiana, must have felt that the Nashville *Christian Advocate* was premature in its statement that the lottery was doomed in the United States because the drift of public sentiment was against it and "no array of once respectable names will give it respectability or save it from the blistering condemnation of honest people." [12] The Louisiana company seemed impregnable. A contemporary reported that it had gained control of the state Democratic Party and was using this to guarantee the continuation of the monopoly; "so thoroughly did they do their work that — they are the absolute masters of every ward boss and every professional politician in the State of Louisiana, whether he be judge, sheriff, constable, treasurer, member of the State Central Committee, member of the parish committee." [13] Time after time attempts were beaten down in the legislature either to abolish the company or charter rivals; no less than four such bills were introduced in the 1880 session.

Even federal authority seemed helpless. To the statement of the Postmaster General that the company was fraudulent, Generals Early and Beauregard replied in a two-column card, "To pronounce this corporation as a fraud does not comport with very clear comprehension of the principles of common sense or official propriety."

With its relatively secure position, shrewd management, and virtual monopoly of sales, the company prospered tremendously. Stockholders reputedly received dividends of 110 per cent in 1887; 120 per cent in 1888; 170 per cent in 1889; and 125 per cent in 1890. [14] Some idea of the firm's magnitude and profitableness can be seen from its own statements. Once a month for ten months a year 100,000 tickets at from two to twenty dollars each were offered for sale. In the other two months the company held "extraordinary drawings" of 100,000 chances priced at from ten to forty dollars each. The amounts of the capital prizes steadily increased until the semi-annual drawings offered a top award of $600,000. Total prize values fluctuated between $265,500 and over $2,000,000, according to the scheme.

A great deal of criticism fell upon the daily drawings. Based upon the ternary system, they usually had seventy-five to seventy-eight numbers in the wheel, of which eleven to fourteen were drawn out. Grouping the original digits by threes made available over 65,000 tickets for sale, retailing from twenty cents to one dollar each, with top awards of approximately $5,000. But two types of chances were sold for these 313 "daily" affairs. One was the regular ticket, and the other was a "policy" or "insurance" ticket, on which the buyer could write his own combination of three numbers. It is doubtful that the Louisiana Lottery Company received any direct return from the latter, but in the popular mind "policy" was considered an integral part of the daily drawing.

It was also the cause of much of the associated disrepute. Certainly "insurance" created the most local complaints, probably because of its greater attractiveness to the lower classes. A clergyman, the Reverend Beverly Carradine of New Orleans' Carondelet Street Methodist Church, asserted that married women "invested" part of their household funds and that clerks surreptitiously "borrowed" from their employers. "To send a servant with money to the market is virtually to send a portion of your money to the lottery," and while the householder might wonder about his skimpy meal, the cook did not.

"Policy" tickets had the advantage of selling for less than a fraction of the cost of a regular chance. There were over a hundred shops in New Orleans usually located in the market district, where they could be bought, and most places sold both types of tickets. A check on a large shop showed that thirty-four people entered in one hour's time — eighteen women, six children between ten and fourteen, and ten men. Twenty-three of the total were Negroes. Since in "policy" a player bet that certain numbers would be drawn or would come out in a prestated order, offices furnished "dream books" and other paraphernalia for the superstitious. Overhead costs for "policy" were practically nothing, for the regular lottery facilities served it also. The total annual income from "policy" in New Orleans alone was estimated at $1,165,000.[15]

Local complaints against the lottery were counteracted by shrewd courting of popular favor with generous gifts for public enterprises and charity. Members of the Howard family became well known for their benefactions. Charles T. Howard, for example, in 1872 bought and converted Metaire Race Course into a beautiful cemetery at a cost of $350,000. Some critics sourly interpreted this move as pique at having been denied membership in the former. Upon his death in 1888 his daughter built and endowed Howard Memorial Library, and the following year Frank T. Howard erected the Confederate Memorial Building in New Orleans. Howard's successor in 1876, Maximilian A. Dauphin, saw to it that the company appeared frequently in the guise of a good angel, as, for instance, in its dramatic role in the floods of 1890.

But such tactics had little influence on national opinion. The admitted fact that 93 per cent of the lottery's revenue came from out-of-state sales — the totals of which were a carefully guarded secret — and the open flaunting of the antilottery laws of other states gave reformers ample ammunition. After 1878 every session of Congress saw bills introduced to end the Louisiana lottery by taxation or other means,[16] eleven such coming in the first session of the Forty-ninth Congress (1885) alone. Petitions descended on Washington from such varied groups as the Louisiana Anti-Lottery League, the Farmers Alliance of North Dakota, the Wage-Worker's Political Alliance, and the Society of Friends of Damascus, Ohio.[17] In 1884 and 1885 attempts to extend the postal ban to newspapers carrying lottery advertisements were defeated on the grounds of restricting freedom of the press.[18] The lottery company was also unsuccessfully challenged in four important court cases between 1879 and 1890.[19]

One by one northern journals ranged themselves in opposition, and several colorful personalities called dramatic attention to the evils of the system.[20] Two of the most outstanding foes outside of Louisiana were Anthony Comstock, agent for the New York Society for Suppression of Vice, and Alexander K. McClure, editor of the Philadelphia *Times*. Comstock proved particularly troublesome, raiding New York offices constantly for the first time in many years. After raids in December 1882, he reported that the Louisiana lottery offices in New York had averaged receipts of $5,176 per day over the previous twenty days. Refusing to be bribed, he almost single-handedly ended lottery business in the city.

In addition to taking direct action, Comstock wrote numerous magazine articles on the subject and exposed the faults of the contemporary lottery in his books, *Frauds Exposed* (1880) and *Traps For the Young* (1883). In chapters with headings such as "The Bogus Lotteries," "Havana and New Brunswick Lotteries," "The Louisiana State Lottery," and "The Lottery Parasite," he repeated the stories of illegality, crime, suicide, poverty, and fraud, concluding that the lottery was "the most extensive and far reaching of all gambling schemes." His campaign in New York was so successful that he was hired by the Post Office Department to investigate lotteries using the mails.[21]

McClure became interested after the Louisiana company had attempted several times to get him to run its illegal advertisements in his newspaper. His investigation proved that not less than $50,000 a year was paid for such services in Pennsylvania. By a test case in a local court he proved the ineffectiveness of the state's statute against lottery advertising, which penalized the advertiser and not the publisher, and secured the passage of a more stringent law in 1883, after a vigorous campaign by his paper. Faced with the subsequent loss of Pennsylvania's lucrative market, President Dauphin of the lottery company instituted a libel suit against McClure in the Pennsylvania courts. It was thrown out on the grounds that Dauphin's business was illegal and could claim no protection from criticism, a decision that was promptly appealed to the United States Supreme Court.

While the case was still pending, Colonel McClure visited the New Orleans Cotton Centennial Exposition of 1885, where he was immediately served with a writ claiming $100,000 damages for libel. Despite advice that state sentiment was with the lottery, McClure decided to fight the suit in the Louisiana courts. The case attracted national publicity during the year's delay before the trial date. Public opinion was swinging so much in McClure's favor that Dauphin decided to compromise, and offered to withdraw both suits and pay the editor $8,500 for costs. McClure accepted the offer, but the damage had already been done to the company's standing.[22]

Everywhere the 1880's brought increasing attacks upon the lottery system. Its old enemy, the *Friend*, accelerated its fight. Articles and editorials reminded Quaker clientele of the query of the annual meeting, "Do you maintain a faithful testimony against . . . encouraging lotteries of any kind?," and that this censure likewise applied to church raffles. The demoralizing effect of the Louisiana lottery was criticized in particular. On June 7, 1884, the journal gleefully headlined McClure's court victory, "To Characterize a Lottery as Robbery not Libelous."

About the same time the *Nation* also entered the fray. Pointing out the lack of progress in excluding lotteries from the mails, it derided the Louisiana firm's claims of being a mere defensive measure against the Havana Lottery or a public benefactor protecting an "infant industry" from the "pauper labor" of Cuba. Instead, the *Nation* argued that Louisiana's high rate of intemperance and illiteracy was the fruit of the lottery. So sharp were its attacks that state pride became involved. B. R. Forman of New Orleans retorted that the blame for the company and the ensuing evils all rested upon the Republican Party. General Sheridan had forced the Republican constitution upon the people in 1868; a Democratic legislature had repealed the lottery provision in 1879 only to have it upheld by a Harvard-trained, New England, Republican, United States judge, appointed by President U.S. Grant. He conveniently forgot to include the constitution and vote in 1879.

Regardless of where the responsibility lay, unfavorable publicity increased action on other fronts. In 1885 the Florida constitution prohibited lotteries, and Utah prohibited them two years later. In 1889 four more states, South Dakota, Washington, Idaho, and Montana made the same provision in their organic law. In the nation's capitol, Representative Henry H. Bingham of Pennsylvania and Senators George F. Edmunds of Vermont and Joseph R. Hawley of Connecticut, friends of McClure, pressed legislation in Congress to close the mails and express companies to lottery materials. In the Forty-ninth Congress twelve such bills were introduced, followed by seven more in the Fiftieth Congress (1887–88).

In a speech in Congress in 1890 Representative Orren C. Moore of New Hampshire gave the annual income and expenses of the Louisiana Lottery Company as follows:[23]

Income

Ten drawings, 1,000,000 tickets at $20 each	$20,000,000
Two drawings, 200,000 tickets at $40 each	8,000,000

Expenses

Prizes, ten drawings	$10,548,000

Prizes, two semi-annual drawings	4,219,200
Commissions to agents	2,000,000
Advertising	2,000,000
All other expenses	1,000,000
Net profit	8,232,800

In the interest of accuracy these figures must be qualified somewhat. In the first place, they apply only after 1888, when the drawings had reached their peak. They also presume that all tickets were sold, which doubtless was not the case. That, of course, might have been offset by the fact that the company retained any prize drawn to an unsold number. The biggest error was in the firm's favor, however, in failure to include the daily drawings. One critic contended that they alone paid all the operating expenses of the business.

President Dauphin reacted to these outside attacks by attempting to entrench his company more firmly in Louisiana. During the disastrous Mississippi River flood in the spring of 1890, $100,000 was offered the governor as aid. When Governor Nicholls refused on the grounds that renewal or extension of the firm's charter was a political issue and acceptance would place the people under an obligation, Dauphin announced on March 17 that the gift had been made directly to the people and apportioned to the various levee districts. Additional gifts were designated: $50,000 to New Orleans, $10,000 to the Fifth Levee District, $1,000 and more if needed to Shreveport, and the right to draw up to $2,500 against the company to Point Coupée and West Baton Rouge parishes. Seven hundred and fifty sacks of cotton seed were furnished to the washed-out farmers of St. Martin Parish, and a Dauphin-chartered boat toured the flood area carrying food and funds and rescuing the distressed. Lottery supporters were loud in their praises of such actions.

But opponents, such as the Reverend Carradine, maintained the company's motives were purely selfish. His pamphlet, *The Louisiana State Lottery Company; Examined and Exposed; Two Addresses and Additional Thoughts* (New Orleans, 1890), packed with ridicule and sarcasm, charged the press with suffering from a new disease, "La-Grippe-de-Greenback-de-la-Lottery." Ticket vendors were "like the frogs of Egypt in their numbers, and . . . in their disgusting ways of leaping on you and crawling into your homes." Citizens might as well save themselves the worry and expense of electing officials since "the Louisiana State Lottery Company is Ruler, Judge, Law-maker and Law-executor, for the fallen State of Louisiana." The Church had been made deaf and dumb by having its ears stuffed with bank notes and its lips sewed up with golden threads. The state had a new church — "The Louisiana State Lottery, Jewish, Catholic, Episcopal, Methodist, Baptist, Presbyterian Church" — which firmly believed in the union of church and state. Among its benefactions, the lottery could not let the people drown, for who would buy its tickets, especially those of the daily drawings, "so they will protect us at every hazard and cost, from the floods of the Mississippi, that they in the future be enabled to plunder us at their leisure." [24]

Undaunted, however, John A. Morris, representing the lottery firm, announced on April 17, 1890, that he would submit a proposition to give the state $500,000 a year instead of the stipulated paltry $40,000. In his message on May 12, Governor Nicholls warned the convening General Assembly that rechartering by constitutional amendment would be a bad move in state politics, a moral outrage against other states, and a continuation of the state's infamous partnership in a gambling operation. To him, the argument that lotteries were a necessary evil was fallacious.[25]

The next day Morris retorted that while his offer for a twenty-five year extension was ample compensation, he was prepared to go to $1,000,000 to supply the "absolute wants of the State." With such pyrotechnics, the Daily Picayune, May 13, 1890, was safe in announcing that rechartering would "be a burning issue" in that session of the legislature.

Closely watched by the nation, the battle began on June 4. House Bill No. 214, authorized by constitutional amendment John A. Morris, his heirs and assigns to conduct lotteries for twenty-five years after January 1, 1894, in return for a payment to the state of $1,000,000 per annum. This sum would be apportioned thus: $350,000 for schools, $350,000 for levees, $150,000 for charitable purposes, $50,000 for Confederate pensions, $100,000 for New Orleans drainage, and the remainder for the general fund. It was a division with widespread voter appeal.

Since the measure required a two-thirds majority, both sides began to organize for the vote. At first a majority of the legislators probably was in opposition and a caucus pledged unremitting opposition. Nevertheless, the group dwindled under tremendous pressure. An enemy of the company and a leading New Orleans lawyer, Edgar H. Farrar, described the tactics: "They subsidized everything there (at the capital) that wealth could buy — newspapers, barrooms, restaurants, houses of prostitution." They sought to intimidate members by threats of exposing their pasts; relatives were used for purposes of influence. As "fast as they captured a member, they set . . . a 'death watch' over him, that is, they had him accompanied night and day by two or three of their henchmen, who effectively prevented all communication with him." [26]

The majority report of the house committee argued the democracy in allowing the people to decide the issue for themselves. Besides, the state needed the money. The minority, on the other hand, stressed the political dangers inherent in the firm and pointed out that the report of the state treasurer showed a surplus for 1890. This group claimed also that if the company paid taxes proportionate to other businesses, the amount would be $1,772,000 annually. After a lengthy struggle, the lottery amendment passed the house despite such "acts of God" as the sudden illness of a new "convert," the paralysis of another supporter, the sickness of the bill's sponsor, and, at the time of voting, one of the most violent rain storms ever seen in Baton Rouge.

Opposition in the senate embraced constitutional, moral, and political issues. Senator Murphy J. Foster of St. Mary declared, "For my country and her honor, for the State and her good name, for her dead and for her living, I vote No." A colleague, Lloyd Posey, replied, "For my country and her poor, for her helpless and insane, for her onward march and future, I vote Yes." After approval of an amendment raising the annual payment to $1,250,000, the bill passed by exactly the two-thirds margin. With house approval of this change, the measure, providing for a vote of the people on the issue in 1892, was sent to the governor on July 1.

Almost immediately Governor Nicholls vetoed the bill on the implication of fraud and that "some other motive for this measure must be found than that her people are unable honorably to carry out for themselves the duty of statehood . . . I place the honor of the State above money . . ." His veto was just as promptly overridden by the house, 66 to 31. Senate supporters, however, faced a grave problem. The measure originally had passed with no votes to

spare, and now one of the backers was critically ill. Unable, therefore, to override the veto, the senate accepted the ruling of its
judiciary committee that executive approval was unnecessary for a
constitutional amendment. The lower house concurred, and the
measure went to the secretary of state for promulgation. That official, however, refused to act because of irregularities in the bill's
passage. Morris then went to court to force submission of the amendment to a vote of the people. Though losing in a lower court, he was
upheld on April 27, 1891, by the state supreme court by a vote of
three to two, thus leaving the final decision on lotteries to the election of 1892.[27]

The struggle naturally had been marked by personal derogation.
Governor Nicholls was accused of narrowness, ingratitude, and in-
consistency on the grounds that he previously had accepted help
from the lottery, and of trying to establish a "ring." Nicholls in-
sinuated that twelve members of the house and four of the senate
had been bought; two other legislators likewise were accused by
the *New Delta*, the antilottery organ. Only one case went to court,
however. Representative A. Joseph St. Amant of Ascension was ar-
rested for having received $16,000 from the company, but the suit
was dismissed on a technicality. Stories of bribery, nevertheless,
were rife throughout the state. Probably the truth was approximated
by a member who later stated that Dauphin "bought up any one
who was for sale. The other side bought up politicians with offices."

Meanwhile this strife at Baton Rouge was reflected in the rest of
the state, both during the fiasco between the governor and the legislature and during the period before the 1892 election. The Reverend
Carradine had lamented in February 1889 the indifference of the
people, saying that, as in the case of slavery, they had become accustomed to lotteries. But the dramatic events of 1890 could hardly
be ignored. From the outset, neither side had had a monopoly on
virtue. The New Orleans *Item*, April 29, 1891, remarked, "Take all
men in Louisiana who are opposed to Lotteries, whether rated by
character, ability, acquirements, property, family or social position,
and they can be matched, man for man, in every characteristic of
excellence, from the friends of the lottery amendment." Supporters
included almost all of the press, those citizens who believed the
company's payments were financially indispensable, and others who
were doubtlessly influenced by personal or political reasons. A con-

temporary commented that the amendment also commanded the solid support of the Negroes and the big New Orleans banks.

In opposition was a solid block of clergymen of various denominations, those people who believed the financial assistance was negated by political and moral evils, and those who saw the issue as means to political preferment. The Anti-Lottery League of Louisiana had been formed on February 28, 1890, in New Orleans by concerned citizens who anticipated the company's seeking a new charter. Interest was so great that a thousand persons attended its first public meeting. It was then that the *New Delta*, printed by the Methodist *Christian Advocate* and edited by C. H. Parker, former crusading editor of the *Picayune*, had been launched. No stone was left unturned to build up state public opinion against the lottery. A ladies auxiliary to the Anti-Lottery League was established under Mrs. William Preston Johnson, wife of the President of Tulane University. The Louisiana Annual Conference of the Methodist Church declared a boycott on all politicians in sympathy with the company and memorialized the state's congressmen for a constitutional amendment prohibiting lotteries in all states. Petitions for the legislature were circulated in New Orleans — "The Legislature cannot, and will not, ignore the prayers of thousands of the best citizens in the land." When the bill for amendment finally passed the legislature, the *Christian Advocate* promptly published, as a roll of honor, the names of the legislators voting against it.[28]

To effect a statewide organization, a convention of antilotteryites was called in Baton Rouge on August 7, 1890. Fifty-three parishes were represented by 956 delegates. There it was decided to battle the lottery simultaneously on two fronts — in Louisiana and in Congress. The Farmers Union strongly hinted it would join the fight. At the close of the meeting, control of the local political struggle was vested in the Democratic Anti-Lottery Executive Committee.

The formation of the Anti-Lottery League had been countered by creation of the Progressive League on July 29, 1890, to foster "all measures calculated to promote the public welfare, particularly in the matter of the improvement of the school and levee systems . . . , to provide for payment of the public debt, and to promote immigration; and with these ends in view, to use all honorable means to secure the adoption . . . of the proposed lottery amendment." New England and other states, as well as the countries of

Europe, had used lotteries when they were poor — and why should Louisiana deny herself such funds? According to the New Orleans *Times-Democrat*, these gentlemen were intelligent, patriotic, and influential men who were aware of the financial situation and were "determined that no false idea of morality, no silly sentimentality shall prevent Louisiana from securing for the next twenty-five years the $1,250,000 per annum offered for a lottery franchise." [29]

Nationally, the division was not so equal. By this time church opinion also had caught up with public opinion and official denunciations of the "octopus" came from national religious organizations. The Methodist General Conference of 1890 denounced the lottery as a national disgrace and stated its determination to aid Louisiana's citizens in ridding themselves of it forever. Southern Baptists in their conventions in 1890 and 1891 wished them "God speed" and pledged "moral sanction." Cardinal James Gibbons of Baltimore issued an encyclical to his people instructing them to work against the lottery.[30] Individual clergymen and congregations of other denominations also were active.

A professor of engineering at the Massachusetts Institute of Technology, Samuel Homer Woodbridge, was destined to serve as one of the main catalytic agents in the struggle. While visiting in New Orleans in the winter of 1890–91, he wrote a letter to the Reverend Lyman Abbott, editor of the *Christian Union* of New York, urging that the Christian forces of the country do something to help end the lottery evil and suggesting that on a fixed day preceding the Louisiana election an appeal should be made from all pulpits to the Christian conscience and purse. The letter was brought to the attention of General George D. Johnston, formerly of the Confederate Army and president of South Carolina's Citadel, who had been sent north by the Anti-Lottery League to seek moral and financial help. Johnston and Woodbridge made many of the plans for the northern campaign. A circular was printed, signed by Bishop Phillips Brooks, Dr. Edward Everett Hale, and other Boston religious leaders, setting the second Sunday of March "as the day of the Church's advance on the foe." The plan, however, was dropped when it was learned that the antilottery forces had gained a small majority of the delegates to the Democratic state convention of Louisiana.

The *Christian Union* served as the coordinator of northern support. Besides conducting a drive to raise funds, it organized a mass meeting in New York in November 1891 with General Johnston, President Seth Low of Columbia University, and former Mayor Abram S. Hewett of New York among the speakers. Levi P. Morton, Vice President of the United States, President Samuel Gompers of the American Federation of Labor, and Episcopal Bishop Henry C. Potter sent letters. The rally was well attended, with over 200 standees. The group not only pledged financial help, but in its resolutions also asked for congressional assistance and for Republican Party influence upon the Negroes of Louisiana, whose votes apparently would be decisive in the 1892 election.[31] Other meetings took place as far west as Seattle and as far north as Lowell and Newburyport, Massachusetts. A Boston gathering received letters from poets John Greenleaf Whittier and Oliver Wendell Holmes and featured such dignitaries as a former governor and the mayor.[32]

But far more important currents had been undermining the lottery on the national scene. In a generation turning more and more to the concept of government regulation as a cure for social maladjustments, exemplified by the Interstate Commerce Act of 1887 and the Sherman Anti-Trust Act of 1890, it was not surprising that many felt the solution of the lottery problem also lay in federal action. The Cincinnati *Commercial Gazette*, July 19, 1890, bluntly called Congress the protector of the lottery and denominated the Louisiana firm the "United States Lottery" since 97 per cent of its revenue came from outside the state. Later it said the name should be the "Congressional Lottery" if the present session ended without action. The New York *Herald* pointed out that the lottery's robbery and demoralization was possible only through use of the mails and that the traffic was no less criminal than polygamy, against which Congress had taken stringent measures. The Philadelphia *Press* called the government's unwitting role a "national shame" and added that congressional action at this time would probably influence Louisiana to deny a new charter.[33] In fact, most antilottery spokesmen were of the opinion that both state and national action would be necessary to destroy the system.

Already sensitive to the situation, President Benjamin Harrison in his first annual message, December 3, 1889, called attention to the unsatisfactory postal laws regarding lotteries and suggested they be amended. But before any action could be taken, public notice was suddenly diverted to the new state of North Dakota where the Louisiana Lottery Company had been secretly active. Almost immediately after statehood was conferred in November, the legislature began consideration of a franchise for the company for approximately $100,000 per annum and 150,000 bushels of seed wheat. Under the covert prodding of George H. Spencer, former United States Senator from Alabama and now the lottery's agent, the poverty of the state and its $539,807 in bonded indebtedness was stressed. As a result, Senate Bill No. 167, or the Landager Lottery Bill, passed the state senate by more than a two-thirds majority before most of the public became aware of what was happening.

Promptly, Governor John Miller organized the opposition, raising funds to fight the measure, circulating petitions, employing detectives to seek evidence of suspected bribery, securing publication of articles in the press, and obtaining letters from prominent businessmen and bankers of St. Paul, Minneapolis, Chicago, and New York. Professor William Patten of the state university and eight other faculty members were so outspoken that the senate retaliated by passing a bill drastically cutting salaries at the institution. A march on Bismarck was organized, composed of representative men of all professions and classes in the state. Pinkerton detectives openly claimed to have amounts and dates of payment, as well as names. Overawed, the lower house postponed the bill indefinitely. According to the Bismarck *Tribune*, February 11, 1890, the lottery proponents decided to drop the measure rather than have it killed, although Pinkerton detectives believed it was to stop further investigations by them.

Credit for the defeat was claimed by many. The governor gave as a cause the fear aroused by the activities of the Pinkertons. *Our Day* put in its bid, because upon learning of the "plot," copies of that magazine were sent to the North Dakota legislature and newspapers. The St. Paul *Pioneer Press* editorialized it was "proud to know it was the chief instrument in exposing the lottery plot in that State, and in preventing the surprise that would have brought the lottery project to success." The Cleveland *Plain-Dealer* argued the move would have been successful if it had not been for Governor Miller and his attorney general. Some believed the whole affair was merely a ruse by Dauphin to frighten the Louisiana legislature, but there were also strong rumors that he had made heavy contributions to the Republican Party in Delaware with the intention of obtaining a license there if his efforts were unsuccessful elsewhere.[34]

This narrow escape severely frightened the nation, and because several months in 1890 had gone by without congressional action, public criticism of the federal government began to mount. Eight proposed laws, including bills to close the mails to newspapers containing lottery advertisements and to forfeit the charter of national banks that guaranteed payment of lottery prizes, had been introduced since the session opened. In March the *Friend* suggested the delay resulted from a strong lottery lobby, and the New York *Times* shortly afterwards stated that the legislation was being prevented by campaign contributions to such an extent that the lottery was becoming a "protected industry." The Philadelphia *Ledger* hinted darkly that Speaker Thomas B. Reed's rules might be holding up a law that "decent opinion" everywhere outside of Louisiana wanted.

Undoubtedly needled by such charges, Postmaster General John Wanamaker wrote to the President on June 28, 1890, that a recent investigation proved that the Washington office of the Louisiana Lottery Company dispatched 50,000 letters per month and that those received might be "safely counted by the ton. What is true of Washington is probably five-fold true of New Orleans." This vast enterprise, he complained, was "terribly demoralizing" to the postal service and caused large outlays for inspectors to trace lost or stolen letters. The temptation to pilfer was exceptionally great as employees assumed such letters contained money whose loss would be difficult to prove. Wanamaker was personally embarrassed that good citizens might think him ignorant of the scope of the lottery activities or else unconcerned. Precisely, he was humiliated that the post-office system was the "principal agent of the lottery" and that every extension of its service spread the harmful power and influence of the company. Yet, under existing laws, he was powerless to do anything to stop it.

Prevailing statutes did fail to give the Postmaster General authority to delay or withhold any ordinary sealed letter which he might believe related to a lottery. Nor could he prevent delivery of registered mail or payment of money orders unless it could be proven that the addressee was actually engaged in conducting a lottery. Warrants were necessary which particularly described the letters to be seized. On one occasion, for example, the lottery company had had its mail addressed to a New Orleans bank to avoid suspicion.[35]

Armed with this information, President Harrison sent a special message to Congress on July 29, 1890, asking for "severe and effective legislation . . . to purge the mails of all letters, newspapers, and circulars relating to the business." He cited the recent effort in North Dakota, the proposed renewal in Louisiana, and the establishment of Mexican lotteries near our borders as making immediate action imperative. It was impossible to contain the lottery within a single state, instead "people of all States are debauched and defrauded." Mail service had become an "effective and profitable medium of intercourse" for the lottery, and the belief was prevalent that "the corrupting touch of those agents [had] been felt by the clerks of the postal service and by some of the police officers of the District." That Washington seemed to have become a sub-headquarters for the company further justified prompt action.[36]

A bill, representing several committee-combined measures, was introduced in the House by Representative John A. Caldwell of Ohio on August 16, 1890. In the debate, much was made of the fact that forty-two of forty-four states had some sort of ban on lotteries and even one of the representatives from Louisiana spoke against the system. With no one defending it, the primary point at issue was the right of the Postmaster General to refuse to deliver mail to an agent of the lottery. The measure passed the House the same day and was reported without amendment to the Senate on September 2 by Philetus Sawyer of Wisconsin. It was passed September 16 without record of any debate. The act became law on September 19 and barred all letters, postal cards, circulars, lists of drawings, tickets, and other materials referring to lotteries from the mails. No check, draft bill, money, postal note, or money order for purchase of chances could be transported; nor any newspaper, circular, or pamphlet listing such activities be carried. Registered letters would be returned unopened. Violations brought a maximum fine of $500 and/or one year in prison.[37]

Postmaster Wanamaker did not wait for the expected decision by the Supreme Court on the law's constitutionality, but put it into effect immediately. A fearless man was appointed postmaster in New Orleans, and thousands of pieces of mail were seized and immense masses of evidence collected. The first arrest in the New Orleans area was made November 5, 1890, when J. Pinckney Smith, business manager of the *Daily States*, was seized for mailing editions containing lottery advertisements. Paul Conrad, who succeeded Dauphin as president of the lottery company in December 1890, was soon involved in a large number of criminal proceedings, particularly for attempting to use an ice company as a blind.

The immensity of the government's action was obvious in that approximately 45 per cent of the entire New Orleans post office business concerned the lottery. Registered letters addressed to the company brought in an average of $11,000,000 annually, or $30,000 a day. An estimated $3,000,000 from all over the world came in yearly in other forms, not including amounts carried by express companies or through New Orleans sales. Wanamaker was able to report fifty-six convictions in the first nine months, and as President Harrison later noted in his second annual address, the new law had "been received with great and deserved popular favor." A check of the press of the period justifies this statement.[38]

The national press gave all aspects of the fight wide coverage and showed that it, too, had brought its conscience up to date. The Postmaster General was quoted in 1891 as saying that of the 2,259 editorials in 850 journals noticed during the past year by his department, 2,172 had been opposed to the lottery.[39] The files of *Public Opinion*, 1890–1892, graphically illustrates the widespread interest, with quoted comments from all sections of the country. The national scope was stressed with appeals to the Louisiana voters not to go against the wishes of the rest of the United States in their 1892 vote. That failing, Congress was exhorted to take a final decisive role. In opposition to these views was the stand that an antilottery law could not be enforced and that proposed remedies violated freedom of the press, states rights, and the liberties of the people.

Numerous magazines opened their columns. *Our Day* featured two Comstock articles, "The Louisiana Lottery, A National Scourge" (November 1889) and "The Louisiana Lottery Octopus" (June 1890). The *Nation* covered the battle seven times in 1890–1892. In March 1890 the *Chautauquan* printed a résumé of the history of lotteries in the United States, and the *Century*'s stand was so vigorous as to call forth the praise of the *Nation*. The *Century* published such articles as "The Lottery's Last Ditch," Clarence C. Buel's

"Degradation of a State," "Will an American State be Guilty of Suicide?" and "The Louisiana Lottery a National Infamy."

Like the *Century,* the *Christian Union* kept a staff correspondent in Louisiana and gave almost a day-by-day account of events in that state, as well as serving as steward for antilottery contributions. In its issue of February 27, 1892, for example, the magazine announced receipt of $746.64 from residents of California, New York, New Jersey, Pennsylvania, Indiana, and Massachusetts during the preceding week. The *Forum* ran two long features in its January 1892 issue, one of which was written by the editor of the *New Delta.* In the next number Horace White, a member of the editorial staff of the New York *Evening Post,* discussed the possibility of killing the lottery by federal taxation. Also in February, the *Charities Review* headlined an article by lawyer Edgar H. Farrar, a Louisiana opponent, on "The Louisiana Lottery: Its History"; Edward Everett Hale vented his anger in *Cosmopolitan;* and Anthony Comstock flayed the company in the *North American Review.* The April *Atlantic Monthly* continued White's taxation theme with an essay by former chief justice Thomas M. Cooley of Michigan. In this sampling of the various articles and editorials can be seen the unconscious beginning of the coming reform cycle, the muckraking era, which reached its hegemony approximately a decade later. Here were attacks upon one of the original "big businesses."

In Louisiana Conrad and his cohorts were losing ground fast in the late months of 1891. All they had left to pin their hopes upon was the Louisiana election of 1892. A great deal needed attention. A contemporary foe of the company asserted that by 1892 the whole bar, "except a few in the pay of the lottery," nine-tenths of the doctors, all of the clergy, "except one or two French priests, one renegade Episcopal minister and one 'piney-woods' Baptist preacher," almost all of the professors and teachers, the organized farmers, and a majority of the great sugar planters and merchants, were opposed to extending the charter.[40]

Bitterness over the issue infected the coincident race for state officers. The Democrats split after a bitter struggle in the state convention in December 1891, and each faction put up a slate of candidates. The antilottery group nominated Murphy J. Foster and Charles Parlange and the recharter advocates named ex-governors Samuel D. McEnery and R. C. Wickliffe as candidates for governor and lieutenant governor respectively. Each combination called itself the regular party organization and the other the "rump." Even the Republicans divided, with the lotteryites under ex-governor W. P. Kellogg supporting Albert Leonard and the opposition under Henry C. Warmoth backing John A. Breaux. A Populist nominee brought the number of gubernatorial candidates to five.

Meanwhile, both schools of thought claimed wide followings. Membership in the Anti-Lottery League had mounted to the "thousands," while the opposing Progressive League announced enrollment of 6,000 in New Orleans alone. Both leagues held political meetings throughout the state. These gatherings usually featured a barbecue and four or five speakers, one or more speaking in French. Excitement mounted almost daily; some episodes of open violence were recorded and rumors were rife in the national and local newspapers that both sides were securing arms. Antilottery forces among the Democrats claimed they were fighting for clean government and that their opponents were trying to win the election by bribery. The Democratic lottery supporters retorted that they were in politics only for defensive purposes and that the antilottery group was making the lottery issue "a gas bag to float its political organization." Both groups claimed to fear a Republican victory if the other were successful. Serious personal charges were made on both sides, involving men as highly placed as Senator Randall Lee Gibson, future Chief Justice of the Supreme Court Edward D. White, and former Speaker of the House and future Secretary of the Treasury John G. Carlisle.[41]

At the same time the test case for the congressional antilottery law had been instituted when in February 1891 George W. Dupre of the *Daily States* notified authorities that he had violated the statute. A similar case was made against John L. Rapier of Mobile, Alabama. On petition for writs of habeas corpus, the cases went to the Supreme Court. The defense contended that lotteries were not *mala in se* and that Congress had no general power over lotteries established in the states or over freedom of the press. In February 1892 the court ruled unanimously that Congress could "designate what may be carried in the mails and what excluded."[42] Following this decision, Conrad notified his employees to observe the law, and began conducting his business by express. Newspapers either printed two editions or used the express to avoid penalty.

Three days after the supreme court's verdict Morris withdrew his bid for a franchise, regardless of the outcome of the April election. It was then argued that the Fosterites no longer had validity for existence and a call was made for Democratic unity. Foster's supporters, however, feared a ruse and announced they were going to stay in the race to make sure the issue did not come up later in a constitutional convention. In the primary on March 22, 1892, the results were so close that both sides were claiming victory five days later. The election committee split, with the majority saying that Foster had won by 549 votes and the minority giving McEnery the victory by 1,570.

McEnery's backers refused to accept the majority report, so the campaign continued unabated until the general election. There the official count gave Foster 79,388 votes and McEnery 47,037. Both sides used the Negro vote extensively and probably on occasion "counted out" the opposition. Foster carried forty-seven parishes and McEnery only twelve. The totals on the lottery amendment were 4,225 for and 157,422 against. These results sealed the fate of the lottery company in the state. The climaxing blow came with the passage by the 1892 legislature of a bill prohibiting ticket sales after December 31, 1893, and providing penalties for drawing, advertising, or soliciting for a lottery.[43]

With its charter soon to expire and a hostile government in Louisiana, the lottery began seriously to look for a new sanctuary. After applications to the Queen of the Hawaiian Islands and to the Mexican, Colombian, and Nicaraguan governments were refused, Honduras was selected as the nominal home. In October 1893 Paul Conrad announced that after January 1, 1894, the business would operate in Honduras under a twenty-five-year contract and that all communications should be addressed to him at Puerto Cortez, care of Central American Express, Port Tampa City, Florida.[44]

Conrad had not, however, given up the American market. An inlet into the United States was provided by a provision in the Florida antilottery law which made it permissible for a state company to print lottery matter, do clerical work, and other "legitimate" business connected with lotteries, although no actual lottery was allowed nor could tickets be drawn in the state. This loophole let Conrad operate from his closely guarded building at Port Tampa, with the drawings being held at Puerto Cortez or at sea on the company-owned steamer *Breakwater*. The firm organized the Central American Express so that tickets and money could be transmitted without conflict with postal authorities. Literature was sent out by express or freight, and almanac and theater-program printers were well paid to run advertisements.[45]

Public alarm over the failure to stop the system alerted its foes to action. Professor Woodbridge prevailed upon the Reverend Lyman Abbott, at that time on the *Outlook,* to lead the fight for another federal law. The national movement was begun during the winter of 1893 by an appeal to about two hundred of the country's best-known citizens by the leading clergymen and residents of Boston. Next a petition written by C. B. Spahr, associate editor of *Outlook,* and signed by twenty-nine university and college presidents, thirty-eight Episcopal bishops, ten Methodist bishops, a cardinal, three archbishops, eight governors, eight former members of Congress, and numerous other dignitaries was sent to Congress. With this went a bill drawn by Austin Abbott, a constitutional lawyer of New York, to end all lottery activity. A national mail campaign followed, and during the second session of the Fifty-third Congress there were over 157 abolition petitions, and thirty more were presented during the next session. A Senate resolution also called for an inquiry into whether or not the Louisiana, or Honduras, Lottery was operating in Florida.

On February 15, 1894, Senator George F. Hoar of Massachusetts presented the memorial and bill to the Senate. The measure was redrafted and reported unanimously to the Senate on April 27, only to lie idle. Steady pressure was brought to bear by the antilottery groups throughout the country, who kept up a constant stream of letters and petitions. Printed information was furnished the religious and secular press by Woodbridge's cohorts. Finally the bill was assigned so low a place on the Senate calendar that it probably could not be reached during the session. Hoar asked unanimous consent to take it up ahead of schedule. He was defeated by George G. Vest of Missouri and Arthur P. Gorman of Maryland, who caused consternation by defending lotteries as allies of the church. But on May 19 the bill was moved up, passed, and sent to the House.

Here the story was much the same after it was reported favorably from committee by Representative Case Broderick of Kansas on July 27. Despite the passage of the Wilson Tariff Act of August 1,

1894, with a section prohibiting importation of any lottery paraphernalia, opponents of the Hoar bill fought a delaying action. Increased pressure was put on the representatives. Religious newspaper subscription rolls, church registers, college catalogs, and other lists were secured, and about 20,000 documents a week were sent out by the Boston headquarters pressing for favorable action in the House. The press was almost in complete agreement in its support. A move for unanimous consent to consider the bill out of turn was first defeated by Walter I. Hayes of Iowa, who was accused of representing the liquor and gambling interests, but he in turn was soon silenced by pressure from his constituents. On a second and third occasion, Robert C. Davey of New Orleans objected, frankly admitting he was instructed to do so by forces in his district and that he would continue his objections.

Apparently this ended the matter, since there was an unwritten rule that a bill failing to be called up on three attempts would not be voted on again. However, Speaker Charles F. Crisp of Georgia favored the measure and privately told Broderick to "watch for and improve any opportunity." It was therefore called up during an absence of Davey, but he arrived in time to object. Time was running out — adjournment was scheduled in ten days. Woodbridge and his friends fought desperately. All religious papers with as many as 5,000 subscribers were sent documents wrapped and stamped with the request that they be forwarded to leading men and women on their lists. Efforts particularly were centered upon the clergy of nine states whose representatives were thought to be uncertain. The legislatures of New Jersey and Massachusetts passed resolutions asking their representatives to do all they could for the bill. Finally, by aid of Speaker Crisp, on March 1, 1895, the bill was called up and passed, but had, to go back to the Senate for approval of a House amendment. More time was lost while Senators Henry Cabot Lodge and Hoar led the fight against Gorman, Vest, and Calvin S. Brice of Ohio. It was finally passed, but was so delayed in engrossing that only ten hours were left for it to receive the President's examination and signature before Congress adjourned.[46] If Postmaster General Wilson S. Bissell had not taken the act and pressed it upon President Cleveland for examination and signature, it probably would have failed to meet the deadline. However, it was signed with only two minutes to spare.[47]

This statute closed all forms of interstate commerce to lottery companies and provided a maximum fine of $1,000 or imprisonment of more than two years for bringing such material into the country or sending it from one state to another. Second offenses were punishable by confinement alone. The law was tested in Champion v. Ames and was upheld as valid under the commerce clause by the Supreme Court in 1903,[48] establishing a precedent used by later legislation excluding obscene literature, impure foods, and so forth, from interstate commerce. Attempts to bring in tickets as personal baggage of lottery agents were halted by successful prosecution in 1907.

Thus ended the legal saga of the American lottery, a pervasive force for over one hundred and sixty years in the drama of America. It had been used to build one-room schoolhouses and to endow university research; to cross creeks and to span rivers; to blaze trails in the wilderness and to construct turnpikes between cities; to clear streams for the fish and to open rivers for ships; to outfit soldiers for war and to build churches for worship. It was a game that expanded to become a national financial institution; a paradoxical temptress, many times a helpmate, but whose vices too often overshadowed her virtues.

Chapter XIV

Conclusions and Present Trends

> Clergymen never seem to realize that if the people cannot
> gamble in the open, they will find other means of doing so.
> This is human nature and two good examples of this were
> prohibition and the black market during war time. A lot-
> tery would create many jobs for vets and drive the racke-
> teers out of this very lucrative business.
>
> — TAX MINDED[1]

By January 1, 1894, the legal lottery in the United States was no
more. In addition to the federal laws, thirty-five states had constitutional prohibitions and most of the remainder had strong statutes
against such schemes. Thus, a device that once could claim country-
wide acceptance was nationally denounced and its supporters muted
by public opinion.

The reasons for this reversal, as well as the original acceptance,
lay in the changing cultural characteristics of American society. The
story of the United States is a history of many frontiers, constantly
shifting and in varying stages of development. The structure and
purpose of the lottery was altered by these changing conditions.
Thus, what began as a simple system on a small scale became a complicated one on a grandiose scale, and coincidentally changed from
an economic expedient to a device primarily aimed at exploitation.
"Good causes" yielded to the gambler's "easy money" as the primary
lure, and the drawings became frankly games of chance.

The earliest lotteries were a natural result of frontier conditions
— merchandising schemes to dispose of property at a time when
normal mediums of exchange were scarce. Then, as the communities
became more organized, so did the lotteries, and official intervention
was made necessary by flagrant abuses. Although by that time there

was less need for this means of retailing goods, other economic problems remained which lotteries could help solve, and consequently only drawings without legislative sanction were banned. There were increasing demands by defense, town and city development, internal improvements, and new churches and schools. Of the approximately 158 lotteries licensed before 1776, 132 benefited civic or state purposes. To a great degree this explained why citizens such as John Hancock, Benjamin Franklin, and George Washington managed lotteries for their communities, thus making valuable contributions to the economy of the provinces.

After the outbreak of the Revolution, the Continental Congress led the way by establishing a lottery to finance the war. For the next few decades the expanding country and population placed new burdens upon state treasuries, and the bulk of such franchises went to churches, schools, and internal improvements. The lottery itself changed little during this period, remaining a local institution, an acceptable and legitimate way of raising money. As practiced, it was still the innocent charmer or, at worst, a necessary evil. However, the system did conceive some of the malpractices it would harbor at a later date, such as the practice of "insurance," which eluded every effort at prohibition, and the lack of managerial responsibility, which necessitated the bonding of managers. A few protests were heard from Quakers and isolated individuals questioning whether the Bible approved use of the lot.

While the lottery had not gone into its metamorphosis, during the confederation and early federal period, the nature of the people and the nation had. Toward 1815, however, the lottery began reflecting the national maturation. The trend in the North was toward making fewer but larger authorizations, since much of the Northeast was growing up, was financially more stable, and the lottery was thought not quite so proper a method to finance reputable projects. Originally it had been considered a tax supplement, but by now most states had, or were in the process of achieving, more adequate methods of taxation. The lottery had also served as almost the only means of tapping small sums of potential investment capital. This function was gradually being assumed by the slowly developing commercial banking system. From only three banks in the United States in 1791, the number mounted to 88 in 1811 and 1,601 by the Civil War. The introduction of the corporation, with its use of stocks and bonds, specialized investment bankers, and "exchanges," expedited the collection of capital funds from many sources. Then, too, the increase in private wealth was reflected in accelerated private benevolence, as old charitable institutions expanded and numerous new ones appeared, robbing the lottery of still another excuse for existence.

The impetus for new drawings shifted to the less sophisticated South and West. Six southern legislatures supplied over half of the franchises issued after 1815. Again the greater proportion was for schools, bridges, canals, river transportation, and roads. The schemes underwent decided changes. Formerly quiet affairs, they were now bought up by brokerage firms with interstate connections, until five or six large companies controlled the national market. Lotteries became a big business with streamlined methods of distribution. Thousands of competing offices sold tickets and "insurance." Drawings were held every day, and citizens invested not only in those of their own community but also in many others.

Coincident with these features was the outbreak of spectacular examples of abuse. State after state experienced cases of mismanagement and of suicides caused by embezzlement of funds to gamble in the lotteries. Public attention focused on the system and closer observation revealed the terrific levy made on the poor by the illegal, but flourishing, trade in "insurance." Correlation between the long lines of petitioners at the bankruptcy courts and participation in these ventures was revealed. The true evil of the lottery became more apparent: its effect upon the participants — their visionary and unreal expectations, debts, disdain for honest labor, and impetus toward crime.

Greater experience with the system also tended to deflate its reputation as a "voluntary tax, cheerfully paid." For one thing, the burden fell most heavily upon those least able to pay it. It is interesting that early labor groups fought such schemes as a pernicious form of taxation. For another, it harmed legitimate business by tying up vast sums for the purpose of raising relatively little. Then, too, with the disassociation from local control, people ceased to identify themselves with the beneficiary and it was easy to lose faith in the directors, to conclude that the only rewards went to the contractors and ticket agents.

These conditions were aggravated by the depression of 1826–1830, and public opinion swung strongly against the lottery. The reform fever was high and all debatable practices were suspect. Most legislators started wondering how soon they could curtail lottery activity without breaking previous commitments. The Panic of 1837 re-emphasized the desire to destroy this "strangling parasite." It is noteworthy that by 1840 twelve of the twenty-six states had taken definite prohibitive action, and a majority of the others were only awaiting the expiration of contracts. Significantly, most states felt so strongly as to write a ban on future authorizations into their constitutions. This trend continued until by the time of the Civil War legal lotteries existed only in Delaware and Kentucky, and in Missouri crooked politicians had made it possible to exploit a repealed charter.

The effect of the Civil War was great upon the people and, in turn, upon the lotteries. The earlier reforming zeal gave way to a blatant materialism. This moral letdown and the postwar economic dislocation bred a revival of lotteries — legal and illegal. An interesting new characteristic was added. The term "lottery" still carried ill repute in the public mind, so the game flourished under new names — as scientific, art, mutual aid, agricultural, and library "associations" — just as in the future the sordid saloon would be reborn as a sophisticated cocktail lounge. It was even more imperative that illegal undertakings assume a protective camouflage, not only from the public but also from the law. Therefore a new variety of lotteries swept the country under the most common denomination of "gift" enterprises, especially tailored to fit loopholes in existing statutes.

But the public and legal agencies were not long fooled. Mississippi's action in repealing its lottery charter and being upheld by the Supreme Court gave lottery opposition a new weapon. Other states changed their laws, driving illicit schemes out of business or underground. In a relatively short time only the gigantic Louisiana State Lottery dominated the scene. With just the slightest claim to public benefaction, but with a near monopoly of the United States market, it ruthlessly exploited all in reach and showed such an utter disregard for law that it became a national problem. So greatly did this "octopus" prosper that it was able to offer a million and a quarter dollars a year for renewal of its franchise.

This phenomenon was occurring at a time when Americans were becoming concerned over the activities of other forms of monopoly. Also, the ripening realization of the need for state cooperation on a national scale made it increasingly obvious that the states could not protect themselves so long as any one of them sanctioned such ventures. Thus there began a concerted effort for federal intervention. The United States government denied use of the mails to the Louisiana company, but had to go even further. In 1895 the all but fatal blow came from the closure of interstate commerce to lottery material.

But human frailties cannot be legislated. The speculative urge and the desire to "get something for nothing" that made such undertakings possible in the past is still alive. A number of foreign countries — Cuba, Panama, Italy, Japan, France, Russia, and Norway, to name only a few — have continued to use this method for revenue. A royal commission set up to investigate Britain's gambling habits in 1950 found public and church opinion taking a very liberal view of almost all forms of gambling. Two Catholic clerics, Cyril Cowderoy, Bishop of Southwark, and Canon Thomas Fitzgerald told the commission that the Church would not oppose a state lottery. In April 1956 Harold MacMillan, Chancellor of the Exchequer, announced a new bond issue with lottery characteristics to give it appeal.[2]

A survey in Australia in 1942 showed that 77 per cent of the voters approved lotteries for hospitals and charity financing. A 1954 public opinion poll showed that 92 per cent of the citizens "down under" had bought lottery tickets and 81 per cent approved of the schemes run by five of Australia's states. Every second person, the poll showed, had won a prize at some time. In 1956, with drawings almost every day, Australians were expected to buy 100,000,000 tickets at a per capita expenditure of about ten dollars in their zeal for prizes as large as $562,500, tax free.[3]

In 1923 Russia banned such schemes but reinstated them in 1930 in cases found worthy by the People's Commissar for Finance. During World War II lotteries ran up to 2,200,000,000 rubles and were paid off in cash and in items as varied as women's clothing. One of the largest modern undertakings was instigated in May 1946 by the Russians in the form of a 20,000,000,000 ruble (nominally $3,774,-000,000) lottery loan. Every citizen was asked to subscribe at least a month's wages in return for non-interest-bearing government bonds whose serial numbers were also chances. One-third of the bonds won cash prizes up to 50,000 rubles ($9,435).[4]

Nor is the idea of lotteries dead in the United States. Newspapers tell of daily arrests in the "numbers" or "policy" rackets, lineal descendants of the old "insurance" game. In "policy" the numbers from 1 through 78 are placed in a little wheel and twelve are drawn out. A player bets that he can write down three, four, or five of them, although the odds against him are 199 to one; 399 to one; and 1,999 to one, respectively. The "numbers" players bet on three-digit numbers from 000 to 999, and the winning number is determined variously by the day's pari-mutuel figures at a race track, the digits that come up in a stock exchange, or some similar figures. The odds are one in 1,000 but the payments as low as 99 to one. Approximately one billion dollars annually is spent on these rackets, with the operators clearing half.[5]

"Bingo," legally defined as a lottery, has become almost a national pastime, and the Federal Communications Commission has been troubled in recent years in trying to draw the line between legitimacy and illegality in countless radio and television "give away" shows. America, moreover, is a big market for outside lotteries. The most famous instance is the Irish Sweepstakes, which earns more than $500,000 annually for the Dublin hospitals and whose tickets find a ready, though illegal, market in this country. The Jamaica Sweepstakes has its fans also; as recently as May 1955 ten thousand envelopes mailed in the British West Indies to Chicago residents were intercepted by post office inspectors because they contained tickets.[6] Foreign winners are played up and romanticized by United States journals in much the same fashion as during the days when such schemes were legitimate.[7]

Signposts marking the widening acceptability of lotteries and kindred games are plentiful. Public opinion already looks with toleration, if not approval, upon church and club raffles, although they are technically illegal. War and soaring governmental debts have led to a rash of proposals that lotteries be legalized. In 1941 a poll by the American Institute of Public Opinion on the desirability of paying the national debt in this fashion found 51 per cent of the respondents in favor of government lotteries, 38 per cent opposed, and 11 per cent expressing no choice. The introduction in Congress of such a bill in 1942 led to a Gallup Poll based on the following query: "Would you favor lotteries run by the federal government to help pay part of the cost of carrying on the war?" Fifty-four per cent answered affirmatively, 37 per cent negatively, and 9

per cent were undecided. If the survey is confined to those expressing a choice, the result would be 60 per cent in favor, a substantial
majority. Those approving did so mainly on the old grounds —
"People are going to gamble anyway, and some of that money might
as well go to the government." Those in opposition declared gambling a sin and held that lotteries would be beneath the dignity of
the government.[8]

Also symptomatic of this changing opinion has been the advocation of national lotteries in bills introduced periodically in Congress.
Such measures in 1934 and 1938 received sufficient support to bring
forth protests from some religious groups.[9] Typical of such bills was
that sponsored in 1949 by Representative L. Cary Clemente of New
York; it would have let post offices sell tickets, winnings would have
been tax free, and the proceeds would have gone for veterans' benefits. Franklin D. Roosevelt favored the institution of a national lottery for charitable ends and pointed to the success of this practice in
Ireland. The idea at times has been supported by such columnists
as John O'Donnell and Arthur Krock, who was quoted as having referred to the period of legal lotteries as a time "when Americans
were sensible." [10] Inclusion of a national lottery plank in the 1956
Republican Party platform was urged on the grounds that it would
add ten billion dollars to federal revenue, providing "a tax cut for
every taxpayer in this country," and would receive "substantial support" from the voters.[11]

Even greater efforts have been made on a state level. The following examples are characteristic. In 1937 Nevada, the only state with
legalized gambling, defeated a constitutional amendment to create
a state lottery, with the gamblers, curiously enough, leading the opposition. A year later a proposed constitutional change sought to
legalize such undertakings in Maryland. The Massachusetts legislature turned down five bills for a state lottery in January 1941. On
December 4, 1948, state senator-elect Vincent E. Hull of New Jersey
announced that at the next session of the Assembly he was introducing such a measure to finance a $180,000,000 veterans' bonus.
The February 1949 all-woman grand jury in Philadelphia pronounced: "Legalization of betting and lotteries would save the commonwealth a great sum of money in the prosecution of these cases
and some form of taxation on lotteries would bring funds into the
commonwealth." In November 1950, after the legislature had

ducked a vote on the issue, Massachusetts voters passed on an initiative petition sponsored by the Massachusetts Society for Old Age Pensions for such a scheme to help finance old-age assistance. The program called for 50 per cent of the revenue to go out in prizes, 15 per cent to be used to aid the blind and dependent children, and the rest to be used for the aged. The organized opposition condemned the project as "leading to corruption and graft," as "a plan for painless prosperity — pie in the sky," and asserted that to raise the required $54,000,000 would necessitate annual purchase of $150's worth of tickets per capita. Though few initiatives have been defeated in Massachusetts, this one was. In December 1952 the city council of New York, over the objection of the council president, Rudolph Halley, unsuccessfully requested Governor Thomas E. Dewey and the legislature to help get the state constitution amended so the city could run lotteries for hospital and medical needs.[12]

Most opposition to these proposals has come from organized church groups. The Federal Council of Churches at its biennial session in 1940 adopted a statement pointing out its concern with the "high-powered propaganda which seeks to extend the vicious influence of this dangerous practice [gambling] by establishing national and state lotteries . . . on the alleged ground that great masses of our people are already indulging in the vices and millions of dollars which are now sent to other lands ought to be kept at home." All pastors and people were exhorted to take a firm stand against such measures. The attitude of the Roman Catholic Church has been less condemnatory but has varied in different dioceses. The *Catholic Encyclopedia* holds lotteries morally objectionable "if carried to excess." However, "if there is no fraud of any sort in the transaction, and if there is some sort of proportion between the price of a ticket and the value of a chance of gaining a prize, a lottery cannot be condemned as in itself immoral." [13]

Of late, however, the biggest and most successful effort has been in the direction of legalization of "bingo" and "raffles." Though both have repeatedly been declared lotteries by state statute and court decisions, the public has come to view them with tolerance. By 1942, for example, bingo had become a political issue in New York and Cincinnati. In the former, after a statement by the police commissioner that bingo and similar games would be viewed as unlawful except when under the auspices of the church, Mayor Fiorello La-Guardia disagreed, holding that if "bingo is unlawful in one place it cannot be lawful in another." In April 1943 Governor Thomas Dewey vetoed a bill to permit local governing bodies to allow bingo permits to religious, social, fraternal, and educational organizations upon petition of 5 per cent of the local voters. In Cincinnati the question split the city government when, in violation of the state constitution and laws, the city fathers voted to permit bingo and the city manager ordered police raids upon those availing themselves of this permission. In 1949 an Illinois state bill for legalization of church bingo was defeated, although Maryland and Connecticut approved bingo under certain conditions. A very bitter battle was fought in New Jersey in 1953 to sanction bingo and raffles for charity and other good causes. Against the referendum were the Methodists, Baptists, Presbyterians, Lutherans, and Episcopalians, as well as the State Federation of Women's Clubs and the New Jersey Congress of Parents and Teachers. Protestants generally agreed with Methodist Bishop Fred P. Corson, who stated that gambling "is just as evil . . . when disguised under the cloak of charity or religion as when it appears openly in the form of slot machines and numbers rackets." Supporters took the stand of the *Advocate,* official newspaper of the Roman Catholic archdiocese of Newark: "It is not gambling but the abuse of gambling that involves an immoral act . . ." The voters then made bingo and raffles respectable by a three-to-one vote.[14]

Bingo was a controversial issue in two states, Michigan and New York, in 1954 and 1955. The Detroit and Michigan Councils of Churches lost their fight to block a popular vote on the question of legalizing charity lotteries and bingo by a constitutional amendment, but were sustained by the voters in 1954. In New York bingo again became a political issue in September 1954, when Deputy Chief Inspector Louis Goldberg, in charge of the police department's morals squad in Brooklyn, was demoted to captain and later forced into retirement allegedly for enforcing the antilottery law against church groups. In that state's gubernatorial election of the same year both parties had planks favoring bingo and similar games by charitable organizations on a local-option basis. The so-called "bingo amendment" to the constitution easily passed the 1955 and 1957 legislatures and, in the later year, was approved by a popular vote of 1,818,353 to 1,175,820. On January 1, 1958, New York became the ninth state to legalize such games.[15]

Many people have become alarmed at these breaks in the dike. Church groups in a number of states have publicly taken an opposing stand. In November 1955 the United Synagogue of America in its code of synagogue practice banned bingo and other games of chance, regardless of state laws. But despite a "clear warning of the church against games of chance," the first nation-wide opinion poll of Methodists showed that over 50 per cent of the respondents saw nothing wrong with bingo. There are authoritative estimates that some twenty million Americans play bingo with "monotonous regularity" in church or professional groups, and an additional forty million play it occasionally. Legally speaking, it may well be the nation's most popular form of gambling, in New York state alone running annually to some $25,000,000. Morris Ploscowe, editor of the Kefauver Crime Report and former Director of the Crime Commission of the American Bar Association, described bingo as "our greatest breeder of lawlessness . . . An integral part of the nation's gambling menace — the total cost of which runs into billions of dollars every year." Virgil W. Peterson, former member of the Federal Bureau of Investigation, Director of the Crime Commission of Chicago, and an editor of the *Journal of Criminal Law and Criminology*, wrote in a recent article concerning church activities of this sort, "These illegal activities and improper pressures [on law enforcement agencies to ignore them] are all justified on the ground that gambling is not immoral per se since the money is used to help others become good law-abiding citizens." Thus the arguments have completed the full circle.[16]

If, as has been estimated, some 54 per cent of all adult Americans will gamble in some form each year, the question naturally arises why this vast revenue cannot be tapped for some good cause by the governments. Since historically the lottery has been the most common mode used, why not re-legalize it? Ignoring all moral implications, it cannot be denied that such ventures once played an important and perhaps a necessary part in the early economic development of this country. Also, it is true that neither side of the argument monopolizes the support of good and honest citizens. But if history teaches anything, a study of the over thirteen hundred legal lotteries[17] held in the United States proves these things: they cost more than they brought in if their total impact on society is reckoned; and that one hundred and sixty years' experience indicates clearly that the most careful supervision cannot eradicate the inevitable abuses in a system particularly susceptible to fraud.

In considering the future of the lottery in the United States, other facts should be remembered. Many an institution has been built on the weakness of man. In the gel of American culture there are many such institutions, some active, some absorbed, and others like the lottery that are dormant. But, importantly, the same nation of people who fostered the lottery and nurtured its growth became in turn the system's destroyer when it grew grotesquely deformed. On the other hand, while the geographical frontiers and their accompanying social atmosphere have disappeared, cultural frontiers are of a regressive nature, subject largely to political and economic cycles. Whether the lottery's abolition was a major reform or part of a recurring cycle is yet to be seen. It is certain, though, the American people will be given ample opportunity to decide.

Bibliographical Essay
Notes
Index

Bibliographical Essay

The principal difficulty in studying American lotteries is the great dispersion of source materials. Although the materials are abundant, few efforts have been made to collect and study them even on the state level. Very early in the lottery's history legislative authorization was required to hold drawings and thus session laws provide the basic evidence of their existence. Sometimes, however, such laws were not incorporated into the general statutes and so must be sought under other titles or connotations. In the descriptions that follow, the most common titles for state session laws are given first, followed by special titles, compilations, indexes, and other primary and secondary sources.

The knowledge that a lottery was authorized can be the only readily accessible information. In some cases apparently no use was made of the franchise, in others the results were never recorded or are yet undiscovered. Contemporary newspapers often prove the only sources of information about the nature of the schemes and sometimes furnish clues to their probable outcome. Schools were a favorite beneficiary and education histories frequently contain valuable information. Magazines furnish evidence chiefly of public opinion after the lottery system became controversial. In the listings that follow no effort has been made to exhaust all the sources used, but merely to indicate those which proved most valuable in this study. Items that furnished only small, but significant, bits of information are referred to in the text or in the notes.

PHYSICAL SURVIVALS

Still extant are surprisingly large amounts of materials associated with the lotteries. Most large libraries and historical societies have consciously or unconsciously acquired lottery tickets, broadsides, and the like. The largest such collection with which the author is acquainted is the Landauer Collection in the New York Historical Society. Additional collections found helpful because of their variety of material were those of the Harvard College Library, Boston Public Library, New York Public Library, the Old State House in Boston, and the Delaware Historical Society. The last named, for example, has an old lottery wheel used for drawings in that state.

GENERAL BIBLIOGRAPHY

In a class by itself as a primary source is the letter-book of Daniel M'Intyre, containing the correspondence of a member of the lottery-contracting firm of J. G. Gregory & Company from November 9, 1844, to January 6, 1847. This firm had interests in many states, and the letters give a good panorama of conditions in those years. When examined by the author, the letter-book was the property of Goodspeed's Book Shop, Boston. Accounts by two reformed gamblers are especially valuable for techniques and chances for fraud: J. H. Green, *An Exposure of the Arts and Miseries of Gambling* (Philadelphia, 1843) and Thomas Doyle, *Five Years in a Lottery Office* (Boston, 1841). Among the books and pamphlets by contemporary reformers, the most helpful are Anthony Comstock's *Frauds Exposed* (New York, 1880) and *Traps for the Young* (1883); Job R. Tyson's *Brief Survey of the Great Extent and Evil Tendencies of the Lottery System as Existing in the United States* (Philadelphia, 1833), probably the best contemporary account, and *Address to the People of Pennsylvania and the United States by the Pennsylvania Society for the Suppression of Lotteries* (Philadelphia, 1834); G. W. Gordon, *Lecture on Lotteries before the Boston Young Men's Society* (Boston, 1833); *Wonderful Advantages of Adventuring in the Lottery* (New York, 1814); *The Lottery Ticket: An American Tale* (Cambridge, 1822; Hartford, 1827); a delightful satire is "Sui Generis" (Thomas Man), *Picture of a Factory Village to Which Are Annexed, Remarks on Lotteries* (Providence, 1833); George Brewster, *An Oration on the Evils of Lotteries* (Brooklyn, 1828); Roland G. Hazard, *Lecture on the Cause of the Decline of Political and National Morality* (Providence, 1841); a rehash of scriptural arguments on the subject is found in *Candid Remarks Addressed to Christians on the Subject of Their Having Concern in Lotteries* (Boston, n.d.); and the relationship between lotteries and poverty is discussed in Society for the Prevention of Pauperism in the City of New York, *Documents Relative to Saving Banks, Intemperance, and Lotteries* (New York, 1819).

Attitudes of religious sects are to be found in the manuscript records of the Historical Foundation of the Presbyterian and Reformed Churches, Montreat, North Carolina; *Journals of the General Conferences of the Methodist Episcopal Church; Discipline of the Society of Friends, Yearly Meetings* by year and state; and the *Proceedings of the Southern Baptist Convention*. Religious periodicals that proved helpful include the *Religious Intelligencer*, XI–XII (1826–27); *Religious Magazine*, I (1833); the *Friend*, I–LXIX (1827–1896), which gives almost weekly coverage of lottery activities; *Friends Review*, V–VIII (1852–1855); *Christian Spectator*, I–X (1819–1828); the *Christian Union*, XLIV–XLV (1891–92), especially good for the fight against the Louisiana Lottery; *American Baptist Magazine*, IV–X (1823–1830); *Connecticut Evangelical Magazine and Religious Intelligencer*, I–VIII (1808–1815); and the *Massachusetts Missionary Magazine*, II (1804).

Among the most useful secular magazines are the *Lottery Exterminator*, I (1842); *Hours At Home*, VII (1868); *North American Review*, IX (1819), XXXVII (1833), CLIV (1892); *Galaxy*, XIII (1872); the *Eye*, I (1808); *Atlantic Monthly*, LXIX (1892); *Hopkinsian Magazine*, II (1826–27); *Monthly Anthology and Boston Review*, III (1806); the *Nation*, XXVIII–LIV (1884–1892); and *Niles' Weekly Register*, XIX–XLV (1820–1834).

Most travelers, coming from countries that also used lotteries, made no comments upon the American variety. Among those who did, the best observations are to be found in Ruben G. Thwaites, *Early Western Travels, 1748–1846*, 32 vols. (Cleveland, 1904–1906); T. H. James, *Rambles in the United States and Canada During the Year 1845* (London, 1847); Edward Dicey, *Six Months in the Federal States*, 2 vols. (London, 1863); James D. Burn, *Three Years among the Working Classes in the United States during the War* (London, 1865); John Bristed, *The Resources of the United States of America* (New York, 1818); and C. D. Arfwedson, *The United States and Canada in 1832, 1833 and 1834*, 2 vols. (London, 1834).

Among the books of a secondary nature that deal with lotteries, John B.

McMaster, *A History of the People of the United States*, 8 vols. (New York, 1883–1913), is the only general survey of American history that shows concern with lotteries. Arthur M. Schlesinger, Sr., *The American as a Reformer* (Cambridge, 1950), is good for putting the crusade against lotteries in its proper historical setting. H. M. Brooks, *Curiosities of the Old Lottery: Gleanings Chiefly from the Old Newspapers of Boston and Salem* (Boston, 1866), and Bella C. Landauer, *Some Early American Lottery Items* (New York, 1928), are good for reproductions of advertisements and tickets. Ben Perley Poore, *The Federal and State Constitutions, Colonial Charters and Other Organic Laws of the United States*, 2 vols. (Washington, 1877), is a convenient source of such information. Francis Emmett Williams, *Lotteries, Laws and Morals* (New York, 1958), gives a brief background, a discussion of the moral issues involved, and the most detailed discussion of modern games defined legally as lotteries. A. A. Freeman, *Lottery Gambling* (n.p., n.d.), is the argument for the defendant in T. J. Commerford *v.* Virginia C. Thompson; it gives a good historical survey as well as throws light upon an important lottery case. Henrietta M. Larson, *Jay Cooke, Private Banker* (Cambridge, 1936) discusses the lottery firm of S. & M. Allen; Fritz Redlich, *The Molding of American Banking: Men and Ideas*, 2 vols. (New York, 1951), shows the role played by lotteries in that business; and Joseph S. Davis, *Essays in the Earlier History of American Corporations*, 2 vols. (Cambridge, 1917), cites the role played by lotteries in the aid of infant corporations. Two popular accounts that feature the novel aspects of lotteries are Eric Bender, *Tickets to Fortune* (New York, 1938), and Herbert Asbury, *Sucker's Progress: An Informal History of Gambling in America from the Colonies to Canfield* (New York, 1938). Information concerning religious points of view are to be found in Anson P. Stokes, *Church and State in the United States*, 3 vols. (New York, 1950); Hunter D. Farish, *The Circuit Rider Dismounts; A Social History of Southern Methodism, 1865–1900* (Richmond, 1938); James M. Buckley, *A History of Methodists in the United States* (New York, 1896); and E. H. Gillette, *History of the Presbyterian Church in the United States of America*, 2 vols. (Philadelphia, 1864).

The most complete monographic study, although making no claim of being definitive, is A. R. Spofford, "Lotteries in American History," American Historical Association, *Annual Report for the Year 1892*. A good short bibliography is in H. M. Muller, "Lotteries," *Reference Shelf*, X (1935), no. 2. A short general survey of legal attitudes is found in William E. Treadway, "Lottery Laws in the United States: A Page from American Legal History," *American Bar Association Journal*, XXXV (1949). Brief articles on the general subject of lotteries include E. N. Vallandingham, "Lotteries in the United States," *Chautauquan*, X (1890); T. H. Ormsbee, "Lotteries — Our First Financing," *American Collector* (November 1938); Howard O. Rogers, "The Lottery in American History," *Americana*, XIII (1919); William C. MacLeod, "The Truth about Lotteries in American History," *South Atlantic Quarterly*, XXXV (1936); and John S. Ezell, "The Lottery in Colonial America," *William and Mary Quarterly*, V (1948), 3rd series. Two articles dealing with lottery contractors are Hugh G. J. Aitken, "Yates & McIntyre: Lottery Managers," *Journal of Economic History*, XIII (1953), and Henrietta M. Larson, "S. & M. Allen — Lottery, Exchange, and Stock Brokerage," *Journal of Economic and Business History*, III (1931).

EUROPEAN BACKGROUND

The two best general accounts of English lotteries are John Ashton, *A History of English Lotteries* (London, 1893), and C. L. Ewen, *Lotteries and Sweepstakes* (London, 1932). Examples of advertisements are found in George Cruikshank, "Lottery Puffs" (2 vols.) and "Caricatures and Other Separate Prints" (8 vols.), both in the Widener Collection, Harvard College Library. General accounts of the Virginia Company Lottery are found in Alexander Brown, *The Genesis of the United States*, 2 vols. (Boston, 1891); *Three Proclamations Concerning the Lottery for Virginia, 1613–1621* (Providence, 1907), which features reproductions as well; and Wesley F. Craven, *Dissolution of the Virginia Company* (New York, 1932). The point of view of the Company, and specific details, can be found in Susan M. Kingsbury, ed., *The Records of the Virginia Company of London*, 4 vols. (Washington, 1906). The royal proclamation in 1769 banning American lotteries without special permission is readily available in Leonard W. Labaree, ed., *Royal Instructions to British Colonial Governors, 1670–1776*, 2 vols. (New York, 1935).

NEW ENGLAND

MASSACHUSETTS. Statutes of enactment are found under many titles, the most common being *Laws of the Commonwealth of Massachusetts, Passed at the Several Sessions of the General Court* (Boston, 1805————); *Laws of the Commonwealth of Massachusetts Passed by the General Court* ———— (Boston); *Resolves Passed by the General Court of the Commonwealth of Massachusetts in* ———— (Boston); *The Acts and Resolves, Public and Private, of the Province of the Massachusetts Bay*, 21 vols. (Boston, 1869–1922); and *Private and Special Statutes of the Commonwealth of Massachusetts*, 21 vols. (Boston, 1805–1913). The Official Papers of Governor Sir Francis Bernard found in the Jared Sparks Manuscripts in Harvard College Library throw light on lottery activity in a crucial period.

Specialized studies of value for specific lotteries include Charles H. J. Douglas, "The Financial History of Massachusetts," Columbia University, *Studies in History, Economics, and Public Law*, vol. I; A. M. Davis, "Papers Relating to the Land Bank of 1740," Colonial Society of Massachusetts, *Publications*, vol. IV; John Noble, "Harvard College Lotteries," Colonial Society of Massachusetts, *Publications*, vol. XXVII; Benjamin Peirce, *A History of Harvard University* (Cambridge, 1833); Josiah Quincy, *The History of Harvard University*, 2 vols. (Boston, 1860); Samuel E. Morison, *Three Centuries of Harvard, 1636–1936* (Cambridge, 1937); and L. W. Spring, *A History of Williams College* (Boston, 1917). A brief survey of Massachusetts lotteries is provided by John S. Ezell, "When Massachusetts Played the Lottery," *New England Quarterly*, XXII (1949). Public opinion and the role played by reformers is found in *The Diary of William Bentley*, 4 vols. (Salem, 1914); Charles Beecher, ed., *Autobiography, Correspondence of Lyman Beecher, D. D.*, 2 vols. (London, 1865); J. C. White, *Personal Reminiscences of Lyman Beecher* (New York, 1882); J. T. Buckingham, *Personal Memoirs and Recollections of Editorial Life*, 2 vols. (Boston, 1852); and Anon., "Peter Chardon Brooks," *New England Historical and Genealogical Register*, vol. IX.

RHODE ISLAND. A quick entry into Rhode Island laws is provided by J. R. Bartlett, comp., *Index to the Printed Acts and Resolves of the General Assembly of the State of Rhode Island and Providence Plantation, 1758–1850* (Providence, 1856). Extremely helpful for the colonial period is J. R. Bartlett, ed., *Records of the Colony of Rhode Island and Providence Plantation in New England*, 10 vols. (Providence, 1856–1865). One of the best accounts of lotteries in any state is J. H. Stiness, "A Century of Lotteries in Rhode Island," State of Rhode Island, *Historical Tracts*, 2nd series, III (1896). Other specialized studies of importance are Walter C. Bronson, *The History of Brown University, 1764–1914* (Providence, 1914); Ruben A. Guild, *Early History of Brown University, Including the Life, Times, and Correspondence of President Manning, 1756–1791* (Providence, 1896); Charles Carroll, *Public Education in Rhode Island* (Providence, 1918); and Hamilton B. Tompkins, "Newport County Lotteries," Newport Historical Society, *Bulletins*, I–II (1912).

CONNECTICUT. The best sources of legal enactments are C. J. Hoadly, ed., *The Public Records of the Colony of Connecticut*, 15 vols. (Hartford, 1850–1890), and his *The Public Records of the State of Connecticut*, 5 vols. (Hartford, 1894–1943). At the time this research was done, the latter extended only to 1784, and for the years after that date the manuscript records of the legislature were used. In addition to such sources as the *Connecticut Journal*, New London *Bee*, and the *Religious Intelligencer*, the following specialized works proved most helpful: Ebenezer Baldwin, *History of Yale College* (New Haven, 1841); Franklin B. Dexter, *Biographical Sketches of the Graduates of Yale College with Annals of the College History*, 6 vols. (New York, 1885–1912); T. R. Trowbridge, "History of Long Wharf in New Haven," New Haven Historical Society, *Papers*, vol. I; and Charles R. Keller, *The Second Great Awakening in Connecticut* (New Haven, 1942). In a class by itself is *Struggles and Triumphs: or, The Life of P. T. Barnum, Written by Himself*, 2 vols. (New York, 1927). Barnum was a lottery ticket seller in Connecticut.

NEW HAMPSHIRE. Authorizations are to be found in *Laws of the State of New Hampshire Passed in the ——— Session of the Legislature* (Concord); *Laws of State of New Hampshire Passed from December Session, 1805, to June Session, 1810, Inclusive* (Concord, 1811); H. H. Metcalf, ed., *Laws of New Hampshire*, 10 vols. (Concord, 1904–1922); and in the journals of the house and senate published at the end of each session. Also valuable is *Documents and Records Relating to New Hampshire*, 37 vols. (Concord, 1867–1939). Good secondary sources with lottery material include Everett S. Stackpole, *History of New Hampshire*, 4 vols. (New York, n.d.); Fredrick Chase and John K. Lord, *A History of Dartmouth College and Town of Hanover*, 2 vols. (Cambridge, 1891); Leon B. Richardson, *History of Dartmouth College*, 2 vols. (Hanover, 1932); George Barstow, *The History of New Hampshire* (Concord, 1842); and Christopher Roberts, *The Middlesex Canal, 1793–1860* (Cambridge, 1938).

VERMONT. The most important sources for Vermont include, *Laws Passed by the Legislature of the State of Vermont at a Session in ——— (Rutland); Journal of the General Assembly of Vermont at Their Session ——— (Bennington); William Slade, Jr., comp., *The Laws of Vermont down to 1824* (Windsor, 1825); E. P. Walton, ed., *Records of the Governor and Council of the State of Vermont*, 8 vols. (Montpelier, 1873); Abby M. Hemenway, ed., *The Vermont Historical Gazetteer*, 5 vols. (Burlington, 1867–1891); and

Zadock Thompson, *History of Vermont, Natural, Civil, and Statistical* (Burlington, 1842).

MAINE. The most helpful legal sources are *Public Acts Passed by the Maine Legislature in Session in* —————— (Portland); *Laws of the State of Maine* (Hollowell, 1821); *Laws of the State of Maine,* 3 vols. (Portland, 1831); *Laws of the State of Maine from 1822–1833,* 2 vols. (Hollowell, 1834); *Private or Special Laws of the State of Maine from 1825 to 1828 Inclusive,* 2 vols. (Augusta, 1842); *Resolves of the Legislature of the State of Maine from 1829 to 1835 Inclusive,* 2 vols. (Augusta, 1842); and *Documents Printed by Order of the Legislature of the State of Maine during its Session A.D. 1835* (Augusta, 1835). An interesting pamphlet by a contemporary opponent of lotteries is F. O. J. Smith ("Civis," *pseud.*), *Dissertation on the Nature and Effects of Lottery Systems, and Principles of Public Policy Relating to Them* (Portland, 1827). Additional background information can be found in James P. Baxter, ed., *Documentary History of the State of Maine,* 24 vols. (Portland, 1916), and William D. Williamson, *The History of the State of Maine,* 2 vols. (Hollowell, 1832).

THE MIDDLE ATLANTIC STATES

NEW YORK. Legislative enactments can be found in *Laws Passed at the* —————— *Session of the Legislature of the State of New York* —————— (Albany); *Journal of the Legislative Council of the Colony of New York* (Albany, 1861); *Laws Passed at the 36th, 37th, and 38th Sessions of the Legislature of the State of New York, Commencing November 1812, and Ending April, 1815,* 3 vols. (Albany, 1815); and Frederick Cook, comp., *Laws of the State of New York Passed at Sessions of the Legislature, 1777–1801,* 5 vols. (Albany, 1886); An excellent source concerning one of the major lottery scandals is Daniel Rogers, *Report of the Trial of Charles N. Baldwin for a Libel, in Publishing Charges of Fraud and Swindling against the Managers and Submanagers of the Medical Society Lottery* (New York, 1818). Source material on the involved story concerning the Union College Lottery is found in Special Committee of the New York Legislature, *Documents Relative to the Dispute between the Trustees of Union College and Yates and McIntyre* (Albany, 1834–1854) and Union College, *Report to the New York Legislature, March, 1849* (n.p., n.d.). Other contemporary sources of value are Society for the Prevention of Pauperism in the City of New York, *Documents Relative to Saving Banks, Intemperance, and Lotteries* (New York, 1819), and John Pintard "Letters to His Daughter," New York Historical Society, *Collections for the Years 1937, 1939,* vols. LXX, LXXII.

Among the more useful secondary items are Alexander C. Flick, ed., *History of the State of New York,* 10 vols. (New York, 1934); *History of Columbia University, 1754–1904* (New York, 1904); Don C. Sowers, "The Financial History of New York State, from 1789 to 1912," Columbia University, *Studies in History, Economics, and Public Law,* vol. LVII; William O. Bourne, *History of the Public School Society of the City of New York* (New York, 1870); Heywood Broun and Margaret Leech, *Anthony Comstock, Roundsman of the Lord* (New York, 1927), which covers the New York career of that bitter enemy of the lotteries; and A. Franklin Ross, *The History of Lotteries in New York* (reprinted from the *Magazine of History,* n.p., n.d.), which gives a brief, incomplete, and sometimes inaccurate survey of New York lotteries.

NEW JERSEY. Legal enactments relative to lotteries can be found in *Laws Passed by the General Assembly of the Province of New Jersey* ——— (Woodbridge); *Acts of the* ——— *General Assembly of the State of New Jersey* (Trenton); *Private and Temporary Acts of the* ——— *General Assembly of New Jersey* (Trenton); and *Laws of the State of New Jersey* (Trenton, 1821). A listing of lotteries can be quickly secured from John Hood, comp., *Index of the Colonial and State Laws of New Jersey Between 1668–1903* (Camden, 1905). Especially valuable are *Documents Relating to the Colonial History of the State of New Jersey* (Newark, 1880–1894), 27 vols., and *Documents Relating to the Revolutionary History of the State of New Jersey*, 3 vols. (Trenton, 1901). Important episodes are covered in the *Journal of the Proceedings at the Second Sitting of the 68th Session of the Legislative Council of New Jersey* (New Brunswick, 1844), and *Proceedings of the New Jersey State Constitutional Convention of 1844* (n.p., 1942). Daniel M'Intyre's "Letterbook" mentioned above is valuable for an insight into the operation of one of New Jersey's largest contracting firms, J. G. Gregory & Company.

Secondary sources of value are Varnum L. Collins, *Princeton* (New York, 1914); William H. S. Demarest, *A History of Rutgers College, 1766–1924* (New Brunswick, 1924); John Maclean, *History of the College of New Jersey, from Its Origin in 1746 to the Commencement of 1854*, 2 vols. (Philadelphia, 1877); David Murry, *History of Education in New Jersey* (Washington, 1899); Edgar J. Fisher, "New Jersey as a Royal Province," Columbia University, *Studies in History, Economics, and Public Law*, vol. XLI; and the story of Alexander Hamilton and the lottery for the Society for Establishing Useful Manufactures is told in J. S. Davis, *Essays in the Earlier History of American Corporations*, 2 vols. (Cambridge, 1917).

PENNSYLVANIA. Legal sources for Pennsylvania lotteries include *Acts of the General Assembly of the Commonwealth of Pennsylvania Passed at a Session Begun* ——— (Harrisburg); *Minutes of the Provincial Council of Pennsylvania*, 16 vols. (Harrisburg, 1852–53); J. T. Mitchell and Henry Flanders, comps., *The Statutes at Large of Pennsylvania From 1682 to 1809*, 18 vols. (Harrisburg, 1895–1915); G. E. Reed, comp., *Pennsylvania Archives*, 120 vols. (Philadelphia, 1852–1935); and *Report of the Committee of Vice and Immorality of the Senate of Pennsylvania, to Whom Were Referred the Message of the Governor and Sundry Memorials Relating to the Abolition of Lotteries* (Philadelphia, 1832).

Primary sources of an unofficial nature include the Benjamin Franklin Papers in the Jared Sparks Manuscripts, Harvard College Library; John F. Watson, *Annals of Philadelphia and Pennsylvania*, 2 vols. (Philadelphia, 1845); *Report of a Committee Appointed to Investigate the Evils of Lotteries, in the Commonwealth of Pennsylvania, and to Suggest a Remedy for the Same* (Philadelphia, 1831) records the findings of a group that later became the Pennsylvania Society for Suppression of Lotteries; *Let Not the Faith, Nor the Laws of the Commonwealth, Be Violated* (n.p., c. 1833) demanded an inquiry into the affairs of the Union Canal Lottery. Special attention should also be given to the two pamphlets of Job R. Tyson mentioned above, as well as the issues of the *Friend* and the *Register of Pennsylvania*.

The most helpful secondary accounts are Ezra Michener, *A Retrospect of Early Quakerism; Being Extracts from the Records of Pennsylvania Yearly Meetings and the Meetings Composing It* (Philadelphia, 1860); Edward P.

Cheyney, *History of the University of Pennsylvania, 1740–1940* (Philadelphia, 1940); Thomas H. Montgomery, *A History of the University of Pennsylvania from its Foundation to A.D. 1770* (Philadelphia, 1900); James H. Morgan, *Dickenson College, The History of One Hundred and Fifty Years, 1783–1933* (Carlisle, 1933); and A. C. Applegarth, "Quakers in Pennsylvania," Johns Hopkins University, *Studies in Historical and Political Science*, 10th series, VIII–IX (1892). There are two studies of lotteries in the state: Irma A. Watts, "Pennsylvania Lotteries of Other Days," *Pennsylvania History*, II (1935), is brief while Asa E. Martin, "Lotteries in Pennsylvania Prior to 1833," *Pennsylvania Magazine of History and Biography*, XLVII–XLVIII (1923–24), is a comprehensive monograph.

DELAWARE. The laws granting lottery franchises can be found in *Minutes of the Council of the Delaware State from 1776 to 1792* (Wilmington, 1887); *Laws of the State of Delaware Passed by the General Assembly* ——— (Dover); *Laws of the State of Delaware, from October 14, 1700, to August 18, 1797*, 2 vols. (New Castle, 1797); and *Laws of State of Delaware*, 4 vols. (Wilmington, 1816). The most useful secondary sources include Henry C. Conrad, *History of State of Delaware* (Wilmington, 1908); Walter A. Powell, *A History of Delaware* (Boston, 1928); J. Thomas Scharf, *History of Delaware*, 2 vols. (Philadelphia, 1888); and Lyman P. Powell, *The History of Education in Delaware* (Washington, 1893). Two articles dealing with Delaware lotteries are: Norman M. MacLeod, "Early State Lotteries Provided Money to Build Jail, College, Churches," Wilmington *Evening Journal–Every Evening*, December 19, 1933, and Jane N. Garrett, "The Delaware College Lotteries, 1818–1845," *Delaware History*, VII (1957).

THE DISTRICT OF COLUMBIA AND THE NATIONAL GOVERNMENT

The most helpful references are the *Congressional Globe* and the *Congressional Record*, especially for the 38th, 40th, 42nd, 44th, 46th, 48th, 49th, 51st, and 53rd sessions of Congress. Peter Force, *American Archives: Containing a Documentary History of the United States of America from the Declaration of Independence, July 4, 1776, to the Definitive Treaty of Peace with Great Britain, September 3, 1783*, 5th series, 3 vols. (Washington, 1848–1853), contains much information on the Continental Lottery. Walter Clark, ed., *Colonial and State Records of North Carolina*, vol. XVI (Goldsboro, 1886–1914), has additional information of value on that scheme. The best sources for District ventures are Andrew Rothwell, *Laws of the Corporation of the City of Washington* (Washington, 1833); Anon., "Writings of Washington Relating to the National Capitol," Columbia Historical Society, *Records*, vol. XVII; Allen C. Clark, "General Roger Chew Weightman, A Mayor of the City of Washington," *ibid.*, XX; the Supreme Court cases, Clark *v.* City of Washington, 12 Wheat. 40, and Cohen *v.* Virginia, 6 Wheat. 264; and Logan Esarey, ed., "Governors, Messages and Papers," State of Indiana, *Historical Collections*, XII. Also of value is James D. Richardson, comp., *A Compilation of the Messages and Papers of the Presidents, 1789–1907*, 11 vols. (Washington, 1908).

The most useful secondary sources included Albert S. Bolles, *The Financial History of the United States, from 1774 to 1789* (New York, 1896); W. B. Bryan, *A History of the National Capitol*, 2 vols. (New York, 1914–1916); William Tindall, *Standard History of the City of Washington* (Knoxville,

1914); Charles Warren, *The Supreme Court in United States History*, 2 vols. (Boston, 1928); and John B. McMaster, *A History of the People of the United States*, vol. II (New York, 1883–1913). See also the material listed under Louisiana for the government's role in the final abolition of lotteries.

THE SOUTH

MARYLAND. Legal enactments concerning lotteries are in *Laws Made and Passed by the General Assembly of the State of Maryland in the Session of* ———— (Annapolis); *Ordinances of the Corporation of the City of Baltimore* (Baltimore, 1801); William Kilty, comp., *The Laws of Maryland*, 2 vols. (Annapolis, 1799–1800); *Laws of Maryland*, 3 vols. (Baltimore, 1811); Clement Dorsey, comp., *The General Public Statutory Law and Public Local Law from 1692 to 1839 Inclusive*, 3 vols. (Baltimore, 1840); *Archives of Maryland*, 61 vols. (Baltimore, 1883–1944); *Proceedings of the Maryland State Convention to Frame a New Constitution, Commenced at Annapolis, November 4, 1850* (Annapolis, 1850); *Debates and Proceedings of the Maryland Reform Convention to Revise the State Constitution*, 2 vols. (Annapolis, 1851); and James W. Harry, *The Maryland Constitution of 1851* (Baltimore, 1902). For quick reference Elihu S. Riley, *A History of the General Assembly of Maryland, 1635–1904* (Baltimore, 1905), is extremely valuable.

Maryland newspapers were especially helpful, with the *Maryland Journal & Baltimore Advertiser, Baltimore Daily Intelligencer,* and the *Federal Gazette & Baltimore Daily Advertiser* being the most useful. Maryland's returns from lotteries can be found in the *United States Commercial and Statistical Register*, I (1839).

Good secondary sources are numerous for the state. Among the most helpful are the following: Hugh S. Hanna, *A Financial History of Maryland, 1789–1848* (Baltimore, 1907), gives a good account of the lottery as a source of state revenue. Jacob H. Hollander, *The Financial History of Baltimore* (Baltimore, 1899) discusses the uses made by that city of its blanket grant to hold lotteries. Colorful background is furnished by two works of J. Thomas Scharf: *The Chronicles of Baltimore* (Baltimore, 1874) and *History of Baltimore City and County from the Earliest Period to the Present Day* (Philadelphia, 1881). Similar information is given in Elihu S. Riley, *"The Ancient City," A History of Annapolis, in Maryland, 1649–1887* (Annapolis, 1887). Two valuable church histories that reflect religious attitudes are William Reynolds, *A Brief History of the First Presbyterian Church of Baltimore* (Baltimore, 1913), and Abdel R. Wentz, *History of the Evangelical Lutheran Church of Frederick, Maryland, 1738–1938* (Harrisburg, Pa., 1938). Eugene F. Cordell, *University of Maryland, 1807–1907*, 2 vols. (New York, 1907), and Bernard C. Steiner, *History of Education in Maryland* (Washington, 1894), are useful in tracing the educational use of lotteries. A brief monograph discussing church lotteries is John S. Ezell, "The Church Took a Chance," *Maryland Historical Magazine*, XLIII (1948).

VIRGINIA. The most common denomination for session laws is *Acts Passed at a General Assembly of the Commonwealth of Virginia Begun and Held at the Capitol in the City of Richmond on* ———— (Richmond). Other sources of a legal nature include *Acts of the General Assembly of a Public and Generally Interesting Nature Passed since the Session of the Assembly which Commenced in the Year One Thousand Eight Hundred and Seven* (Richmond, 1812); William W. Hening, comp., *The Statutes at Large; Being a Collection of all the Laws of Virginia from the First Session of the Legislature, in the Year 1619,* 13 vols. (Philadelphia, 1823); Samuel Shepherd, comp., *The Statutes at Large of Virginia from October Session 1792, to December Session 1806, Inclusive,* 3 vols. (Richmond, 1835–1836); *Journal of the House of Delegates of Virginia, Session* ——— (Richmond); and H. R. McIlwaine, ed., *Journals of the House of Burgesses, 1752–1755, 1756–1758* (Richmond, 1909). Jefferson's petition and list of Virginia lotteries is found in A. A. Lipscomb, ed., *Writings of Thomas Jefferson,* vol. XVII. (Washington, 1903). Supplementary information can be found in Philip A. Bruce, *History of the University of Virginia, 1818–1919,* 4 vols. (New York, 1920); Alfred J. Morrison, *The College of Hampden-Sidney* (Richmond, 1912); and W. A. Maddox, *The Free School Idea in Virginia Before the Civil War* (New York, 1918).

NORTH CAROLINA. Primary information on North Carolina lotteries can be found in *Laws of North Carolina Passed at the General Assembly in the Year* ——— (Raleigh); Walter Clark, ed., *Colonial and State Records of North Carolina,* 30 vols. (Goldsboro, 1886–1914); Charles L. Coon, ed., *North Carolina Schools and Academies, 1790–1840; A Documentary History* (Raleigh, 1915) and his *The Beginnings of Public Education in North Carolina; A Documentary History,* 2 vols. (Raleigh, 1908); and Hugh T. Lefler, ed., *North Carolina History Told by Contemporaries* (Chapel Hill, 1934). Also of value are Kemp P. Battle, *History of the University of North Carolina,* 2 vols. (Raleigh, 1907); and M. C. S. Noble, *A History of the Public Schools of North Carolina* (Chapel Hill, 1930).

SOUTH CAROLINA. Primary sources for legal enactments include *Acts, Ordinances, and Resolves of the General Assembly of the State of South Carolina Passed in the Year* ——— (Columbia); Alexander Edwards, comp., *Ordinances of the City Council of Charleston, in the State of South Carolina, Passed Since the Incorporation of the City* (Charleston, 1802); *Reports and Resolutions of the General Assembly of South Carolina Passed at its Regular Session* ——— (Columbia); *Acts of the General Assembly of South Carolina, 1791–1804,* 2 vols. (Columbia, 1808); and Thomas Cooper and D. J. McCord, eds., *Statutes at Large of South Carolina,* 10 vols. (Columbia, 1836–1841). Also helpful were O. J. Bond, *The Story of the Citadel* (Richmond, 1936); J. H. Easterby, *A History of the College of Charleston* (Charleston, 1935); and Hennig Cohen, *The South Carolina Gazette 1732–1775* (Columbia, 1953).

GEORGIA. Session acts can be found under the denomination of *Acts of the General Assembly of the State of Georgia Passed in* ——— (Milledgeville, ———). The most useful collections are Horatio Marbury and W. H. Crawford, comps., *Digest of the Laws of the State of Georgia 1755–1800* (Savannah, 1802); A. S. Clayton, comp., *A Compilation of the Laws of the State of Georgia Passed by the Legislature, 1800–1810* (Augusta, 1812); L. Q. C. Lamar, comp., *A Compilation of the Laws of the State of Georgia, Passed by the Legislature since the Year 1810 to the Year 1819, Inclusive* (Augusta, 1821); W. C. Dawson, comp., *Compilation of the Laws of the State of Georgia, 1819–1829* (Milledgeville, 1831); and O. H. Prince, comp., *A Digest of the Laws of the State of Georgia* (Athens, 1837). Other primary material of value is *The Colonial Records of the State of Georgia,* 26 vols. (Atlanta, 1904–1916); and *The Revolutionary Records of the State of Georgia,* 3 vols.

(Atlanta, 1908). Important monographs include Thomas Gamble, Jr., *A History of the City Government of Savannah, Georgia, from 1790 to 1901* (n.p., n.d.), and Elbert W. G. Boogher, *Secondary Education in Georgia, 1732–1858* (Philadelphia, 1933). The latter contains a list of lotteries granted for schools. The most useful state history is Amanda Johnson, *Georgia as Colony and State* (Atlanta, 1938).

FLORIDA. The few authorizations made in that state can be found in *Laws of the Legislative Council of the Territory of Florida Passed at the ——— Session* (Tallahassee); Cecil Johnson, *British West Florida, 1763–1783* (New Haven, 1943); and Caroline M. Brevard, *A History of Florida From the Treaty of 1763 to Our Times*, 2 vols. (Deland, 1924).

ALABAMA. The major primary sources for Alabama are *Acts Passed at the ——— Session of the General Assembly of the Territory of Alabama* (St. Stephens); *Acts Passed at the Annual Session of the General Assembly of the State of Alabama ———* (Tuscaloosa); Harry Toulmin, comp., *Digest of the Laws of the State of Alabama: Containing the Statutes and Resolutions in Force at the End of the General Assembly in January 1823* (Cahawba, 1823); J. C. Aikin, comp., *A Digest of the Laws of the State of Alabama, Containing all the Statutes of a Public and General Nature in Force at the Close of the Session of the General Assembly in January 1833* (Philadelphia, 1833); and C. C. Clay, comp., *A Digest of the Laws of the State of Alabama, Containing all the Statutes of a Public and General Nature in Force at the Close of the Session of the General Assembly in February 1843* (Tuskaloosa [sic], 1843).

MISSISSIPPI. Legal enactments concerning lotteries are to be found in *Statutes of the Territory of Mississippi* (Natchez, 1816); *Acts of the Legislature of the State of Mississippi ———* (Jackson); *The Revised Code of the Laws of Mississippi, in Which are Comprised All Such Acts of the General Assembly of a Public Nature, as Were in Force at the End of the Year 1823* (Natchez, 1824); T. J. F. Alden and J. S. Hoesen, comps., *A Digest of the Laws of Mississippi* (New York, 1839); and Rena Humphreys and Mamie Owen, comps., *Index of Session Acts, 1817–1865* (Jackson, 1937). The best secondary sources are two works by Dunbar Rowland: *Encyclopedia of Mississippi History*, 2 vols. (Madison, Wisc., 1907), and *History of Mississippi: The Heart of the South*, 2 vols. (Chicago, 1925).

LOUISIANA. Legal sources for Louisiana lotteries include *Acts of the ——— Session of the ——— Legislature of the State of Louisiana held in ———* (New Orleans); Francois X. Martin, comp., *A General Digest of the Acts of the Legislature of the Late Territory of Orleans*, 2 vols. (New Orleans, 1816); L. M. Lislet, comp., *A General Digest of the Acts of the Legislature of Louisiana: Passed from the Year 1804 to 1827 Inclusive*, 2 vols. (New Orleans, 1828); and Meinrad Greiner, *The Louisiana Digest, 1804–1841*, 2 vols. (New Orleans, 1841).

Other primary materials, especially for the late Louisiana Lottery, are numerous. Among the most helpful contemporary accounts are: Beverly Carradine, *The Louisiana State Lottery Company, Examined and Exposed* (New Orleans, 1890); Edgar H. Farrar, "The Louisiana Lottery: Its History," *Charities Review*, I (1892); C. C. Buel, "The Degradation of a State," *Century*, XXI (1892); Anthony Comstock, "The Louisiana Lottery, A National Scourge," *Our Day*, IV (1889); Anthony Comstock, "The Louisiana Lottery Octopus," *ibid.*, V (1890), and "Lotteries and Gambling," *North American Review*, CLIV

(1892); Frank McGloin, "Shall Its Charter be Renewed?" *Forum*, XII (1892); and J. C. Wickliffe, "A History of the Company," *ibid*. Extremely valuable for the fight for federal action is S. H. Woodbridge, "Anti-Lottery Campaign: The Overthrow of the Louisiana Lottery — An Address First Delivered Before the Association of Collegiate Alumnae of Boston." This dramatic account by one of the leaders was apparently mimeographed in 1921 and can be found in the Harvard College Library. Periodicals that give full coverage of the fight are the *Friend*, LII–LXIX (1879–1895); *Century*, XX–XXI (1891–92); *Christian Union*, XLIV–XLV (1891–92); the *Nation*, XXXVIII–LIV (1884–1892); and *Public Opinion*, IX–XIII (1890–1892).

The mass of secondary material is almost overwhelming. The most useful, however, are Alcée Fortier, *A History of Louisiana*, 4 vols. (New York, 1904); Edwin W. Fay, *The History of Education in Louisiana* (Washington, 1898); Walter L. Fleming, *Louisiana State University, 1860–1896* (Baton Rouge, 1936); Thomas E. Dabney, *One Hundred Great Years: The Story of the Times-Picayune from its Founding to 1940* (Baton Rouge, 1944); the extremely valuable Marshall Cushing, *The Story of Our Post Office* (Boston, 1893), with a detailed account of the effort to close the mails to the lottery. Julian Ralph, *Dixie, or Southern Scenes and Sketches* (New York, 1896), describes a drawing of the Louisiana Lottery; T. Harry Williams, *P. G. T. Beauregard, Napoleon in Gray* (Baton Rouge, 1954), discusses the role of that former general in the lottery company; and Richard Harding Davis, *Three Gringos in Venezuela and Central America* (New York, 1896), describes the lottery in exile. There are two good monographic studies of the Louisiana Lottery: B. C. Alwes, "The History of the Louisiana State Lottery Company," *Louisiana Historical Quarterly*, XXVII (1944), and G. W. McGinty, "The Louisiana Lottery Company," *Southwestern Social Science Quarterly*, XX (1940).

KENTUCKY. The best sources of information include *Acts of the Legislature of Kentucky* ——— (Frankfort); *Journal of the Senate of the State of Kentucky* ——— (Frankfort); C. S. Morehead and Mason Brown, comps., *A Digest of the Statute Laws of Kentucky*, 2 vols. (Frankfort, 1834); *Journal and Proceedings of the Convention of the State of Kentucky* (Frankfort, 1849); Richard H. Collins, *History of Kentucky*, 2 vols. (Louisville, 1924); William E. Connelley and E. M. Coulter, *History of Kentucky*, 5 vols. (New York, 1922); Robert and Johanna Peter, *Transylvania University: Its Origin, Rise, Decline, and Fall* (Filson Club Publication no. 1, Louisville, 1896); and House of Representatives, *Executive Documents*, 46th Congress, 2nd session (1879–80), doc. 22.

TENNESSEE. The best primary sources are *Journal of the Proceedings of the Legislative Council of the Territory of the United States of America, South of the River Ohio*, ——— (Knoxville); *Journal of the Proceedings of the House of Representatives of the Territory of the United States of America, South of the River Ohio*, ——— (Knoxville); *Acts of a General or Public Nature Passed at the* ——— *Session of the* ——— *General Assembly* (Knoxville); *Acts of a Local or Private Nature Passed at the* ——— *Session of the* ——— *General Assembly* (Nashville); Edward Scott, comp., *Laws of the State of Tennessee from 1715 to the Year 1820 Inclusive*, 2 vols. (Knoxville, 1821); John Haywood and Robert L. Cobb, comps., *The Statute Laws of Tennessee* (Knoxville, 1831); and R. L. Caruthers and A. O. P. Nickolson, *A Compilation of the Statutes of Tennessee from Commencement of the Government to the Present Time* (Nashville, 1836).

Secondary accounts containing lottery information are John T. Moore and Austin P. Foster, *Tennessee, the Volunteer State, 1769–1923,* 4 vols. (Knoxville, 1923); James Phelan, *History of Tennessee: The Making of a State* (Boston, 1888); Douglas C. McMurtie, *An Early Tennessee Paper Mill* (Chicago, 1933); and Joshua W. Caldwell, *Studies in the Constitutional History of Tennessee* (Cincinnati, 1895).

MISSOURI. The most helpful sources for this state are *Laws of a Public and General Nature of the State of Missouri Passed Between the Years, 1824 and 1836,* 2 vols. (Jefferson City, 1842); *Laws of the Territory and State of Missouri up to the Year 1836,* 2 vols. (Jefferson City, 1842). The best of the secondary accounts of a broad nature is H. L. Conrad, ed., *Encyclopedia of the History of Missouri,* 6 vols. (St. Louis, 1901). See also Walter B. Stevens, *Centennial History of Missouri,* 6 vols. (St. Louis, 1921), and two articles by the same author in the *Missouri Historical Review:* "The Missouri Tavern," XV (1921), and "New Journalism in Missouri," XVIII (1924). For the Austin scheme, see Eugene C. Barker, ed., "The Austin Papers," American Historical Association, *Annual Report for the Year 1919,* vol. II.

THE NORTHWEST AND WEST

OHIO. Material on Ohio lotteries can be found in the *Journals* of the house and senate published for each session; *Acts of a General Nature Passed at the* ———— *General Assembly of the State of Ohio* (Columbus); *Acts of a Local Nature Passed at the* ———— *General Assembly of the State of Ohio* (Columbus); "Annals of Cleveland, 1818–1935; A Digest of the Newspaper Record of Events and Opinions," multigraphed by a Cleveland W.P.A. project in 1938; Ernest L. Bogart, *Financial History of Ohio* (Urbana-Champaign, 1912); Emilius O. Randall and Daniel J. Ryan, *History of Ohio,* 5 vols. (New York, 1912); and James H. Kennedy, *A History of the City of Cleveland, 1796–1896* (Cleveland, 1896).

INDIANA. The best sources for this state include Francis S. Philbrick, "The Laws of the Indiana Territory, 1801–1809," Illinois State Historical Library, *Collections,* vol. XXI; Louis B. Eubank and Dorothy Riker, comps., "The Laws of the Indiana Territory, 1809–1816," State of Indiana, *Historical Collections,* vol. XX; *Laws of the State of Indiana Passed at the* ———— *Session of the General Assembly of Indiana* (Indianapolis); *Report of the Debates and Proceedings of the Convention for the Revision of the Constitution of the State of Indiana, 1850,* 2 vols. (Indianapolis, 1850); and George S. Cottman, *Centennial History and Handbook of Indiana* (Indianapolis, 1915).

ILLINOIS. The few lotteries in this state can be found in *Laws Passed at the* ———— *General Assembly of the State of Illinois* (Vandalia) and G. Koehler, "Lottery Authorized in 1819 by the State of Illinois to Raise Funds for Improving Public Health by Draining the Ponds in the American Bottoms," Illinois State Historical Library, *Publications,* vol. XXXV.

MICHIGAN. The most useful sources for this state are *Laws of the Territory of Michigan,* 4 vols. (Lansing, 1871–1884); *Journal of the Legislative Council of the Territory of Michigan* ———— (Detroit); *The Revised Statutes of the State of Michigan* (Detroit, 1876); James V. Campbell, *Outlines of the Po-*

litical History of Michigan (Detroit, 1876); and Silas Farmer, *The History of Detroit and Michigan* (Detroit, 1884).

NORTH DAKOTA. No lotteries were authorized in this state, but it is important because of the efforts of the Louisiana Lottery Company to gain a charter. Therefore most of the sources for the state have previously been listed under Louisiana. A good local source is Clement A. Lounsberry, *Early History of North Dakota* (Washington, 1919). An incomplete transcript of the reports of the Pinkerton detectives can be found in the state historical society.

ARIZONA. The story of its one effort is told in Richard E. Sloan and Ward R. Adams, *History of Arizona,* 4 vols. (Phoenix, 1930).

CALIFORNIA. The most useful sources for this state include *The Statutes of California Passed at the* ———— *Session of the Legislature* (Sacramento); Samuel Garfielde and F. A. Snyder, comps., *Laws of the State of California* (Boston, 1853); John R. Browne, ed., *Report of the Debates of the Convention of California on the Formation of the State Constitution, in September and October, 1849* (Washington, 1850); and Theodore H. Hittell, *History of California,* 4 vols. (San Francisco, 1885–1897).

Notes

I. THE BACKGROUND OF THE LOTTERY

1. Numbers 26:56.
2. Paul A. Fino, "Let's Legalize Gambling," *Coronet*, XXIX (November 1955), 61–64.
3. Quoted by Edwin R. A. Seligman, *Principles of Economics* (New York, 1906), 564.
4. "Lotteries," *Encyclopaedia Britannica* (11th ed.), XVII, 20–22; John Ashton, *A History of English Lotteries* (London, 1893), 2–4.
5. "Lotteries," *loc. cit.*
6. *Ibid.*
7. Ashton, 4–16.
8. *Three Proclamations Concerning the Lottery for Virginia, 1613–1621* (Providence, 1907), 1.
9. *Ibid.*
10. *Ibid.*
11. Alexander Brown, *The Genesis of the United States* (Boston, 1891), II, 555.
12. *Three Proclamations*, 2.
13. Hyder Edward Rollins, ed., *The Pepys Ballads* (Cambridge, 1929), quoted in the *William and Mary Quarterly*, 3rd series, V (April 1948), 259.
14. *Three Proclamations*, 2. Considerable information concerning the company's methods of conducting their lotteries can be found in the records of their suit against one of their collectors, William Leveson, to force him to pay in his returns. Susan Kingsbury, *Records of the Virginia Company of London* (Washington, 1906), III, 50–51, 54–57.
15. *Three Proclamations*, 2.
16. *Ibid.*, 2–3 (including the first reproduction).
17. Brown, 687, 691.
18. *Three Proclamations* (second reproduction).
19. Kingsbury, III, 67.
20. Quoted by Wesley F. Craven, *Dissolution of the Virginia Company* (New York, 1932), 149.
21. Kingsbury, I, 279, 390.
22. *Ibid.*, 411–412. Spelling of the words plantation and malignant has been modernized for convenience of the printer.
23. *Three Proclamations* (third reproduction).
24. Craven, 184; A. R. Spofford, "Lotteries in American History," American Historical Association, *Annual Report for the Year 1892*, 174.
25. *Three Proclamations*, 4; Kingsbury, I, 390, 396–397, 492–493.
26. Kingsbury, I, 556; Brown, II, 575.
27. Kingsbury, III, 47–48.
28. Ashton, 40–41.

29. *Ibid.*, 287–292.
30. "Lotteries," *loc. cit.*, 20–22.
31. Ashton, 224–265.

II. THE LOTTERY CROSSES TO AMERICA

1. Increase Mather, *A Testimony against Several Prophane and Superstitious Customs Now Practiced in New England* (London, 1687), 13.
2. Thomas Jefferson, *Writings,* edited by A. A. Lipscomb (Washington, 1903), XVII, 450.
3. State of New Jersey, *Documents Relating to the Colonial History* (Newark, 1880–1894), XX, 575–576.
4. *Ibid.*, XI, 122–123.
5. Anon., "The Virginia Gazette," *William and Mary College Quarterly Historical Magazine,* 1st series, XXVII (1919), 301; Robert H. Land, "The First Williamsburg Theater," *ibid.*, 3rd series, V (1948), 369–370.
6. An orrery is a type of planetarium. State of New Jersey, XX, 537–541.
7. Photostat of the Petties' Island Lottery broadside is in the collection of the Boston Public Library. This is undated; but Bella C. Landauer, *Some Early American Lottery Items* (New York, 1928), 2, assigns the date, 1772.
8. Jared Ingersoll, "Papers," New Haven Colony Historical Society, *Papers,* IX, 242–243.
9. William Strahan and David Hall, "Correspondence," *Pennsylvania Magazine of History and Biography,* X, 327–331.
10. Quoted by Lady Edgar, *A Colonial Governor in Maryland* (New York, 1912), 263, 265. Dr. Upton Scott was Sharpe's American physician.
11. Thomas Adams, "Letters, 1768–1775," *Virginia Magazine of History and Biography,* XXIII, 52.
12. Quoted by W. C. Bronson, *The History of Brown University, 1764–1914* (Providence, 1914), 37, 59.
13. Guiljelmi Amesij, *De Conscientia, et Euis Iure vel Casibus* (Amstelodami, 1630), libri quinque, 159; William Ames, *Works* (London, 1643), Book IV, chap. xxiii, 60–61; S. E. Baldwin, "The Ecclesiastical Constitution of Yale College," New Haven Colony Historical Society, *Papers,* III, 434. A Latin copy in Harvard College Library is autographed by Richard Wensley, 1681, an undergraduate.
14. Catherine P. Hargrave, *A History of Playing Cards* (Boston, 1930), 323–324.
15. Mather, 13–14.
16. "Diary," Massachusetts Historical Society, *Collections,* 7th series, VII, pt. 1, p. 202.
17. As quoted by George W. Gordon, *Lecture on Lotteries before the Boston Young Men's Society* (Boston, 1833), 10.
18. Boston, 1713, pp. 14–15.
19. For an example of Quaker opposition to lotteries in England, see George Fox, *Journal,* edited by Norman Penney (Cambridge, 1911), I, 187, note 2.
20. Quoted by A. C. Applegarth, "Quakers in Pennsylvania," Johns Hopkins University, *Studies in Historical and Political Science,* 10th series, VIII, 32, 37–38.

21. Quoted by Ezra Michener, *A Retrospect of Early Quakerism* (Philadelphia, 1860), 361.

22. Samuel Sewall, "Letter Book," Massachusetts Historical Society, *Collections*, 6th series, II, 102–103.

23. New York stated in the preamble of an act against lotteries in 1747 that private lotteries were of "pernicious Consequences" to the public because they encouraged "Numbers of Laboring People to Assemble together at Taverns where such Lotteries are usually Set on Foot and Drawn."

24. Landauer (photostatic copy of the printed law).

25. In 1747 the law expired and was re-enacted with the same penalties.

26. Colony of Connecticut, *Public Records*, edited by C. J. Hoadly (Hartford, 1894), VII, 147, 161.

27. Michener, 361–363.

28. See the letter of Governor William Shirley of Massachusetts, May 2, 1756, requesting that Governor R. H. Morris of Pennsylvania do this for a Connecticut church. Provincial Council of Pennsylvania, *Minutes* (Harrisburg, 1852–1853), VII, 112–113.

29. Province of Massachusetts Bay, *The Acts and Resolves, Public and Private* (Boston, 1874), II, 663–664.

30. A convenient source of these advertisements is the section of State of New Jersey, *Documents Relating to the Colonial History* (Newark, 1880–1894), entitled "Extracts from American Newspapers."

31. *Ibid.*, XIX, 141.

32. The preceding quotations are from *ibid.*, XX, 320–321, 324–325, 332–333.

33. Provincial Council of Pennsylvania, *Minutes*, VIII, 339–341.

34. For examples of the prevalence of raffles in South Carolina, see Hennig Cohen, *The South Carolina Gazette 1732–1775* (Columbia, S.C., 1953), 75–85. The author cites no raffles after 1762.

35. E. S. Stackpole, *A History of New Hampshire* (New York, n.d.), II, 26–27.

36. The Byrd lottery was given legal sanction in November 1781, in order to confirm the titles of those who had won land. W. W. Hening, comp., *The Statutes at Large, being a Collection of all the Laws of Virginia from the First Session of the Legislature in the Year 1619* (Philadelphia, 1823), X, 446.

37. State of North Carolina, *Colonial and State Records* (Goldsboro, N.C., 1886–1914), VIII, 185–186. Authorization was not required until 1780.

38. State of Delaware, *Laws, from October 14, 1700, to August 18, 1797* (New Castle, 1797), I, 504–506.

39. Part of the advertisement in the *Maryland Gazette*, July 7, 1761.

40. State of New Jersey, *Documents*, X, 509.

III. AUTHORIZED LOTTERIES IN COLONIAL AMERICA

1. St. Denis Le Cadet, *The Lottery, A Poem* (Baltimore, 1815), 14.

2. The first authorized lotteries in Massachusetts, New York, and Virginia, for example, were for that purpose.

3. State of Pennsylvania, *Statutes at Large from 1628–1801*, compiled by J. T. Mitchell and Henry Flanders (Harrisburg, 1895–1911), VI, 382–384.

4. *Ibid.*, VI, 384–391.

5. Province of Massachusetts Bay, *The Acts and Resolves, Public and Private* (Boston, 1874), III, 195.

6. The directors included Samuel Watts, John Quincy, James Bowdoin, Robert Hale, and Thomas Hutchinson.

7. Thomas Doyle, *Five Years in a Lottery Office* (Boston, 1841), 11.

8. Benjamin Franklin Papers, in Jared Sparks Manuscripts, XVIII, 65, in the Harvard College Library.

9. Broadside in the collection of the New York Public Library. The 1746 lottery was probably not held because of the war and the lack of success of the fortification venture.

10. Manuscript letter, without date or address, in the Boston Public Library. Internal evidence supports the view that this reference is to the New York lottery, voted in December 1746, for King's College.

11. F. B. Dexter, *Biographical Sketches of the Graduates of Yale College with Annals of the College History* (New York, 1885), 103, 140; Ebenezer Baldwin, *History of Yale College* (New Haven, 1841), 65, 323. Four tickets for this lottery are in the Harvard College Library.

12. *History of Columbia University 1754–1904* (New York, 1904), 3–4.

13. John Maclean, *History of the College of New Jersey* (Philadelphia, 1877), I, 136–137.

14. Though Bernard gave the date as 1754, the correct date was 1757. Official Papers of Governor Sir Francis Bernard, Jared Sparks Manuscripts, IV, 268–269, Harvard College Library. Germantown later became Braintree.

15. These were the churches of St. James and St. Philip. State of North Carolina, *Colonial and State Records* (Goldsboro, N.C., 1886–1914), VI, 32–33.

16. *Journal of the Legislative Council of the Colony of New York* (Albany, 1861), 1379.

17. John Woolman, *Journal and Essays*, edited by Amelia M. Gummere (New York, 1922), 236.

18. Quoted by Eric Bender, *Tickets to Fortune* (New York, 1938), 111.

19. The Boston Public Library collection has twelve tickets in this lottery signed by Hancock. A ticket in the second class was endorsed by him as part owner.

20. This delayed the drawing until January 1764, when it took place in Nassau Hall.

21. In addition to the others, there were lotteries for repairing a Providence highway, paving in North Providence, recompensing W. & H. Wall for loss of merchandise by fire, rebuilding a bridge over Woonsocket Falls, repairing a road leading from Providence into Connecticut, and constructing a pond near Shoreham.

22. W. C. Bronson, *History of Brown University* (Providence, 1914), 37; Manning was the one later rebuffed by his English friend when seeking sales assistance. See above, Chapter II.

23. Maryland Historical Society, *Archives of Maryland* (Baltimore, 1883–1944), XIV, 384.

24. *Ibid.*, XIV, 391.

25. Governor Bernard, *loc. cit.*, IX, 186–187.

26. Quoted by C. H. J. Douglas, "The Financial History of Massachusetts,"

in Columbia University, *Studies in History, Economics and Public Law* (New York, 1897), I, 100–101.

27. Governor Bernard, *loc. cit.*, II, 56–57.

28. *Ibid.*, 60–62.

29. State of New Jersey, *Documents Relating to the Colonial History* (Newark, 1880–1894), IX, 443–444, 446–447, 458.

30. Provincial Council of Pennsylvania, *Minutes* (Harrisburg, 1852–53), IX, 638–640.

31. *Ibid.*, 636–637.

32. Leonard W. Labaree, ed., *Royal Instructions to the British Colonial Governors, 1670–1776* (New York, 1935), I, 200.

33. John Ashton, *A History of English Lotteries* (London, 1893), 72–86.

34. One of Connecticut's three licenses, that for Long Wharf, was probably never held. See T. R. Trowbridge, "History of Long Wharf in New Haven," New Haven Colony Historical Society, *Papers*, I, 93–95.

35. It is not clear why the instructions of 1771 were necessary.

36. Frederick Chase and J. K. Lord, *A History of Dartmouth College* (Cambridge, 1891), I, 276.

37. Quoted by Ezra Michener, *A Retrospect of Early Quakerism* (Philadelphia, 1860), 363.

38. Since there is no record of authorization, it must be assumed that the joint lottery of 1773 for two Trenton churches was held without permission. Trenton Historical Society, *A History of Trenton 1679–1929* (Princeton, 1929), I, 109.

39. All was not clear sailing, as evidenced by Princeton's becoming involved in a serious controversy over one of the larger prizes, which, it seems, the college could not pay for lack of ready cash. A compromise was finally reached in 1780.

40. On April 13, 1772, a lottery was drawn to raise £600 for a "Reformed German Church." There is no evidence that it was authorized.

41. *Census of the Inhabitants of the Colony of Rhode Island and Providence Plantations, 1774*, edited by John R. Bartlett (Providence, 1858), 239.

IV. WAR AND CONFEDERATION DAYS

1. This was a proverb taught Boston school children, according to Theodore Sedgwick, *Hints to My Countrymen* (New York, 1826), 203.

2. Quoted in the brief of the appellee, Champion v. Ames, 106 U.S. 22–23. It is of interest that England, too, used lotteries to finance the war.

3. James Warren and John Adams, "Letters," Massachusetts Historical Society, *Collections*, LXXII, 309.

4. North Carolina records give an indication of the money paid out in prizes. The large amounts involved probably help explain the project's failure. The people could not support it. State of North Carolina, *Colonial and State Records* (Goldsboro, N.C., 1886–1914), XVI, 354.

5. *Maryland Journal*, April 29, 1780.

6. "Incidents in the History of York, Pennsylvania, 1778," *Pennsylvania Magazine of History and Biography*, XVI, 434.

7. Quoted by C. H. J. Douglas, "The Financial History of Massachusetts,"

Columbia University, *Studies in History, Economics and Public Law*, I, 110–111.

8. Quoted by H. B. Tompkins, "Newport County Lotteries," Newport Historical Society, *Bulletins*, II, 2–3.

9. Quoted by J. B. Wilbur, *Ira Allen* (Boston, 1928), I, 182.

10. Douglas, 116.

11. Edward Channing, *A History of the United States* (New York, 1905–1930), IV, 24–27.

12. *Maryland Journal & Baltimore Advertiser*, November 20, 24, and December 8, 1789.

13. State of New Hampshire, *Documents and Records* (Concord, 1867–1939), XIII, 559–560.

14. State of North Carolina, *Records*, XXIV, 821.

15. General Assembly of South Carolina, *Acts, Ordinances, and Resolves Passed in the Year 1784* (Charleston, n.d.), 58.

16. Such was educational financing in the 1780's!

17. John B. McMaster, *A History of the People of the United States* (New York, 1883–1913), I, 297.

18. State of New Hampshire, *Documents and Records*, XIII, 229.

19. An interesting list of the expenses of this lottery, even down to the cost of "wax and thread," is found in the records of the Harvard Corporation.

20. State of Pennsylvania, *The Statutes at Large, 1682–1801*, compiled by J. T. Mitchell and Henry Flanders (Harrisburg, 1895–1911), XIII, 277.

21. This does not include the Maryland lotteries mentioned, since that state did not require legal sanction, nor any that might have been held under the blanket approval given by North Carolina to school lotteries in 1780 nor those held by Charleston, South Carolina, under its grant.

V. A PERIOD OF TRANSMUTATION

1. Written in 1776. Adam Smith, *An Inquiry into the Nature and Causes of the Wealth of Nations* (London, 1786), I, 164–165.

2. For a detailed description of American national characteristics, see A. M. Schlesinger, *Paths to the Present* (New York, 1949), 1–22.

3. This phrase was used by the Reverend Wakely to describe the purchase of a lottery ticket by a church. J. B. Wakely, *Lost Chapters Recovered from the Early History of American Methodism* (New York, 1858), 344.

4. Fritz Redlich, *The Molding of American Banking: Men and Ideas* (New York, 1951), part II, p. 327. The relationship between lotteries and the development of investment banking is seen in England also. John Ashton, *A History of English Lotteries* (London, 1893).

5. Henrietta M. Larson, "S. & M. Allen—Lottery, Exchange, and Stock Brokerage," *Journal of Economic and Business History*, III (May 1931), 425–430, 435–436.

6. *Struggles and Triumphs: Or the Life of P. T. Barnum, Written by Himself* (New York, 1927), I, 44–47, 53–56, 70, 82, 84–85, 87, 95.

7. The letter-book of Daniel M'Intyre, associate of J. G. Gregory & Co., one of the large contractors, shows that the lottery men maintained active lobbies in most of the state capitals and did not hesitate to use money to smooth their path. Although M'Intyre is referring to events in 1845–46, there

is no reason to believe that he is describing a new practice. The letters also show the difficulty of enforcing antilottery laws. This volume, covering from November 9, 1844, to January 6, 1847, was in 1947 the property of Goodspeed's Book Shop, Boston, Massachusetts.

8. Hugh G. J. Aitken, "Yates & McIntyre: Lottery Managers," *The Journal of Economic History,* XIII (1953), 38–39.

9. State of New York, *Laws Passed at the 56th Session of the Legislature, 1829* (Albany, 1829), 567–583, contains a legislative report on the activities of this firm.

10. Gilbert & Dean's was a big lottery office in Boston. Quoted in Colonial Society of Massachusetts, *Publications,* XIII, 156.

11. In the Old State House collection, Boston, Massachusetts.

12. Quoted by J. H. Stiness, "A Century of Lotteries in Rhode Island," State of Rhode Island, *Historical Tracts,* 2nd series, III, 90.

13. Boston *Independent Chronical,* April 6, 1808.

14. Boston *Repertory,* March 24, 1809.

15. Quoted by H. M. Brooks, *Curiosities of the Old Lottery* (Boston, 1886), 44.

16. Salem *Gazette,* May 24, 1812.

17. Quoted by Stiness, *loc. cit.,* 87–88.

18. Salem *Gazette,* December 25, 1812.

19. For examples of frauds of this sort, see G. W. Gordon, *Lecture on Lotteries* (Boston, 1833), 33; "Civis," *Dissertation on the Nature and Effects of Lottery Systems* (Portland, Maine, 1827), 24.

20. Quoted by Brooks, 16–17.

21. Benjamin Franklin, *Works,* compiled by John Bigelow (New York, 1904), II, 227–228.

22. For a full account of the ternary combination system, see Thomas Doyle, *Five Years in a Lottery Office* (Boston, 1841), 18–20.

23. The new Philadelphia Arcade found difficulty in renting its offices because *nine* lottery agents had moved in and other businessmen did not want to share the building with them. Boston *Daily Advertiser,* September 12, 1827.

24. Concerning the importance of lotteries, Edward Channing wrote, "Indeed until the multiplication of stocks and bonds provided an outlet for speculative desire, lotteries maintained their place despite reformers, legislatures, and courts of law." Henrietta M. Larson writes in a similar vein: "There was a veritable crusade against lotteries, but I am inclined to think that not the reformers but the development of machinery for the sale of shares in corporations was responsible for the decline of lotteries." Edward Channing, *A History of the United States* (New York, 1905–1930), V, 198; Larson, *loc. cit.,* III, 431n.

VI. THE LOTTERY AS AN AID TO GOVERNMENT

1. Broadside by T. Kidder advertising the Harvard College Lottery, July 9, 1812; Boston Public Library collection.

2. In addition to chartering lotteries for their own use, some states, as noted in the previous chapter, required that an out-of-state lottery hold a drawing for their benefit as the price of being allowed to sell its tickets.

3. Blodget wrote the first American statistical work, *Economica.*

4. See the letter of Lewis Bond, River Raisin, March 12, 1804, asking the fate of his tickets, Pioneer Society of Michigan, *Collections*, XXXVII, 434.

5. George Washington, "Writings Relating to the National Capital," Columbia Historical Society, *Records*, XVII, 91.

6. Quoted by William Tindall, *Standard History of the City of Washington* (Knoxville, 1914), 165.

7. Washington, *loc. cit.*, XVII, 95–96.

8. Tindall, 165–167. On May 6, 1794, Washington again wrote Lear, saying that he understood little Lincoln Lear was planning to live in the federal city if the ticket produced a prize. He was sorry to tell him that his award (ten dollars) would "hardly build him a baby house." "Mr. Blo - - - t's agency in this lottery will it is to be feared be more productive of thorns than roses." Washington, *loc. cit.*, XVII, 101.

9. Quoted by Allan Nevins, ed., *American Press Opinion, Washington to Coolidge* (New York, 1928), 25.

10. Quoted by Charles Warren, *The Supreme Court in United States History* (Boston, 1928), I, 548.

11. Some of the Baltimore lotteries seem to have been originated not from the grant of the lottery power but in the grant of power to accomplish such things. See *Ordinances of the Corporation of the City of Baltimore* (Baltimore, 1801), 219, and J. H. Hollander, *Financial History of Baltimore* (Baltimore, 1899).

12. William D. Hoyt, Jr., "Robert Mills and the Washington Monument in Baltimore," *Maryland Historical Magazine*, XXXIV (June, 1939), 144; "Pickering's Letter on Washington," *Tyler's Historical Quarterly and Genealogical Magazine*, VII (1926), 44.

13. This is only an approximation as the individual lotteries held by Baltimore and Charleston, South Carolina, under their blanket grants, are counted as only two authorizations.

VII. INTERNAL IMPROVEMENTS

1. From an announcement for the New Hampshire Union Canal Lottery, Boston *Daily Advertiser*, November 8, 1814.

2. Managers' receipt book for this lottery is in the Boston Public Library.

3. By the proceeds of this lottery the canal, begun in 1793, had its bed lowered several feet and the famous incline where boats were carted 230 feet with a vertical lift of fifty-three feet was replaced by five locks.

4. A copy of this report can be found in G. W. Gordon, *Lecture on Lotteries before the Boston Young Men's Society* (Boston, 1833), 63–67.

5. Justin Winsor, *The Memorial History of Boston* (Boston, 1881), IV, 116.

6. Harvard College Library collection.

7. T. R. Trowbridge, "History of Long Wharf in New Haven," New Haven Historical Society, *Papers*, I, 93–95.

8. Christopher Roberts, *The Middlesex Canal, 1793–1860* (Cambridge, 1938), Appendix G, 206–208; State of New Hampshire, *Journal of the House of Representatives, 1827* (Concord, 1827), 145, 236; *ibid.*, 1829, 67, 126–127.

9. Five of these were passed before 1790. Zadock Thompson, *History of Vermont, Natural, Civil and Statistical* (Burlington, 1842), part II, 222–223.

10. Gordon, 31.

11. James P. Baxter, ed., *Documentary History of the State of Maine* (Portland, 1916), XXII, 224–227, 309–310, 372–374.

12. Gordon, 31.

13. State of Maine, *Documents Printed by Order of the Legislature During its Session A.D. 1835* (Augusta, 1835), no. 34, pp. 1–6.

14. D. C. Sowers, "The Financial History of New York State from 1789 to 1912," Columbia University, *Studies in History, Economics, and Public Law,* LVII, 136.

15. For the story of this squabble, see Anon., *Let Not the Faith, Nor the Laws of the Commonwealth be Violated* (N.p., c. 1833); Committee Appointed to Investigate the Evils of Lotteries in the Commonwealth of Pennsylvania, and to Suggest a Remedy for the Same, *Report* (Philadelphia, 1831); Committee on Vice and Immorality of the Senate of Pennsylvania, to Whom Were Referred the Message of the Governor and Sundry Memorials Relating to the Abolition of Lotteries, *Report* (Philadelphia, 1832); Samuel Hazard, ed., *The Register of Pennsylvania,* I (1828), 111–112, VII (1831), 157–160, IX (1834), 121–125, 129–137, 149–152, 165–169. For a list of the classes, contractors, number of tickets, prices, and prizes, see Job R. Tyson, *Address to the People of Pennsylvania and the United States* (Philadelphia, 1834), 10, 88–92.

16. "Petition of Mason L. Weems," *Tyler's Quarterly Historical and Genealogical Magazine,* V (1923), 237–238.

17. W. E. Connelley and E. M. Coulter, *History of Kentucky* (New York, 1922), I, 494, II, 724; R. H. Collins, *History of Kentucky* (Louisville, 1924), I, 26, 539.

18. *Tennessee Historical Magazine,* VII (1924), 282–283; Legislative Council of the Territory of the United States of America, South of the River Ohio, *Journal of Proceedings, 1795* (Knoxville, 1795), 5.

19. For the story of this lottery, see *Missouri Historical Review,* VII (1913), 160; XVIII (1924), 200; H. L. Conrad, "Lotteries," *Encyclopedia of the History of Missouri* (St. Louis, 1901), IV, 113–114.

20. The Cleveland, Ohio, *Herald,* January 3, 1845, gives a list of the numbers drawn.

21. E. C. Barker, ed., "The Austin Papers," American Historical Association, *Annual Report for the Year 1919,* vol. II, part I, pp. 267–271, 281–283, 285–286.

22. For details of Ohio lotteries, see E. L. Bogart, *Financial History of Ohio* (Urbana-Champaign, 1912), 330; E. O. Randall and D. J. Ryan, *History of Ohio* (New York, 1912), 61–63; J. H. Kennedy, *A History of the City of Cleveland, 1796–1896* (Cleveland, 1896), 134–136.

23. G. Koehler, "Lottery Authorized in 1819 by the State of Illinois," Illinois State Historical Library, *Publications,* XXXV, 195–200.

24. Pioneer Society of the State of Michigan, *Collections,* XXXVI (1908), 594; XXXVII (1909–10), 108. For a comment on the 1829 lottery, see C. E. Carter, ed., "The Territory of Michigan 1829–1837," *The Territorial Papers of the United States* (Washington, 1934——), 100.

25. Again, these figures are, at best, an educated guess and represent a minimum because of the difficulty of multiple grants and the fact that often no specific limit was set on the amount that could be raised for a single project.

VIII. CHURCHES AND SCHOOLS

1. Circulating Library Lottery. *Maryland Journal & Baltimore Advertiser,* May 15, 1789.

2. This figure is, at best, an educated guess complicated by the fact, for example, that a single Kentucky law allowed every academy in the state to hold a lottery, and in some states lotteries were held for the benefit of the entire educational system.

3. These were the states of Rhode Island, Connecticut, New York, New Jersey, Pennsylvania, Delaware, Maryland, Virginia, North Carolina, South Carolina, Georgia, Mississippi, Louisiana, and Kentucky.

4. For a discussion of church lotteries in Maryland, see John S. Ezell, "The Church Took a Chance," *Maryland Historical Magazine,* XLIII (December 1948), 266ff.

5. *Federal Gazette & Baltimore Daily Advertiser,* July 1, October 14, 1803.

6. *Connecticut Journal,* February 12, 1801; New London *Bee,* February 11, September 30, 1801.

7. (Lexington) *Kentucky Gazette,* February 16, 1793.

8. American Catholic Historical Society of Philadelphia, *Records,* XLIII (September 1932), 237.

9. The story of this lottery is told in Samuel E. Morison, *Three Centuries of Harvard, 1636–1936* (Cambridge, Mass., 1937), 173; William Bentley, *Diary* (Salem, Mass., 1914), II, 97; H. M. Brooks, *Curiosities of the Old Lottery* (Boston, 1886), 51–53; and John Noble, "Harvard College Lotteries," Colonial Society of Massachusetts, *Publications,* XXVII (1927–1930), 169–182.

10. Broadside for "Gilbert & Dean's Lottery Office." Boston Public Library.

11. Frederick Chase and J. K. Lord, *A History of Dartmouth College* (Cambridge, Mass., 1891), I, 579, 612–613, 627–629, and L. B. Richardson, *History of Dartmouth College* (Hanover, 1932), I, 228.

12. W. C. Bronson, *The History of Brown University, 1764–1914* (Providence, 1914), 143–144.

13. Charles Carroll, *Public Education in Rhode Island* (Providence, 1918), 283.

14. The Botanical Gardens comprised twenty acres in the area now lying between Fifth Avenue and the Avenue of the Americas and Forty-seventh and Fifty-first streets.

15. The remaining part of this story will be told in Chapter XI.

16. W. O. Bourne, *History of the Public School Society of the City of New York* (New York, 1870), 107, 627–628.

17. W. H. S. Demarest, *A History of Rutgers College, 1766–1924* (New Brunswick, N. J., 1924), 231–234, 263–267.

18. The school was later called Delaware College and after 1921 became the University of Delaware. L. P. Powell, *The History of Education in Delaware* (Washington, 1893), 47, 82, 89, 103, 106–107; Henry C. Conrad, *History of the State of Delaware* (Wilmington, 1908), III, 798; Jane N. Garrett, "The Delaware College Lotteries, 1818–1845," *Delaware History,* VII (1957), 305, 306, 311. The lottery was managed at various times by Yates & McIntyre, D. S. Gregory, and J. G. Gregory and Company.

19. *Federal Gazette & Baltimore Daily Advertiser*, November 1, 1809.

20. E. F. Cordell, *University of Maryland, 1807–1907* (New York, 1907), I, 30–31.

21. B. C. Steiner, *History of Education in Maryland* (Washington, 1894), 84, 96, 119, 170–172, 245.

22. For an advertisement of this unusual type of lottery, see *Federal Gazette & Baltimore Daily Advertiser*, March 14, 1804.

23. A description of the state's role can be found in H. S. Hanna, *A Financial History of Maryland, 1789–1848* (Baltimore, 1907), 58–60, 129.

24. For this plan, see W. A. Maddox, "The Free School Idea in Virginia before the Civil War," Teachers College, Columbia University, *Contributions to Education*, no. 93 (New York, 1918), 45–46, 49–51. For the Literary Fund Report, see House of Delegates of Virginia, *Journal of the Session, 1821–1822* (Richmond, 1822), Tables B and C of the governor's letter to the legislature on the Literary Fund (unpaged).

25. House of Delegates of Virginia, *Journal of the Session of 1847–1848* (Richmond, 1847 [*sic*]), 289–290.

26. William and Mary College, *Quarterly Historical Magazine*, 2nd series, V (1925), 121–124.

27. Thomas Jefferson, *Writings*, edited by A. A. Lipscomb (Washington, 1903), XIX, 362–364; P. A. Bruce, *History of the University of Virginia, 1819–1919* (New York, 1920), 124–125, 178.

28. K. P. Battle, *History of the University of North Carolina* (Raleigh, 1907), I, 126–128.

29. M. C. S. Noble, *A History of the Public Schools of North Carolina* (Chapel Hill, 1930), 45, 136; see also, C. L. Coon, *The Beginnings of Public Education in North Carolina, a Documentary History, 1790–1840* (Raleigh, 1908), and C. L. Coon, *North Carolina Schools and Academies, 1790–1840, A Documentary History* (Raleigh, 1915).

30. J. H. Easterby, *A History of the College of Charleston* (Charleston, S. C., 1935), 19, 41, 65, 343.

31. E. W. G. Boogher, *Secondary Education in Georgia, 1732–1859* (Philadelphia, 1933), 106–108.

32. E. Merton Coulter, *College Life in the Old South* (New York, 1928), 52, 151.

33. Dunbar Rowland, *History of Mississippi, The Heart of the South* (Chicago, 1925), I, 385; C. S. Sydnor, *A Gentleman of the Old Natchez Region, Benjamin L. C. Wailes* (Durham, N. C., 1938), 48–49; Mississippi Historical Society, *Publications*, II, 183–184.

34. E. W. Fay, *The History of Education in Louisiana* (Washington, 1898), 29–31, 54, 63; W. L. Fleming, *Louisiana State University, 1860–1896* (Baton Rouge, 1936), 12–13.

35. Robert Peter, *History of Transylvania University* (Louisville, 1896), 32; R. H. Collins, *History of Kentucky* (Louisville, 1924), I, 30, 41, 78; House of Representatives, *Executive Documents*, 46th Congress, 2nd session (1879–80), XII, document no. 22.

36. Jefferson, *Writings*, XII, 386.

37. J. M. Miller, *The Genesis of Western Culture* (Columbus, Ohio, 1938), 71–72; B. W. Bond, Jr., *The Civilization of the Old Northwest* (New York,

1934), 429; E. O. Randall and D. J. Ryan, *History of Ohio* (New York, 1912), III, 62–63.

38. F. S. Philbrick, "The Laws of the Indiana Territory, 1801–1809," Illinois State Historical Library, *Collections*, XXI, 183–184; G. S. Cottman, *Centennial History and Handbook of Indiana* (Indianapolis, 1915), 56.

39. Pioneer Society of the State of Michigan, *Collections*, VII, 36–40.

IX. PRIVATE AND SEMI-PRIVATE LOTTERIES

1. St. Denis Le Cadet, *The Lottery, A Poem* (Baltimore, 1815), 15.

2. Thomas Jefferson, *Notes on the State of Virginia*, edited by Paul L. Ford (Brooklyn, 1894), 202–203.

3. William Bentley, *Diary* (Salem, Mass., 1914), I, 236–238.

4. There is no evidence that this permission was ever given.

5. J. S. Davis, *Essays in the Earlier History of American Corporations* (Cambridge, 1917), I, 385, 428–429, 442, 447–449.

6. State of New Jersey, *Journal of the Proceedings of the Legislative Council Convened at Trenton, 1843–1844* (New Brunswick, 1844), 292.

7. The Jefferson lottery will be discussed under Virginia authorizations.

8. Thomas Jefferson, *Writings*, edited by A. A. Lipscomb (Washington, 1903), XVI, 157–158.

9. *Ibid.*, XVII, 448–465.

10. With the failure of the lottery, Jefferson's property was sold in 1827–28 and the real estate in 1829. His daughter was penniless until the legislatures of Virginia and South Carolina later voted her a gift of $10,000 each. James Madison, *Letters and Other Writings* (Philadelphia, 1865), III, 538–539, 617–618; *Niles' Weekly Register*, XXX (July 29, 1826), 390–391; Herbert Asbury, *Sucker's Progress* (New York, 1938), 74–76.

11. Walter Clark, ed., *The State Records of North Carolina* (Goldsboro, 1905–1906) XXV, 94–95.

12. W. H. Hoyt, ed., *The Papers of Archibald D. Murphey* (Raleigh, 1914), I, 357; C. L. Coon, *The Beginnings of Public Education in North Carolina, A Documentary History, 1790–1840* (Raleigh, 1908), 286, 298–299, 384, 529–531.

13. T. E. Dabney, *One Hundred Great Years: The Story of the Times-Picayune from its Founding to 1940* (Baton Rouge, 1944), 50, 342; Asbury, 80.

14. D. C. McMurtie, *An Early Tennessee Paper Mill* (Chicago, 1933), 3–5.

15. L. B. Eubanks and Dorothy Riker, "The Laws of the Indiana Territory, 1809–1816," State of Indiana, *Historical Collections*, XX, 105–106; G. S. Cottman, *Centennial History and Handbook of Indiana* (Indianapolis, 1915), 56.

16. Works Progress Administration, *History of Journalism in San Francisco* (Project 100008, O.P. 665–08–3–12, n.p., 1939), II, 111–117.

17. The figure of 186 is inconclusive since Louisiana gave a blanket approval for sale of property in this manner merely for payment of a fixed percentage to the state, and Alabama passed a blanket act for all Masonic lodges. It also does not include the numerous schemes that were held in other states without consent.

X. THE SHIFT IN PUBLIC OPINION

1. Quoted by Bella C. Landauer, *Some Early American Lottery Items* (New York, 1928), 2 (Foreword).

2. John Bach McMaster, *The History of the People of the United States, from the Revolution to the Civil War* (New York, 1883–1913), I, 587–588.

3. Jeremy Belknap, "Papers," Massachusetts Historical Society, *Collections*, Fifth series, III, 217, 251. It is surprising the idea did not occur to Hamilton to use a national lottery in light of his sponsorship of a lottery for the New Jersey Society for Useful Manufactures in 1791.

4. H. B. Tompkins, "Newport County Lotteries," Newport Historical Society, *Bulletins*, II (1912), 11.

5. William Bentley, *Diary* (Salem, Mass., 1914), I, 138–139, 157–158, 189, 231, 237–238, 248, 258, 263, 357.

6. H. M. Brooks, *Curiosities of the Old Lottery* (Boston, 1886), 57–58.

7. Bentley, I, 83, 97.

8. Quoted by John Noble, "Harvard College Lotteries," Colonial Society of Massachusetts, *Publications*, XXVII, 171n.

9. Quoted by A. F. Ross, *The History of Lotteries in New York* (reprinted from the *Magazine of History*), 11.

10. J. B. Wakely, *Lost Chapters Recovered from the Early History of American Methodism* (New York, 1858), 344.

11. Robert B. Semple, *A History of the Rise and Progress of the Baptist in Virginia* (Richmond, 1894), 118–119, 124–125.

12. Society of Friends, *Rules of Discipline of the Yearly Meeting Held on Rhode Island, for New England* (New Bedford, Mass., 1809), 52; Society of Friends, *Discipline of the Yearly Meeting of Friends, Held in New York and Adopted, in the Sixth Month, 1810* (New York, 1826), 54.

13. W. H. Foote, *Sketches of North Carolina, Historical and Biographical, Illustrative of the Principles of a Portion of Her Early Settlers* (New York, 1846), 468.

14. General Conference of the Methodist Episcopal Church, *Journals* (New York, n.d.), I (1796–1836), 120–121; J. M. Buckley, *A History of the Methodists in the United States* (New York, 1896), 340. The matter was not brought up in 1816. Perhaps one reason for Methodist leniency was that John Wesley had had no strong feelings on the matter. On October 29, 1787, he wrote David Gorden, "I never myself bought a lottery ticket; but I blame not those that do . . ." John Wesley, *Letters*, edited by John Telford (London, 1931), VIII, 20.

15. Noble, *loc. cit.*, 170n.

16. "On Casting Lots," *Massachusetts Missionary Magazine*, II (1804), 303–311.

17. "The Lottery Ticket," *Companion and Weekly Miscellany*, I (1804–1805), 85–87.

18. *Evening Fireside*, I (1804–1805), 116–117.

19. "Lotteries," *Monthly Anthology and Boston Review*, III (1806), 630.

20. Obadiah Optic, "Lotteries," *Eye*, I (1808), 87–89, 217–219, 229–231.

21. "Priscus," "On the Lawfulness and Expediency of Lotteries," *Connecticut Evangelical Magazine and Religious Intelligencer*, IV (1811), 99–104.

22. Quoted by G. L. Kittredge, *The Old Farmer and His Almanack* (Cambridge, Mass. 1920), 90.

23. *Wonderful Advantages of Adventuring in the Lottery* (New York, 1814).

24. Quoted by Mary E. Young, "The Creek Frauds: A Study in Conscience and Corruption," *Mississippi Valley Historical Review*, XLII (December 1955), 423–424.

25. Quoted in the *Lottery Exterminator*, vol. I (1842), no. 1, 2nd edition, p. 16; for a modern discussion of this problem, see W. C. McLeod, "The Truth About Lotteries in American History," *South Atlantic Quarterly*, XXXV (1936), 201–211.

26. McMaster, IV, 528–529; Blanche D. Coll, "The Baltimore Society for the Prevention of Pauperism, 1820–1822," *American Historical Review*, LXI (October 1955), 84.

27. Information concerning this trial is taken from Daniel Rogers, *Report of the Trial of Charles N. Baldwin for a Libel* (New York, 1818), and Thomas Doyle, *Five Years in a Lottery Office* (Boston, 1841), 14–17.

28. John Pintard, "Letters to His Daughter," New York Historical Society, *Collections for the Year 1937*, LXX, 153–154, 157.

29. Society for the Prevention of Pauperism, *Documents Relative to Saving Banks, Intemperance and Lotteries* (New York, 1819), 23–26.

30. Ross, 32–34; D. C. Sowers, "The Financial History of New York State from 1789 to 1912," in Columbia University, *Studies in History, Economics, and Public Law*, LVII, 136.

31. Quoted by "A Journalist," *Memoirs of James Gordon Bennett and His Times* (New York, 1855), 58.

32. "Civis" (F. O. J. Smith), *Dissertation on the Nature and Effects of Lottery Systems, and Principles of Public Policy Relating to Them* (Portland, Maine, 1827), 29n.

33. Allan Nevins, *The Evening Post: A Century of Journalism* (New York, 1922), 71–72.

34. John Gallison, "Prevention of Crimes," *North American Review*, IX (1819) 301–302.

35. T. F. Buxton, *An Inquiry, Whether Crime and Misery Are Produced or Prevented by Our Present System of Prison Discipline* (London, 1813). A play by Samuel Beazley of England, "The Lottery Ticket and the Lawyer's Clerk," was produced from "thirty-five to more than sixty times" in this country. It concerned the last drawing in England but did not oppose the system. The American version of 1828 was almost identical with the English version of 1827. Samuel Beazley, *The Lottery Ticket and the Lawyer's Clerk* (New York, 1828); R. L. Rush, *The Literature of the Middle Western Frontier* (New York, 1926), I, 420.

36. *The Resources of the United States of America* (New York, 1818), 435–436.

37. Ruben G. Thwaites, ed., *Early Western Travels, 1748–1846* (Cleveland, 1904–1906), IV, 69, 216; XII, 125, 303.

38. *The United States and Canada in 1832, 1833, and 1834* (London, 1834), I, 231. None made any reference to the fight for abolition in the states.

39. Theodore Sedgwick, *Hints to My Countrymen* (New York, 1826), 69–71. Other examples of this approach are *Christian Spectator*, VIII (1826), 323–324; *United States Literary Gazette*, IV (1826), 414–417; *Niles' Weekly Register*, XXXIV (June 14, 1828), 253; *The Friend*, VII (1833), 89–90. Most who used England as an example contrasted France.

40. Job R. Tyson, *Address to the People of Pennsylvania and the United States* (Philadelphia, 1834), 3–4.

41. Anon., "Peter Chardon Brooks," *New England Historical and Genealogical Register*, IX, 21–26; for a copy of the report of the joint committee, see

G. W. Gordon, *Lecture on Lotteries before the Boston Young Men's Society* (Boston, 1833), 63–67.

42. Anon., *The Lottery Ticket: An American Tale* (Cambridge, 1822).

43. *American Baptist Magazine*, IV (January 1823), 15–16.

44. Quoted by J. H. Stiness, "A Century of Lotteries in Rhode Island," State of Rhode Island, *Historical Tracts*, 2nd series, III, 72.

45. A. R. Wentz, *History of the Evangelical Lutheran Church of Frederick, Maryland, 1738–1938* (Harrisburg, 1938), 201–202.

46. *Ibid.*, 202. It would be interesting to know if the church's failure to get a license after several efforts had any influence on this change of attitude.

47. 10 Wheaton 395; 12 Wheaton 40.

48. C. L. Coon, *The Beginnings of Public Education in North Carolina, A Documentary History, 1790–1840* (Raleigh, 1908), 277–278, 288, 352.

49. *Ibid.*, 330–338.

50. *Niles' Weekly Register*, XXXI (September 23, 1826), 57; "Civis," 24.

51. C. R. Keller, *The Second Great Awakening in Connecticut* (New Haven, 1942), 160.

52. *Religious Intelligencer*, XI (1826–1827), 346, 378, 396–397, 685, 731, 747–748.

53. *Christian Spectator*, VIII (1826), 196–198, 323–324; IX (1827), 54, 71–79, 121–125.

54. Quoted by the *Religious Intelligencer*, XI (1826–27), 625.

55. Lyman Beecher, *Autobiography*, edited by Charles Beecher (London, 1865), II, 144–146; A. B. Darling, *Political Changes in Massachusetts, 1824–1848* (New Haven, 1925), 55.

56. J. C. White, *Personal Reminiscences of Lyman Beecher* (New York, 1882), 13–15.

57. *Hopkinsian Magazine*, II (1826–27), 508–509.

58. See above, note 32.

59. Both Granger and Spencer had outstanding reform records and were leaders in the anti-Masonic fight.

60. Special Committee of the New York Legislature, *Documents Relative to the Dispute between the Trustees of Union College and Yates and McIntyre* (New York, 1834), paragraphs 141–152.

61. Nevins, 132.

62. A. C. Flick, ed., *History of the State of New York* (New York, 1934), VI, 216.

63. W. O. Bourne, *History of the Public School Society of the City of New York* (New York, 1870), 107.

64. Pintard, *loc. cit.*, LXXII, 2–3.

65. George Brewster, *An Oration on the Evils of Lotteries* (Brooklyn, 1828).

66. Hugh G. J. Aitken, "Yates & McIntyre: Lottery Managers," *Journal of Economic History*, XIII (1953), 44, 49, 52.

67. *Christian Spectator*, X (1828), 168, 224, 402–403.

68. Samuel Hazard, ed., *Register of Pennsylvania*, I (1828), 111–112.

69. J. R. Commons and others, *History of Labour in the United States* (New York, 1918), I, 217, 223; J. R. Commons, ed., *A Documentary History of American Industrial Society* (Cleveland, 1910–11), V, 119.

70. Job R. Tyson, *Brief Survey of the Great Extent and Evil Tendencies of*

the Lottery System as Existing in the United States (Philadelphia, 1833), Appendix, 98.

XI. THE FIGHT FOR ABOLITION

1. "The Lay of the Last Lottery" (sung to the tune of " 'Tis the Last Rose of Summer"). An English lottery advertisement found in the Widener Collection, Harvard College Library, in George Cruikshank, *Lottery Puffs,* II. Pages are unnumbered.

2. For a characterization and discussion of the forces and elements acting upon reform movements, see Arthur M. Schlesinger, *The American as Reformer* (Cambridge, Mass., 1950).

3. E. H. Gillette, *History of the Presbyterian Church in America* (Philadelphia, 1864), II, 365. See also the resolution of the Harmony, South Carolina, Presbytery, November 26, 1830, that this resolution on lotteries be read in its churches. Manuscript of Harmony Presbytery (1830–1848) in the collection of the Historical Foundation of the Presbyterian and Reformed Churches, Montreat, North Carolina.

4. General Conference of the Methodist Episcopal Church, *Journals* (New York, n.d.), I, 373.

5. *Journal of the Franklin Institute,* VIII (1831), 26–28.

6. For the report of the jury, see G. W. Gordon, *Lecture on Lotteries before the Boston Young Men's Society* (Boston, 1833), Appendix, 75.

7. Special Committee of the New York Legislature, *Documents Relative to the Dispute between the Trustees of Union College and Yates and McIntyre* (New York, 1834), paragraphs 396–397.

8. State of Pennsylvania, *Archives,* compiled by G. E. Reed (Harrisburg, 1900), 4th series, V, 959–961. Wolf was a close personal friend of Robert Vaux, the Quaker reformer.

9. Samuel Hazard, ed., *Register of Pennsylvania,* VII (1831), 157–160.

10. *The Friend,* II (1829), 148; III (1830), 76.

11. *Ibid.,* IV (1831), 104, 338–339; V (1831–1832), 37, 65–66.

12. Committee Appointed to Investigate the Evils of Lotteries, in the Commonwealth of Pennsylvania, and to Suggest a Remedy for the Same, *Report* (Philadelphia, 1831), 3–4, 8–16. To the efforts of this organization must be given much of the credit for the ending of lotteries, not only in Pennsylvania, but also throughout the country.

13. Hazard, *Register,* IX (1832), 121–125, 129–137.

14. *Ibid.,* 165–169.

15. Committee on Vice and Immorality of the Senate of Pennsylvania, *Report* (Philadelphia, 1832), 3–15.

16. Anon., *Let Not the Faith, Nor the Laws of the Commonwealth, Be Violated* (n.p., c. 1833).

17. Job R. Tyson, *A Brief Survey of the Great Extent and Evil Tendencies of the Lottery System as Existing in the United States* (Philadelphia, 1833), 67–68.

18. *Niles' Weekly Register,* XLII (March 31, 1832), 81.

19. Tyson, *Brief Survey,* p. iii.

20. Toland was a member of the original antilottery group.

21. *The Friend,* VI (1833), 151–152.

22. Joseph T. Buckingham, *Personal Memoirs and Recollections of Editorial Life* (Boston, 1852), II, 231. The governor's message can be found in General Court of Massachusetts, *Resolves Passed in 1832* (Boston, 1833), 332–335. See also, Gordon, Appendix, 68–69.

23. Buckingham, II, 231–236; Gordon, Appendix, 69–70; Tyson, *Brief Survey,* Appendix, 103–105

24. See, "Lotteries," *North American Review,* XXXVII (1833), 494–501; *Religious Magazine,* I (1833), 76–86.

25. Boston, n.d.

26. State of Maine, *Documents Printed by Order of the Legislature During Its Session A.D. 1835* (Augusta, 1835), no. 34, pp. 1–6; State of Maine, *Resolves of the Legislature from 1829–1835 Inclusive* (Augusta, 1842), II, 723–727.

27. Tyson, *Brief Survey,* 77–78; Job R. Tyson, *Address to the People of Pennsylvania and the United States by the Pennsylvania Society for the Suppression of Lotteries* (Philadelphia, 1834), 7–8.

28. Tyson, *Brief Survey,* 76.

29. "Sui Generis" (Thomas Man), *Picture of a Factory Village to Which Are Annexed, Remarks on Lotteries* (Providence, 1833), 122, 127, 130–131, 133–134.

30. Special Committee of the New York Legislature, *Documents,* paragraphs 396–397.

31. Union College, *Report to the New York Legislature, 1849* (n.p., n.d.).

32. C. D. Arfwedson, *The United States and Canada in 1832, 1833, and 1834* (London, 1834), I, 231.

33. *The Friend,* VI (1833), 176, 184, 256; VII (1834), 48; Tyson, *Brief Survey,* 76–78. *The Friend,* November 16, 1833, reported the formation in Richmond of a Society to Suppress Gambling, but no specific mention was made of lotteries.

34. *The Friend,* V (1831–32), 65; P. M. O'Brien, *The Story of the Sun* (New York, 1918), 37; "The Lottery," *Ladies Companion,* VII (1837), 81–84; "The Lottery Ticket," *Gentleman's Magazine,* III (1838), 224–225; "The Lottery Ticket: A True Narrative," *New Yorker,* VII (1839), 388–389; "Oliver Goldsmith's Nephew and the Lottery Ticket," *Corsair,* I (1839), 407–409.

35. Tyson, *Address to the People,* 7; *The Friend,* VII (1834), 160; Hazard, *Register,* XIV (1834), 96. A list of the members of the society are found in Tyson, *Address to the People,* 15.

36. Charles Carroll, *Public Education in Rhode Island* (Providence, 1918), 284–285; J. H. Stiness, "A Century of Lotteries in Rhode Island," State of Rhode Island, *Historical Tracts,* 2nd series, III, 80–83. Titus is also interesting for his role in Dorr's Rebellion and his sentiments as seen on the back of his lottery ticket (see above, p. 194).

37. J. W. Caldwell, *Studies in the Constitutional History of Tennessee* (Cincinnati, 1895), 119–120; *ibid.,* 2nd ed. (1907), 208–209; Wallace McClure, *State Constitution Making with Especial Reference to Tennessee* (Nashville, 1916), 446; R. L. Caruthers and A. O. P. Nickolson, *A Compilation of the Statutes of Tennessee* (Nashville, 1836), 446.

38. E. S. Riley, *A History of the General Assembly of Maryland, 1635–1904* (Baltimore, 1905), 358; H. S. Hanna, *A Financial History of Maryland, 1789–1848* (Baltimore, 1907), 59–60; Clement Dorsey, comp., *The General Public*

Statutory Law and Public Local Law of the State of Maryland from 1692 to 1839 Inclusive (Baltimore, 1840), II, 1211.

39. *The Friend,* IX (1836), 117; Hanna, 59.

40. Samuel Hazard, *United States Commercial and Statistical Register,* I (1839), 352.

41. Manuscript minutes of the Charleston Union Presbytery, 1822–1850, in the Historical Foundation of the Presbyterian and Reformed Churches, Montreat, North Carolina.

42. *The Friend,* VII (1834), 128; Hosea Holcombe, *Baptists in Alabama* (Philadelphia, 1840), 155.

43. E. Merton Coulter, *College Life in the Old South* (New York, 1928), 151.

44. For an account of the skirmish over lotteries, see Jesse Turner, "The Constitution of 1836," Arkansas Historical Association, *Publications,* III, 110.

45. Society of Friends, *The Discipline of the Indiana Yearly Meeting, Revised in the Year 1838* (Cincinnati, 1839), 35.

46. Works Progress Administration, *Annals of Cleveland, 1818–1935: A Digest of the Newspaper Record of Events and Opinions* (Cleveland, 1938), "1835," abstracts 121–125. For example, among the lotteries advertised in 1839 were the New Jersey, Wheeling, Maryland, Leesburg, and Richmond Academy.

47. Mrs. J. Thayer, "The Lottery Ticket," *Boston Weekly Magazine,* II (April 11, 1840), 233–234, 241–242; Thomas Doyle, *Five Years in a Lottery Office* (Boston, 1841), 12.

48. Copies of this petition are found in Stiness, *loc. cit.,* 110–116; Doyle, Appendix, 53ff; and the *Lottery Exterminator,* I (April 1842), no. 1, 2nd ed., 16ff.

49. Stiness, *loc. cit.,* 85–87, 117–123. For a brief account of the fight in the convention of 1842, see Carroll, 285.

50. William Reynolds, *A Brief History of the First Presbyterian Church of Baltimore* (Baltimore, 1913), 6–7.

51. H. L. Conrad, ed., "Lotteries," *Encyclopedia of the History of Missouri* (St. Louis, 1901), IV, 113–114; W. B. Stevens, *Centennial History of Missouri* (St. Louis, 1921), II, 480–481, 601–602.

52. William Garrett, *Reminiscences of Public Men in Alabama* (Atlanta, 1872), 608–609.

53. Legislative Council of the State of New Jersey, *Journal of the Proceedings for the Second Sitting of the 68th Session* (New Brunswick, 1844), 148, 280, 292; New Jersey State Constitutional Convention of 1844, *Proceedings,* edited by Writers Project of the W.P.A. (n.p. 1942), 336, 545–546, 620. Of interest is the fact that both Whigs and Democrats were represented among the antilottery leaders, as were also the Baptist, Methodist, Presbyterian, and Episcopal churches.

54. The activities of J. G. Gregory & Co., from November 9, 1844, through January 6, 1847, are covered in the manuscript letter-book of Daniel M'Intyre. This was the property of Goodspeed's Book Shop, Boston, in 1947. For the quotations cited, see letters of December 11 and 31, 1846.

55. T. H. James, *Rambles in the United States and Canada During the Year 1845* (London, 1847), 195. See also, Allan Nevins, ed., *The Diary of Philip Hone* (New York, 1936), 793, for an account of a lottery held in New York for benefit of the starving Irish in 1847.

56. General Assembly of South Carolina, *Reports and Resolutions Passed at the Regular Session of 1846* (Columbia, 1846), 181–182.

57. M. M. Quaife, "The Struggle over Ratification 1846–1847," State Historical Society of Wisconsin, *Publications*, XXVIII (1920), 366, 481, 602, 682.

58. J. R. Browne, *Report of the Debates of the Convention of California, on the Formation of the State Constitution, In September and October, 1849* (Washington, 1850), 90–93.

59. *The Friend*, XXI (1848), 136. A letter from M'Intyre to Gregory, February 3, 1846, reported efforts to influence the Maryland legislature. M'Intyre letter-book.

60. State of Maryland, *Proceedings of the Convention to Frame a New Constitution* (Annapolis, 1850), 62, 122, 155, 299; Maryland Reform Convention to Revise the State Constitution, *Debates and Proceedings* (Annapolis, 1851), I, 11, 18, 307–309, 399; II, 836–837.

61. State of Indiana, *Report of the Debate and Proceedings of the Convention for the Revision of the Constitution* (Indianapolis, 1850), II, 1286, 1294, 2076.

62. M. C. S. Noble, *A History of the Public Schools of North Carolina* (Chapel Hill, 1930), 136; John R. Logan, *Sketches, Historical and Biographical of the Broad River and King's Mountain Baptist Associations, from 1800 to 1882* (Shelby, N.C., 1887), 82.

63. For the slight skirmish in Minnesota and Oregon, see William Anderson and Albert J. Lobb, *A History of the Constitution of Minnesota* (Minneapolis, 1921), 120, 218, and C. H. Carey, *The Oregon Constitution and Proceedings and Debates of the Constitutional Convention of 1857* (Salem, 1926), 367–368, 426.

64. The *Blue Hen's Chickens* was published in Wilmington by William T. Jeandell and Francis Vincent. M'Intyre letter-book, May 11, 15, 20, 1846.

65. For examples of opposition to lotteries at this time, see *Friend's Review*, V (1852), 344; VIII (1855), 394–395; Wilmington *Delaware Republican*, December 13, 16, 1858. The $750,000 was to be shared by four railroads, two academies, a courthouse, and a Methodist church. The last drawing for which a record has been found was in 1863. Norman M. MacLeod, "Early State Lotteries Provided Money to Build Jail, Colleges, Churches," Wilmington *Evening Journal–Every Evening*, December 19, 1933; *Friend's Review*, XII (1859), 582; *The Friend*, XXXII (1859), 176, 184, 258.

66. State of Kentucky, *Journal and Proceedings of the Constitutional Convention* (Frankfort, 1849), 75; R. H. Collins, *History of Kentucky* (Louisville, 1924), I, 78.

67. *Gospel Doctrine, Selections from the Sermons and Writings of Joseph F. Smith*, 3rd ed. (Salt Lake, 1920), 407–410.

68. Vol. XXXIII (1860), pp. 231–232.

XII. THE CIVIL WAR AND THE POSTWAR REVIVAL

1. Advertisement for a new variety of lottery. *De Bow's Review*, July 1869, advertising section.

2. Edward Dicey, *Six Months in the Federal States* (London, 1862), II, 73, 102–103.

3. James D. Burn, *Three Years among the Working Classes in the United States During the War* (London, 1865), 65.

4. T. E. Dabney, *One Hundred Great Years: The Story of the Times-Picayune* (Baton Rouge, 1944), 133–135.

5. W. B. Stevens, "The Missouri Tavern," *Missouri Historical Review*, XV (1921), 255.

6. *Congressional Globe*, 38th Congress, 1st session (1863–64), 1816, 1852; Appendix, 225, 226. The breakdown of these taxes is found in the *Forum*, XII (1892), 807–809.

7. H. L. Conrad, ed., "Lotteries," *Encyclopedia of the History of Missouri* (St. Louis, 1901), IV, 114; W. B. Stevens, *Centennial History of Missouri* (St. Louis, 1921), II, 480–481; W. B. Stevens, "New Journalism in Missouri," *Missouri Historical Review*, XVIII (1924), 200.

8. W. E. Connelley and E. M. Coulter, *History of Kentucky* (New York, 1922), II, 1005; House of Representatives, *Executive Documents*, 46th Congress, 2nd session (1879–80), XII, document 22; Anthony Comstock, *Frauds Exposed* (New York, 1880), 329–334; *Public Opinion*, XIII (1892), 378. For Simmons' activities, see Herbert Asbury, *Sucker's Progress* (New York, 1938), 98–106. For Vincennes University, see G. S. Cottman, *Centennial History and Handbook of Indiana* (Indianapolis, 1915), 56.

9. Quoted from the Montgomery, Alabama, *Advertiser* by H. D. Farish, *The Circuit Rider Dismounts: A Social History of Southern Methodism, 1865–1900* (Richmond, 1938), 358n.

10. By law the Mississippi venture could give land, books, paintings, etc., as prizes. William E. Treadway, "Lottery Laws in the United States: A Page from American Legal History," *American Bar Association Journal*, XXXV (May 1949), 388. Dunbar Rowland, ed., "Lotteries," *Encyclopedia of Mississippi History* (Madison, Wisc., 1907), II, 120; Stone *v.* Mississippi, 101 U.S. 814 (1879); H. L. Carson, *The Supreme Court of the United States* (Philadelphia, 1892), II, 523–524; Charles Warren, *The Supreme Court in United States History* (Boston, 1928), II, 619.

11. T. H. Hittel, *History of California* (San Francisco, 1885–1897), IV, 433–434, 499, 506; R. E. Sloan and W. R. Adams, *History of Arizona* (Phoenix, 1930), II, 27–28, 34.

12. For the advertisement quoted above, see the advertising section of *De Bow's Review*, July 1869. For an early article exposing such schemes, see "Gift Enterprises," *Hours at Home*, VII (1868), 494–500.

13. Bessie L. Pierce, *A History of Chicago* (New York, 1940), II, 433.

14. United States Senate, *Miscellaneous Documents*, 39th Congress, 1st session (1865), document 57.

15. "The Round Table," *Boston Review*, VI (1866), 158–160; "Lotteries and Raffles," *ibid.*, 496–511.

16. William A. Butler, *Mrs. Limber's Raffle* (New York, 1876).

17. *Congressional Globe*, 40th Congress, 2nd session (1867–68), 4412; Appendix, 552.

18. For a discussion of early federal lottery laws, see A. A. Freeman, *Lottery Gambling* (Argument for the defendant in T. J. Commerford *v.* Virginia C. Thompson, U.S. Circuit Court, Sixth Judicial Circuit), 350; Champion *v.* Ames, 106 U.S. 8; *Congressional Globe*, 42nd Congress, 2nd session (1871–72), Appendix 787, 790, 797.

19. Quoted by Dashiel T. Grayson, *A Digest of the Proceedings of the Conventions and Councils in the Diocese of Virginia* (Richmond, 1883), 319–320.

20. Freeman, 348.

21. Quoted by A. K. McClure, *Our Presidents and How We Make Them* (New York, 1900), 259.

22. *Congressional Globe*, 44th Congress, 1st session (1876), IV, 3655–3656, 4261–4264; Freeman, 339–340; 1 Fed. Rep. 417 (1880).

23. House of Representatives, *Executive Documents*, 46th Congress, 2nd session, document 22. Edward Crapsey, "The Nether Side of New York," *Galaxy*, XIII (April 1872), 489–497, shows the effects of this revival of activity upon New York. He states there was scarcely a street in the city where dealers could not be found in their "Exchange Offices," that the average numbers of offices in the city was 350, and that there had been only one raid against them in five years.

24. The word "Louisiana" was favored because that state had the only legal lottery at the time. Marshall Cushing, *The Story of Our Post Office* (Boston, 1893), 538–541, 552.

XIII. THE LOUISIANA LOTTERY

1. One of the thinly disguised advertisements used by the exiled Louisiana Lottery in the late 1890's. Quoted by Richard Harding Davis, *Three Gringos in Venezuela and Central America* (New York, 1896), 29–30.

2. G. W. McGinty, "The Louisiana Lottery Company," *Southwestern Social Science Quarterly*, XX (March 1940), 330; B. C. Alwes, "The History of the Louisiana State Lottery Company," *Louisiana Historical Quarterly*, XXVII (October 1944), 970–971.

3. H. O. Rogers, "The Lottery in American History," *Americana*, XIII (1919), 48; A. R. Spofford, "Lotteries in American History," American Historical Association, *Annual Report for the Year 1892*, p. 190; E. H. Farrar, "The Louisiana Lottery; Its History," *Charities Review*, I (1892), 148. Morrissey, member of Congress, was the boss of New York gambling and Simmons was one of the biggest "policy" men in the United States and was later identified with the Kentucky Lottery. Herbert Asbury, *Sucker's Progress* (New York, 1938), 98–100, 360–375.

4. Alwes, *loc. cit.*, 971–973.

5. Farrar, *loc. cit.*, 143, 148; C. C. Buel, "The Degradation of a State," *Century*, XXI (1892), 622–623; Rogers, *loc. cit.*, 48–49; McGinty, *loc. cit.*, 331; Alwes, *loc. cit.*, 974–976.

6. See advertisement in *De Bow's Review*, February 1869, advertising section.

7. For the *Advocate*'s role, see H. D. Farish, *The Circuit Rider Dismounts: A Social History of Southern Methodism, 1865–1900* (Richmond, 1938), 358ff; for the story of the *Picayune*, see T. E. Dabney, *One Hundred Great Years: The Story of the Times-Picayune* (Baton Rouge, 1944), 255. A suit against the *Democrat* reached $90,000 before being dropped when the lottery company gained control of the paper. McGinty, *loc. cit.*, 335.

8. McGinty, *loc. cit.*, 334; Alwes, *loc. cit.*, 980–981, 984–985.

9. A grand jury in 1878 did recommend that the attorney general investigate the company's right to a legal existence. McGinty, *loc. cit.*, 334. Dabney, 241, 342–343.

10. McGinty, *loc. cit.*, 335; Alwes, *loc. cit.*, 985–988. One curious charge

was that the company had been responsible for police raids in Philadelphia and New York against the rival Kentucky Lottery.

11. The best account of the convention is Alwes, *loc. cit.*, 998–1001. See also Farrar, *loc. cit.*, 144–145; Dabney, 282; Spofford, *loc. cit.*, 191–192; Rogers, *loc. cit.*, 49–50; and McGinty, *loc. cit.*, 338.

12. Quoted by *The Friend*, LII (1879), 406.

13. Quotation from Farrar, *loc. cit.*, 145.

14. Buel, *loc. cit.*, 624.

15. For good accounts of the daily drawings and "policy," see Marshall Cushing, *The Story of Our Post Office* (Boston, 1893), 516, 518–520; McGinty, *loc. cit.*, 341; Alwes, *loc. cit.*, 1021–1024. Julian Ralph, correspondent for *Harpers*, left a vivid description of a regular drawing in *Dixie, or Southern Scenes and Sketches* (New York, 1896), 73–76.

16. Champion *v.* Ames, 106 U.S. 8. For examples of these measures, see House bills 3827 (1879), 6552 (1880), 4960 (1881) and Senate bills 1017 (1883) and 1018 (1884).

17. *Congressional Record*, 51st Congress, 1st session (1889–90), XXI, 4641, 6287, 6465, 8185, 8841, 8904, 9701.

18. House of Representatives, *Reports for the 48th Congress, 1st Session, 1883–1884*, III, document 826; Senate, *Reports for the 49th Congress, 1st Session, 1885–1886*, I, document 11.

19. For a brief summary of the issues involved and the verdicts, see Alwes, *loc. cit.*, 1007–1010.

20. For examples of press opinion, see issues after 1890 of *The Friend*, *Nation*, *Our Day*, *Chautauquan*, *Public Opinion*, *Century*, *Christian Union*, *Charities Review*, *North American Review*, *Atlantic Monthly*, *Cosmopolitan*, and *Forum*.

21. For Comstock's activities, see Heywood Broun and Margaret Leech, *Anthony Comstock, Roundsman of the Lord* (New York, 1927), 194–206; Anthony Comstock, *Frauds Exposed* (New York, 1880), 133ff; and *Traps for the Young* (New York, 1883), 58–95. According to his biographers, Comstock was offered bribes consisting of an annual check for $25,000 to his society and a trip to Europe for himself and his wife. This failing, wires were pulled to have him removed.

22. A. K. McClure, *Recollections of Half a Century* (Salem, Mass., 1902), 173–183; Harry Thurston Peck, "Twenty Years of the Republic," *Bookman*, XXI (1905), 299–301.

23. *Congressional Record*, 51st Congress, 1st session (1889–90), XXI, 8706–8713.

24. For a modern discussion of these charities, see Alwes, *loc. cit.*, 1027–1029.

25. Nicholls' message is found in Louisiana House of Representatives, *Journal, 1890* (Baton Rouge, 1891), 7–32. *The Friend* reported, September 28, 1889, that the lottery company offered to pay the $12,000,000 state debt if its charter were extended for fifty years.

26. Farrar, *loc. cit.*, 146.

27. Alcée Fortier, *A History of Louisiana* (New York, 1904), IV, 220–223; Alwes, *loc. cit.*, 1030–1052; McGinty, *loc. cit.*, 342–345; Dabney, 344–346; Rogers, *loc. cit.*, 51–54. Dramatic accounts of the legislative fight are also found in Farrar, *loc. cit.*, 146–147; *Century*, XX (1891), 631–632, XXI (1892), 620–629; and *Forum*, XII (1892), 571–576.

28. Farish, 359–361.

29. Quoted by *Public Opinion*, IX (1890), 407.

30. J. M. Buckley, *A History of Methodists in the United States* (New York, 1896), 643; Farish, 359; *Deseret Weekly*, February 6, 1892; *Proceedings of the Southern Baptist Convention, 1890* (Atlanta, 1890), 40; *ibid.*, 1891, 36.

31. *Christian Union*, XLIV (1891), 818–819, 997; for Woodbridge's role, see Anson P. Stokes, *Church and State in the United States* (New York, 1950), II, 298.

32. *Christian Union*, XLV (1892), 221, 277, 282, 372.

33. Newspaper references here are based on *Public Opinion*, IX (1890), 341, 405–407.

34. An incomplete transcript of the reports of the Pinkerton detectives is in the files of the North Dakota State Historical Society. For other accounts of this fight, see Grand Forks *Herald*, February 23, 1958; H. A. Gibbons, *John Wanamaker* (New York, 1926), I, 315; Beverly Carradine, *The Louisiana State Lottery Company; Examined and Exposed; Two Addresses and Additional Thoughts*, Crescent City Anti-Series I, no. 1 (New Orleans, 1890), 4, 21–22, 30; C. A. Lounsberry, *Early History of North Dakota* (Washington, 1919), 422–425; *Congressional Record*, 51st Congress, 1st session (1889–90), XXI, 8718–8719; Nina Wishek, *Along the Trails of Yesterday: A Story of McIntosh County* (n.p., 1941), 137; Anthony Comstock, "The Louisiana Lottery Octopus," *Our Day*, V (1890), 472–477; *Public Opinion*, IX (1890), 405–406, 570; Cushing, 560–561; *The Friend*, LXIII (1890), 255. The tickets for the lottery company had been printed in Wilmington for years.

35. Cushing, 523–524; James D. Richardson, ed., *Messages and Papers of the Presidents of the United States* (Washington, 1908), IX, 44.

36. Richardson, IX, 80–81.

37. W. A. Richardson, ed., *Supplement to the Revised Statutes of the United States*, 2nd ed. (Washington, 1891), I, 803–804; *Congressional Record*, 51st Congress, 1st session (1889–90), XXI, 8698–8721, 9510, 10085.

38. Richardson, *Messages and Papers*, IX, 116; Gibbons, I, 314–315; Cushing, 521. For press opinion, see *Public Opinion*, IX (1890), 570–571. Federal authorities were also successful against the Juarez Lottery Company of Mexico, presided over by General John S. Mosby.

39. Buel, *loc. cit.*, 630–631.

40. Farrar, *loc. cit.*, 151.

41. Alwes, *loc. cit.*, 1063–1066; Gustavus Myers, *History of the Supreme Court of the United States* (Chicago, 1918), 703–708; James A. Barnes, *John G. Carlisle* (New York, 1931), 521.

42. *Ex parte* Dupre, Rapier, 143 U.S. 110.

43. The story of the election of 1892 has been told in detail by many authors. Among the best are Alwes, *loc. cit.*, 1085–1097; Dabney, 345–346; *Christian Union*, XLIV (1891), 965, 1021–1022, 1053; *ibid.*, XLV (1892), 60–62; *Forum*, XII (1892), 572–576; Farrar, *loc. cit.*, 147–148; Fortier, IV, 224–225; G. M. Reynolds, *Machine Politics in New Orleans, 1897–1926* (New York, 1936), 23–25.

44. The best account of the exiled lottery, including a description of a drawing, is in Davis, 33–38, 43–44, 50–55. American churches kept a close watch on its activities. After exulting over "the destruction of that gigantic engine of Satan" in their 1892 convention, Southern Baptists in 1894 offered

their sympathies and prayers in behalf of the people of Florida in their struggle with the "octopus."

45. Federal Writers Project, *Florida: A Guide to the State* (New York, 1939), 520; *Congressional Record*, 53rd Congress, 2nd session (1894), XXVI, 2356–2357.

46. The power of the President to sign a bill after Congress' adjournment was not specifically established until 1932 (Edwards *v.* United States, 286 U.S. 482). For a discussion of this problem, see L. F. Schmeckebier, "Approval of Bills after Adjournment of Congress," *American Political Science Review,* XXXIII (February 1939), 52.

47. A highly dramatic account of the fight on this bill is found in S. H. Woodbridge, "The Anti-Lottery Campaign" (an address first delivered before the Association of Collegiate Alumnae of Boston and apparently first mimeographed in 1921; a copy is in the Harvard College Library). See also *The Friend,* LXVIII (1895), 294, and Stokes, II, 299–300; *Congressional Record,* 53rd Congress, 2nd session (1894), XXVI, 2211, 4312–4314, 4986, 7941, 8129; *ibid.,* 3rd session (1895), XXVII, 3013, 3039, 3100–3101, 3144.

48. Champion *v.* Ames, 188 U.S. 321.

XIV. CONCLUSIONS AND PRESENT TRENDS

1. Letter to the editor, Boston *Traveler,* February 27, 1947.

2. Oklahoma City *Daily Oklahoman,* March 9, 1950; New York *Times,* June 19, 1956, p. 5.

3. Birmingham, Alabama, *News,* February 1, 1942; Oklahoma City *Times,* October 6, 1954; "Australia," *Time,* LXVII (January 23, 1956), 26.

4. "Chances for Comrades," *Time,* LVIII (May 13, 1946), 38–40.

5. Earnest Havemann, "Gambling in the United States," *Life,* XXVIII (June 19, 1950), 96ff.

6. "Winners Every Time," *Time,* LXVII (April 4, 1955), 71–72; Oklahoma City *Times,* May 19, 1955.

7. See, for examples, "13 Million to One," *Time,* LXIV (March 31, 1952), the story of a French Catholic priest winning thirteen million francs; "Winner of Big Lottery [Italy] Loses Ambitious Wife," Oklahoma City *Times,* August 19, 1955; and the story of a Japanese housewife winning one million yen, *Daily Oklahoman,* December 2, 1954.

8. Birmingham *News,* February 1, 1942.

9. See, for example, *Annal of the Southern Baptist Convention, 1934* (n.p., n.d.), 112; *ibid., 1938,* 115–116.

10. Oklahoma City *Times,* May 14, 1949; Grace G. Tully, "Stories and Anecdotes about F.D.R., My Boss," *Ladies Home Journal,* LXVI (July 1949), 46.

11. Oklahoma City *Times,* August 8, 1956. For other recent proposals, see also Paul A. Fino, "The Case for a National Lottery," *American Magazine,* CLVIII (August 1954), 19ff, and "Let's Legalize Gambling," *Coronet,* XXXIX (November 1955), 61ff; T. F. James, "Gambling Boom in America," *Cosmopolitan,* CXLV (July 1958), 26ff; and New York *Times,* January 24, 1957, p. 22.

12. Anson P. Stokes, *Church and State in the United States* (New York, 1950), II, 299, 301; *Daily Oklahoman,* December 5, 1948; Oklahoma City

Times, March 5, 1949, October 26, 1950, December 12, 1952; Richard G. Lillard, *Desert Challenge: An Interpretation of Nevada* (New York, 1942), 85–86.

13. Stokes, II, 299–302; T. Slater, "Lottery," *Catholic Encyclopedia* (New York, 1910), IX, 366.

14. Stokes, II, 302–303; Oklahoma City *Times,* November 4, 1953; "Bingo," *Time,* LXII (November 16, 1953), 81.

15. These states were Vermont, Connecticut, New Hampshire, Minnesota, Maine, Rhode Island, Maryland, and New Jersey. "Bingo an Issue in Two States," *Presbyterian Life,* VII (October 2, 1954), 30; *Daily Oklahoman,* January 2, 1955; Don Romero, "Bingo — Shame of the Churches," *Christian Herald* (January, 1955), 22ff; New York *Times,* December 30, 1956–December 8, 1957.

16. Oklahoma City *Times,* November 17, 1955; "Words and Works," *Time,* LXVII (January 9, 1956), 42; Romero, *loc. cit.,* 18ff; Bill Davidson, "Bingo Is Getting Too Big," *Reader's Digest,* LXVI (March, 1955), 102ff.

17. My tabulation reaches 1,371, not including the fifty-odd ventures held in Pennsylvania by quasi-legal authority, Maryland schemes before authorization was required, or the unknown numbers held under blanket grants given by Kentucky to academies and artists, Alabama to Masons, North Carolina to printers, and Louisiana to sellers of property. Other conditions of listing have been enumerated in the text. This total applies to authorizations only, not to the number of classes or drawings.

Index